Public Sector Organizations

Editors: **B. Guy Peters**, Maurice Falk Professor of Government, Pittsburgh University, USA, and **Geert Bouckaert**, Professor at the Public Management Institute, Katholieke Universiteit Leuven, Belgium

Organizations are the building blocks of governments. The role of organizations, formal and informal, is most readily apparent in public bureaucracy, but all the institutions of the public sector are composed of organizations, or have some organizational characteristics that affect their performance. Therefore, if scholars want to understand how governments work, a very good place to start is at the level of the organizations involved in delivering services. Likewise, if practitioners want to understand how to be effective in the public sector, they would be well-advised to consider examining the role of organizations and how to make the organizations more effective.

This series will publish research-based books concerned with organizations in the public sector and will cover such issues as: the autonomy of public sector organizations, networks and network analysis, bureaucratic politics; organizational change and leadership and methodology for studying organizations.

Titles include:

Cristopher Ballinas Valdes
POLITICAL STRUGGLES AND THE FORGING OF AUTONOMOUS GOVERNMENT AGENCIES

Geert Bouckaert, B. Guy Peters and Koen Verhoest
THE COORDINATION OF PUBLIC SECTOR ORGANIZATIONS
Shifting Patterns of Public Management

Leslie A. Pal
FRONTIERS OF GOVERNANCE
The OECD and Global Public Management Reform

Amanda Smullen
TRANSLATING AGENCY REFORM
Rhetoric and Culture in Comparative Perspective

Koen Verhoest, Paul G. Roness, Bram Verschuere, Kristin Rubecksen and Muiris MacCarthaigh
AUTONOMY AND CONTROL OF STATE AGENCIES
Comparing States and Agencies

Koen Verhoest, Sandra Van Thiel, Per Lægreid and Geert Bouckaert (*editors*)
GOVERNMENT AGENCIES
Practices and Lessons from 30 Countries

Public Sector Organizations Series
Series Standing Order ISBN 978–0–230–22034–8 (Hardback) 978–0–230–22035–5 (Paperback)
(*outside North America only*)

You can receive future titles in this series as they are published by placing a standing order. Please contact your bookseller or, in case of difficulty, write to us at the address below with your name and address, the title of the series and the ISBN quoted above.

Customer Services Department, Macmillan Distribution Ltd, Houndmills, Basingstoke, Hampshire RG21 6XS, England

Frontiers of Governance

The OECD and Global Public Management Reform

Leslie A. Pal

Chancellor's Professor, School of Public Policy and Administration, Carleton University, Canada

First published 2012 by
PALGRAVE MACMILLAN

Palgrave Macmillan in the UK is an imprint of Macmillan Publishers Limited, registered in England, company number 785998, of Houndmills, Basingstoke, Hampshire RG21 6XS.

Palgrave Macmillan in the US is a division of St Martin's Press LLC, 175 Fifth Avenue, New York, NY 10010.

Palgrave Macmillan is the global academic imprint of the above companies and has companies and representatives throughout the world.

Palgrave® and Macmillan® are registered trademarks in the United States, the United Kingdom, Europe and other countries

ISBN 978–0–230–30930–2

This book is printed on paper suitable for recycling and made from fully managed and sustained forest sources. Logging, pulping and manufacturing processes are expected to conform to the environmental regulations of the country of origin.

A catalogue record for this book is available from the British Library.

A catalogue record for this book is available from the Library of Congress.

10   9   8   7   6   5   4   3   2   1
21   20   19   18   17   16   15   14   13   12

Printed and bound in Great Britain by
CPI Antony Rowe, Chippenham and Eastbourne

Contents

List of Tables

List of Figures

List of Abbreviations/Acronyms

ABA	American Bar Association
ACN	Anti-Corruption Network (OECD)
ADB	Asian Development Bank
APEC	Asia-Pacific Economic Cooperation
BERI	Business Environmental Risk Intelligence
BIAC	Business and Industry Advisory Committee (OECD)
BRIC's	Brazil, Russian Federation, India, China
CCN	Committee on Cooperation with Non-Members (OECD)
CCNM	Centre for Cooperation with Non-Members (OECD)
CEE	Central and Eastern Europe
CEEC	Committee of European Economic Cooperation
COFOG	Classifications of the Functions of Government
CoG	Network of Senior Officials from Centres of Government (OECD)
DAC	Development Assistance Committee (OECD)
DAF	Directorate for Financial and Enterprise Affairs (OECD)
DCD	Development Cooperation Directorate (OECD)
EBRD	European Bank for Reconstruction and Development
EC	European Commission
ECB	European Central Bank
ECO	Economics Department (OECD)
EDRC	Economic Development and Review Committee (OECD)
EE5	Enhanced engagement countries (OECD – Brazil, China, India, Indonesia, South Africa)
EGOV	Network of Senior E-Government Officials (OECD)
EI	Employment insurance
ENPI	European Neighbourhood and Partnership Instrument
EU	European Union
FATF	Financial Action Task Force
FDI	Foreign Direct Investment
G20	Group of 20 Leading Economies
GaaG	Government at a Glance (OECD)
GOV	Directorate for Public Governance and Territorial Development
GOVNET	Network on Governance (OECD)
HRM	Human resource management
IAIS	International Association of Insurance Supervisors
IASIA	International Association of Schools and Institutes of Administration
IDB	Inter-American Development Bank

IFP	International Futures Programme (OECD)
IGO	International governmental organization
IIAS	International Institute for Administrative Sciences
ILO	International Labour Organization
IMF	International Monetary Fund
IOSCO	International Organization for Securities Commissions
JAPMI	Joint Activity on Public Management Improvement (OECD)
LGI	Local Governance Initiative
MAI	Multilateral Agreement on Investment
MCM	Ministerial Council Meeting (OECD)
MG	Modernising Government
MENA	Middle East and North Africa (OECD)
NATO	North Atlantic Treaty Organization
NDP	New Democratic Party (Canada)
NEDAP	New Partnership for Africa's Development
NGO	Non-governmental organization
NISPAcee	Network of Institutes and Schools of Public Administration in Central and Eastern Europe
NPM	New public management
OAS	Organization of American States
OECD	Organisation for Economic Cooperation and Development
OEEC	Organisation for European Economic Cooperation
OGBS	Offshore Group of Banking Supervisors
OSCE	Organization for Security and Cooperation in Europe
PB	Policy Brief
PEMWP	Public Employment and Management Working Party (OECD)
PGC	Public Governance Committee (OECD)
PHARE	Poland and Hungary: Assistance for Restructuring their Economies
PISA	Programme for International Student Assessment (OECD)
PUMA	Public Management Directorate (OECD) Public Management Committee (OECD)
REG	Working Party on Regulatory Management and Reform (OECD)
RPC	Regulatory Policy Committee (OECD)
SBO	Working Party of Senior Budget Officials (OECD)
SG	Secretary-General of OECD
SIGMA	Support for Improvement in Governance and Management (OECD)
TAP	Technical Assistance Programme (OECD)
TDPC	Territorial Development Policy Committee (OECD)
TECO	Technical Cooperation Committee (OECD)
TUAC	Trade Union Advisory Committee (OECD)
UAE	United Arab Emirates

UN	United Nations
UNDP	United Nations Development Programme
UNDESA	United Nations Department of Economic and Social Affairs
UNECA	United Nations Economic Commission for Africa
UNPAD	United Nations Public Administration Division
UNPAN	United Nations Public Administration Network
USAID	United States Agency for International Development
VC	Voluntary contribution (OECD)
WB	World Bank
WCO	World Customs Organization
WTO	World Trade Organization

Preface

Strolling down the Avenue Victor Hugo in Paris to where it meets the Avenue Henri Martin, one turns left on the small, quiet rue de Franqueville. The street reflects the *haute bourgeois* character of this 16th *arrondissement* neighbourhood – four-storey, impeccable solid stone apartment buildings, only a few cars, the occasional pedestrian walking a typically diminutive, fluffy Parisian dog. On the right is a modernish but tasteful building that runs along the street to the corner, at rue André Pascal. Here the building is attached to a small, gated chateau. The casual tourist might assume that a slightly eccentric French baron had decided to build an Olympic-sized swimming pool next door to his home.

In fact, the Château de la Muette and its adjoining conference centre are the headquarters of the Organisation for Economic Cooperation and Development (OECD). It has an annual budget of Euro 320 million, and some 2,500 permanent (very bright, professional) staff who churn out over 250 publications, research studies, and reports annually. Almost 45,000 senior public servants from the OECD's 34 member states (as well as non-member states) walk through its doors each year, attending conferences, committee meetings and working and expert groups that oversee the Secretariat, and occasionally coming to agreements on conventions, standards, and "best" or "good" practices. In its first incarnation in 1948 as the Organisation for European Economic Cooperation (OEEC), it was originally established to manage American and Canadian aid under the Marshall Plan to help re-build Europe, liberalize trade, develop a European Payments Union, and eventually construct the foundations of the European Common Market. The original 18 members were: Austria, Belgium, Denmark, France, Greece, Iceland, Ireland, Italy, Luxembourg, Netherlands, Norway, Portugal, Spain, Sweden, Switzerland, Turkey, United Kingdom, and Western Germany. The OEEC was replaced by the OECD in 1961, with the intent of creating a world-wide body (Canada and the United States were added as OECD members). Its founding convention stated that the new organization was dedicated: "(a) to achieve the highest sustainable economic growth and employment and a rising standard of living in Member countries, while maintaining financial stability, and thus to contribute to the development of the world economy; (b) to contribute to sound economic expansion in Member as well as non-member countries in the process of economic development; and (c) to contribute to the expansion of world trade on a multilateral, non-discriminatory basis in accordance with international obligations".

The modern OECD has 34 members,[1] is reviewing the possible accession of Russia, and is seeking "enhanced engagement" with Brazil, China, India,

Indonesia, and South Africa. The OECD is clearly the "rich countries club": in 2009 its members accounted for 71.9 per cent of the world's Gross National Income, 60.5 per cent of world trade, and 94.9 per cent of world official development assistance (OECD 2009a: 6). Its mandate has grown considerably beyond economic growth and trade: the OECD is essentially the world's largest think tank, producing research on everything from agriculture, energy, health, education, and the environment, to e-government and biotechnology.

This book is about one important strand of the OECD's work: governance and public management, which is overseen by one of the OECD Secretariat's 12 directorates, GOV (Public Governance and Territorial Development), and by three of its committees, with membership of representatives of member states and some non-member-states: the Public Governance Committee, the Territorial Development Policy Committee, and the Regulatory Policy Committee. The fact that governance is only one of a myriad of activities in the OECD belies its importance, both for the OECD itself and for governments around the world. "Governance" has become a popular concept both in and out of academe, denoting a focus not just on "government" but on the entire apparatus – both governmental and non-governmental – whereby governments steer themselves and their societies. "Public management" is about the tools and techniques whereby states organize their administrative structures, and includes everything from the hiring of civil servants to the quality of public services. Together, they comprise the sinews of societal self-management. Without effective governance, almost everything else in a modern society becomes either impossible or dysfunctional: tax collection, health and social services, education, public transit, sewage disposal and garbage collection. This is clear in the case of failed states such as Somalia, Sudan, and Zimbabwe, which head *Foreign Policy*'s annual List of Failed States. These countries cannot control their borders, are marked by violence and corruption, and their people live in abject misery. But it is also true in more developed, democratic states: the economic crisis of 2008–2010 revealed major flaws in financial regulation in the United States, the United Kingdom, and Iceland. The sovereign debt crisis in Greece was in part due to its mismanagement of public funds in previous years. Governance matters.

Governance, networks and the OECD

In one sense, this interest in governance – or effective public administration and public sector management – is as old as the modern state itself. In the United States, for example, the Progressive movement in the early part of the 20th century aimed at ridding local governments and cities of corrupt, nepotistic and ethnically dominated political "machines" and at introducing professional and politically neutral administration (Hofstadter 1963). The American Society for Public Administration was established in

1939. Canada introduced a Civil Service Act in 1918 to ensure a merit-based, non-partisan federal public service (Roberts 1996). France's École nationale d'administration was established in 1945 and was designed to produce the very best and the very brightest of higher government (and private sector) managers. In Britain, a less formal but equally effective system evolved wherein the highest cadres of the civil service were recruited from "Oxbridge" and staffed an administrative system that was loyal to crown and government, but non-partisan and expected to implement policies and programmes efficiently and effectively. This system was exported throughout the Commonwealth, to variable success.

The post-World War II context for governance, however, was different in at least four ways from this more traditional concern about effective public management, and the OECD's work needs to be situated within that evolving context. First, the 15 years after 1945 were dominated by the rebuilding of Western Europe. This was primarily about infrastructure and industry, but also involved the reconstruction of governments, administrative systems, and key policies around trade and common markets. As noted earlier, the OEEC was a primary instrument of that reconstruction, and was succeeded by the OECD in 1961 with a broader mandate of economic development through public policies that enhanced trade and effective economic policies. Second, coinciding with this early reconstruction effort but extending beyond it to 1990, was the Cold War. It framed governance issues in terms of a "clash of systems" and of "democracy". Both the West and the Soviet Union tried in subtle and not-so-subtle ways to demonstrate the superiority of both their economic and their governance systems in producing everything from full employment to refrigerators. Proxy wars throughout Africa, Asia and Latin America were maneuvers by the two superpowers to spread either socialism or democracy, ironically often resulting in cleptocratic dictatorships or brutal military regimes. This clash of systems was then in the 1980s refracted internally within the West itself, as conservative-minded governments in New Zealand (Labour Prime Minister Lange), Britain (Prime Minister Thatcher), and the United States (President Reagan) sought to shake off what they claimed was the sclerosis of two decades of left-leaning and quasi-socialist public policy. They sought to reinvigorate capitalism through deregulation and smaller government with an eye to defeating the "evil empire".

As an organization, the OECD was not directly involved in this conflict of systems, but its membership at the time consisted of the leading capitalist nations, and so their broader preoccupations inevitably filtered through the organization. For example, at a conference in Madrid in 1979, the OECD added "public sector reform" as formal item for research and development. It became much more involved in the public management reform agenda in the 1990s as a result of the collapse of the Soviet Union, the end of the Cold War, a new reconstruction of central and Eastern Europe, and a sense that even in this moment of triumph over the Soviet Union, Western states themselves were facing turbulence and instability (e.g., increasing budgetary deficits).

This was the third way in which the context for work on governance and public management differed from the historical tradition of trying to build effective, national public bureaucracies. In 1990 the OECD established a directorate in its Secretariat entitled PUMA (public management), which produced a synoptic report in 1995 entitled *Governance in Transition*. This captured both what was happening in the "transition" countries of central and Eastern Europe as well the new pressures on established democratic states. The European challenge was to introduce capitalism and all that that entailed in terms of privatization of state assets, deregulation, stock exchanges and a host of other standard market institutions. But it soon became clear that economic reform without governance reform – both in the political system and in the administrative system – would not get very far. The OECD in this period became somewhat of a cheerleader for freer market systems both in central Europe and the rest of the world, as well as for leaner governance through the adoption of practices termed the "new public management". It became active in proffering management advice and reform in central and Eastern Europe through a partnership with the European Union under a programme called SIGMA. But the reform agenda was broader than Europe, and extended both to OECD members and the world at large. The frame of reference became "modernising government", the title of a 2005 report that surveyed public management trends, pressures and best practices in the developed world. The argument was that these governments were facing broadly similar challenges, from declines in public trust and legitimacy, to rising expenditures and public demands, to new technologies and mechanisms of service delivery.

This forms the backdrop for the fourth important contextual difference in the contemporary emphasis on governance and management. The traditional emphasis had been on reforming and improving public management within single nation-states and on the basis of national legal traditions such as common versus Roman law. By the late 1990s and into the 2000s, the emphasis was both systemic and increasingly global. The systemic dimension was reflected in the increasingly entrenched assumption that, despite national constitutional and historical differences, there are basic and common dimensions to "good governance" that can be transferred from successful states to less successful ones. The clearest and most explicit example of this is the process of European Union (EU) accession. In the successive expansions of the past decade, and for the ones on the horizon, aspiring states must agree to and incorporate the *acquis communautaire*, a body of some 31 chapters of laws and regulations that form the foundation of an EU "system" of governance and public policy.

Another example is the shift among development agencies in the late 1990s to a greater appreciation of the importance of governance, and to the idea that "best practices" of democratic governance could be measured, benchmarked, and circulated or transferred. The World Bank, for instance, signalled a change from an agenda purely focused on economic development to one that emphasized governance factors with a conference in 1991 on "good governance". In 1996, then World Bank President James Wolfensohn issued a statement reversing the Bank's policy (as outlined in its charter) not to address political factors in development such as corruption. This was followed in 1997 with its annual report entitled *The State in a Changing World*. The UNDP's 2002 Human Development Report, *Deepening Democracy in a Fragmented World*, was inspired by the idea "that politics is as important to successful development as economics". In 2003 the European Commission published a draft manual on good governance: "There is widely acknowledged evidence that development cooperation has not succeeded in reducing poverty in recent years. One fundamental reason has been identified as poor governance, which most people can recognise when they see it". The OECD itself, through its Development Assistance Committee (DAC), which oversees almost all the world's bilateral development aid, issued a report in 1996 entitled *Shaping the 21st Century: The Contribution to Development Cooperation*, focusing on capacity-building. This entailed priorities for "effective, democratic and accountable governance, the protection of human rights and respect for the rule of law". The point is that what emerged in this period was a sense in which good governance and effective public management were central to economic development and prosperity, that they could be measured and assessed, and that their core elements (e.g., transparency, anti-corruption measures, a professional public service) were <u>systemic</u> elements of effective regimes that could be studied and transplanted in a process of "modernization".

The global dimension of this fourth contextual factor is related to but distinct from the systemic character of governance reform. Economic globalization, despite occasional setbacks, has grown steadily since 1950. According to the World Bank, total world exports grew by an annual average rate of 6 per cent between 1950 and 2006. Foreign direct investment and capital flows also grew exponentially. Coupled with the rise of Brazil, Russia, India and especially China (the "BRICs") both in terms of imports and exports, along with other developing countries, this has created a truly global economic trading and financial system. While that system has generated prosperity, it has also created vulnerabilities and turbulence. The 1998 Asian financial crisis spread a contagion of financial instability throughout the world. That crisis was eclipsed in 2008 with the financial crisis that started with housing bubbles in the United States but spread rapidly through the developed economies, plunging almost the entire world into recession, and destabilizing the Euro and consequently the EU.

A globalized economy needs some form of globalized coordination that, even if it falls short of a "global government", implies some sort of regime of global governance, in several senses. The first is coordination. The 2008 global financial crisis had to be addressed globally, and so the G20 emerged as a key instrument for both developed and leading developing countries such as China and India, to orchestrate their stimulus packages as well as their financial regulatory practices. The OECD was invited to participate in the G20 in 2008 and provide research support on key global issues, and so became a member of the global "steering system". The second sense of global governance is harmonization of governance and management regimes, as well as key policy regimes. Foreign investors in developing countries, for example, look to certain basic practices in anti-corruption and tax regimes. Countries wishing to attract foreign investment know this, and want to demonstrate that they meet "world standards" in policy and public management. There are now hundreds of indexes on a myriad of aspects of governance and policy, often ranking and rating countries, and countries that wish to attract investment or expand trade to developed economies are fully aware that their internal systems need to meet basic standards (Buduru & Pal 2010). In this way, the global "market" for governance reform and best practices has increased exponentially as a result of economic globalization.

So, in summary, the current context for public management and governance reform is significantly different from traditional, nation-state based reform efforts of the past. While national differences are respected or at least acknowledged, there is a strong sense that good governance and effective public management reflect "systems" or "models" of elements with basic standards or practices. *Governance in Transition* (1995) and *Modernising Government: The Way Forward* (2005) were two key OECD contributions to this development, but the World Bank and others have also generated models, standards, best practices, agreements, conventions, and recommendations around systemic reform. This should not be overstated to imply some sort of coordinated agenda (indeed, as we will see in a moment, there is considerable competition) of reform, or complete insensitivity to local circumstances. But it is part of a global conversation that has grown in the last 15 years about comparing regimes, discussing best practices, and transferring those practices.

This conversation and this dynamic have emerged through the growth of a global network around public sector reform (Pal & Ireland 2009). This is important since a loosely coordinated form of "isomorphic governance" has emerged in the past 20 years, without however the benefit of any single design. These network dynamics will be discussed in greater detail in subsequent chapters, but it is impossible to fully understand the OECD without grasping how this network has emerged and how it operates. The emergence was in large part due to the factors discussed above – the gradual and then rapid emergence in the 1990s of a realization that governance matters a great deal to economic performance and prosperity. Ronald Reagan and Margaret Thatcher provided the bully pulpits whereby a message of governance reform (in the direction of smaller government, less taxation, less interference) could gain sustained attention. International governmental organizations (IGOs) like the World Bank, the UNDP, the UN and the OECD began to contribute conceptual frameworks and ideas about effective public management.

The public administration and public policy academic communities were bubbling with ideas and debates as well, and many of their members circulated through national administrations as well as the research arms of IGOs. These academic communities were by no means constrained by national boundaries, and this is what made the spread of their ideas more powerful and ubiquitous. The International Institute for Administrative Sciences (IIAS), for example, was founded in 1930. It is affiliated with the International Association of Schools and Institutes of Administration (IASIA), which has an international membership of academic institutions as well as civil service ministries. Another example is the Network of Institutes and Schools of Public Administration in Central and Eastern Europe (NISPAcee). It was established in 1994 to enhance public administration teaching, research and practice in the region, and brought together academics and practitioners both in the region, the EU and the United States. These academic communities have often been sustained by foundations, most prominently the Soros Foundation, which funded the Open Society Institute and its networks throughout central and Eastern Europe as well as southern Europe and central Asia (Eisfeld & Pal 2010).

Network elements or nodes may emerge, but to become true networks, they must interact and interconnect. Three examples will demonstrate the networked character of this global constellation of actors around public management reform. UNPAN is the United Nations Public Administration Network, established in 1999, with the mission to be "a global networking tool that connects relevant international, regional, subregional, and national institutions worldwide for the promotion of better public administration". It meets in plenary every three years, and has a Committee of Experts that meets annually. NISPAcee provides a second and third example. From its founding in 1994 to 2011 it was financially supported by the Local Government Initiative (LGI), which is part of the Soros Foundation's work in the region. When NISPAcee was created, it worked closely with the National Association of Schools of Public Affairs and Administration (US) through faculty exchanges, which were funded by USAID. At the 18th Annual NISPAcee conference in Warsaw in May 2010, there was a panel on the internationalization of public administration education. The panelists, all well known to each other and by the audience were: Allan Rosenbaum (President, IASIA), Alexei Tikhomirov (Division of Public Administration and Development Management, UNDESA – UNPAN), Rolet Loretan (Director General, IIAS), Adrian Ionescu (Director, LGI), Pan Suk Kim (Vice President, Asian Association of Public Administration), and Meredith Newman (President, American Society for Public Administration). There was nothing sinister in this, but it shows that there is a visible and vibrant global network around governance and public administration and management, a network that does not merely exist in the abstract, but that connects, converses, communicates and collaborates.

The OECD is an important node in this network, and has been identified as a key contributor to governance debates on new public management as well as a host of other governance and management topics in the past 20 years. We mentioned some of its unique characteristics at the outset. It has an enormous research capacity that eclipses that of other members of the network. The various professional associations, for example, conduct little or no research on their own, though they may stimulate and publish research through conferences and working groups or research committees. The OECD is a formal international entity, with ambassadorial representation from 34 member states. In this respect, again, it is different from professional associations, and even organizations like UNPAN. This can be an advantage, in that the OECD enjoys the prestige of being an organization of leading, developed countries. But it can also complicate life on the research front, since there are foreign policy dimensions to its research work (e.g., reports that might impugn the sovereign dignity of a member or non-member state). Unlike the development banks, it provides no loans or grants, and so has no other leverage than the quality of its ideas and its key advantage in being a dense nodal point for the interaction of a highly skilled research cadre in the Secretariat and senior practitioners/officials. Other organizations try to bridge the research/practice divide as well, but only the OECD enjoys the status of being an organ of those practitioners and their states. This means a steady circulation of officials through the OECD system, representing their states, as well as a capacity for the OECD to act as a mirror and sounding board for issues that are preoccupying its members. Angel Gurría, the current Secretary-General of the OECD, gives some 160 speeches a year, and is constantly visiting member states and asking them "what keeps them up at night, what is their worst nightmare?"[2]

Some of these characteristics translate into distinct advantages. But the OECD is not without its own challenges, in part due both to the enhanced interest in governance and public management, and to the growth and development of the global network dedicated to it. The "market" for governance advice has grown tremendously in the past 20 years, but the field of "suppliers" in the network has also grown. Whereas in 1995 the OECD was almost alone in conducting and circulating its research on comparative governance and public management systems, the field has become crowded with other IGOs, international professional associations, foundations, think tanks, NGOs, and even private actors (e.g., political risk assessment agencies). When asked what is the major challenge facing the OECD, Gurría responded: "Relevance, relevance, relevance". Some of the OECD's recent strategic initiatives, such as expanding its membership and enhancing engagement with non-member states, have been in response to this challenge.

Themes and contributions

This book will explore three themes in relation to the OECD. The first is the growing "market" for good governance and public management reform since the mid-1900s. The OECD has been an important part of that market, both as a supplier and a *demandeur*. The market has become crowded in the past five years, and the OECD has had to change and evolve in order to retain and enhance its relevance. We have highlighted a few points in the development of this market here, but Chapter 1 will go into greater depth on how governance and public management emerged as a focal point for development assistance and as a perceived linchpin for economic development in advanced states. Other chapters will touch on the theme in terms of how that market is evolving, and the pressures it places on the OECD as an organization engaged in policy transfer.

The second theme is the specific tools of policy transfer used by the OECD (e.g., peer review, accession) – how they work, their limitations and contradictions, and how they are shaped, fashioned and used within the OECD and its member and non-member states. We have noted that the OECD has an almost unrivalled capacity to conduct a type of research that uniquely combines theory and practice – research that can claim to have "insider" knowledge about what is actually going on in leading countries, but informed by social science theory and a mountain of databases and previous research. There is a complicated and nuanced process behind this research effort, a process that is critical to the OECD's influence. By tracking these tools and their underlying logic, we can see more clearly how influence can be exercised through non-coercive instruments or "soft tools".

The third theme is the scope and extent of global governance networks, and the way in which they operate. The OECD provides a window into one important part of the network, and helps us understand its connections to the other parts. We will see both cooperative dimensions to the network, as well as competitive ones. The OECD is an interesting intersection of at least three key global governance networks: its own membership of the leading 34 economies in the world, the G20, and a host of non-members with which it interacts (e.g., it has recently conducted studies for the Chinese government on its economy, and provides advice to Middle East states through MENA). The modern world is chaotic and turbulent, but whatever order it has comes from interlaced networks of governance institutions.

The book makes several contributions.

1. It is the first detailed and sustained analysis of the OECD's role in global governance reform. The literature on the OECD as a whole is surprisingly meager, and while there is work on its role in social policy, the governance and public management file has been almost ignored.

2. It is based in large part on confidential interviews with OECD Secretariat officials, ambassadors, government officials working on committees, and several national country OECD secretariats. Some interviews were on the record, and so noted, but others are simply cited by codes. Most of those interviews were with OECD officials, former officials, and country delegation members. This is a unique data source for analysis – almost all other work on the OECD is based almost entirely on document analysis. As a methodology, confidential interviews also has its weaknesses – it cannot be easily replicated by other researchers, interview data may be biased and memories flawed, and interviewees may have their own personal axes to grind and agendas to promote. The replication issue can easily be addressed – the book's focus was the GOV directorate, its three committees, and a subset of delegation members. The problem of bias was addressed by conducting four waves of interviews that posed similar questions on key themes, building up a collage of responses that goes beyond a single person's memory or recollection. Points of fact where double-checked with primary documentary evidence where available. Even if there remain limitations and small flaws, the wealth of detailed and internal information that was gathered would simply have been impossible without the guarantee of confidentiality. In total, 63 interviews were conducted between May 2010 and June 2011.
3. It analyses an institution that is quintessentially a "globally networked" organization. This should provide insights and lessons about global networks more generally.
4. It casts fresh light on governance and public management drivers and tendencies around the world, both in terms of their roots in the 1990s and more contemporary emphases and approaches.

No book of this scope could be done alone, and I have a long list of people and organizations to thank. My first debt is to the OECD itself and to members of the GOV committees, the GOV directorate, other directorates and units within the organization, and the excellent staff at the OECD Library and Archives. They were all unfailingly helpful and open. In some cases I requested access to classified materials or confidential committee meetings, and while there was initial reluctance simply due to organizational practice, in all cases I was eventually accommodated. Delegation members who were interviewed gave generously of their time and were often refreshingly candid in their views and reflections. As well, several Canadian officials and ex-officials connected with the OECD were also generous and insightful, and in particular members of the Permanent Delegation of Canada to the OECD.

The funds to undertake the research were provided by the Social Sciences and Humanities Research Council of Canada, grant no. 410-2007-2056.

Several colleagues provided inspiration, guidance and helpful criticism as the book evolved from a germinating idea to a reality: Pertti Alasuutari, who shared his knowledge of international organizations, policy transfer, and the OECD; David Elder, who provided an early introduction to former colleagues at the OECD; Rianne Mahon, who started me on the project with the invitation to present a paper at a conference that she organized in 2007; and Graeme Auld, a colleague at the School who read most of the manuscript and provided helpful comments as well as fresh thoughts and approaches. As well, I benefitted greatly from presenting versions or parts of chapters to several conferences of the Canadian Political Science Association, NISPAcee, the International Studies Association, and the International Political Science Association, as well as invited lectures at St. Francis Xavier University (Canada), the University of Tampere (Finland), and the Higher School of Economics (Moscow and Nizhny Novgorod). My deepest and most special thanks are to my colleague and friend Rainer Eisfeld, who went through every chapter with his characteristically eagle editorial eye, both correcting small errors and providing big ideas that vastly improved the book.

The book would simply not have been possible without the hard work of several research assistants over the past two years: Bohdan Buduru, Nicolas Falvo, Marian Gure, Derek Ireland, Tamara Krawchenko, Ha Nguyen, Matthew Pal, and Will Sternberg. The editorial team at Palgrave provided collegial and thoroughly professional support throughout the writing and publication of the book.

Finally, deep thanks to my family. They tolerated long and frequent absences as I conducted field research and interviews, and supported me through the usual stresses of completing a manuscript of this length and complexity.

1
Frontiers of Governance and the OECD as an International Organization

Angel Gurría, appointed OECD Secretary-General (SG) in 2006, is the first to hold the position from a developing country – he served as Mexico's Minister of Foreign Affairs and subsequently as Minister of Finance and Public Credit in the 1990s. He is relaxed for our interview, but still gives the impression of coiled energy. I ask him where the OECD's agenda comes from, and he paints a portrait of an unusual organization:

> There are many sources. One of them of course is the Secretariat including myself, because we're always talking to ministers, to prime ministers, to presidents. Last year I saw about 140 ministers individually ... and about 42 leaders individually. I made about 160 speeches. We're always trying to reach out ... . The idea is to get back the results, what are they worried about, what can we do for you, what is important for you, how can we do it. What is going to hit you in the face in one years' time, two years' time? Five years? What is your greatest nightmare, what keeps you awake at night that can suddenly come and haunt you and that is going to forever change your society ... . You know, these things. We get them from them. So I am a source. My deputies are a source. The directors are a source ... . Now, there's also of course the Council, which is formed by governments, by representatives, who have their own concerns. Sometimes the members of the council individually, personally have a concern or knowledge, and sometimes they represent their countries. Then of course the Ministerial Council Meeting. The Ministerial Council Meeting which gets together once a year, for which we prepare the ground [and] we ask for guidance about policy. I prepare every year a paper called Strategic Orientations, which is public. And the Strategic Orientations becomes the subject of the discussion for priorities and strategy at this time. So, this is what I would call the top-down inputs. And then of course what makes us different, and I think better, is that we have more than 100 bodies, meaning the committees. And these committees are formed by experts from the different countries, not by bureaucrats, not by officials of the OECD, but by officials

in the 31 or sometimes 40 member countries, sometimes a committee has 60 members even though we only have 31 [members], and they will be discussing taxes or education or health or budgets, or nanotechnology or higher education … . And they will be saying yes, OK, but education is a very big name, it encompasses too many things. Higher education encompasses too many things. Even "universities" is too many things. Now, how do you focus on what do you want, what do we tell the OECD, what do we tell the directors to focus on, because it's what keeps us awake at night. So we have a discussion and we get our marching orders and six months later or two years later we produce the piece of research that was asked of us. And then, third, there are the events, realities – which presents us with challenges every day.[1]

Gurría's sketch is one of a member organization – its members are states – but one that is research- and problem-driven. Gurría himself almost ceaselessly travels the globe, but OECD staff – both permanent and on secondment – undertake missions to other countries on a regular basis for reviews, research, consultations, conferences and workshops. It is a responsive organization – it receives its agenda through a tango, danced by the Ministerial Council and the Secretariat, but also by keeping its ear to the ground and responding to "what haunts governments at night". It also looks ahead and works for years in vineyards neglected or ignored by its member states, building up expertise and knowledge, being ready to offer advice based on substantial and extensive research.

The OECD is an international governmental organization (IGO), a type of organization that has grown in importance and influence over domestic policy in the last 50 years, but it has its own special and unique features. It is an organization deliberately engaged in policy transfer – its mandate is to support free markets, trade, capitalist economic development, and democratic institutions around the world. As the next chapter shows, it has developed interesting criteria on membership as well as engagement in order to meet this mandate. As noted in the Preface, this book is not about the entire organization, only its role in global public management reform and modernization. We touched on that movement lightly there, but will explore it in more detail in this chapter. In the next chapter we examine the emergence of governance and public management as a core area of OECD activity and research. While Chapter 3 will describe the inner workings of GOV and its committees, this chapter will outline the broad structure of the OECD and how it operates.

Emergence of governance and public management as a "policy area"

Governments are organizations, and all organizations look internally from time to time to increase efficiency and improve capacity. The Preface described, for example, the early 20th century reform movements and the establishment of professional associations of public managers. We also highlighted four distinguishing features in the post-1945 era: the priority of rebuilding Europe, the Cold War and the "clash of systems", the rise in the 1980s of "new public management" (NPM), and the emergence of the idea that – however "soft" – there nonetheless are common and global standards of "good governance".

What essentially happened over this period was the emergence of public sector reform as a core policy area of global, not merely national, concern – something to which states would have to pay constant and sustained attention. This was due to an emerging sense of the importance of governance, the increasing challenges to governments themselves (e.g., more citizen demands, more competition, more fiscal pressures), and the imperative of "modernization". We come back to this theme of "modernization" in the book's conclusion, but it had a deep gravitational pull on public sector reform discussions in the 1990s and 2000s. Now, with the financial crisis of 2008 and its continuing impact on many countries, the discussion has shifted to "survival" and "growth".

So, public sector reform was not ignored before the 1990s, but it was considered either an internal national matter (e.g., the United States underwent reform under the Carter administration, Canada in the late 1980s with its PS2000), or something involving piecemeal rather than systemic reform.[2] The two important changes that occurred were in the IGO donor community, and in thinking about NPM. On the IGO community, Roberts notes that before "the 1990s, many development specialists, particularly those affiliated with major organizations like the World Bank, paid little attention to the ways in which the design of state institutions affected economic growth. But this changed in the 1990s. The World Bank in particular developed an enthusiasm for the improvement of 'institutional capability' in poorer nations" (Roberts 2010: 15). The roots of this change among IGOs (we discuss the OECD specifically in the next chapter) in fact go back to the 1970s.

Caiden notes that the first attempt at collaboration around governance issues was at a conference organized by the Committee on Comparative Politics of the US Social Science Research Council at Stanford in 1962 (Caiden 1991: 57–70). Its title was "Bureaucracy and Political Development" and was marked by strong doubts about exporting Weberian (i.e., hierarchical, rule-bound) bureaucratic models to developing countries. This was followed by another seminar in mid-1963, organized by the Comparative Administration Group of the American Society for Public Administration. Again, there were critiques that American efforts at reform should encourage rule of law, freedom of expression rather than public administration reform per se – the overarching agenda was democratic, not bureaucratic. In 1966 the US Foreign Assistance Act was amended along these lines, to emphasize the importance of democratic reform. The first global meeting of experts on major administrative reform was in 1971, organized by UNPAD (United Nations Public Administration Division). It was held at the Institute of Development Studies in the UK, and its focus was on reform in developing countries. The conclusion was that there was a need for more international cooperation. Then in 1979 the US hosted an International Conference on Improving Public Management and Performance, co-sponsored by the American Consortium for International Public Administration and the International Institute of Administrative Sciences. While the purpose of the conference was to support continuing involvement and work by the international community, the financial crisis shortly afterwards re-directed the focus on cutback management. Caiden argues that international cooperation abruptly ended and countries were left to their own devices. International agencies continued to make modest efforts on internationalization – the World Bank added a Management and Development Series to its working paper series in the early 1980s, and the IMF included some public sector-related issues in its Occasional Papers series on taxation.

The seminal World Bank 1997 report, *The State in a Changing World*, marked an important change in the donor community's view of the importance of governance for development, but in fact the first wisps were evident as early as its 1983 *World Development Report* (World Bank 1983), the sixth in a series that had been launched in 1987. This was the first volume to look closely at public administration and management. The report concentrated on public enterprise, project management, and the management of the public service. While public administration professionals thought that some parts of the report were *jejeune*, it was still acknowledged as "provocative" in its argument that governments are administrative instruments that affect markets, and should be relied upon more by developing countries (Murray 1983). Turner and Hulme note that the report reinforced the idea that: "A state was no longer credible (and might even be without credit!) unless it had an ongoing programme of administrative reform" (Turner & Hulme 1997: 105). Despite these ambiguities, the report emphasized the importance of effective and efficient public management in achieving economic development, albeit more as a handmaiden to macroeconomic policy than a key driver in its own right. The following quotes give a flavour of the report's approach, one in which governance and public management are important ingredients in economic development, and should be the targets of reform and improvement:

> To bring performance into line with potential, governments must play a central role in ensuring:
> - A stable macroeconomic environment, by adopting sustainable monetary, fiscal, and foreign exchange policies
> - A system of incentives that encourages resources to be allocated efficiently and used optimally
> - A pattern of growth whereby benefits are widely shared. Since the world is beset with uncertainty, governments need the flexibility to respond to unforeseen events and to resolve the inevitable conflicts between competing interest groups. (World Bank 1983: 41)

Training is widely advocated but often poorly executed. Before 1950 most developing countries had only limited training facilities. Over the next thirty years, aid donors directed large quantities of aid to training public officials in developing countries and to building training institutions inside and outside governments:

- Five regional and intergovernmental training institutions have been established in Africa, Asia, and Latin America – three under UN auspices – to support public service training.

- The United Nations, the United States government, and the Ford Foundation are estimated to have spent roughly $250 million in support of institutions for training in public administration alone during 1951–62. (World Bank 1983: 106)

It is easy to prescribe what is needed for successful management of the public service. It is much less easy to adapt these requirements to the cultural and political environment of individual countries. Unless management techniques are designed to take explicit account of these cultural influences, however, they will fall far short of their potential. Although practices evolved in developed countries can be used in many developing countries, they need to be tailored to local realities. And it is just as important to identify and develop indigenous management principles. (World Bank 1983: 113)

We see in these excerpts an intellectual tug-of-war between pure market principles and a growing sense of the importance of governing institutions. The report closed with "lessons learned", and one of them was that policies "are relevant only if there is the institutional capacity to carry them out" (World Bank 1983: 126). The evolution of the World Bank in the ensuing years was remarkable. By its 1997 World Development Report, *The State in a Changing World*, it was trumpeting the importance of sound governance institutions to economic development (World Bank 1997). It strived to re-invent itself as a "knowledge bank" (Stone 2000, 2003; Stone & Wright 2007) and institutions, governance, and public management became new priorities. In reality, this was a far cry from the "Washington consensus" of the late 1980s (Williamson 1993; Rodrik 2006; Weaver & Leiteritz 2005). In this it may have gone further than most other IGOs at the time, but it is a clear illustration of a tectonic shift in thinking.

The other shoe to drop in this period was a change in public management theory. As "theory" of course, much of it was being generated in academe, but we should not ignore the rivulets of debate that flowed between academe and IGOs and back. We will see this dynamic in subsequent chapters on the OECD, but the change in theory was something that migrated smoothly between academic thinkers and international organizations (Farazmand 2004). Under the banner of NPM there was a sea-change in thinking about how government and public management should be organized. The typically cited "leaders" in this "revolution" were New Zealand

(Boston 1996; Aucoin 1995), and the United Kingdom (Savoie 1994). Of equal interest in the discussion of NPM was how it spread and how deeply it was affecting governments around the world. "Since the 1980s, a global reform movement in public management has been vigorously underway" (Kettl 2005: 1). Peters and Pierre noted: "Except perhaps during major wars there never has been the extent of administrative reform and reorganization that has been occurring during the period from approximately 1975 onward" (Peters & Pierre 2001: 1).

The NPM literature is voluminous. For an overview see Lane (2000) and Christensen and Laegreid (2002, 2008) and Dunleavy et al (2005). There are conflicting interpretations of what NPM actually meant (its high tide has passed with the financial crisis of 2008 and the need for governments to be more active and interventionist (Pal 2011b), but also because of a renewed sense of the public value of government (Denhardt & Denhardt 2003). Common provides a useful summary of the key elements of NPM (see Table 1.1).

The broad agreement that public management reform was occurring around the world was part of a larger debate about the causes and consequences of that reform. There were occasional observations in the literature on the effect of IGOs, principally the public administration section (PUMA) of the OECD. Hood (1998: 202) for example noted that international organizations like the OECD and the World Bank had a vested interest in arguing on behalf of "best practice" models that they would then have a role in fostering and supporting. Premfors argued that the dominant narrative of public sector reform had been developed by PUMA and that it had "been very successful in stimulating interest and debate among both member governments and wider audiences and in formulating and propagating a particular mode of thinking about administrative reform" (Premfors 1998: 142). Other observers agreed: "PUMA has been one of the nodal points in an international network, bringing together civil servants, management consultants and academics (an occasionally politicians themselves) who are interested in public management. It has helped shape what has now become an international 'community of discourse' about public management reform ... . The World Bank, the IMF and the Commonwealth Institute have also been international disseminators of management reform ideas" (Pollitt & Bouckaert 2004: 20–21). Larmour traces the role of IGOs in exporting NPM policy ideas to the Pacific Islands, but also notes that: "The OECD took an active role in standardizing these ideas and disseminating them through conferences, publications, and an annual report on developments. NPM ideas were originally justified in terms of the special conditions of Western Europe and the United States: complex liberal economies that could no longer be regulated by command and control; and sophisticated users of public services, who wanted to exercise choice. Nevertheless, NPM's critique of insensitive and inefficient state planning and of self-interested officialdom had intuitive appeal in many postcommunist and developing countries" (Larmour 2005: 98–99).

Table 1.1 New Public Management "Model"

Reform	Meaning
STRUCTURE	**Organizational Decentralization**
1. Creation of single purpose agencies	Separate policy from execution (horizontal decentralization)
2. New forms of organization	Flattening hierarchies
3. Territorial/geographical decentralization	Vertical decentralization
4. Reduce number of departments/agencies	Streamline organization structure
5. Quasi-privatization	Blurring public/private divide – "flexibility to explore alternatives to public provision"
6. Contracting out (market testing)	Create and manage competitive environments
PROCESS	**Introduce private sector management techniques**
7. Corporatization/strong organizational leadership	"Hands on" management enjoying greater visibility, accountability and discretion
8. Strategic management	Business and corporate planning
9. Decisions made close to/at point of service delivery	Managerial decentralization

Table 1.1 New Public Management "Model" – *continued*

Reform	Meaning
Budgetary Process	
10. Performance measurement	Stress on and use of outpouts (or outcomes)
11. Create internal markets	Separation of purchasing and providing functions
12. Cost-centre creation	Devolved budgeting
13. Use of cost rather than expenditure	Focus on actual costs rather than volume budgeting
14. End annuality	Freedom to retain savings
15. Use of budgets for planning/control	"Top-down" budgeting
16. Use of output measures and volume targets in budgets	More detailed budgetary scrutiny against targets
17. Cost-saving incentives	To encourage managers to make efficient use of resources
18. Trading funds	Revenue retained from user charges
19. Resource accounting	Accrual accounting
20. Greater evaluation through audit	Establishment of independent auditing bodies
21. Bulk budgeting	Greater flexibility within budgetary parameters
22. Purchasing deregulation	Avoid central procurement agencies

Table 1.1 New Public Management "Model" – *continued*

Reform	Meaning
Human Resource Management	
23. Change reward structure	Pay to reflect "market" conditions
24. Performance related/merit pay	Pay to reflect performance
25. Performance contracts	Tenure determined by performance
26. Appraisal based on performance	Monitoring by performance
27. Personnel deregulation	Covers the elimination of a range of civil service controls
28. Weaken trade union power	Strengthen managerial discretion
29. Quality management	Deprofessionalization
30. Programme review	Systematic analysis of costs and benefits of individual programmes
31. Consumerist mechanisms	e.g., Citizen's Charters
32. PR and marketing	Establish market identity for public organizations
33. Integrated service delivery	Includes "one stop shops" and case management
34. Foster greater transparency	Public as monitors of services

Source: Common 2001: 49–50

However, for the most part, explanations of the global public management movement tended to emphasize functional reasons such as modernization or democratization (Lynn Jr 2001). Gradually, the focus shifted from reforms in individual countries to the dynamics of the spread of reform ideas. That sharpened the focus on IGOs.

International government organizations and policy transfer

The collapse of the Soviet Union created the potential and the imperative for a massive transfer of policies and institutions to the newly formed states, especially in central and Eastern Europe (CEE). Somewhat surprisingly, researchers from 1991 to roughly 1995 who focused on the region tended to stress the importance of different communist legacies and internal, domestic factors as determining the reform path that different countries would take. In 1996 Schmitter (1996) commented that most work in the field had ignored international pressures, and that it was time to look more seriously at them. Crawford and Lijphart (1997) echoed the re-thinking in posing two models of transition in CEE, one based on Leninist legacies and the other on functionalist pressures of liberalization:

> In sum, this first cut at the evidence suggests that neither the Leninist legacy nor the imperatives of liberalization provides an adequate approach to the study of post-Communist political and economic change. Not all past legacies have become politically relevant. Although among elites, cultural legacies of passivity and intolerance seem to be losing their power in the political process, other legacies, such as the incomplete process of nation-building, are undermining liberalization in many areas. Some institutional legacies provide support for liberalization, and some immediate circumstances, rather than legacies, have worked to undermine economic and political liberalization. We must therefore turn to explanations that provide a more nuanced view of how past legacies and current circumstances interact to explain particular outcomes in the process of regime change. (Crawford & Lijphart 1997: 31)

The realization that there needed to be a better link between domestic policy processes and international or transnational policy networks was arising in the international relations literature as well. Risse-Kappen argued that the "interaction between international norms and institutions, on the one hand, and domestic politics, on the other, is not yet fully understood; work in this area has just begun" (Risse-Kappen 1995: 31). At the same time, the potential importance of IGOs as venues or sites for policy diffusion and lobbying was also being recognized:

> International institutions are then expected to facilitate the access of transnational actors to the national policy-making processes. International

regimes and organizations are likely to increase the availability of channels which transnational actors can use to target national governments in order to influence policies. INGOs [international governmental organizations] and transgovernmental networks lobbying governments can do so more easily in the framework of international institutions. To a certain degree, international regimes and organizations are likely to reduce the differences in filtering effects of the various types of domestic structures. Even countries with state-dominated domestic structures such as France are probably unable to cut themselves off from demands of transnational actors when dealing with international institutions. International regimes and organizations would then provide channels into the national political systems which domestic structures might otherwise limit. (Risse-Kappen 1995: 31; see also Risse-Kappen 1994)

Within a few years, however, the impact of IGOs and international policy transfer to the region was better appreciated. Schimmelfennig observed that "In the aftermath of the Central and Eastern European revolutions and the breakdown of communism, the CEECs [Central and Eastern European Countries] have turned to international organisations for guidance and assistance in their political and economic transformation, and international organizations have become strongly involved in the domestic politics of the CEECs, the restructuring of domestic institutions, and the entire spectrum of material policies" (Schimmelfennig 2002: 1). At the same time, however, he also claimed that the role of these organizations "has rarely been analyzed in a systematic, theory-oriented, and comparative way" (ibid.).

Smith agreed that "Western actors have played an unprecedented, active role in promoting democracy in Eastern Europe, using a variety of instruments. These actors include Western governments, multilateral organizations, nongovernmental organizations (NGOs), and foundations" (Smith 2001: 31). In examining the EU, the OSCE, the Council of Europe, and NATO – organizations focused more on democracy than on economic reform – she argued that while there was general consensus in the West to support democratization, there was no clear definition of what that meant, and it varied country by country, without overt coordination, and some conflicting objectives such as how best to introduce market mechanisms. She argued that more resources and energy were put into liberalization of markets and economic reform than democratization. However, her focus was on democratization, and she has only two or three references to attempts to reform public administration.

One of the best overviews of the impact of international organizations in the region was by Jacoby (2001: 169). Grounding himself explicitly in the literature on lesson-drawing and policy borrowing (discussed below), he pointed out that it assumes that innovation "is both voluntaristic and done against a background of fairly stable domestic institutions". The situation in CEE, however, was one where international actors aggressively promoted certain models in the context of massive shifts in domestic political and economic institutions. Nor were domestic elites simply passive recipients of these models – they had their own local challenges to face and so actively negotiated the importation of these models to suit their own interests.

As it was, elite borrowing of Western institutional designs had a political logic that satisfied multiple constituencies. First, borrowing appeared to be a relatively easy way to design new structures without the uncertainty and time costs of experimentation. Second, by seeming to promise suitable substitutes, such borrowing made it much easier to jettison the widely discredited institutions of the recently fallen Marxist-Leninist regimes. Third, imitating "proven" Western Structures seemed to promise national elites a kind of "legitimacy windfall" vis-à-vis their own polities, with whom they had fragile ties of loyalty and trust. Fourth, copying Western structures seemed likely to reassure both Western investors and Western political figures, whose investments and aid elites sought to help achieve democratic capitalism. To oversimplify, the first two grounds might be seen as reasons of administrative convenience, while the latter two involved strategies of coalition building. (Jacoby 2001: 173)

IGOs and single-country technical assistance programmes in the early 1990s focused first on economic development (Wedel 1998; Pickel 1997; Nello 2001), in tandem with political democratization, realizing that economic changes were not sustainable – or indeed feasible – without properly functioning institutions. While the initial emphasis was on politics – parties, elections, the judiciary, constitutionalism, participation – it was almost immediately clear that administrative reform would be required if effective and efficient public policies could be eventually expected in the newly emerging countries. Nunberg (1999) provided a useful overview of a decade of reform in the CEE. After 2000, and certainly by the time the EU went through two rounds of accession, the reform trajectories of the former Soviet Union states in the CEE began to diverge significantly (Àgh 2003).

The Nunberg study, conducted for the World Bank, reviewed Poland, Romania, Hungary, Russia, and the German Democratic Republic. She argued that the priority on economic and political reform tended to slow the pace of administrative reform, partly because of the overwhelming urgency of economic reforms, but also possibly due to a "wave of anti-statism that was both a reaction to the delegitimization of the communist state as well as a prevailing intellectual wind blowing in from influential quarters of the developed world" (Nunberg 1999: 1). Nunberg's conclusions on policy borrowing with respect of public sector management models were:

> The models and motivations driving the direction of ministerial restructuring vary, but the transfer or importation of foreign institutional arrangements appears to have been widespread. ... In addition, foreign models also have penetrated CEE countries through the delivery of expatriate tech-

nical assistance. The restructuring of ministerial machinery also has been significant, both through help to specific departments or particular functions within ministries or through head-to-toe "re-engineering" of entire agencies. ... Finally, perhaps the greatest influence from abroad comes as a function of CEE countries' quest to join the EU. Conformity to EU standards increasingly has driven the reorganization of ministerial functions. Hungary's Ministry of Interior based the design of many of its new service functions on EU norms. And, of course, Poland's bold and decisive 1996 administrative reform initiative was no doubt largely driven by the government's recognition that administrative modernization would be key to the country's successful entry into the EU. (Nunberg 1999: 246)

All of this raises the issue of policy transfer or diffusion. It is central to the OECD story, since that is the OECD's basic line of business: to absorb policy experiences, reflect on them, research them, and then refract them back to member countries (and increasingly to a global audience of non-members) as "lessons" or benchmarks. The literature on policy transfer has developed a variety of categories of diffusion and transfer in an attempt to clarify what is actually going on when policies migrate. Rose provided the seminal contribution to this work in 1993, focusing on what he called "lesson-drawing" in public policy, and explicitly highlighted the role of IGOs:

Intergovernmental and international organizations encourage exchange of ideas between countries with similar levels of economic resources. The European Community and OECD encourage exchanges among advanced industrial nations. The collapse of the Communist system is creating a group of more than a dozen states that may learn from each other ways to make a transition to the market economy and democracy. The IMF promotes lessons drawn from the experience of countries that have large foreign debts, and the World Bank and many United Nations agencies focus on programs of concern to developing countries. (Rose 1993: 105)

Bennett's work (1991, 1992, 1997) was a sustained attempt to explore policy transfer or diffusion. In one work, for example, he analysed models of cross-national diffusion of policy around three public administration innovations: the institution of the ombudsman, freedom of information legislation and data protection (information privacy) law. He concluded that there was no one method of diffusion, but that there were different dynamics of adoption: lesson-drawing (where governments see a problem and borrow an existing solution – essentially a rationalist problem-solving and borrowing procedure), legitimation (referring to other international examples to satisfy domestic critics), and harmonization. The later is facilitated by IGOs: with respect to data privacy, the nature of the problems of transborder data flows impelled legislation spearheaded by the OECD and the Council of Europe in 1981 that then "became a powerful, if not determining, incentive for adoption: failure to act would have meant an inability to ratify the Council of Europe Convention, an exclusion from the 'club' within which personal data could be legitimately communicated, thus causing adverse economic consequences especially for the service sector" (Bennett 1997: 228). This insight was supported by Dolowitz and Marsh (1996, 2000):

> [I]nternational governing organizations (IGOs), such as the OECD, G-7, IMF and the UN and its various agencies, are increasingly playing a role in the spread of ideas, programs and institutions around the globe. These organizations influence national policy-makers directly, through their policies and loan conditions, and indirectly, through the information and policies spread at their conferences and reports. (Dolowitz & Marsh 2000: 11)

Policy transfer and diffusion is not uniquely associated with contemporary globalization – in the late 19th century, after the Meiji restoration, the Japanese attempted to modernize their administrative systems and economy (Westney 1987) – but there is a close connection nonetheless, for several reasons (Evans 2004: 32; Cerny 1997). To begin with, the post-World War II settlement created a host of international organizations – the IMF, the World Bank, and the OEEC being among the most prominent – and they were clearly in the policy transfer business in order to create a broadly capitalist and liberal-democratic global order. Communications and travel technology dramatically improved in the same period, making it literally possible to both know about what other countries were doing in different policy fields, and directly meet and exchange ideas. This is absolutely critical for an organization like the OECD, that is essentially an "idea broker" (more on this below). Finally, the increasing complexity of systems at the global level – for example, trade regimes – makes coordination and borrowing increasingly important as well.

But how to frame this process? Evans points out that the literature has generated a variety of terms, all broadly similar, but with slight differences in emphasis: bandwagonning, convergence, diffusion, emulation, policy learning, social-learning, and lesson-drawing (Evans 2009a: 238). A recent contribution by Simmons et al (2008b) examines the global diffusion of markets and democracy through a lens that highlights four causal mechanisms of diffusion or transfer: coercion, competition, learning, and emulation. Their approach closely parallels others in the field (Evans 2004; Common 2001), and we will rely on it to cast light on how diffusion occurs.

Coercion can be applied by governments, international organizations, even NGOs, and can be subtle or overt: threats of physical force, economic pressures, and other instruments can be applied by more powerful actors against weaker ones. They cite the World Bank, the IMF and the EU as prime examples of organizations that can extract compliance through conditionalities. Countries that seek financial support must meet the policy standards imposed by these organizations. This is essentially a hierarchical and centralized form of transfer.

Competition involves states adopting "market friendly" policies and institutions because this will make their markets attractive to investors. If competitors have lower tax rates, or simplified regulatory regimes, and consequently improved economic performance, other countries need to follow suit or be left behind. Simmons et al argue that the competitive dynamic seems to work more prominently around economic policy, but there is some evidence that investors also sometimes prefer certain institutional arrangements. This form of diffusion is decentralized and uncoordinated, and hence is a different pathway when compared with coercive mechanisms.

Policy learning is a mechanism whereby countries draw lessons, based on observation and rational assessment of efficacy, from other countries' experiences, and then apply those experiences in their own context, quite likely with some modification in the process of "institutional transplantation" (De Jong et al 2002).

Emulation is a mechanism of diffusion drawn from sociological research that emphasizes that borrowing takes place within a shared set of meanings as to appropriate social actors, societal goals, and means for achieving those goals. As Simmons et al argue: "While policymakers see themselves as collectively trying to divine the 'best practice' in each policy area, and see policy as evolving toward more and more effective forms, in fact policymakers are seldom able to judge whether a popular new policy improves upon the status quo" (2008c: 32). Emulation relies on voluntary adoption of new policies in a context where "followers" typically are ready to copy the example of countries or IGOs considered to be "leading". Emulation has a strong element of bounded rationality – policymakers cannot really be certain about the empirical efficacy of many policies – so they make the best guesses that they can, but also take their cues from who is defined as "leading" and what is defined as a "best practice".

The OECD is a member-based organization and has few instruments or tools to enforce compliance. Consequently, unlike the World Bank or the IMF, it has little capacity to enforce conditionalities, though this is not necessarily a weakness. Woods points out that "borrowing governments seldom actually do as they are told" (Woods 2006: 4), and Vreeland claims that this is one reason the OECD has maintained its "pristine reputation" compared to the IMF (Vreeland 2007). Coercion is not an option. However, the other three mechanisms do characterize the OECD's mode of operation. First, member states and even non-member states often use the OECD to develop either formal or informal/consensual standards or benchmarks. These "rules of the game" ensure a level playing field but also help countries as they compete for investment – China, for example, has had several OECD reviews, through several *Economic Surveys* and peer reviews on agricultural policy, education, innovation and the environment. Second, lesson-drawing is at the heart of the way in which the OECD operates. We discuss this in detail in Chapter 4, but the unique character of the OECD is given by the fact that thousands of public servants from its member states, as well as observers, come to meetings to exchange experiences and learn what other countries are doing in their areas of policy expertise. Almost all committee meetings are confidential, and so lesson-drawing can take place in a secure or "safe" environment where public servants can be frank with each other. Finally, emulation is also a key OECD mechanism. We will see in the next chapter and in more detail in Chapter 4 that the OECD often uses the language of "best practices" or "trends" or "leaders and laggards". This is a powerful tool in creating impressions about standards and practices on the cutting edge, on shared solutions, or broadly shared values and objectives. Lee and Strang (2008) argue in their case study on the international diffusion of public sector downsizing in OECD countries that learning as emulation is the best fit with the case, and Simmons et al say that they were surprised at the "the strength of emulation-style mechanisms in several policy areas, including economic policies, that traditionally are analyzed in strictly rationalist and materialist ways" (2008a: 353–354).

Work on policy diffusion also routinely highlights another important transfer mechanism: the role of policy professionals, academics, intergovernmental organizations and NGOs (Simmons et al 2008c: 35). These "epistemic communities" (Haas 1992) help to define problems and frame solutions for those problems, and become key promoters and sellers of policy, effectively the human side of the policy transfer network (Evans 2004; Common 2001: 35; Dunlop 2009). The OECD is a "bundle" of epistemic communities of experts and practitioners around almost every important public policy field from education to the environment, and again this is its unique strength. Of the 2,500 permanent staff in the OECD's Secretariat, about 800 are senior-level analysts, and they are among the best subject-matter experts in the world. They constantly travel and meet counterparts; they continually network in conferences and meetings. The very *raison d'être* of the organization is policy development, policy learning, and policy transfers through learning, research, and emulation.

We now turn to a more detailed portrait of the OECD as an organization. Its history and its focus on governance are discussed in the next chapter, and Chapter 3 looks closely at the GOV directorate's structure and activities.

The OECD as an organization

The next chapter provides a history of the OECD (with a special focus on governance and public management). This section probes more deeply into what kind of international organization the OECD is. We have already mentioned that it is a member-based organization, and that it specializes in the interaction and exploration and mutual sharing of its members and increasingly a wide audience of non-members. But we can dig a little more deeply.

First, on its status as an IGO. Barnett and Finnemore (1999, 2004) have provided the best clues to understanding these organizations. Their work has focused on IGOs that can actually make rules – international law and hard standards – on a global scale, and so they do not address the OECD directly since it rarely makes rules. However, they make several key points about IGOs. These organizations are not merely ciphers for their member states – they are bureaucracies in their own right, and develop agendas and objectives that do not necessarily coincide with those of their members (we address this in Chapter 5). They note that the authority of IGOs "often consists of telling people what is the right thing to do" (Barnett & Finnemore 2004: 20), but also that IGOs can rarely demand obedience – they engage in self-effacement, purporting only to uphold values: "The authority of [IGOs], and bureaucracies generally, therefore, lies in their ability to present themselves as impersonal and neutral – as not exercising power but instead serving others" (Barnett & Finnemore 2004: 21). ... "[IGOs] are often authoritative because of their expertise. ... Specialized knowledge derived from training or experience persuades us to confer on experts, and the bureaucracies that house them, the authority to make judgements and solve problems" (Barnett & Finnemore 2004: 24). And in an important observation that links the role of IGOs back to the discussion above about policy diffusion, they argue:

> Having established rules and norms, [IGOs] are eager to spread the benefits of their expertise and often act as conveyor belts for the transmission of norms and models of good political behavior. There is nothing accidental or unintended about this role. Officials in [IGOs] often insist that part of their mission is to spread, inculcate, and enforce global values and norms. They are the missionaries of our time. Armed with a notion of progress, an idea of how to create a better life, and some understanding of the conversion process, many [IGO] staff have as their stated purpose to shape state action by establishing best practices and by articulating and transmitting norms that define what constitutes acceptable and legitimate state behavior. (Barnett & Finnemore 2004: 33)

The OECD reflects these characteristics, perhaps more acutely than most other IGOs. As Porter and Webb point out, the "OECD can be seen as a paradigmatic example of an identity-defining international organization. Its primary impact comes through efforts to develop and promote international norms for social and economic policy ... . It defines standards of appropriate behaviour for states that seek to identify themselves as modern, liberal, market-friendly, and efficient" (2008: 44). Marcussen has explored the way in which the OECD plays the "idea game". He notes how Thorkil Kristensen, the first SG of the OECD, argued that the core of the organization's work was a process of continuing consultation involving "regular discussion between officials coming from their capitals, regular examinations of the policies of each individual member country, studies undertaken by expert groups on problems of special interest, [and] formal or informal recommendations to countries" (quoted in Marcussen 2004: 15).

According to Kristensen, the OECD serves the role of an "ideational artist" which "formulates, tests and diffuses new policy ideas", as well as an "ideational arbitrator", facilitating consultation and mutual learning and education over repeated encounters (Aubrey 1967). In all this, it is clear that the OECD is a preeminent example of a "networked" organization at the international level. Indeed, in its 50th Anniversary Vision Statement, released in May 2011, the SG explicitly underscored "our resolve to make the OECD a more effective and inclusive global policy network" (OECD 2011c).

The idea of conceptualizing domestic policy processes in terms of networks – rather than institutions – can be traced back at least to the early and mid-1970s in Heclo and Wildavsky's work challenging the idea that American public policy was the product of rigid "iron triangles" (Heclo 1978; Heclo & Wildavsky 1978). Instead they suggested the more fluid concept of "issue networks". But the idea of conceptualizing policy processes in terms of networks did not gain traction until the 1990s – in 1991 Marin and Mayntz called the idea of policy networks a "new key term" (1991: 11), but one which was being identified as one of the most important conceptual innovations in recent studies of the policy process (Atkinson & Coleman 1992: 158; Thatcher 1998). Nonetheless, the concept's utility has been hotly debated (Dowding 1995, 2001; Marsh & Smith 2001; Klijn & Skelcher 2007; Rhodes 2007; Börzel 1998) in its application to domestic policy processes. As remarkable as it seems, it took some time for the concept to migrate into the study of international relations – in part because of the discipline's traditional emphasis on "realist" perspectives that privileged dominant powers. Haas's invention of the term "epistemic communities" (Haas 1992) opened the door not only to seeing non-state actors as important in shaping global order and global policy priorities (Risse-Kappen 1995), but also to the role of ideas in international policy-making and how they – and their sponsors – can shape global policy outcomes (Risse-Kappen 1994).

As policy issues increasingly get driven upward to the international level, and as government officials and NGOs increasingly respond by connecting to counterparts everywhere around the globe, the idea that policy networks are primarily domestic is being re-thought. Domestic human rights groups, for example, now are routinely connected to international networks, as are groups organized around population issues, economic development, and the environment. To some extent, this non-governmental global associational system was deliberately fostered and nurtured. International agencies such as the UN, for example, particularly in the 1990s, "accelerated the global associational revolution by affirming the right of nongovernmental actors to participate in shaping national and global policies on the environment, population, human rights, economic development, and women" (Batliwala 2002: 394). International UN conferences on the environment (Rio in 1992), human rights (Vienna in 1993), population (Cairo in 1994), social policy (Copenhagen in 1995), women (Beijing in 1995), and housing and cities (Istanbul in 1996) became platforms for the development of international networks of activists. The OECD had its own encounter with global civil society in the late 1990s around the Multilateral Agreement on Investment that it was championing. The effort was defeated by activists in 1998, leading the OECD two years later to launch the Annual Forum, a meeting that brings together government, business and civil society representatives (Woodward 2009: 37).

In addition to NGOs and activists, of course, there are more formal organizations and institutions, including IGOs. Professional associations, foundations, and think tanks generate ideas that enter the flow through publications and conferences; NGOs like Transparency International or Global Integrity produce measures and assessments through indicators and other publications, and their ideas flow into the stream as well; state aid and technical assistance agencies and IGOs can apply somewhat more coercive instruments such as conditionality, or mount training programmes that transfer standards and norms directly to recipient groups of public officials. Stone calls these organizations "transfer agents" (2002, 2004, 2008), thus nicely connecting networks to the dynamics of policy transfer and diffusion discussed earlier.

What do networks – and networked organizations look like? What are their characteristics? The contrast should be with traditional organizations or bureaucracies – including states and market organizations (e.g., business firms). For the purposes of our analysis of the OECD, we highlight ten key characteristics of networks. These will guide the rest of the book.

1. Networks are non-hierarchal, or as organizations, at least very "flat", without excessive layers. This means that "orders" and "commands" are not their basic vocabulary, certainly not in the sense that they are determined "above" and sent "down".
2. Networks consist of interconnected nodes. These nodes may be "individuals, groups, organisations, or states" (Kahler 2009: 3). The interconnections may be strong (repeated interactions and flows) or weak (episodic interactions with relatively low volume of exchange).
3. Network nodes need not all be equal, despite the flatness and lack of hierarchy. As long as the other characteristics of networks are respected and maintained, networks can embrace "larger" and "smaller" members (Watts 1999, 2003).
4. Network links and connections consist of exchanges. Our interest here is in organizations like the OECD, or global public policy networks. For networks of this type, "a key feature ... is a shared problem on which there is an exchange of information, debate, disagreement, persuasion and a search for solutions and appropriate policy responses" (Stone 2004: 560).

5. Networks in which the primary exchanges are information (as opposed to money or goods or services) have specific characteristics in themselves. They tend to be <u>open</u> because information has the quality that its value increases with wider dissemination. They tend to focus on the <u>quality</u> of their information and exchanges, since information is so potentially abundant that only quality information will be used. They tend to be <u>search</u> organizations, since information gets stale quickly, and the value of interconnections for members of the network is the exchange and accumulation of new information.

6. Networks are typically voluntary. Membership is not coerced, though more structured networks can set rules for membership. But these rules tend to be quite loose, since part of the value of the network to its members comes from a diversity of participants.

7. Network's prefer norms to rules, though they can occasionally arrive at rules that apply to most if not all members. Norms emerge from interaction, are usually unenforceable, but become embedded as a form of both network governance and the "product" the network produces to deal with the problems identified by the network in the first place.

8. Networks have no single, final arbiters. To the extent that networks render "decisions" they do so through complex interactions and interconnections and exchanges. Rather than arbiters, networks tend to rely on brokers. Brokers rely on trust.

9. Networks are flexible, often in a condition of flux, change, decline and growth. They can have some institutional boundaries and inner architecture, but in comparison to more hierarchical organizations, they are closer to clouds or schools of fish – they have discernable shape, but are always in motion.

10. Networks are embedded in environments, and those environments can influence network growth and development, as networks – either unconsciously (e.g., a school of fish reconfiguring itself in the face of a predator) or deliberately – adapt and develop.

The OECD, its structure and practices, reflect and express each one of these characteristics. As we noted earlier in canvassing the descriptions of what kind of organization the OECD is, the various terms – ideational artist, ideational arbitrator, playing the idea game – are essentially euphemisms for a networked organization. The only explicit mentions of the OECD as being a networked organization are Stone's (Stone 2004: 130) and Evans (he picks up on Stone) and calls the OECD a "committed agent of policy transfer" (Evans 2009c: 257). We shall see in subsequent chapters that the OECD exemplifies all the key network characteristics. In the early stages of its development, in a more hierarchical international system, being a networked organization was in some respects to the OECD's detriment – it sometimes appeared weak and redundant. But in a global system where networks matter a great deal, as do information flows, these same characteristics have emerged as strengths.

Its network characteristics are inscribed in its very structure. We will explore some other aspects of its structure in the next two chapters, but here we can provide an overview and some bearings on its architecture. We have already mentioned that the OECD is a member organization, at time of writing consisting of 34 member states. Table 1.2 shows the members as of 2011, with their contributions to the OECD's core budget. These contributions come in two parts, one as a base fee linked to national income, and a fee reflecting an equal share of a fixed percentage of the budget (Part 1 of the budget). In addition, members may put forward sums to cover areas or projects of interest (Part 2 of the budget). Peer reviews are paid for by the countries under review.

The OECD has three core components (see Figures 1.1 and 1.2 below). The first is the Council, consisting of one diplomatic representative from each member country, and a representative of the European Commission (non-voting). The Council is chaired by the SG, and meets regularly to oversee the OECD's work and set it broad agenda. Once a year there is a Ministerial Council Meeting (MCM – with elected chairs). Each country sends a delegation to the MCM, and there are invited observers, other government officials, OECD social partners, policy experts and others. The MCM sets the broad direction for the organization. Council now (since 2006) has three sub-committees: a budget committee, an executive committee (for non-budget items), and external relations committee (to deal with enhanced engagement). These all have full representation of members, but there is also a number of smaller committees with only a handful of countries. The tradition in the OECD was to take decisions by consensus, with ballots only in rare occasions, and even then members could abstain. This was relaxed in 2006 with a provision that certain decisions could be passed by qualified majorities.

The real day-to-day work of the OECD takes place in its committees. The committee structure is fluid and can be changed as new needs arise (the GOV committee system is discussed in detail in Chapter 3). Committee membership consists of a subset of member states, and in some cases non-members, and can be attended by non-members and invited observers. In 2011, these together amounted to over 200 bodies. The meetings of the main committees usually take place once or twice a year, some four or five, and the on-going work is done by the Secretariat and the country delegations. Some committees, however, like the Economic and Development Review Committee (supported by the Economics Department) meet over 25 times a year.[3] Each directorate in the OECD supports one or a number of main committees, but other working groups, or groups of experts can be assembled and delegated as the main committee decides (GOV supports the Public Governance Committee, the Territorial Development Policy Committee, and the Regulatory Policy Committee). Working Groups are more on-going, whereas Expert Committees are assembled usually for a single issue. The main committees are listed in Table 1.3.

Table 1.2   OECD Membership and Budget Contributions (2011)

Country	Year of Accession	Contribution to OECD Core (Part 1) Budget (per cent)
Australia	1971	2.39
Austria	1961	1.25
Belgium	1961	1.50
Canada	1961	3.54
Chile	2010	1.43
Czech Republic	1995	0.68
Denmark	1961	1.08
Estonia	2010	1.43
Finland	1969	0.93
France	1961	6.46
Germany	1961	8.38
Greece	1961	1.06
Hungary	1996	0.57
Iceland	1961	0.23
Ireland	1961	0.82
Israel	2010	1.43
Italy	1962	5.14
Japan	1964	12.22
Korea	1996	2.40
Luxembourg	1961	0.29
Mexico	1994	2.39
Netherlands	1961	2.16
New Zealand	1973	0.59
Norway	1961	1.32
Poland	1996	1.28
Portugal	1961	0.85
Russian Federation	[under review for accession]	n/a
Slovak Republic	2000	0.36
Slovenia	2010	1.43
Spain	1961	3.73
Sweden	1961	1.38
Switzerland	1961	1.56
Turkey	1961	1.23
United Kingdom	1961	6.28
United States	1961	22.21

Source: OECD, Member Countries Budget Contributions for 2011, available at
http://www.oecd.org/document/14/0,3746,en_2649_201185_31420750_1_1_1_1,00.html
(accessed 22 June 2011, and OECD, List of OECD Member Countries – Ratification of the
Convention on the OECD, available at
http://www.oecd.org/document/58/0,3746,en_2649_201185_1889402_1_1_1_1,00.html
(accessed 22 June 2011).
The OECD core (Part 1) budget for 2011 was Euro 342 million. The Part 1 budget is about 50 per
cent of the total OECD budget, and based on a mix of an equal share and a share proportional
to size of GDP. Part 2 of the budget is for special purpose bodies (e.g., the International Energy
Agency) and specific projects, and is funded by contributions.

The Council and its committees are supported by the OECD Secretariat. It consists of the SG and some 2,500 permanent staff, the core of whom are policy experts in the diverse fields within which the OECD is involved. As well, for special projects, public servants or experts from member states are seconded to Paris for fixed terms to produce research reports or participate in reviews. In addition to this general Secretariat, there are semi-autonomous bodies that consist of centres for policy dialogues with other states (e.g., the Development Centre is a forum for the OECD and developing countries; the Sahel and West Africa Club encourages regional dialogue between West African countries and OECD members) and so are not completely under the authority of the OECD.

Finally there is the growing network of relations with civil society, mentioned earlier, through the Annual Forum and Global Forums and participation in some OECD committees. This is an extension beyond the two non-governmental fora that were originally linked to the OECD: the TUAC (Trade Union Advisory Committee) and the BIAC (the Business and Industry Advisory Committee).

This overview shows some of the complexity of the OECD, but only scratches the surface. It is a hybrid organization, unusual among IGOs, in that it is half diplomatic and half think-tank. This means that the overlay of the Council is ambassadorial, with representatives of member states having to exercise all the prerogatives and obligations of an international body. There is inevitable pomp and circumstance, formality and protocol. At the same time there is the SG and a Secretariat. The SG has a responsibility to drive the organization, view the horizon, determine directions and steer the agenda. The SG reports to Council, but also chairs its meetings, and has the latitude and authority to meet with world leaders and represent the OECD. As noted above, the SG has his own Office, consisting of routine bureaus such as Legal Affairs, but also more substantive ones like the Centre for Co-operation with Non-Members, and so has some latitude to develop an independent agenda within those resources. Because the committees are nominated by member countries, they have the imprimatur of member country, or diplomatic, representation. In most cases, the committees consist of senior officials from member states. This combination of seniority and diplomacy gives the committees a substantial status in reference to the Council and the SG. Committees "drive the organisation",[4] but at the same time, since most meet so infrequently, their supporting directorates end up developing most of the substance of their agendas. The agenda-setting process within the OECD is accordingly complex – it is neither dominated by member states nor by the Secretariat and its directorates. While there is a times tension between the two components, they "can be seen as mutually constitutive" (Trondal et al 2010: 73).

The OECD directorates support their committees, and given the committees' relative autonomy and status, they are naturally as oriented to them as

Table 1.3   OECD Main Committees

Chemicals Committee

Committee for Agriculture

Committee for Information, Computer and Communications Policy

Committee for Scientific and Technological Policy

Committee on Consumer Policy

Committee on Financial Markets

Committee on Fiscal Affairs

Committee on Industry, Innovation and Entrepreneurship

Committee on Statistics

Competition Committee

Coordinating Committee on Remuneration

Corporate Governance Committee

Development Assistance Committee

Economic and Development Review Committee

Economic Policy Committee

Education Policy Committee

Employment, Labour and Social Affairs Committee

Environment Policy Committee

Fisheries Committee

Health Committee

Insurance and Private Pensions Committee

Investment Committee

Joint OECD/ITF Transport Research Committee

Public Governance Committee

Regulatory Policy Commttee

Steel Committee

Steering Committee for Nuclear Energy

Territorial Development Policy Committee

Tourism Committee

Trade Committee

Source: OECD, On-Line Guide to OECD Intergovernmental Activity, available at
http://webnet.oecd.org/oecdgroups/Bodies/ListByNameView.aspx (accessed on 22 June 2011).
The web page list includes eight bodies not listed here since they are centres, programmes,
boards, forums, or Council entities that work quite differently than bona fide committees.

Figure 1.1   Core Elements of the OECD

Who drives the OECD's work?

Council
Oversight and strategic direction
Representatives of member countries and of the European
Commission: decisions taken by consensus

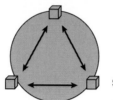

Committees   **Secretariat**

Discussion and implementation   *Analysis and proposals*
Representatives of member countries and of   Secretary-General
countries with Observer status work with the   Deputy Secretaries-General
OECD Secretariat on specific issues   Directorates

Source: OECD, *Who Does What?*, available at http://www.oecd.org/pages/0,3417,en_36734052_
36761791_1_1_1_1_1,00.html (accessed on 22 June 2011).

Figure 1.2   OECD Secretariat

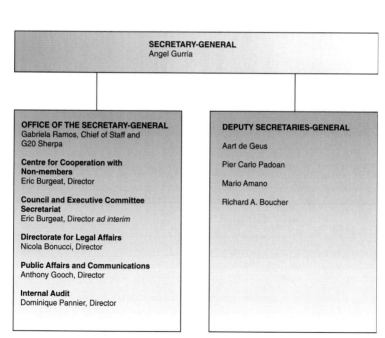

Figure 1.2   OECD Secretariat – *continued*

SPECIAL BODIES

Development Centre	International Energy Agency	Nuclear Energy Agency
Mario Pezzini Director	Nobuo Tanaka Executive Director	Luis Ech varri Director General

DIRECTORATES

Development Cooperation Directorate	Economics Department	Directorate for Education	Directorate for Employment, Labour and Social Affairs	Centre for Entrepreneurship, SMEs and Local Development
Jon Lomoy Director	Pier Carlo Padoan Chief Economist	Barbara Ischinger Director	John P. Martin Director	Sergio Arzeni Director
Environment Directorate	Executive Directorate	Directorate for Financial and Enterprise Affairs	Directorate for Public Governance and Territorial Development	Directorate for Science, Technology and Industry
Simon Upton Director	Patrick van Haute Director	Carolyn Ervin Director	Rolf Alter Director	Andrew Wyckoff Director
Statistics Directorate	Centre for Tax Policy and Administration	Trade and Agriculture Directorate		
Martine Durand Director	Jeffrey Owens Director	Ken Ash Director		

SPECIAL ENTITIES

Africa Partnership Forum	Financial Action Task Force	International Transport Forum	Partnership for Democratic Governance	Sahel and West Africa Club
David Batt Director	Rick McDonell Head of Secretariat	Jack Short Secretary General	Jerzy Pomianowski Head of Advisory Unit	Laurent Bossard Director

Source: OECD, *Secretary-General's Report to Ministers, 2011*, available at http://www.oecd.org/dataoecd/56/6/48066007.pdf (accessed on 22 June 2011).

they are to the organization – the SG – as a whole. As well, committees have several working groups and expert committees working on different subjects within their mandate. This makes for a highly decentralized organization. There are annual agendas and overviews, but the directorates have much wider latitude to determine their own work than is characteristic of most international organizations. Within the directorates, the permanent staff is quite small, and is supplemented by secondments from countries depending on projects. Once projects end, the seconded staff leave. This means an almost constant churn and turnover of personnel within an already decentralized organization. The seconded staff are paid by the OECD, but are still seen as representing their host countries, and so a diplomatic shadow is cast even over subject-matter experts. Finally, much of the work of the OECD involves analysing the policy records of member and non-member states, often through peer review (discussed in detail in Chapter 4). All such reviews are at the request of the host country, but in reviewing a "country" one inevitably gets entangled in diplomatic protocol. Being both objective and critical under these circumstances is a constant challenge.

Conclusion

In one of the first empirical studies of the OECD's, and specifically PUMA's, role in policy transfer, Peters noted that "individual member countries want to appear as modern and innovative as possible to their peers" (1997: 85). Sharing experiences and transferring ideas has also taken place outside of the OECD context at least since the mid-1990s (Laking & Norman 2007), and increasingly this global promotion of policy change has depended on "knowledge banks" (Evans 2009b) like the OECD. But this transfer does not happen magically. A global movement and architecture of public sector reform has depended on several key developments.

The first and most obvious is the appreciation that institutions matter. As we saw in this chapter, and we will see more in the next, it took some time for this sensitivity to develop, as strange as it sounds today. This is not to say that public sector reform of one sort or the other had not occurred before the mid-1990s. Canada, for example, launched a major public sector review, the Royal Commission on Government Organization (the Glassco Commission) in 1960. The commissioners visited the US and the UK, and released five volumes of reports between 1962 and 1963. But as we noted above, there was a palpable acceleration of reform, not just within single countries, but also as a global movement, in the 1980s and beyond. And just as important, international organizations got into the game and began to deliberately position themselves as transfer agents of change.

As well, countries also had to be willing to borrow and to learn. In coercive circumstances, such as conditionalities tied to aid, countries have little choice, though they can still maneuver and in practice ignore those conditions. Voluntary acceptance of transfer is another thing, and as we noted may be a matter of competition, of policy learning, or of emulation. Emulation turns out to be a surprisingly important element in voluntary borrowing. As Peters notes, countries want to appear modern and innovative. This theme of "modernity" will be taken up in the conclusion to this book, but it is a powerful driver of policy transfer in public sector reform, particularly in the OECD context. As a member-based institution, one that represents the "leading countries" in the world (historically, the richest and most advanced in Western Europe and North America) it sets benchmarks and "best practices". No member state wishes to seem "behind" the others, particularly given the diplomatic context we noted above – all members are equal sovereign states, and so in principle should be equivalent in their practices. The realities are always different of course, from actual GDPs to member contributions, and the OECD has been very careful to always acknowledge that different country circumstances will lead to acceptable variations in practices. But the fig leaf of equal status, despite varying local conditions, inevitably leads to a sense of wanting to be among the best of the club. Unlike the UN or the World Bank, the OECD is explicitly driven to measure, compare and contrast. It generates endless reports on "best practices" and "lessons" in almost every conceivable field of public policy, including governance and public sector modernization. This succeeds for two reasons. Members support the effort, since they are interested in what works best. But members are also prepared to take their medicine, primarily because it is peers from other member countries that administer it. We discuss the complexities of this in Chapter 4 on the OECD's tools, but peer review is possibly the most important foundation of the OECD's activities.

Finally, a global movement cannot exist without a global network. The next chapter shows how TECO and PUMA (forerunners to GOV) built a global network around public sector reform, but here we can highlight the core elements. Some of these were deliberate – the early leaders in the OECD knew well that they were building a networked organization in the sense of having a global membership and using the tools of exchange and peer review. Somewhat less consciously, they designed a flat organization that could not command, but could cajole. It had small and large nodes, thus expanding network power. It focused on the exchange of information, was voluntary, and issued norms rather than rules. It adapted to massive changes in its environment, from oil shocks to the collapse of the Soviet Union. None of this was foreordained, and successive SGs have struggled to keep the organization relevant, alive and healthy. But they had the good fortune – they might not agree with this assessment, given the sometimes intractable difficulties of dealing with an organization simultaneously as decentralized and as protocol-dominated as the OECD – of steering a clipper, not a tank.

2
Governance and its Emergence in the OECD

The weather on 5 June 1947 was warm and sunny, a congenial setting for the 15,000 guests assembled in Harvard Yard for the university's first normal commencement after the end of the war. One of the honorary degree recipients was Secretary of State, George C. Marshall, and he appeared distinctly nervous just before he was to give his address at the afternoon alumni association meeting. Marshall had had a brilliant military career, becoming Army Chief of Staff in 1939 just at the outbreak of war in Europe, and had been the US Ambassador to China when he was recalled by President Truman to become Secretary of State. No one in the audience expected anything but an ordinary commencement speech, including the President of Harvard, James B. Conant, who had entertained Marshall the evening before. Marshall's delivery was described as flat and sometimes inaudible, but when it was over less than 20 minutes later, he had laid the foundation for what came to be known as the Marshall Plan, the foundation for a new partnership between the United States and war-torn Europe (Smith 1962).

The Marshall Plan channelled over $12 billion ($117 billion in 2011 US dollars, using the Consumer Price Index) to Western Europe between 1947 and 1951 to enable those countries to rebuild their economies. Economic historians now dispute whether this money was actually necessary or whether it had the real effect of stimulating European recovery, but our interest here is in the governance dimension of the initiative. While the Marshall Plan is usually regarded through an economic lens, as an economic recovery plan, it was just as important for its institutional effects, not the least of which was the creation of the Organisation for European Economic Cooperation (OEEC), the predecessor to the OECD. Partly through accident and partly through design, the OEEC developed many practices and procedures that would carry over into the OECD and provide its distinctive profile as an international governmental organization. Moreover, the Plan was deeply inspired by the emerging Cold War tensions with the Soviet Union, and was intended to provide a defence – through economic and institutional recovery along market-capitalist and democratic lines – against communism. Much the same rationale emerged in 1960 when the OECD emerged from the ashes of the OEEC. A close look at the early history of the OEEC and the birth of the OECD shows that governance issues were always at the heart of the organization, though not so much as a matter of practical advice to member and non-member states, which developed in the 1990s, but as a function of its very existence and ultimate purpose.

This chapter examines the emergence of governance as a key organizational theme and eventually a prime area of exchange, research, and analysis in the OECD. It begins with a short history of the Marshall Plan and the OEEC, and the creation of the OECD itself in 1960–1961. The second section reviews the first incarnation of a governance focus in the OECD in its Technical Cooperation Committee (TECO) and its evolution into the Public Management Committee (supported by the PUMA directorate in the OECD Secretariat) in 1990, and in 2002 into the Public Governance Committee (which works closely with the Territorial Development Policy Committee and the Regulatory Policy Committee – all three are supported now by the GOV directorate in the OECD Secretariat). The trajectory of this development – a stronger focus on providing advice to governments on promising practices, surveying governance trends, and encouraging "good governance" (what this means is still being debated) as a key ingredient to economic growth – paralleling developments we described in Chapter 1. As we noted there, public sector management and governance were emerging themes among international governmental organizations as early as the 1980s (and as we shall see below, even earlier in the OECD), but came forcefully into their own as distinct foci for reform efforts in the 1990s. The third section of the chapter looks at how the OECD as an organization is navigating a world in which governance is recognized as a key ingredient to economic and social development, but in which there are many more competing organizations that can offer similar services and products (Trondal et al 2010: 85–86). This sets the stage for the next chapter, which looks in detail at GOV, its committees and networks.

Marshall Plan and the OEEC

Europe in 1947 was scarcely any different than immediately after the end of the war two years earlier. Rationing was still in place, as were black markets; transportation and infrastructure were still mostly in ruins, and refugees were still being resettled. Trade among European nations and between them and the United States was low and hampered by dollar shortages and an inability to reintegrate Germany with the other European economies that needed its coal and steel, as well as it markets (Judt 2001: 3). The United States had recognized the imperative of economic reconstruction after the war (both for its own trade interests as for those of the Europeans), and up to the inception of the Marshall Plan had already contributed some $9 billion under various programmes. But this money had been ad hoc, without any strategic design or overarching administration, and since Europeans could not count on it each year, had not induced them to move ahead on substantial and radical restructuring of their economies.

Political considerations also played an important role in persuading Marshall and the Truman administration that a new, bolder approach was necessary. By 1947 the "onward march of Communism appeared to many to be inexorable" (Judt 2001: 3). Communists were participating in governments in France, Italy, and Belgium, and Communist parties were rapidly solidifying their grip on Eastern Europe. Marshall himself had led the American delegation to the Moscow Foreign Ministers' Conference in April 1947, scarcely two months before his Harvard speech, and came away convinced that the Soviet Union was trying to impede European recovery, and that the United States needed to take strong action (Smith 1962). Most importantly, this action would be driven by a political or governance vision of an integrated Europe (it is unclear how much of this, at least initially, was about "Western Europe" – Marshall aid was offered to the Soviet Union and its satellites but was turned down), and not simply a recovery of single European states and economies. "In promoting Western Europe as a large, unified, and open economic space, the United States sought to create (or at least encourage the creation of) a European market in its own image. ... The Americans thus foresaw the future of Western Europe in much the same way as it assessed its own past: as one based on economic prosperity and social harmony driven by the operation of a large, effective, and free internal market" (Cini 2001: 16). This interest in integration had not been an element of American policy towards Europe from 1945 to 1947, but began to be actively discussed and eventually was reflected in Marshall's Harvard speech. By 1947, according to Hogan, the internal debates within the American administration had settled on a synthesis that essentially aimed to "remake Western Europe in the likeness of the United States". Its key components were the principle of federalism (in the European case transposed into an integrated market supervised by supranational institutions), a free single market, Keynesian macroeconomic management, and American production techniques (Hogan 1987: 22–23). Or as Marshall put it in his speech, the "purpose should be the revival of a working economy in the world so as to permit the emergence of political and social conditions in which free institutions can exist" (Griffiths 1997a: 258).

Two other important governance dimensions were embedded in Marshall's speech and what would eventually become the formal programme of aid, the Economic Recovery Programme. First, it was the European nations themselves who would draw up their individual and collective recovery plans. Marshall stated that it would be neither "fitting nor efficacious" for the Americans to unilaterally draw up a plan for European recovery. This included the overall level of aid as well as its distribution. Second, the United States strongly emphasized the "institutionalization of cooperation" (Cini 2001: 21) that would go beyond ad hoc multilateral meetings. This was a key source of pressure for the creation of the OEEC, which some European states, like Britain, resisted.

On 12 July 1947 the European states (with the exception of Spain, under Franco) were invited to a conference in Paris to develop a plan to be conveyed to the Americans. At this meeting they established the Committee of European Economic Cooperation (CEEC) that developed priorities for reconstruction and asked for $19 billion from the United States. Negotiations ensued, with a final agreement of $12 billion to $17 billion, starting on 1 April 1948 (Barbezat 1997: 34). Discussions over the new permanent European body to oversee the Economic Recovery Plan's disbursements started in January 1948, and the CEEC met again in March 1948 to discuss a draft charter for the organization. That charter was signed on 16 April 1948, establishing the OEEC. Its founding members were: Austria, Belgium, Denmark, France, Greece, Iceland, Ireland, Italy, Luxembourg, the Netherlands, Norway, Portugal, Sweden, Switzerland, Turkey, the United Kingdom, and Western Germany (Canada and the United States became associate members in June 1950). The struggle over the design of the organization had been over whether it would be a genuinely supranational body with independent decision-making powers (something the French wanted) or simply a coordinating entity dominated by national governments (something the British wanted). The British won, and the OEEC emerged from the negotiations as a considerably weaker body than the Americans had hoped (Hogan 1987: 127). A Council, comprised of all members, met regularly, sometimes at the Ministerial level, but usually with high officials, and all decisions would have to be unanimous (though members could abstain from a decision). There was a Secretary-General (SG), but only with limited powers. Day-to-day decision-making (though subordinated to the Council) was handled by an Executive Committee consisting of seven members elected by Council. It could also strike committees to examine specific matters. Much of this architecture was adopted by the OECD when it was established in 1961.

The OEEC's mandate was economic recovery, an on-going challenge even after the end of the Marshall Plan in 1951. The two key problems were currency convertibility among the European states, and reduction of trade barriers. Both of these were achieved by 1958 (Wolfe 2008: 26; Reichlin 1995), making the OEEC redundant as an instrument of European economic coordination. There remained interest, however, in some sort of organization to orchestrate trans-Atlantic economic cooperation, but the OEEC was not suited to the task. First, it had been established to administer American aid, but the trans-Atlantic partners were much more equal now and that had to be reflected in a new organization. Second, the Cold War context had evolved and the battle lines were now, with decolonization, as much North-South as East-West, but the "OEEC was poorly situated to assist the developing world"

(Woodward 2009: 17). But, just as the United States was contemplating some sort of renewed vehicle for trans-Atlantic cooperation, the OEEC imploded due to acrimony between members who had joined the European Economic Community (based on the 1958 Treaty of Rome – Belgium, France, West Germany, Italy, Luxembourg, and the Netherlands) and the others. The December 1958 OEEC Council meeting was its last.

Negotiations continued however, propelled by a summit meeting of the Presidents of the United States and France, the West German Chancellor, and the British Prime Minister, calling for continued cooperation over development aid and trade, and suggesting a convening of countries (the Executive Committee of the OEEC and the European Economic Commission) to discuss the matter (OECD 1963), and eventually, with the establishment of a Group of Four on Economic Organization to recommend a revised OEEC. It reported on 7 April 1960 and recommended the establishment of the OECD, with Canada and the United States as full members. The report was reviled by some countries (particularly the Nordic states), and generated various objections, principally over whether OEEC acts would automatically be annulled, or carried over into the new organization, and the OECD's competence on trade matters (Griffiths 1997b). Differences were finally resolved, and the convention was signed in Paris on 14 December 1960. It had 20 members (the original OEEC members, plus Spain, Canada and the United States). The convention went into effect on 30 September 1961, and the first Ministerial Council was held in December 1961. The former Danish finance Minister, Thorkil Kristensen, became the OECD's first SG.

Article 1 of the Convention stated the objectives of the new organisation:

> The aims of the Organisation for Economic Co-operation and Development (hereinafter called the "Organisation") shall be to promote policies designed:
> (a) to achieve the highest sustainable economic growth and employment and a rising standard of living in Member countries, while maintaining financial stability, and thus to contribute to the development of the world economy;
> (b) to contribute to sound economic expansion in Member as well as non-Member countries in the process of economic development; and
> (c) to contribute to the expansion of world trade on a multilateral, non-discriminatory basis in accordance with international obligations.
> (OECD)

These were to be achieved through information exchange (and a commitment by members to submit information "necessary for the accomplishment of its tasks"), consultations, studies, projects, cooperation, and – "where appropriate" – coordinated action. As Woodward points out, this remit was sufficiently broad that it eventually provided a justification for "the OECD's involvement with almost every facet of economic and social life", but also made it vulnerable to duplication because it had no clearly defined focus or exclusive policy field (Woodward 2009: 4). As he states, this "has resulted in an extraordinarily elastic body whose functional domain is in perpetual flux" (Woodward 2009: 4).

Nonetheless, the Convention and its annexes (see (OECD 1963) make it clear that the OECD was to be originally focused on economic development in the narrower sense of the term – trade, balance of payments, scientific research, energy, labour, and a host of specific sectors such as oil, iron and steel, textiles, hides and skins, and cement. But an important dimension of this, and indeed one of the drivers in creating a new organization from the OEEC, was overseas aid and technical assistance to non-members. The preamble to the Convention stated that the signatories believed "that the economically more advanced nations should co-operate in assisting to the best of their ability the countries in process of economic development" and to that end created a Development Assistance Committee (DAC) and a Technical Cooperation Committee (TECO). We will not be examining the DAC in detail in this book, since its focus is on financial aid to developing countries (the world's principal donor countries are in the OECD, and the DAC became a source of information and policy analysis, as well as a pressure point on countries) but it also reflected, as we noted above, a political and governance concern at the heart of the organization: if newly de-colonized countries were not assisted financially and technically, they might not take the democratic, capitalist path to development. TECO was originally designed to provide technical economic advice and manage a wide range of operational projects that mirrored the different sectors of the OECD, but evolved over time into a directorate focused on public sector management and governance. An important point to keep in mind is that the focus on governance and public management did not arise organically within the OECD. As we noted earlier in Chapter 1, public administration, public management, and most recently governance, were not considered primary targets of international intervention, at least not in their own right. The focus was on market and economic development. The emphasis on public management had to be constructed, developed, and to a certain extent invented by its protagonists in the Secretariat and relevant committees.

From TECO to PUMA to GOV

In 1955 the OEEC approved a programme to help "less developed" member countries in Europe – the original recipients were southern Italy, Greece, and Turkey, which were joined in turn by Yugoslavia (1959), Spain (1960), Iceland (1961) and Portugal (1963). With the withdrawal of Italy in 1963 and Iceland in 1965, the geographical group for the OECD successor programme consisted of Greece, Portugal, Spain, Turkey and Yugoslavia. The

OEEC programme was carried over to the OECD through articles 1(b) and 2(e) of the OECD Convention in promising technical assistance for development. The OEEC had had several operational grant programmes for economic development, mostly managed by its subsidiary body, the European Productivity Agency – but the new OECD was not envisioned as an operational agency. Therefore, all operational programmes were terminated, with the exception of a newly created (simply imported from the OEEC, but in a more formal sense because of the provisions in the Convention) "Technical Assistance Program" or TAP, that was overseen by the Technical Cooperation Committee, or TECO, established in 1960 (OECD August 12, 1969). The committee's original title was the "Technical Assistance Committee", but there was some sense that the term "assistance" was condescending, and so the next year the committee's name was changed (Domergue 1968: 13). This was important, since it signalled that this type of technical assistance – to members of the organization – was different from technical assistance to third world, developing countries. It gave TECO more latitude, but also affected the nature of the work, allowing the programmes to "avoid the technical assistance dogmas of third world assistance".[1] The rationale for keeping TAP was two-fold: to support countries/ regions that were behind the rest of the OECD in terms of economic development, and to protect Europe's southern flank from disorder and possible vulnerabilities to communists. The TAP programme was initially aimed at Portugal, Spain, Greece, Turkey, Yugoslavia (considered strategically important), southern Italy and Iceland. The first five countries were in varying degrees, either dictatorships or in some respects autocracies, and this contributed to the low priority with which TECO and its administrative support within the Secretariat were regarded within the OECD. Nonetheless, the view was "better colonels than communists" and TECO was in part designed to channel expertise to these countries while the rest of the OECD turned a blind eye.[2] The target countries put forward their own projects, which covered a wide spectrum from economic planning, both regional and national; state corporations; agriculture, industry; science; education; institutes of statistics; civil service management; and selected technical issues like irrigation, fruit and vegetable production, and even sheep-breeding (Sahlin-Andersson 2000). While some projects involved capacity-building in public management, on the whole the TAP was about advice (technical experts and study tours), education, and infrastructure projects.[3] Most of the staff in the Technical Cooperation Service were contract managers rather than subject-matter experts, and the fact that it was a "service" rather than a directorate with the OECD Secretariat also signalled its lower, almost "pariah" status.[4]

By the late 1960s TAP and TECO looked, from within the OECD, less and less relevant. Internal reviews cast doubt on the scattered nature of the projects, and openly wondered if the target countries actually needed assistance – in the previous decade all of them had developed quite rapidly.[5]

Since TECO was not a treaty committee (like DAC), it only had five-year renewable mandates. A review was undertaken in 1970. The US was against continuing with the programme, the UK had reservations, but only the Japanese were entirely negative. Most other OECD members were not opposed to its continuation.[6] Recipient countries were asked for their views on the continuation of the programme, and predictably they were supportive, and asked for multi-year rather than annual appropriations.[7] The programme was approved for another five years, with considerably higher financial contributions by the recipients to the cost of activities,[8] with similar complaints about lack of focus, scattered projects, and declining funding due to inflation. As well, the OECD was maturing, and the model of technical assistance and aid was gradually being "replaced by the growing sense of interdependence between all the Organisation's membership. New forms of co-operation therefore had to be developed, which substituted a relationship of solidarity in place of the old donor-recipient relationship" (OECD 1977). In 1972 Derry Ormond, the newly appointed Acting Director of the Technical Cooperation Service, was asked to conduct a review of the programme, but in fact was directed to wind down the organization (both the service and the committee) by 1975.[9]

TECO was saved from extinction by several factors. The first was the oil shock in 1973, and in particular its anticipated effect on Greece, Portugal and Spain. The three countries had for years been relying heavily on remittances, and the shock would not only lower those remittances, but also possibly stimulate mass re-migrations, for example thousands of Turkish "gastarbeiter" back to Turkey. Some form of technical assistance was going to be needed as these countries struggled to respond to the crisis. A second, key factor was the sudden collapse of the dictatorial regimes in the TECO countries in 1974 and 1975. Greece had been governed by a military dictatorship (the "Colonel's Regime") since 1967. It collapsed in 1974 due to bungled machinations over Cyprus and bloody suppression of protests. Turkey had had a military coup in 1971, but the military preferred to orchestrate from behind the scenes, and so there had continued to be elections amid escalating terrorist chaos. In 1973 the Republican People's Party (considered a socialist or centre-left party) unexpectedly won power. Portugal was even more complicated. Antonio Salazar had been dictator since 1932, and died in 1970, succeeded by Marcelo Caetano. The military was fed up with fighting anti-colonial wars in Portugal's "overseas provinces" in Africa (Mozambique, Angola, Guinea-Bissau, Cape Verde, São Tomé and Principe), and so led a non-violent overthrow of the regime in 1974 (the "Carnation Revolution") that established democracy. The colonies were immediately granted independence, leading to nearly one million persons of Portuguese descent returning to Portugal as refugees. In Spain, Francisco Franco had been dictator since 1936. He became ill in 1974, and transferred rule to King Juan Carlos. He recovered, but then died in 1975, and Juan Carlos carefully guided

Spain towards democracy. These dramatic changes suddenly made the four sleepy dictatorial clients of TECO newly important as democratic members of the OECD.[10] TECO now appeared potentially and newly relevant – it knew the countries, had been working in them for years, and it was clear that they would need support and assistance to be able to develop in the emerging new economic context, as well as to avoid communist takeovers.

A third factor was that TECO had been gradually re-orienting its activities in 1973 and 1974 away from sectoral projects and towards public administration. Ironically, this was stimulated in part by the SG's office. An advisor there had become convinced in the early 1970s that the capacity to implement programmes by government agencies was critical to economic development, and persuaded the SG to launch an initiative entitled the "Secretary-General's Experimental Activity on Innovative Structures and Procedures in Government". This resulted in only three meetings, and then was terminated without a final report or any publications.[11] However, Ormond and his colleagues felt that the initiative was especially valid in the southern European countries, and decided to recommend to the Committee and Council that more of TECO's activities be shifted towards public administration projects, particularly joint projects that would engage all the TECO countries but also progressively begin to bring in more non-TECO members of the OECD. This strategy, which put all participants on an equal footing, created the basis of a constituency within the organization for work on public management reform.

So, instead of being dissolved, TECO and the Service were steadily re-shaped and re-focused as of early 1975. The main changes were:

- The Service was to help national officials think through how different policy alternatives could be developed and implemented.
- Whereas previously, the TECO remit had been almost limitless, it would now focus on rural development, industrial promotion, human resources and urban management.
- Activities would be practically oriented, and act as "incentive for national officials to bring about change, rather than to produce reports". There would be country activities serving special requests for technical support from Greece, Portugal, Turkey and Yugoslavia, as well as joint activities, where those countries as well as any other Member countries could participate in addressing a common problem. To highlight this evolution away from the donor-recipient model, the program was renamed as the "Co-operative Action Programme". (OECD 1977)

There were two other important changes. One was an explicit recognition that TECO's focus was on public management, and that it would be "undertaking activities generally focused on improving the responsiveness and effectiveness of public service".[12] As we noted above, the public management or governance theme had been at the heart of both the OEEC and the founding of the OECD, but not as a specific area of activity or expertise as such. Economic development stimulated through the OECD would, the logic argued, lead to prosperity and to commensurate liberal-democratic institutions. TECO, of course, had in practice focused on the management of projects, since it did not have experts in each of the substantive areas in which projects were undertaken (e.g., agriculture). But its activities had nonetheless been typically framed in terms of technical assistance. Its first expert meeting on public administration only took place in 1973. This signals a process of discovery and search for an organizational mandate. Ormond, before he took over as Acting Director of TECO, had been responsible for the Turkey programme, and his experience there and in Greece had convinced him that the real issue in these countries was less one of technical capacity than of administration and management. Accordingly, he had launched an initiative to develop a public administration programme at the Middle East Technical University. Advertisements were posted around the world, and a professor at the University of Wisconsin, Ravi Kapil, responded and came to Ankara to teach in the new programme for five years. Once his contract was over, Ormond recruited him to Paris. It was Kapil who (at least within TECO) coined the term "public management" as the key mandate of TECO, to distinguish it from more classical public administration. He went on to become Deputy Director of the service.

The 1975 re-shaping signalled that, from the Council's point of view, TECO had a special expertise within the OECD: "Thus the work of the Service has acquired a distinct specialization in what has come to be termed as 'public management'." To take an example, a land improvement activity may be undertaken not only for the immediate benefits it may bring to people living and farming in the vicinity, but more important, because it may lead to a reworking of the government's own institutions and decision taking processes – that is its managerial capacities – for carrying out and supporting such activities" (OECD 1977: 3). In its project work, special "attention would be paid to improving the responsiveness and effectiveness of public service in dealing with both the routine public administration tasks as well as in managing the development process" (OECD 1977: 3). The focus on management was also reflected "in those activities whose direct purpose is to help governments to sort out the ways in which they manage their own administration for instance as regards using computers or improving public personnel policies. ... A glance at these activities shows that support is being provided for such vital functions as policy development, resource allocation, planning and programming, management practice and organisational development" (OECD 1977: 7).

The second change – less a change than a re-affirmation – was in the ways in which the new TECO would work. We noted that the OEEC had developed a committee-council-secretariat architecture from the beginning, in large part because of some fears that the organization would become too powerful, and because the very purpose of the organization – as a member-based organization – was cooperation and hence exchange. The OECD inherited this structure and ethos. The new TECO would build on this tradition in moving away from the technical assistance, donor-recipient model. The joint activity framework was designed to support thinking about longer-term problems of organization and institutional structure facing any member country, not just the targeted countries. It would provide a chance to exchange experiences on other countries' solutions and the organizational designs for those solutions. This form of networked collaboration, exchange, and mutual learning became the basis of both PUMA's and GOV's approach to stimulating debates about public management reform.

Even given these positive developments, more work was needed to build TECO into the "public management" arm of the OECD.[13] In 1976 Ormond hired Bob Bonwitt, a recent graduate of the London Business School (Masters in Economics), to develop a strategy to solidify TECO's role in public administration/public management within the OECD. The strategy had to consider four elements: financial resources, attitudes of target countries, broader support throughout the OECD, and products and substance. The financial problem was that most of TECO's budget was for projects and operations, but they needed to build subject-matter expertise, and so shift funds among projects. Target countries had to be convinced that money should be moved from the Ministry of Agriculture, for example, to central agencies for public administration reform. Broader support throughout the OECD was important in order to end TECO's appearance as a programme geared simply to poor, southern European countries. The solution was to develop more joint activities involving a range of member states – both to help the poorer countries, but also to engage the richer ones, and hence broaden the range of expertise and experience around public management reform. This was not as easy as it sounded. Today, while sensitivities around the borrowing and transfer of public management practices remain, most countries are open to and interested in learning from the experience of others. In the late 1970s, the attitude was much more one of "we have nothing to learn from the [French, the Brits, the United States]". The product and substance challenge was about how exactly to define what TECO would be doing in the public management field without stepping on the toes of other directorates within the OECD (though other directorates appreciated the importance of institutions). Again, this was not as simple as it might sound. Public administration at the time was not an internationalized discipline (the International Institute of Administrative Sciences came closest to an international network, but it was primarily a network of universities), and its focus was overwhelming on traditional areas such as civil service classification and training. TECO staff adopted the approach of providing "horizontal" advice and analyses – i.e., looking at administrative functions such as human resource management or budgeting or service delivery, which cut across vertical ministries. This also provided them with an insight as to who their clients in domestic governments would be: centres of government (e.g., prime ministers' and cabinet offices, secretaries general of government), public service commissions or civil service bureaus, ministries of public administration, budget ministries and audit agencies. One gets a sense of the experimentation and adventure that all this entailed from a 1977 letter by Kapil:

> [The Technical Cooperation Service] has for some time been reviewing its work in the field of public administration reform in OECD Member countries. ... The Technical Cooperation Committee has approved the inclusion of a joint project (meaning an inter-governmental cooperative project) to examine the kinds of change and adaptation which the public management systems of our countries should be making to cope with emerging changes in society, economy and the polity. The theme, I have to confess, is vast and complex, and the search for the most efficacious way by which an organization like the OECD can be of help, not easy.[14]

TECO held its first ever symposium on public management in Madrid on 5–9 February 1979, and it was instructive both for how the public management/governance theme was being addressed in other countries, and how it was becoming a broader movement. Just as important, however, was how the issue of governance and public management was being framed. As we saw in the last chapter, public sector reform as an area of policy was not self-evident, especially for an organization dedicated to economic development and dominated by economists. The link or connections between economic growth, effective economic policy and public management had to be established and argued. The first oil shock, stagflation, growing deficits, and the sheer size of the public sector by the mid-1970s had put public sector reform on the agenda of many countries, but the 1979 OECD meeting was one of the first major high-level conferences on the topic (though the United Nations Public Administrative Division had organized a conference in 1971, and the UK had had several tri-annual conferences on the training and development of senior civil servants in Europe; also see the examples from (Caiden 1991) cited in Chapter 1), and represented an important sea-change in how public sector reform was to be addressed. As Caiden argues, while of course there had been reform efforts in the 1960s, they had been piecemeal. It was now time, in the 1970s, to see it "as a continuous activity, institutionalized somewhere within government, professionally staffed, given adequate resources, allowed sufficient time, and politically supported so that reforms do not just spin their wheels but make a real impact on the conduct of public business" (Caiden 1991: 16).

The symposium was designed to identify elements of a work plan, and had participation from all 21 member countries consisting of "mainly senior administrators from national agencies with responsibility for improving public management", and opened by the US cabinet member responsible for the US civil service reform just enacted (OECD 1980b: 5). It was clear from various remarks at the symposium that something important had changed in the international, political and economic context that was now driving a new appreciation of the importance of public management. In a theme that was to become a leitmotif for OECD reports on governance and public management for the next 20 years – especially *Governance in Transition* (1995a), discussed below – the symposium rapporteur, Dwight Ink, noted that governing OECD countries had become more challenging for several key reasons. Their societies were more complex. External issues such as the oil shocks and economic turbulence were generating pressures. There was also an abiding contradiction at the heart of OECD policy frameworks: publics (and elected officials) were demanding lower taxes, but without a commensurate reduction in services. The only way out was greater efficiency, and not only to deal with the practical fiscal problem, but to ensure public support through effectiveness. In his opening remarks, Gérard Eldin, the deputy SG of the OECD, noted that the "changing national and international economic environment is a real challenge to governments, and must be accompanied by a re-examination of administrative procedures and structures so that new functions may be assumed and coherent and effective action taken" (OECD 1980b: 44). He called for "continuous systematic attention to the ability of the public administrative system to change and adjust itself" and for a priority "to re-examining the structures and machinery of administration and of the public sector in its broad sense". Both Ink and Eldin were drawing a connection between economic performance, growth, stability, public trust and public management and governance. This connection is largely taken for granted today, but was unusual in this period, as we noted above, in the sense that this was the beginning of not merely piecemeal tinkering with administrative processes, but an attempt to think systematically. As Ink put it: "Given these considerations it is a natural extension of the OECD's work in the field of economic policy formulation that the machinery of government should, itself, be subject to study". (OECD 1980b: 5)

The symposium resulted in a list of substantive issues of wide interest to members, and became the backbone of an agenda of research and consultation for TECO for the next decade, and indeed beyond, since many of the same issues continue to occupy GOV today. They were: problems of management change in government organizations; personnel policy, particularly for senior civil servants; budget systems; political-administrative interface; reprivatization and reliance on market mechanisms; decentralization and/or devolution of decision-making and administrative responsibility; the problem of policy advice; simplification of administrative processes (OECD 1980b: 20–21). The symposium also yielded some strategies on how to push the reform project ahead. In addition to the usual suggestions for more (focused) workshops, participants proposed a variety of what today we would call "network" strategies, ones which have become the basic tools of OECD work: information exchange and diffusion; response to specific requests from countries for support in specific administrative problem areas; and the first example of what eventually became country reports: "One possible way to stimulate such activities is to encourage interested countries to prepare country papers on their administrative change problems and issues. Then, a 'counter group', appointed by the OECD with approval of the Member country, could study the situation and make comments and alternative proposals" (OECD 1980b: 23). Two key "constituency groups" were formed on this basis, and still operate in GOV: the Centres of Government (CoG) meeting of officials, and the Senior Budget Officials network.

The Madrid symposium also was the basis for the development of a new programme within TECO – built around the Joint Activities on Public Management Innovation (JAPMI), which Ormond, Kapil, and Bonwitt decided should be governed by a steering committee of senior government officials from the central management agencies in member countries, and which would be able to call on well known international experts, such as Aaron Wildavsky and Yehetzkel Dror (both of whom had worked with TECO in the past). The conference and the steering committee helped TECO develop a new and unique agenda of research and projects around "horizontal" public management themes: human resource management, citizen-administrative relations, budgeting, regulation, and public services, to name a few. For example, TECO produced a remarkable and pioneering series of publications on service delivery, well anticipating – and probably stimulating – national reviews of service standards and the importance of citizen-centred services (the research was started in the early 1980s, yielding publications a few years later; for example see (OECD 1987). But perhaps most importantly, the symposium and its aftermath of new projects gave TECO a stronger claim to be a serious and unique component of the OECD, with impressive networks of senior officials.

Even though the 1975 redesign of TECO had been intended to move away from the technical assistance model, it was still partly engaged in that approach – sending experts, providing advice on specific problems. But by the late 1980s, JAPMI had more or less absorbed all the other technical assistance projects under TECO, and in the review leading up to the 1990 renewal, it was clear that a new structure was needed – TECO still has some members with a "donor mentality", (paternalistic, demanding conditionalities) but the Technical Cooperation Service had moved strongly into public management and joint activities. A rationale was developed in a 1989 internal document entitled "Serving the Economy Better", which was the basis for a new Public Management Committee to replace TECO, and a new Public Management (PUMA) Service to replace the Technical Cooperation Service (PUMA was to be the first new committee to be established since the founding of the OECD in 1961). "Serving the Economy Better" was released for general distribution in 1991. It summarized the Public Management Committee's reflections on the issue of public sector reform, and it laid out an ambitious approach to the issue. This is important because the OECD and PUMA in particular have routinely been accused in the academic literature of being a standard-bearer for NPM (Premfors 1998; Sahlin-Andersson 2000; Hansen et al 2002). Halligan refers to "the OECD's fixation on NPM" (Halligan 2010: 134), while Pierre claims that PUMA was involved in the "propagation of NPM-style reform" (Pierre 2010: 193). To some extent that was true, and almost inevitably so since so many key OECD members were going through a series of NPM reforms – PUMA could hardly have opposed them. On the other hand, this document at least acknowledged a more nuanced view of what an agenda of public sector reform might entail. It is notable, however, that the language of "trends" and "broad directions" crept into this document whereas it had been largely absent in the TECO period. TECO had emphasized the uniqueness of each country's case, its specific challenges and history and institutions. "Serving the Economy" did some of the same, but also claimed that "the evidence of the Committee's activities and its annual surveys of public management developments suggest that countries share a degree of common understanding of the nature of the problem and are following the same broad direction of change" (OECD 1991: 2).

In this document, the importance of public management to economic performance is unequivocal: "Efficient and effective public management is vital to national economic development and competitiveness" (OECD 1991: 3).

But the importance of the public sector cannot be expressed by simple measures of size. The public sector, acting on behalf of political authorities, affects every part of the economy and society. Its effectiveness conditions, to a large extent, economic development and sustains political and social cohesion. The public sector is responsible for the legal and administrative environment in which private business activity takes place. It affects production decisions and costs through a myriad of regulatory controls, services, transfers, taxes and tax reliefs. It alters patterns of demand by redistributing income. It is also a large purchaser in the private economy and thereby affects overall resource allocation. It influences national economic efficiency, the rate of technological and organisational innovation, the direction and speed of structural adjustment, and the cost, to users, of unpriced resources like the environment. (OECD 1991: 7)

The report identified two main concerns in the reform movement in the past two decades: reducing taxes and cutting expenditures to deal with deficits, which in turn were followed by waves of privatization and deregulation. However, the report criticized an over-emphasis on expenditure cuts and efficiency, noting that an effective public sector might actually require some new investments, such as training and support for senior personnel. Instead, it recommended that the goal of public management reform should be "to raise cost-effectiveness in the framework of public law and political accountability". This in turn would require a "managerial approach" with a focus on achieving specific goals and performance standards rather than just complying with administrative rules. Claiming to have discerned a trend (an NPM trend, in effect) the report argued that a "common feature is to introduce a more contractual, participative, discretionary style of relationship: between levels of hierarchy; between control agencies and operating units; and between producing units, be they public or private". (OECD 1991: 11) Most governments were working to raise the performance of public organizations and make greater use of the private sector. But the report was cautious about how far this could go without undermining important and cherished principles of administrative organization and public law. The report urged a balance between the two, arguing that there were limits to privatization, reliance on market-type mechanisms, and the efficiency of the private sector. PUMA was not writing a blank, NPM cheque.

The report closed with an agenda for reform in the 1990s:

- Greater understanding of where public, private or mixed production can be used and of how the public and private sectors interact;
- Better ways of measuring performance, and ensuring control and accountability;
- Improved management and development of human and physical resources of the public sector;
- Adaptation of the decision making and rule-setting processes of government (and the interaction with the legal system);
- Better quality of information so that public sectors can learn from each other, exchange experience and compare performance;
- An enhanced capacity at the centre of government, to guide the overall evolution of the public sector and harmonise the efforts of the central management agencies. (OECD 1991: 18)

This was an ambitious agenda – PUMA would provide information and analysis on public management, facilitate contact and exchange, and issue reports and research (between 1990 and 1995 it produced some 60 such reports). As a background paper later released by the Public Management Committee in 1999 stated: "Beginning with its first mandate in 1961, PUMA work was seen as technical assistance... . But as the 1980s progressed, it became clear that the public management orthodoxies being put forward were themselves under considerable challenge. This gave rise to a substantial change in direction in the OECD's work in this area. In 1990, the Council took the organization out of technical assistance and into public management. The focus shifted to information sharing. It has followed this course for the past decade, acting as one of the world's most important catalysts to innovation and reform of government administration" (OECD Public Management Service and Public Management Committee 1999: 3).

Within a year of its founding, however, PUMA found itself in the middle of the largest structural adjustment exercise in history – the collapse of the Soviet Union and the creation of new, post-communist states throughout central and Eastern Europe (CEE).[15] Economic change and the introduction of markets and private property were the first order of business for organizations like the World Bank and the IMF. The EU and the OECD also decided to respond, but the question was how? PUMA, like the rest of the OECD secretariat, existed primarily to serve its members, and did not have (at that time) mechanisms for outreach or substantial engagement with non-members. The EU almost immediately held out the possibility of eventual membership to the new states, depending on deep economic and political reforms, but it had no expertise in the area of public management, and no experience in assisting accession of countries going through such upheavals.

The original OECD response to the collapse was confused, and it could really only give policy support, though initially there was some thought that PUMA could once again become an arm of OECD technical assistance. This alarmed the PUMA directorate, since it would have seemed to be going back into ancient TECO history.[16] Moreover, there was little prospect of many of the former Soviet states becoming OECD members any time soon (though the Czech Republic acceded in 1995, Hungary and Poland in 1996, and the Slovak Republic in 2000), and so the organization had no leverage. The EU, on the other hand, was compelled to respond more vigorously, and had the funds for major spending programmes. It could also offer the real prospect of eventual membership, an incentive that could attract compliance and cooperation from the CEE. So the two organizations had a common purpose, but different capacities. Something was needed to ignite a partnership.[17]

Ravi Kapil happened to be at a conference in Brussels in 1991 to give a presentation on TECO and PUMA, and afterwards a person from the European Commission (EC) approached him, said he was impressed since the EC did not have this sort of expertise, and wondered if the two organizations might cooperate. Kapil returned to Paris, reported to Derry Ormond, who then dispatched Bob Bonwitt to Brussels within a few days to see what might be worked out. On his return, they pitched the idea of a cooperative programme between PHARE and the OECD around public management reform to the SG. He approved it within 24 hours. Accordingly, the OECD and the EU began negotiations in July 1991 and signed an agreement later that year. SIGMA itself was launched in 1992, guided by a jointly agreed "Programme Orientation" document.[18] It was focused on Bulgaria, Czech and Slovak Federal Republic, Hungary, Poland, and Romania. The concerns about "tainting" PUMA once again as a technical assistance agency led to positioning SIGMA within the directorate, but giving it a separate status. It could draw on the expertise of the rest of the group, and naturally the two sides cooperated in various ways, but there was a "firewall" nonetheless. It also helped that SIGMA had a separate source of funding through the EU (some OECD members contributed funds as well).

The "Programme Orientation" document reveals several important aspects of the way in which public management reform was being thought about in this period (OECD 1992).[19] The Mission Statement, for example, read: "Support the development of efficient and effective public institutions which can sustain market economies, provide a base for democratic pluralist systems of governance and implement public policies". To achieve this, SIGMA would aim to: "build up central government capabilities to develop and co-ordinate policies, to manage the evolution of public institutions and the public service, to carry out resource management and control functions; encourage central management agencies to promote reform in public bodies responsible for delivering public services in priority areas" (n.p.). The programme echoed the same emphasis on the importance of public institutions and administration for a functioning market economy as the "Serving the Economy" document had earlier:

> The transformation of public institutions is instrumental, indeed crucial, to the success of transition to democratic systems of governance and market economies. The transition process itself, both policy formulation and implementation, depends on functioning public institutions. The goal of transition – a State functioning much as in OECD countries – implies that there should be well-performing bureaucracies to support policy-making, to manage cost-effectively and without abuse of power. The provision and production of publicly provided goods and services, and to set the framework conditions in which private economic activity takes place, (see the recent report by the OECD PUMA Committee on Serving the Economy Better. Paris. 1991). Functioning public institutions are necessary to the survivability and stability of democracy. (p. 4)

It noted that shortly after 1989, "the focus of attention of Western support has been on economic transition and less attention has been given to the problems of public institutions". But now, donors and multilateral institutions "recognise, if belatedly, that public administration is a constraint on progress and it is now being given some priority" (p. 8). The problems were enormous: legacies of communism in the state system, efficient collection of taxes and management of expenditures, mechanisms for policy steering through the bureaucracy and with political leaders, rule of law and the legal systems themselves. Under these circumstances, it was recommended that a strategy be adopted to focus on just a few key, defined areas.

1. strengthen policy-making capacities, improve quality of legislation, introduce implementation planning, improve the ability of governments to direct resources to priorities while respecting budget limits;

2. enhance the ability of the public and governments to guide and control administrative activity and keep a balance between the extent of administrative discretion and the instruments of control;
3. ensure that a firm base of "rule of law" institutions is established as soon as possible;
4. create a limited core of stable, institutionalized, competent, neutral professional public servants who have an ethical framework and a "public service mentality".

Using a tactic of "selective radicalism" ("bring about radical change in a few areas where interdependencies will force other parts of the system to respond"), in each of the four areas SIGMA would draw on various PUMA activities and networks (e.g., work on Regulatory Management and Reform and on Human Resource Management, the network of Senior Budget Officials). We noted earlier than an important shift occurred when public sector reform went from being an ad hoc, piecemeal and disjointed process to a policy field in its own right to be undertaken strategically and continuously. The SIGMA document reflected the new thinking: "Transformation of public institutions needs to be elevated to the status of a <u>policy domain</u>" (p. 14, emphasis in original). Despite the risk of isolation, the document recommended the creation of reform units located at the centre of each government. The methods of work were drawn directly and explicitly from the PUMA experience: programmes would be responsive and supportive of national needs, would avoid the importation of foreign models, would provide "frameworks for analysis, expert (wherever possible locally recruited) support for analysis, peer reviews and assessment or 'examinations' by independent experts" (p. 15).

The traditional PUMA method of working was through activities and research on specific sectors or problems, projects and networks. But in 1995 it released the first synoptic review of broad governance issues among its members – *Governance in Transition*. It was a significant document for several reasons. First, it was the culmination of the first five years of PUMA's mandate, and was intended to be its major product for that period. Second, it was seminal, since no such broad review of public management reform or modernization had been attempted before by any research group. Third, it is universally recognized as having been uniquely influential, particularly in popularizing NPM. The document in some respects represents the high tide of NPM within PUMA[20] (we discuss this at greater length in Chapter 5), but by the mid-1990s the organization as a whole had come to be known as strongly in favour of structural adjustment and supply-side economics (Woodward 2009: 28–30; Sullivan 1997: 55).

Governance in Transition (OECD 1995a) had a tone of naked urgency and radicalism that one rarely finds in reports by international organizations. Its key premise was that a combination of fiscal pressures, rising public demands, falling public trust, and increasing global economic competition was creating a policy environment "marked by great turbulence, uncertainty and an accelerating pace of change" in which traditional "governance structures and managerial responses are increasingly ineffectual" (p. 15). Half measures were out of the question; only "fundamental change" would do. While the report acknowledged that countries had responded to these challenges differently, and that there was no single best model of governance, nonetheless it was possible to identify "common reform trends". Principal among these trends was a focus on results and performance in terms of efficiency, effectiveness, and quality of service, and decentralization of public management.

The environment facing governments was described bleakly, like a sermon to dinosaurs on the cusp of the first ice age: "Organisations that do not learn to adapt themselves to ever-faster, multi-fronted change atrophy until external forces transform them. Governments no less than business have to adapt to an environment that is becoming more turbulent, complex and difficult to predict. Global transformations, caused by, among other things, developments in technology, communications and trade, demand new abilities. Flexibility and nimbleness have become key objectives. Inherited forms of governance appear outmoded and inflexible" (p. 21). The report declined to use the term "crisis" to describe this new environment, but it allowed that current pressures were considerable, and that those to come would be "at least equally impressive and challenging" (p. 22).

The bulk of the report was divided into chapters describing major reform efforts in the following areas: devolving authority; performance and accountability; developing competition and choice; service; human resources management; information technology; regulation; and strengthening steering functions. It acknowledged that countries differ at the level of individual reforms, but it asserted that nonetheless there was a "remarkable degree of convergence overall" with "clear patterns of reform" (p. 25). The report had no doubts about the radical nature of these changes. They amounted to a "paradigm shift". The "fundamental, comprehensive nature of the changes described represents a move to a new order" (p. 27). Unsurprisingly, the report noted that change on this scale would inevitably generate resistance, and so devoted a chapter to implementing reform, highlighting the fact that public management reform is "a long haul, not a quick fix" (p. 80).[21]

Governance in Transition helped consolidate PUMA's reputation as a leading centre on public management reform, but the OECD as a whole was enjoying increased legitimacy after a period in the 1980s of severe challenges to its role on the world stage. Until the late 1980s, the OECD continued to be seen as a promoter of Keynesian economic policies (Sullivan 1997: 7; Woodward 2004: 27–28). It was frozen out of G7 Summit meetings, and was dismissed by President Ronald Reagan and Prime Minister Margaret Thatcher as being "too Keynesian" (Woodward 2004: 28). It was also facing competition in areas of traditional strength, such as development (the World Bank), macroeconomic coordination (the G7), and European integration (the Single European Act of

1986). The collapse of the Soviet Union in 1989 was an even more powerful threat to the organization, SIGMA notwithstanding. As we noted earlier, the OEEC and the OECD had been designed and established very much within a Cold War context of promoting capitalism and democracy, and coordinating the economic policies of the major economies of the world. Without that rationale – especially the coordination role, which changed from active collaboration to the development of a common policy culture (Wolfe 2008: 36) – and without a clear focus or powerful policy tools, the OECD looked increasingly irrelevant.

Jean-Claude Paye became SG in October 1984: "During his tenure, the newfound predilection for 'structural' and supply side policies partially resurrected interest in the OECD. Having dissected them for a quarter of a century or more, the OECD had a comparative advantage in subjects like labor markets, taxation, competition policy, environmental sustainability, technology, education, health, and public sector governance that were suddenly in vogue" (Woodward 2004: 29). Donald Johnston succeeded Paye as SG in July 1996, and launched an aggressive campaign to modernize the OECD through "internal reorganization, outreach to non-members and civil society, and enlargement" (Woodward 2004: 34). Johnston had decided in 1997 to streamline PUMA and re-focus governance within the organization (he also streamlined other directorates within the OECD). Derry Ormond retired in 1998, and the day he left, Johnston announced a 50 per cent reduction in PUMA staff. Johnston actually tried to abolish PUMA, but was overruled by the Council.[22] Bob Bonwitt was appointed as acting director for six months. He was succeeded in the next four years by five different directors (Ying 2005). In 2002 Odile Sallard was appointed director of (now) GOV, and she served until 2009, succeeded by Rolf Alter, who had been deputy-director of GOV before becoming Chief of Staff for SG Angel Gurría.

It was Johnston's decision in 2002 to amalgamate PUMA with the Territorial Development Service into one directorate – GOV – serving the two committees. GOV still serves the two committees – the Public Governance Committee and the Territorial Development Policy Committee – as well as the Regulatory Policy Committee when it was created in 2009. We discuss GOV in detail in the next chapter, but it is worth highlighting some salient points about it here. The creation of GOV was, within the OECD, a re-shuffling of deck chairs to some extent and a streamlining of Secretariat staff. But the context in 2002 and afterwards was quite different than the context that had shaped TECO and PUMA. TECO, despite its evolution and changes in the mid-1970s, was a technical assistance and donor-aid organization. PUMA rose from it with the aspiration of becoming more of a knowledge bank and analytical centre, but it was birthed in the context of the end of the Cold War, and consequently had a strong focus on Europe (through SIGMA, but through its members as well, notwithstanding the influence of Australia, Canada, and New Zealand), and the NPM flavour of the times. By the time that GOV was created, the context was completely different. Johnston had injected new priorities of enlargement and engagement with non-members, and had emphasized the OECD's unique role in knowledge creation, management, dissemination, and horizontal research. These were and are the OECD's comparative advantages, and GOV reflected this shift by reinforcing its analytical focus. But that focus was no longer anchored in NPM, as PUMA had been in 1995. The world had moved on in public management theory and practice (Pollitt & Bouckaert 2004; Radin 2006; Pollitt et al 2007; Pollitt 2001), and the reality of speaking to a global audience of members as well as non-members meant that GOV had to broaden its approach. Whereas PUMA's mandate as articulated in 1994 by the OECD Council was focused on "the quality and cost-effectiveness of public sector management", the GOV mandate now included strategic governance challenges, performance of public institutions, and a focus on the elements of good governance (e.g., transparency, accountability, effective intervention in society and markets to promote competition as well as social cohesion) (Ying 2005).

One additional way of charting this organizational evolution from TECO to PUMA and the rise of a public management focus is to see the shifting activities for the two organizations at a more microscopic level over the 25 year time span focused on above. Table 2.1 does that, based on OECD Annual Reports from 1970 to 1995.

We can see that up to the mid-1970s TECO programming was a mix of technical projects around things like livestock breeding and public administration training either with public servants or in the universities – or even helping develop post-secondary institutions to help deliver this training. Then came the change to the "Co-operative Action Programme" in 1974–1975 and a much tighter focus on public administration that continued to build through the second half of the decade. But even the report for 1979 displayed the schizophrenic character of TECO. The opening paragraph to the TECO section ran: "The Co-operative Action Programme has special responsibility to respond to the needs and concerns of less industrialized Member countries and Yugoslavia, and to provide opportunities through joint activities for governmental interchange with the full range of Member countries. It further provides a vehicle for carrying out specifically technical and operational work as a complement to the discussions held in the Organisation's policy committee. The principal field of activity is public management and administration" (OECD 1980a: 91). The effects of the Madrid symposium were becoming clear by 1981, however, as the focus continued to sharpen on central government and senior policy and budgeting officials in the public service. The next year the programme was renamed to "Technical Co-operation and Public Management". By 1984 there were no longer any "technical assistance" projects of the old style (e.g., in agriculture or industry). TECO was now almost exclusively engaged in study projects or events around the high themes of public management: policy advice, implementation,

Table 2.1 Programme Activities, TECO to PUMA, 1970–1995

ACTIVITY YEAR	MAIN PROGRAMME HEADING	ACTIVITIES (SAMPLES)/COMMENTS
1970	Technical Cooperation	• Country activities include: Greece: livestock development, marketing of fruits and vegetables; development of a new University of Patras; Portugal: review of the Civil Service structure, development planning and programming; Spain: training senior civil servants, regional development policies and methods; Turkey: training for the management of State enterprises, university development; Yugoslavia: emigration, tourism development, problems in the steel industry. • Comment: The report notes that over the period 1970–1973 there would be a 25 per cent reduction in OECD contributions to the programme, offset by financial contributions from the target countries. The principles and procedures of the programme would be reviewed in 1973.
1971	Technical Cooperation	• Country activities include: Greece: land use planning; modernization of fruit and vegetable growing techniques; modernization of central and regional public administration; Portugal: studies in the development of essential infrastructure, development of an active manpower policy; Spain: re-organization of the iron and steel sector of the Asurias, aid with teaching in the National School of Public Administration and the Seville School for Industrial Engineering; Turkey: review of national accounting methods, training young university graduates in the special subjects of economics, statistics, public administration and management; Yugoslavia: transportation planning and operational research, assistance in drawing up the development plan for the Kosovo region.

Table 2.1 Programme Activities, TECO to PUMA, 1970–1995 – *continued*

ACTIVITY YEAR	MAIN PROGRAMME HEADING	ACTIVITIES (SAMPLES)/COMMENTS
1972	Technical Cooperation	• Country activities included: <u>Greece</u>: studies on fruit and vegetable growing techniques, pilot farms for improved animal husbandry, information systems for the civil service; <u>Portugal</u>: analysis of the road network of the Lisbon area, organizing courses in national accounting; <u>Spain</u>: coordination of a farm management course and preparation of a course on vine growing and marketing, the National School of Public Administration; <u>Turkey</u>: study of the market possibilities for selected Turkish industries in the EEC countries, improvement of national income estimates, higher education development; <u>Yugoslavia</u>: planning of an improved communications system in Croatia, research institutes involved in economic policy-making. • <u>Comment</u>: The report noted that emphasis "was put on the wish of beneficiary countries to explore certain common problems. On occasion, cooperation was initiated with a few other Member countries, either because they shared the same difficulties or because they had special experience to offer".
1973	Technical Cooperation	• <u>Comment</u>: This was the first year that the report was organized around thematic areas rather than the recipient countries themselves. As well, it noted that while the programme was being extended for another three years, the Council's review has "pointed up the gathering awareness of the need to reappraise the relative value of projects and working methods ...". Planning and management headed the list, stating that public administrative "reform and related training continued to be a major theme ...". The other themes were human resources, sectoral development (modernization of agriculture and industry) and technology transfer and science policy.
1974	Technical Cooperation	• <u>Comment</u>: The Technical Cooperation Programme was renamed the "Cooperative Action Programme" with the main thrust being "improvements in public administration ...". Each of the main theme areas now had an orientation towards public administration and management, though there were still technical projects on issues like meat processing and technological transfer in pharmaceutical chemicals.

Table 2.1 Programme Activities, TECO to PUMA, 1970–1995 – *continued*

ACTIVITY YEAR	MAIN PROGRAMME HEADING	ACTIVITIES (SAMPLES)/COMMENTS
1975	Technical Cooperation	• <u>Comment</u>: The report notes that while the traditional pattern of single-country projects will continue, they will be progressively linked "closer in style and substance to joint action" and that the shared focus of the six thematic areas would be "public management by promoting improved procedures, decision-making processes, or organizational change in the working of government".
1976	Technical Cooperation	• <u>Comment</u>: Resettlement of Portuguese repatriates from former overseas colonies is mentioned in terms of the management challenges for housing and international assistance. For the first time, a report makes mention of the combined and simultaneous challenges of high inflation and high unemployment. The six theme areas are: public management, urban management, industry and technology, rural investment and development, emigration and employment, and education.
1977	Technical Cooperation	• <u>Comment</u>: The economic slowdown in 1977 called into question standards models of industrial development, and "the Programme therefore continued to focus on public management capabilities. Many of its activities involved work to improve decision-making techniques and procedures, whether for multi-purpose investment projects, technology choice, or managing the public administration itself".
1978	Technical Cooperation	• <u>Comment</u>: The previous two reports had mentioned efforts to help governments cope with new technologies, and this volume referred to the Joint Activity on Computer Utilization in Public Administration, which this year funded a study on computer hardware and software acquisition. Also mentioned was the creation of the "Joint Activities on Public Management Innovation" (JAPMI) and preparation for the February 1979 symposium in Madrid.

Table 2.1 Programme Activities, TECO to PUMA, 1970–1995 – *continued*

ACTIVITY YEAR	MAIN PROGRAMME HEADING	ACTIVITIES (SAMPLES)/COMMENTS
1979	Technical Cooperation	• <u>Comment</u>: With the five-year renewal of the Programme came a reaffirmation of the "distinctive character of the Technical Cooperation Committee" with its focus on public management. In previous reports the focus had been on improvement, technical development and training, but for the first time there is explicit mention of a theme in TECO's work being about how to "bring about change and reform in public administration at all levels of government so as to increase effectiveness, efficiency, and responsiveness in public services". The 1979 Madrid symposium is cited as a catalyst for a renewed programme focus and a fresh range of activities in the field. For the first time, a report mentions the importance of providing support to develop policy analysis capacity.
1980	Technical Cooperation	• <u>Comment</u>: The public management theme had a special focus on the central government level, and on control of public expenditures, with a first mention of the network of Senior Budget Officials.
1981	Technical Cooperation	• <u>Comment</u>: While mention was made in 1978 of powerful interest groups complicating the work of government, that factor ("the conflicting pressures exerted by powerful interests") is combined as a particular challenge with scarce public resources. The legacy of the 1979 Madrid symposium is clear in a tighter focus on central administration as part of the public management theme, in particular with reference to policy formulation and management of resources. Also, for the first time there is mention of non-governmental policy research and analysis organizations.

Table 2.1 Programme Activities, TECO to PUMA, 1970–1995 – *continued*

ACTIVITY YEAR	MAIN PROGRAMME HEADING	ACTIVITIES (SAMPLES)/COMMENTS
1982	Technical Cooperation and Public Management	• <u>Comment</u>: The JAPMI Steering Committee to review the TECO programme of work, which "has found itself responding to the concerns about the role, size, effectiveness, and manageability of the public sector; and about respective public and private responsibilities for carrying policies through to effective action". The list of themes is now more attuned to public management than to technical projects: policy research and advice to governments, decision-making procedures and techniques, management of financial and human resources, information issues and systems, role and responsibilities of public and private sectors, citizen-administration relations.
1983	Technical Cooperation and Public Management	• <u>Comment</u>: No major innovations from 1982, with the same themes, though with somewhat greater emphasis on citizen-administration relations.
1984	Technical Cooperation and Public Management	• <u>Comment</u>: There is virtually no mention of technical assistance projects in favour of a fresh mandate to promote joint studies and exchange from a public management perspective on the following themes: improving policy formation processes, improving policy implementation and effectiveness, improving resource allocation and expenditure control, improving relationships between different levels of government.
1985	Technical Cooperation and Public Management	• <u>Comment</u>: Two innovations were the first Survey of Public Management Initiatives by the OECD, something that was continued in later years, and the change in the TECO committee to include a majority of officials responsible for machinery of government in their countries.
1986	Technical Cooperation and Public Management	• <u>Comment</u>: A second public management survey was conducted, which showed that the dominant concerns among OECD countries were decentralization of authority coupled with increased accountability, greater use of market discipline in public service provision, simplification of structures and rules, and improvement in policy cohesiveness. There was also a new study on public services (*Administration as Service: The Public As Client*, published in 1987).

Table 2.1 Programme Activities, TECO to PUMA, 1970–1995 – *continued*

ACTIVITY YEAR	MAIN PROGRAMME HEADING	ACTIVITIES (SAMPLES)/COMMENTS
1987	Technical Cooperation and Public Management	• Comment: No major changes from the previous year, except for the completion of several key studies on citizen-centred service.
1988	Technical Cooperation and Public Management	• Comment: In this report, the theme of relationship between the citizen and the administration heads the list, based on further development of concepts and conclusions contained in the 1987 *Administration as Service: The Public As Client.* One new activity stemming from this previous work was on the management of regulatory reform.
1989	Public Management	• Comment: The decision was taken to change the name of the committee to "Public Management Committee" (PUMA), and "Technical Co-operation" was dropped from the programme title. This entailed a focus on three new areas of action: effectiveness and efficiency of the machinery of government, formulation and coordination of government policy, and budgeting and management of public sector resources. However, the list of actual projects differed little from previous years.
1990	Public Management	• Comment: The programme of work for this year was the first under PUMA's new mandate, and reflected a "unifying purpose" to "clarify and strengthen the linkage between economic performance and efficient, effective and flexible public sector management". Activities now congealed into a coherent public management framework: management of policy-making, budgeting, market-type mechanisms and public services, regulatory review, management of human resources, management of information technology, and rural public management.
1991	Public Management	• Comment: Serving the Economy Better is released, and makes a stronger link between public management and economic performance. SIGMA is launched.
1992	Public Management	• Comment: No significant change from previous year, though a mention of the link between public sector reform and "structural adjustment".

Table 2.1 Programme Activities, TECO to PUMA, 1970–1995 – *continued*

ACTIVITY YEAR	MAIN PROGRAMME HEADING	ACTIVITIES (SAMPLES)/COMMENTS
1993	Public Management	• <u>Comment</u>: The same broad themes and activities are mentioned as in previous years, but there is also mention of the circulation to member states of the first draft of *Governance in Transition*, and how the report concludes "that despite successes in many areas, reforms need to be pushed further and progress monitored and evaluated more systematically".
1994	Public Management	• <u>Comment</u>: No major changes in themes or activities from the previous year, though echoes from *Governance in Transition* are there in references to the rise in challenges, stresses, pressures and demands.
1995	Public Management	• <u>Comment</u>: No major changes in themes or activities from the previous year, with the exception of a new programme on ethics in the public service. However, first (in terms of OECD-speak) mentions of terms that would become part of the public management vocabulary: regulatory quality, administrative burden, fiscal consolidation, performance management, and ethics in the public service.

Source: OECD, *Activities of the OECD* for years 1970–1990, and OECD, *Annual Reports* for years 1991–1995. The "Activities" were essentially annual reports, but the title was changed in 1991. Until 1995 these reports were quite detailed, but afterwards became much thinner and less useful as a record of activities. The focus of this summary is TECO to the consolidation of PUMA, and draws only on those 2–3 page sections in each report dealing with TECO or PUMA. The publication year of each of the reports is the year following the reported year, i.e., the report for 1975 was published in 1976, and so on. All reports are available at the OECD Library, Paris.

resource management, and relations among levels of government. New ground was broken in the late 1980s with surveys of public management among member states, a major study on citizen-centred service, and work on the management of regulatory reform. As we noted, the directorate and its committee were changed to PUMA in 1989. Some aspect of NPM language did indeed begin to creep into the report around this time – more emphasis on performance, market-style service provision, budgetary control, flexible pay systems, but as we argued above, this was not the whole story. A more sombre tone had been established by the mid-1990s, echoing themes in *Governance in Transition*. By that point, however, the transition from TECO to PUMA was complete, and PUMA's agenda – developed over the previous decade as it severed its umbilical cord to technical assistance, became the "DNA" of GOV.

Outreach and governance

As we noted earlier, the OECD began a serious outreach campaign to non-members in the 1990s. The Development Centre had been the vehicle for relations with non-members to that point, but under SG Paye a series of new initiatives were launched. Two of them were directly related to the new states in central and Eastern Europe: the Centre for Cooperation with European Economies in Transition (it was directly engaged with SIGMA, and had pre-dated it, having been created in March 1990), and the Partners in Transition programme (launched in 1991, and managed by the Centre for Cooperation with European Economies in Transition). The Dynamic Non-Member Economies opened connections to Asia and Latin America, and eventually (1995) became the Emerging Market Economy Forum. Donald Johnston as SG consolidated these efforts in 1998 by creating the Centre for Cooperation with Non-Members (CCNM). Global forums for discussions with non-members on specific policy fields like education and agriculture were launched in 2001, and in 2000 the OECD inaugurated the Annual Forum with representatives of international NGOs and civil society (including businesses and government). Angel Gurría, who became SG in 2006, continued to build on these outreach efforts by pursuing an aggressive accession strategy that saw Chile, Estonia, Israel, and Slovenia accede in 2010, with the Russian Federation under review.[23]

We will consider the MENA (Middle East and North Africa) as a case study of outreach and a tool used by the OECD in Chapter 4. At this stage, we simply want to explore the OECD's broader strategy of outreach and its impacts on GOV. As we noted in Chapter 1, a key characteristic of the OECD – one that in essence it pioneered for international organizations – is its networked nature. However, in the 1980s and 1990s this seemed increasingly anachronistic. The OECD had no big stick, and no apparent leverage except as an idea broker, and increasingly the global market of ideas was being saturated with new organizations and new initiatives by other organizations (e.g., the World Bank and the Global Development Network). But there was a clear line of thinking extending from Paye to Gurría that realized that the OECD's relevance depended on the scope of its networks and the range of its members. If the new world trading order depended on China, Brazil, India and Russia, not having those countries in the fold in some fashion ultimately reduced the OECD's influence. For the purposes of this book, the more important element in this outreach is the way in which it spreads a common policy culture. As we noted in Chapter 1, this does not mean homogenization. It does mean common sets of standards within which there can be variation, but the variation is modulated and governed by those standards, producing a global policy architecture.

Donald Johnston launched a focused review of OECD enlargement and outreach (later dubbed enhanced engagement, focusing on Brazil, China, India, Indonesia, and South Africa) in 2002 at a retreat of OECD Heads of Delegation, which culminated in a strategy document in 2004 (OECD 2004). He called for a "more inclusive, more diverse OECD" that would grow in relevance in a new global context where the old membership's dominance on the world's economic stage was waning. The report was quite frank about past expansion and current pressures:

> All the countries that joined after 1990, and the majority of those wishing to join, are transition or emerging economies. Taken from a historical perspective, it is apparent that the desire for membership in the OECD reflects the respective country's wish to establish itself as a member of a community of nations committed to democratic as well as market-oriented institutions and policies. The OECD is faced with having to take a decision on how to deal with such political aspirations. In fact, it has procrastinated on this point for a number of years, sometimes delaying a response to countries that have expressed an interest in membership. (p. 7)

It was also frank about previous expansion: it had been largely ad hoc and demand driven, and moreover there was a temptation to decide accession requests on the basis of politics, without a strategic vision. The report highlighted the importance of peer review and learning as a characteristic of the OECD, and used it as a foundation for thinking about strategy. On the one hand, the OECD was grounded in a membership of shared values, so that learning could at least take place within a common frame: "Like-mindedness (broadly shared values) is important in this regard because only countries where democratic principles are well-entrenched in the beliefs and values of the people and founded in formal legislation and rules are in a position to add value significantly to OECD's peer learning process. There is little doubt that the search for solutions to some of the complex problems faced by OECD countries is inextricably linked to the values of our societies" (p. 13).

However, the list of truly "like-minded countries" would be relatively short, and moreover part of the process was not simply learning from other countries but influencing their domestic policies. In leveraging its influence, the OECD should be looking to "significant players" as well as the "like-minded". The criteria for "like-minded" countries were:

Fundamental yardsticks:
- market-based economy
- democratic principles

Other relevant yardsticks (no hierarchy involved):
- basic economic performance (per capita income levels as an indicator of the capacity to contribute to peer learning)
- good governance and rule of law
- human rights
- active participation in other relevant international and regional organizations
- provision of development assistance initiatives
- observance of "OECD *acquis*" (p. 17)

The criteria for "significant players" were: "a country that has the capacity to contribute effectively to peer learning/influencing across all key OECD committees or whose policies matter for Members because they have, through economic interdependence, significant impact on the economic, social and environmental performance of OECD countries as well as on the shaping of the international economic order" (p. 17). Finally, the report noted that the OECD was also a global organization (a "pathfinder of globalization") and so global considerations should also be factored into the accession process: would new members bring a diversity of approaches to common problems within the broad frame of "like-mindedness"? Based on these criteria, the report proposed a new, more pro-active accession and enlargement process, wherein the OECD itself determined likely accession candidates, in light of a new concept of the "OECD *acquis*", obviously modelled on the EU. The idea of an *acquis* was itself a departure, since previous applicants had been considered on their own merits and specific procedures. The OECD *acquis* could include at minimum the small number of legal instruments adopted within the OECD framework, but could also include broad policies shared by OECD members (though within this "sharing" there would be considerable variation), and the peer-review process itself. Ultimately, the advice of the OECD's Directorate for Legal Affairs was that the OECD *acquis* consisted of three elements: (1) acceptance of the obligations in the OECD Convention and acceptance of all internal rules, (2) acceptance (though reservations are permitted within the OECD framework) of all substantive OECD instruments, and (3) the position of applicant countries *vis-à-vis* other major international agreements to which most if not all OECD members are signatories.[24]

The Strategy paper was subsequently supplemented by a formal guide for future accessions (OECD 2007c), and eventually by roadmaps, reviews and recommendations for the accession of Chile, Slovenia, Estonia, Israel, and the Russian Federation. What did this mean for GOV and the accession criteria around public management and public sector performance? In essence, it encouraged a more systematic view or framework on governance reform. With a wider range of interactions with non-members, GOV and its committees "noted the increasing demand by non-member economies for cooperation and a common framework could make professional debate clearer and more focused around specific PGC lessons and experiences" (OECD 2007a: 3). As well, with the new emphasis on enlargement and on enhanced engagement, GOV needed better and more systematic screening mechanisms, replacing the more ad hoc and applicant-specific approach of the past. However, such a systematic framework could not pretend to suggest that there were firm and clear OECD standards of governance – the framework would have to distinguish between goals, on which there was "solid consensus" and institutional arrangements, "which are illustrative but where there are few single first best options".

In a fascinating exercise, GOV had to start from first principles – what is the "public sector" and how broad should the notion of "public sector reform" be – should it, for example include all public governance issues such as accountability to parliament? The decision was to structure the guiding elements in line with work underway to develop "Government at a Glance" (GaaG – discussed in detail in Chapter 4), and use GaaG's classification system to determine what constituted the public sector. Table 2.2 provides a schema that guided GOV's thinking on what the appropriate domain of its reviews and advice would be:

Table 2.2 Summary of the "Public Domain" – A National Accounts Perspective

The "public domain"	General government	Institutional domain	Public sector	Private sector
	General government	Central governments	Public sector	
	General government	State governments	Public sector	
	General government	Local governments	Public sector	
	General government	Social security funds	Public sector	
		Other public sector	Public sector	
		Private sector in the public domain		Private sector
		Other private sector		Private sector

Source: OECD 2007a: 5.

Then there was the delicate issue of policy transfer. The committee was well aware of the pitfalls of trying to transfer experiences from one context to another. It developed a hierarchy of transfer possibilities. First, broad governance arrangements (e.g., media, nature of parliamentary oversight) – these were inherently constitutional and cultural, and so transfer would be both challenging and open to charges that the OECD was meddling in national political affairs. Second, technical goals of public management reform – these are reasonably consistent and with fewer political sensitivities. Third, public management institutional arrangements – mechanisms to achieve those goals which could be discussed without too many political sensitivities. But how would the OECD's work relate to that of other multilateral or country agencies involved in governance reform? Most of these other organizations rely on indicators as the foundation for their analyses (Buduru & Pal 2010) whereas

> The OECD starts from a very different position. It is in the fortunate position of building on the experiences of practitioners from a "club" of member and non-member policy makers. Thus it can obtain consensus about the significance of diverse developments in public management, allowing the development of a genuine empirical base rather than theory-based or technical-assistance driven approaches and recommendations. Second, through specifying the units of analysis in some detail it is able to ensure that the conceptual basis for the discussion is clear. (OECD 2007a: 7)

Having developed a concept of the "public sector", GOV and the PGC listed eight Building Blocks – along with goals, institutional arrangements, and existing OECD instruments, that constitute a "grid" or *acquis* in the governance area: budget practices and procedures; human resource management; integrity in the public sector; internal and external reporting; e-government readiness; centre of government; management of regulatory quality; multi-level governance. The details are presented in Appendix 1. Those details show GOV's sense of what constitutes good governance. While there certainly is flexibility, these criteria are not empty. They reflect the theme identified in Chapter 1 of "loosely coordinated governance". If states increasingly emulate these goals and institutional structures, they operate within a consistent "system of rules", whatever their peculiarities and distinctive institutional configurations. Moreover, as we discuss in Chapter 5, GOV's building blocks in this document are supplemented by other instruments, for example, around anti-corruption and lobbying.

The PGC updated its global strategy in April 2010 for the period 2010–2014 (OECD 2010c). In addition to the existing pillars of participation and dissemination, the document recommended further efforts at capacity-building: "This dimension is already part of the MENA program and also PGC peer reviews, such as the review of human resource management in Brazil's federal government. In addition, a capacity building dimension can better help PGC governance perspectives, practices, guidelines and recommendations take root". It methods would include: "accession, enhanced engagement, observership, global fora, and regional programmes". The graduation of countries from observer status to fully acceded members of the OECD meant that the number of observers would go down, somewhat below the average of other committees. Now that the OECD had a firm global strategy of expansion, the PGC felt that it should relax some of the caution it had exercised in the past over too many observers (making committee business possibly less efficient) and expand its roster of observers to include "some if not all of the remaining EE (enhanced engagement) partners". It concluded that despite successful efforts in the last five years, "engagement with non-member countries could be further developed in order to reach its full potential". It noted that the relevance of public governance in a country's economic health and government performance, however, "is becoming increasingly accepted, especially given the current global economic context", rendering the PGC's "activities even more timely and appropriate".

Conclusion

The OECD's roots in the OEEC were nourished in Europe. In 1961, with the establishment of the OECD itself, those roots spread to a trans-Atlantic alliance. By 2010 they spread further, and the OECD was engaged globally, with an aggressive programme of expanded membership and enhanced engagement with single key countries (e.g., Indonesia) and regions (e.g., MENA). The OECD's mandate covers almost every conceivable policy area, but this chapter has shown how central governance is to its mission, though that centrality has varied at times. It was originally established to foster economic development in Europe and later free markets around the world, but it was one of the first international organizations to recognize that economic performance could not be divorced from an efficient and effective public sector. In that sense, governance and public management reform and modernization are inscribed in the organization's DNA.

The chapter also shows the origins of other key elements in the OECD's genome. It was a membership-based organization, but one in which the US deliberately stepped away from the creation of OEEC, except to provide funds. Its internal rivalries meant that its Secretariat was weak, and its agenda driven by member-dominated committees. It had, in the OEEC, what Woodward has called a core "palliative" function – help and assistance. The OEEC cajoled and coordinated – through its members – but it could never dictate. That characteristic was inherited by the OECD, which deliberately expanded its activities to begin to engage with non-members. This softened its "soft powers" even more. Once the OECD gradually reduced its technical assistance activities

– starting, as we saw, in the mid-1970s with the re-shaping of TECO – it had no coercive arrows left in its quiver. The techniques it pioneered then remain the basic tools it uses today, though on a wider canvas.

We can also see the three themes of this book reflected in the narrative of the OECD's history, though with interesting wrinkles. As we noted in Chapter 1, the emergence of public sector reform as a policy field – as opposed to a terrain of piecemeal tinkering – took time and was not fully appreciated by international governmental organizations until the mid-1970s, at the earliest. The UN Public Administration Network had held a workshop in 1971, but had failed to pursue governance and public sector reform as a priority. The OECD held its public management symposium in 1979 in Madrid. TECO continued its research through the 1980s, even while senior staff in the OECD began to doubt the directorate's efficacy. The transformation into PUMA and the release of *Governance in Transition* put the OECD squarely at the head of international thinking about public management and reform. By the late 1990s PUMA had found its voice. In GOV and its associated committees, the OECD's public management function has become a truly networked operation. The recent OECD globalization strategy has expanded GOV's activities to partners under enhanced engagement, as well as accession states, and a host of observers. It is active in every region of the world (for example, there exists a senior budget officials group in every continent). But it carries no big stick. It draws upon, and refracts and amplifies, the mental energies of thousands of senior public servants and subject-matter specialists around the world.

In this it also casts lights on the other two themes of this book. It is hard to imagine the modern world without international governmental organizations – in aid, trade, international agreements of one sort or another. Though the OECD is unique, it is not alone. Indeed, though it went through a "through" of despondency and apparent irrelevance in the 1980s, and continues under SG Angel Gurría to fight to keep that relevance, the organization is deeply entangled in a mesh of international organizations that, however fitfully, keep world order. We return to this theme in the book's conclusion, but we here have glimpses of how order can be created without hierarchy. It starts with harmonic resonance around rules, practices and standards, and gradually it herds cats to come to rest in roughly the same place.

Finally, we see in this history the struggle over policy transfer. The literature reviewed in Chapter 1 shows a growing maturity and nuance in gauging how policy transfer actually can happen, but there has been virtually no analysis "from the inside". How do organizations like the OECD wrestle with policy transfer? The texts and the interview data show that people in "policy transfer institutions" – of which the OECD is a prime example – are not stupid. They fully know that experiences from one country cannot simply be "transferred" to another. Culture, history, institutions and constitutional practices differ too much. And yet ... and yet ... policy transfer is the OECD's business. How to create the necessary incentives? How to transfer with delicacy and diligence? We saw that, contrary to its NPM-warrior image, in the 1970s TECO was quite sensitive and realistic about inappropriate transfer. By the mid-1990s, when NPM had its ascendancy, PUMA acknowledged varieties of governance experiences, but began to highlight "trends" and "consensus". By the time "Building Blocks" was released, a more robust but still flexible framework was developed for what it meant to be in the "OECD family". Accession simply put an accent on that. What did it mean to be "aligned" with OECD practices? And in fact, did it matter that much in terms of the OECD's higher objective of influencing the global economy? For example, Russia suffers clear deficits in terms of open government, free media, and corruption. But if Russia is granted accession, it will be in the tent, not outside.[25] As an OECD member it will perforce influence allied states – all part of the vast former Soviet Union – to behave as it does. With this one member, the OECD tightens is soft embrace on a quarter of the globe.

Appendix 1   Thematic building blocks for guiding elements on public governance and management in global relations

Chapter 1: Budget practices and procedures

Technical goals of public management reforms	Institutional arrangements
OECD governments are seeking...	In order to achieve these goals, budgeting and public expenditures systems generally comprise...
1. Aggregate fiscal discipline	
• to control the government's total expenditures in the short-, medium- and long-term at a level consistent with optimal economic and social development	• Appropriately designed and enforceable fiscal rules; • Medium-term expenditure frameworks; • Long-term budget sustainability projections, including potential fiscal risks; • Mechanisms to ensure the use of prudent economic assumptions; • Systems to prevent the undermining of fiscal discipline through the abuse of tax expenditures and off-budget expenditures
2. Effective allocation and reallocation of resources	
• to establish priorities within the budget, including the capacity to shift resources from old priorities to new ones, or from less to more productive uses, in correspondence with the government's policy objectives	• Appropriate division of responsibilities between the central budget bureau and spending ministries (top-down arrangements); • Performance and results information systems in order to evaluate programmes; • Systems to ensure the accurate measurement of the cost of government, including the use of accruals where appropriate; • Capacity to perform periodic government-wide programme review initiatives

Chapter 1: **Budget practices and procedures** – *continued*

Technical goals of public management reforms	Institutional arrangements
OECD governments are seeking...	In order to achieve these goals, budgeting and public expenditures systems generally comprise...

3. Promotion of efficient delivery of services

• to progressively reduce the cost of producing the goods and services for which resources are provided	• A system for automatically extracting productivity dividends from spending ministries; • Mechanisms to reduce and reform central management controls and review organizational structures in order to give managers more flexibility; • Programmes to regularly subject government provision to outsourcing and other market-type mechanisms; • Systems to consider public-private partnerships as alternatives to traditional government provision; • Incentive-based systems to improve cash management and asset (capital) management

4. Budget transparency and accountability

• to subject all aspects of the budgeting and public expenditures system to outside scrutiny and challenge	• A timely schedule for the publication of all relevant fiscal information in a user-friendly form; • Sufficient time for deliberation in parliament together with independent capacity to provide effective oversight; • New techniques and outreach mechanisms to inform the public and civil society organizations of the nature of fiscal conditions currently and in the future; • Peer reviews to regularly assess the budgeting and public expenditures system.

Existing OECD Instrument: 2001 OECD BEST PRACTICES FOR BUDGET TRANSPARENCY **Existing PGC Guidance:** none

Chapter 2: Human Resource Management (HRM)

Technical goals of public management reforms	Institutional arrangements
OECD governments are seeking...	In order to achieve these goals, human resource management systems generally comprise...

1. Workforce planning and management

• To attain a core public service that is appropriately skilled, sized and remunerated; and whose composition is adaptable to changes in productivity and needs;	• Workforce planning and management arrangements that contribute to... • providing opportunities and incentives for measuring and achieving productivity gains (e.g. through recruitment, staff development and compensation arrangements); • deterring unplanned long-term growth in the costs of public employment; • ensuring that staff profiles are monitored and developed and that capacity is allocated to priority areas; • providing capacity to manage change in the workforce (e.g. through integration of HRM into organizations' strategic planning);

2. Core values

• to attain a core public service • that has a core group of staff who share common values and is responsive to new priorities within the limits of legality; • that earns respect from the public for its merit and probity; • that has a "whole of government" perspective;	• public service legislation and practices that contribute to: • preserving institutional memory, continuity, probity, merit, and a whole of government perspective, without creating undue rigidity; • making the machinery of government "legible", with clear accountabilities but the possibility for change in response to new responsibilities and service delivery requirements. • oversight arrangements that contribute to ensuring: • that public officials are appointed on merit and maintain integrity in public decision-making and public trust in government; • an effective political-administrative interface; • institutional arrangements that contribute to striking a balance between supporting "new" values such as performance, efficiency and diversity and preserving "traditional" values (e.g. impartiality, legality...).

3. Staff performance and capacity

• to attain a core public service that comprises staff who strive for delivering quality goods and services at minimum cost, within organizations with clear objectives and appropriate autonomy and authority;	• selection and appointment arrangements that contribute to deliver the "right" staff; • performance information concerning service delivery that contributes to informing all aspects of the employment cycle (including recruitment and promotion arrangements, pay and other compensation incentives, disciplinary and termination arrangements); • a fit between HRM and financial delegation that contributes to agency incentives for performance; • various employment regimes (core civil service, senior civil service and contracted staff) that contribute to collectively contributing to staff incentives for performance.

Existing OECD Instruments: none
Existing PGC Guidance: OECD Country Peer Reviews of Human Resource Management, GOV/PGC/PEM(2006)7.

Chapter 3: Integrity and Corruption Resistance

OECD governments promote integrity and enhance corruption resistance in public institutions in order to maintain confidence in public decision-making and a level playing field for businesses

Technical goals of public management reforms	Institutional arrangements
OECD governments are seeking...	In order to achieve these goals integrity and corruption resistance systems generally comprise...

1. Standards of behaviour for conduct

• To attain a core public service in line with a modern mission of the public service	• Updated core values, principles, standards of conduct for public officials in order to meet public expectations • adequate forms (in legislation, codes of conduct, guidelines, etc) for effective applications of values, principles and standards

2. Implementation and monitoring compliance

• To ensure that implementing mechanisms are integrated into overall management • To ensure that effective transparency and accountability mechanisms enables public scrutiny of conduct	• professional socialization and application of core values and integrity standards in daily processes through communication, training, advice, guidance, leadership, staff involvement, etc • Monitoring of compliance and detect irregularities and systemic weaknesses through management mechanisms and independent reviews • Enforcement of standards and timely and just sanctions in case of breaches of standards through investigation and prosecution

3. Corruption resistance in risk areas

• To identify risk areas • To anticipate emerging problems and shift attention from enforcement to prevention	• Mapping out of activities and sectors vulnerable to corruption • Mitigation of risk by tailored prohibitions and restrictions, stricter control and procedures for reporting corruption

4. Assessment of implementation and impact

• To provide relevant and credible data for policy makers and the wider public	• Methodologies and procedures to collect relevant and credible data on implementation and impact of integrity measures • Procedures to properly integrate collected data in the policy cycle

Existing OECD Instruments: 1998 Recommendation on Improving Ethical Conduct in the Public Service 2003 Recommendation on Guidelines for Managing Conflict of Interest in the Public Service

Existing (or forthcoming) PGC Guidance:

Public procurement – a forthcoming publication maps out good practices for integrity in public procurement from both member and non-member countries. Country experts called for a checklist for policymakers.

Post-public employment – a good practice handbook is under preparation.

Lobbying – draft principles for enhancing transparency and accountability in lobbying will be reviewed in June.

Ethics Infrastructure and Assessment Framework, see at
http://www.oecd.org/document/19/0,2340,en_2649_34135_35822611_1_1_1_1,00.html

Chapter 4: Internal and External Reporting: Open Government

Building an open government is an objective shared by OECD countries that provides an essential ingredient for democratic governance, social stability and economic development. Open government covers basically three main elements: transparency, accessibility and responsiveness

Technical goals of public management reforms	Institutional arrangements
OECD governments are seeking...	In order to achieve these goals arrangements to support open government policies generally comprise...

1. Transparency

• To ensure that governments actions, and the individuals responsible for those actions, will be exposed to public scrutiny and challenge	• Laws providing access to information • Effective (electronic) systems (e.g. registers) allowing people to identify and retrieve any government information they may seek • Publication of annual reports, performance data, strategic plans, legislative timetables etc • Standards to ensure quality, consistency and coherence of information

2. Accessibility

• To ensure that government services and information on its activities will be readily accessible to anyone, at anytime, and anywhere, in a user-friendly way	• Administrative laws defining the basic conditions for citizens' access and mechanisms for holding administrative authorities accountable for their decisions. • Independent institutions (e.g. ombudsman) for oversight, and to enforce the citizens rights to access information • citizens' or service charters with the aim of providing high quality, easily accessed and customer-centred public services for citizens and business • Cutting through "red tape" by reducing administrative burdens and one-stop shops (physical and electronic), providing assistance and advice in complying with regulations • E-government arrangements to reduce costs and provide 24/7 access to government information and online services • Multi-channel approach to guarantee users a choice between on-line and off-line information, transactions and services

3. Responsiveness

• To ensure that government will be responsive to new ideas, demands and needs	• Tools, rules and procedures for public consultation and/or active participation at all stages of the policy process, e.g. regulatory impact assessment, participatory budgeting • Integration of results of consultation and participation in established decision-making processes, and feedback to participants.

4. Inclusiveness

• To ensure a wide variety of different people as possible can interact with government	• Lower barriers for people who are willing, but unable to interact with government • Provide incentives for people who are able, but unwilling to interact with government

Existing OECD Instruments: none

Existing PGC Guidance: Citizens as Partners: Information, Consultation and Public Participation in Policy-Making

Ten guiding principles for successful on-line consultation: to be found in box 1. On pages 10–11 of the report "promise and problems of e-democracy". See http://publications.oecd.org/acrobatebook/4204011E.PDF

Checklist for evaluating public participation: box 0.2. pages 16–17 in "evaluating public participation in policy making" http://publications.oecd.org/acrobatebook/ 4205101E.PDF

Guiding principles for successful information, consultation and active participation of citizens in policy-making. Page 15 of the report on citizens as partners, see http://publications.oecd.org/acrobatebook/4201131E.PDF

Chapter 5: E-government Readiness

E-government is more about government than about "e". As a tool to achieve better government and enable governments to deliver better and smarter services, e-government offers potential solutions across the whole of government and for the benefit of the whole of public sector. For governments to becoming e-government ready, it is a question of addressing a broad range of public governance issues involving all parts of the public sector and its users such as citizens and businesses.

Technical goals of public management reforms	Institutional arrangements
OECD governments are seeking to...	To achieve these goals arrangements to support E-government readiness generally comprise...

1. E-government vision and operational strategic goals:

• Raise awareness and achieve commitment. • Ensure policy integration with public sector transformation goals and Information Society goals. • Develop Information Society skills and competencies.	• Programmes to promote the positive impact of e-government on efficiency, service quality and citizen engagement and trust. • E-government strategies aligned with broader policy and service delivery goals. • Strategies to develop a broad range of competencies to engage in e-government decision.

2. Establishment of framework conditions for e-government:

• Create and adopt legislative and budgetary frameworks which support the implementation of e-government goals. • Identify and address digital divides, infrastructure deficiencies and society-wide ICT skills and competency deficiencies.	• Legislation supporting the development of e-government within areas for example: e-procurement, re-use of public data, e-commerce, liberalization of telecommunications markets, e-signatures, e-invoicing, privacy, and data protection. • Budgeting mechanisms supporting collaborative approaches to e-government. • Common public sector infrastructure policy to ensure horizontal and vertical integration and interoperability of e-government. • Programmes to address the country's digital divides

3. Development of e-government leadership:

• Ensure strong political and top-management support to e-government development and implementation. • Create (a) simple e-government organization(s) within the public sector which have clear responsibilities and competencies to achieve a whole-of-public-sector e-government development and implementation.	• Strategic tools to achieve strong political commitments to e-government strategies, goals, and outcomes within governments themselves and with Parliaments. • Reorganize programmes to better accommodate the cross-public-sector nature of e-government.

4. Effective and efficient implementation of e-government:

• Ensure the usage of the necessary management tools for tracking e-government development. • Create clear and transparent policies for using private sector competencies and capacities and the development skills and competencies within the public sector itself.	• common public sector monitoring and evaluation concepts, delivering mechanisms, and incentives, to ensure timely feedback on progress and status. • clear and transparent policies for using private sector competencies and capacities through e.g. outsourcing, "arms length agencies", and public-private partnerships and develop and implement human resource development policies and action plans which address identified lacks of ICT competencies and skills within the public sector.

Chapter 5: **E-government Readiness** – *continued*

Technical goals of public management reforms	Institutional arrangements
OECD governments are seeking to...	To achieve these goals arrangements to support E-government readiness generally comprise...

5. Setting up of effective e-government collaboration frameworks:

• Improve back-office efficiency and effectiveness. • Improve user-friendliness and interoperability. • Ensure interconnectivity.	• Common business processes. • Front-office and back-office standardization in order to achieve an improved user-friendliness of front-office e-government services. • Common public sector enterprise architecture and service multi-channel delivery strategies.

6. Improving service delivery outputs and outcomes by:

• Provide relevant and needed e-government services to citizens, businesses, and governments themselves. • Ensure a high user take-up and improve user satisfaction of e-services.	• Services and systems focused on the most common transactions and based around the needs of the user. • User research and cost-benefit analysis as an element in deciding whether an e-government investment potentially can deliver sufficient quantitative and qualitative benefits to governments.

Existing OECD Instruments: none

Existing PGC Guidance:

Analytical framework and methodology to conduct E-government Reviews of OECD countries (presented and discussed at the meeting of the Informal E-Government Steering Group on 15 December 2003).

Checklist for E-Government Leaders (2003), policy brief
http://www.oecd.org/dataoecd/ 62/58/11923037.pdf

Checklist to Evaluate the Economic Case of E-Government (Annex to Chapter 4 of the OECD report E-government for Better Government)

Chapter 6: Centres of Government

The Centre of Government is the body or group of bodies that provide direct support and advice to the Head of Government and the Council of Ministers for decision-making.

Technical goals of public management reforms	Institutional arrangements
OECD governments are seeking...	In order to achieve these goals arrangements at the centre of government generally comprise...

1. Interface between political and administrative levels

• To provide advice for final decision makers • To ensure continuity of procedure, policy and implementation • To ensure stability of structure and maintain the "institutional memory"	*Depending on the structure of the central executive (collegial, presidential or hybrid system)* • A Government Office (a generic term that refers to the administrative body that serves the head of the government and the Council of Ministers) • Sometimes with an additional • A Prime Minister Office (office that serves specifically the head of the government, normally the Prime Minister) • Staffing of these offices is balanced between civil servants and political appointees.

2. Coordination for decision-making

• to ensure a "whole of government" perspective both inside and outside government • to ensure policy coherence and quality • to reconcile conflicting interests and activities between government entities.	• policy coordination, policy advice, and conflict resolution • legal functions • logistical and technical support of the Council of Ministers • support of the Prime Minister while representing the government • monitoring functions • coordination of government-wide communication • Centre of Government pursues the above roles throughout the entire policy cycle, from agenda setting through to evaluation, (NB: not all Centres of Government pursue all of these roles!)

3. Preparation for future challenges

• to help government identify and prepare for future challenges (e.g. risk management, governance in the knowledge society, the impact of ICTs on decision-making)	• A strategic planning unit that coordinates among strategic bodies throughout the administration in most governments.

Existing OECD Instruments: none

Existing PGC Guidance: none

Chapter 7: Management of Regulatory Quality

OECD governments promote regulatory quality performance to improve national economies and enhance their ability to change:

Technical goals of public management reforms	Institutional arrangements
OECD governments are seeking...	To achieve these goals regulatory quality management arrangements generally comprise...

1. Broad programmes of regulatory reform adopted at the political level

• to establish clear objectives and frameworks for implementation • to consider key elements of regulatory policy – policies, tools and institutions – as a whole	• clear responsibilities for assuring regulatory quality including application of policies for regulatory reform at all levels • an adequate institutional framework and resources, with adequately staffed and trained staff • systems to manage regulatory resources effectively and to discharge enforcement responsibilities

2. Capacity to access and review regulatory impacts

• to improve the stock of existing and the quality of new regulation • to achieve net welfare benefits taking into account of environmental and social as well as of economic policy objectives	• regulatory impact analysis (RIA) integrated into the development, review and revision of significant regulations • RIA and ex-post evaluation applied from the point of view of those affected rather than of the regulation • alternatives to regulation when appropriate

3. Transparent and non-discriminatory regulatory institutions and processes

• to ensure that the public interest is not subordinated to those of regulated entities and stakeholders • to include measures to promote integrity	• regulatory quality criteria such as transparency, non-discrimination and efficiency to regulation inside government • public registries of regulations • interactive websites on rule-making information available to the public and able to receive public comments on regulatory matters • transparent and non-discriminatory administrative procedures for applying regulations as regulatory decisions

4. linkages with other policy objectives

• evaluate and assess linkages with other policy objectives	• assessment of risk to public and to public policy as fully and transparently as possible • effective and credible coordination mechanisms • scope for regulatory quality broadened to include public services • targeted reviews of regulation where change will yield the highest and most visible benefits

Existing OECD Instruments:
1995 OECD Reference Checklist for Regulatory Decision-Making

2005 OECD Guiding Principles for Regulatory Quality and Performance Available at: http://www.oecd.org/dataoecd/24/6/34976533.pdf

Existing PGC and GRP Guidance:

APEC-OECD Integrated Checklist on Regulatory Reform Available at: http://www.oecd. org/dataoecd/41/9/34989455.pdf

Chapter 8: Multi-level Governance

Technical goals of public management reforms	Institutional arrangements
OECD governments are seeking...	In order to achieve these goals, arrangements to support multi-level governance generally comprise...

1. Multi-level governance frameworks, implementation and capacity	
• to build a clear framework for multi-level governance	• transparent and coherent distribution of functions, avoiding fiscal and territorial imbalances
	• contract-type vertical coordination mechanisms to ensure that roles and obligations are clearly defined between the centre and the regions with agreed objectives and clear targets
	• incentives for local and regional governments to be active in regional development
• to promote effective implementation through cooperation and coordination among subnational governments	• incentive mechanisms for cooperation among municipalities and among regions to improve strategic planning and resource sharing and to make service delivery more cost effective
• to build technical and administrative capacity at local and regional level	• technical and administrative capacity building for personnel and processes in administrations responsible for policy planning and implementation
	• grants and transfers creating incentives for local governments to improve their policy-making capacities

2. Relations and cooperation between levels of government for key core function of public management: Example: Central/Regional/Local Cooperation in Human Resource Management.	
• To achieve a balance between autonomy and a common framework across devolved governments. This balance contributes to: • ensuring that the HRM responsibilities of subnational governments matches their devolved functions; • promoting a flexible civil service able to adapt to local priorities without undermining a level of coherence for the whole of government;	• Intergovernmental relationships contribute to providing: • a clear demarcation of responsibilities between central government staff and staff in other levels of government; • devolved or decentralized budget and establishment control; • subnational government with recruitment authority, responsibility for subnational performance management arrangements and pay policy; • central control over subnational HR arrangements when necessary and within clear guidelines; • Arrangements for staff mobility between governments contribute to providing opportunities for sharing experiences between governments – and the development of a common set of values. • Shared evaluations of the effectiveness of HRM arrangements at national/federal and subnational government level contribute to providing opportunities for mutual learning.

Existing OECD Instruments: none

Existing TDPC Guidance: Innovation and Effectiveness in Territorial Development Policy, High Level Meeting; Martigny, Switzerland, June 2003.

Source: OECD 2007a.

3
Public Management and Governance in the OECD

The mist was gently lifting from the Piazza San Marco, Venice, in the early morning on Monday, 15 November 2010. Pigeons and tourists were beginning to appear in the eerie quiet and echoes of a city without cars that rests on a lagoon, criss-crossed by canals. In the higher-end hotels near the Piazza, delegations from 37 countries – OECD members, as well as Brazil, South Africa, Egypt, Morocco, Estonia, Russia and Ukraine – were finishing breakfast and readying for the day's Ministerial Meeting of the Public Governance Committee (PGC) of the OECD. There were 26 ministerial-level attendees, four civil society organizations (e.g., Transparency International), and of course representatives from the GOV Secretariat. Gingerly climbing onto bobbing water taxis, they crossed the Grand Canal to the Isola di San Giorgio Maggiore for the first such meeting since 2005, a meeting that would determine the direction of OECD work on governance for the next five years. The next day, the PGC (consisting of delegates appointed by member countries) would meet for a day to absorb the Ministerial's conclusions, and engage in discussion over two country reports. By Tuesday evening almost all the international diplomats and public servants had left, and Venice was returned to its tourists, pigeons, and miniscule local population. But a global public sector reform agenda had been forged.

In Chapter 2 we focused on the evolution of TECO, PUMA and GOV because they were and are the epicentre in the OECD in analysing and dissecting public sector reform and public management, and this Ministerial meeting was entirely a GOV event. We saw how the successive directorates and departments had to carve out an agenda, find clients, and establish legitimacy within the overall organization. Their solution was to seize on horizontal issues. Regulation, budgets, human resource management – these were areas of public management and governance that were not being addressed in the organization. The rest of the various parts of the OECD focus on specific policy areas – trade and agriculture, science and technology, education, tax policy. But in a real sense the entire mandate of the OECD is public management – Donald Johnston, Secretary-General (SG) 1996–2006, notes that "The OECD is in a way, all about governance".[1] Its mandate in Article 1 of the Convention is "to promote policies" to help develop the world economy. While various directorates work on everything from agriculture and trade to science and technology, in one way or another these are all about governance, at least at the policy level.

So, as important as the Ministerial was, focusing on GOV (as we did in the last chapter) actually would ignore the other governance and management aspects of the OECD as an organization. However, if every policy field is a field of public management advice, this would turn into a book about the OECD as a whole. Our strategy therefore will be to zero-in on those arms of the OECD that are clearly dedicated to broad public sector reform, even if they are outside GOV but supported by it. GOV is the focal point, but it is increasingly embedded in and supportive of a web of governance-related initiatives and programmes throughout the OECD. In this chapter we will discuss the following. First, we examine GOV, its structure and activities (both the directorate and the committees), and use the Venice Ministerial and PGC meetings as a lens on understanding the OECD's new global strategy on public sector reform. Second, we look at SIGMA (Support for Improvement in Governance and Management) – the OECD/EU effort to deal with the collapse of states in central and Eastern Europe that was launched in 1991 and has evolved in tandem with changes in the EU. While in principle it is part of the GOV directorate, SIGMA (due to independent funding) is in practice quite distinct and autonomous. Finally, we move outside of GOV to other key parts of the OECD to provide examples of how they contribute to public management reform and the governance agenda. We will review three initiatives in the SG's office that have been undertaken over the past years: the CCNM (the Centre for Cooperation with Non-Members – part of an earlier global strategy that now has been re-centred in the current outreach and globalization strategy), the International Futures Programme, and an initiative around "Making Reform Happen". Then we look briefly at three other directorates with mandates that address governance issues: development cooperation (DAC), financial and enterprise affairs (DAF), and economics (ECO).

GOV: Directorate and committees

The GOV Directorate was created in 2002 through an amalgamation of PUMA and the Territorial Development Service. It initially supported two committees – the Public Management Committee (later renamed the Public Governance Committee or PGC) and the Territorial Development Policy Committee (TDPC). The Regulatory Policy Committee (RPC) was created and added in 2009, elevating the importance of work on regulation that had been conducted for years in a Working Party. In large part GOV's creation was a rationalization of resources within the Secretariat – this was a lean period for the OECD, and as SG, Donald Johnston had a mandate to streamline the organization. The TDPC had never been particularly strong or well-focused, and so the marriage of the two under a new Secretariat was intended to give it better support.[2] This belied the turbulence that both the OECD and PUMA/GOV were undergoing in the period. The OECD faced severe budget pressures in the late 1990s. Between 1996 and 1999, the organization's budget was reduced by approximately 18 per cent. As Johnston himself noted: "Members did not deliver the budget stability they promised would follow the reductions. Instead, the staff have had to deal with further cuts and repeated job uncertainty at the end of each year, in addition to the upheaval of the move and adapting to new ways of working".[3]

PUMA was almost abolished in 1998, survived, but suffered a substantial cut in staff.[4] Between 1998 and 2002 there were five successive heads of PUMA/GOV until the appointment of Odile Sallard in February 2002. Sallard had been the Acting Director of the Territorial Development Service (launched in 1995 to support "place-based" economic policies) and had been tasked with creating TDPC (which she did, in 1999), but it had proved a difficult assignment, and so the joining of the committees within a new directorate was not entirely a cost-cutting measure, but was also intended to realign public management reform efforts. Though the new directorate was called GOV, its key committee remained PUMA until 2004, when it was changed to the Public Governance Committee (PGC). Dropping the PUMA name was a difficult decision. Directorate staff had worked hard for more than 20 years to carve out a space for public management within the OECD, and while "governance" was a new and popular term, it did not have the global brand recognition of PUMA.

As outlined in Chapter 2, while the PGC and GOV inherited the same broad areas of focus that had been at the core of PUMA – e.g., budgets, centres of government, regulation – they were also to adopt a more strategic perspective around modern challenges to governance, transparency and the accountability of public institutions. PUMA had been more "internally oriented", and the change was supported by some committee members who wanted a broader focus on issues like citizen engagement and results and performance. Committee members also supported the change since it would consolidate governance issues in the OECD and perhaps give them more weight within the organization.[5] The PUMA committee mandate for 2000–2004 was expanded to include the following tasks:

- To identify and help address the emerging forces and trends which constitute strategic governance challenges;
- To assist members and non-members to raise the performance of their public institutions so that they are better equipped to manage those forces;
- To focus on key elements of good governance framework including: developing capacities for more coherent and globalized policies, delivering on policy commitments in a changing world, institutionalizing

transparency, honesty and accountability in government, intervening effectively in society and markets to achieve public policies and promote competition as well as social cohesion.[6]

This mandate was expanded further with the new OECD strategy of enlargement. As noted in Chapter 2, the process of enlargement and enhanced engagement by 2007 led the PGC to develop a broad concept of a "grid" or *acquis* in the governance area: budget practices and procedures; human resource management; integrity in the public sector; internal and external reporting; e-government readiness; centre of government; management of regulatory quality; multi-level governance (OECD 2007a).

These activities represent the formal mandate of GOV, but for budgetary reasons the directorate has had to broaden its scope. The OECD budget consists of two components. Part 1 consists of country contributions to the base budget paid by all members according to a formula consisting of a portion related to relative size of the national economy and a portion shared equally. Part 2 of the budget is for special purpose bodies (e.g., the International Energy Agency) and specific projects, and is funded by contributions (e.g., Programme for International Student Assessment, or PISA). Both Part I and Part II budgets can contain "voluntary contributions" (or "VCs") for specific projects. Part I contributions came under severe strain in the early 2000s relative to the overall budget, and so GOV, like other directorates and the OECD as a whole, began to search more assiduously for "voluntary contributions". These come in a variety of forms: special projects that particular governments might be interested in supporting; or projects such as country reviews that are paid for by host countries. Projects funded through voluntary contributions are quite frequently solicited at the director or departmental level within a directorate. This contributes to the further decentralization of the OECD as an organization that we discuss in more detail shortly, but also to a certain degree of internal competition over funding through special projects. Moreover, since by now a substantial portion of OECD (and GOV) funding comes through voluntary contributions, the proportion of permanent staff is quite small. In fact, in 2010–2011 the distinction between "permanent" and "project" staff eroded almost completely – partly due to the fact that more and more staff with longer tenure spend a significant portion of their time working on projects.[7] Many staff now are hired on a project basis, and when the project is over, are let go. This leads to organizational churn, and some criticism that the quality of work has suffered since there is less depth of experience among OECD staff, though it should be noted that the annual quantity of reports and reviews (see below for an analysis) produced by the directorate is substantial (virtually every GOV publication is written by directorate staff – the role of committees is to review, comment and negotiate more delicate political points). The other point that this highlights is that as a result of

Figure 3.1 GOV Directorate Structure (2011)

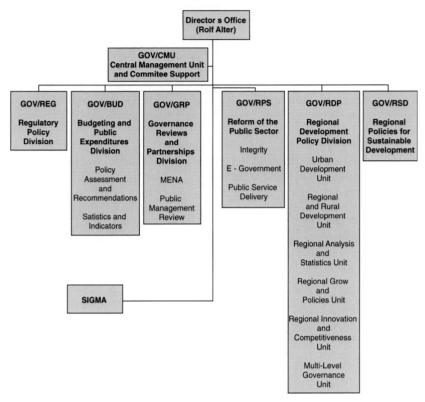

Source: OECD, Public Governance and Territorial Development Directorate, June 2011.
Reproduced with permission.

budget pressures and the logic of voluntary contributions, much of the OECD actually behaves more like a private consulting firm soliciting contracts.

Figure 3.1 shows the organizational structure of the GOV directorate as of June 2011. The directorate is divided into six divisions, as well as SIGMA. Four of the six divisions are further sub-divided into units (the Regulatory Policy Division and the Regional Policies for Sustainable Development Division are not). The largest division in terms of staff (staff listings are not shown in the figure) is the Regional Development Policy division (at 34), followed by the Regulatory Policy division at 18. However, another way to read the chart is to see that two divisions (GOV/RDP and GOV/RSD) essentially support the TDPC, while the GOV/REG division supports the RPC. The three remaining divisions essentially support different aspects of the work of the PGC. It is important to appreciate that the directorate as a whole is relatively small in terms of staff – just counting the six divisions and the director's office, as of June 2011 they amounted to 119 people. Moreover, the workflow in the directorate is more fluid than one would presume from the siloed divisions – individual staff will contribute portions of their time to projects that might not be housed within their divisions.

GOV focuses on the following themes: budgeting and public governance, e-government, ethics and corruption, governance dialogue with non-members, public employment and management, regional development and regulatory management and reform. These themes correspond to the work of the different committees, networks and working groups of the GOV directorate, with all groups participating in dialogue with non-members. A quantitative analysis of the content of publications of the GOV directorate by theme up to 2010, shows that approximately 27 per cent of all content was focused on public employment and management, closely followed by regulatory management and reform (approximately 24 per cent of all content – see Figures 3.2 and 3.3). By this measure, regional development accounts for approximately 19 per cent of content followed by budgeting and public expenditures (13 per cent), ethics and corruption (6 per cent), governance

Figure 3.2   GOV Output by Policy Theme (by count, all years to 07/10)

Percentage of all content by policy area out of total (947)

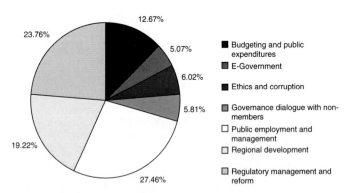

Source: OECD. Public Governance and Territorial Development (GOV) – Publications and documents, web resource, accessed 30/07/10 from http://www.oecd.org/findDocument/0,3354,en_2649_33735_1_1_1_1_1,00.html

Note: This chart depicts publication and documents by count for the core activity areas of GOV (all years available up to June 2010). The core areas of GOV activity are: budgeting and public expenditures, e-government, ethics and corruption in the public sector, governance dialogue with non-members, public employment and management, regional development, regulatory management and reform.

This chart depicts publications (major) by percentage of total for all years by core area. Total number of publications: 947.

Figure 3.3   GOV Output by Country

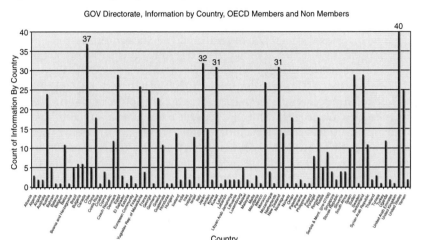

GOV Directorate, Information by Country, OECD Members and Non Members

Note: This chart represents all "information by country" for the GOV Directorate for both member and non-members as of June 2010. Information by country includes all publications and documents content types (e.g., country surveys, publications, questionnaires, reports).

80 per cent of all information by country is for OECD members (official), with the remainder being for non-members. This gives an indication of the level of engagement with non-member countries.

Source: OECD. GOV Directorate – Information by Country, OECD web resource, accessed 30/07/10 from http://www.oecd.org/infobycountry/0,3380,en_2649_33735_1_1_1_1,00.html

dialogue with non-members (6 per cent) and e-government (5 per cent). A further analysis of content-by-country shows that 80 per cent of all content (e.g., publications and documents) is understandably focused on OECD member countries, with the remainder on non-members. For all content-by-country, the United Kingdom, Canada, Italy, Korea and New Zealand stand out as having the greatest amount of content. This is notable in that it signifies considerable engagement by these countries within the OECD on governance issues. For example, Canada has been particularly active through OECD territorial reviews.

As we argued in Chapter 1, the OECD is a hybrid, highly decentralized organization. It is "hybrid" because it combines the qualities of a think tank and an international diplomatic organization. The Council consists of diplomatic country representatives, in all cases senior people, often with substantial public service careers. In this sense they have broad policy expertise, but are not necessarily equipped to substantively comment upon or critique the myriad products and publications that come up for their approval. Typically, they help set the broad agenda for the organization, represent country interests (especially around budgetary items), and from time to time weigh in on key priorities. The SG chairs Council meetings, but has real scope to develop his own agenda for the organization, with the aid of the SG's office and of course the rest of the Secretariat. The Council effectively acts as the OECD's "board" and the SG and the Secretariat act as its permanent functionaries. As in all organizations with this structure, there is always a creative tension between the parties, but diplomatic niceties and the OECD's positioning on the international stage add a layer of protocol and sometimes even intrigue (e.g., the lobbying around voting for a new SG). Once a year the OECD holds a Ministerial Council Meeting (MCM) with ministers from member states. This is the key agenda-setting meeting for the OECD as a whole. As well, there are "sectoral Ministerials" throughout the year where ministers responsible for specific policy areas meet to share experiences and set the agenda for their specific committees and directorates. The Ministerial for GOV and its committees, for example, occurs about every five years, the last one being in Venice, Italy on 15 November 2010 (see below for more detail on the meeting itself).

Then there is the committee system. As the OECD itself notes: "Through its committee structure the OECD's substantive policy agenda and outputs respond directly to the needs of, and are closely monitored by, senior policy officials from capitals in a way that may be unique among international organisations. It is these committees that produce the outputs of the OECD, the policy advice, guidelines, principles ('soft law') and best practices. The working methods of the committees are one of the institution's hallmarks, the source of its added value and the support it enjoys in capitals".[8] Chapter 1 listed the OECD committees, each of which (or in groups) is supported by a directorate in the Secretariat. The committees consist as well of senior representatives of states, but usually with more substantive expertise in the committee's subject matter and from specific ministries responsible for that subject matter. Council appoints committee chairs, but vice-chairs are elected by the committee members. The Chair and vice-chairs together form (with other members of the committee) the "Bureau" for that committee – effectively an executive committee.[9] Committees "drive the OECD" because they are the key point of contact for each directorate, which in principle take instructions from their committees. So the committees have a mix of substantive expertise, but, since each member is appointed by a state (and states have complete latitude on whom they appoint) they also reflect the diplomatic dynamics that are evident in the Council. For example, committees reach decision by consensus, though member states may abstain from voting. Each committee in turn typically (though not always) has Working Parties and Expert Groups that work on specific aspects of the committee's mandate. These entities consist almost entirely of subject-matter experts. How these committees and their entities are structured is largely up to them, as is how frequently they meet and (more or less) the subjects that they will tackle. The subsidiary bodies are less formal than committees – the latter primarily consist of state represent-atives (even though they are public servants) while the subsidiary bodies consist primarily of subject-matter experts in a specific field (who typically are also public servants). The relations among committees and their subsidiary bodies are generally quite loose. The former chair of one expert committee noted that relations with the PGC were "virtually non-existent".[10] The sub-sidiary bodes have substantial latitude in developing their work plans – they can commission external studies, find funding from member states for parti-cular projects, commission surveys from the Secretariat. Sometimes they are used as sounding boards for specific studies done by the directorates (see the PGC meeting discussion below).

This makes for a highly variable architecture throughout the OECD – each committee is structured differently, has different observers (along with mem-ber states), sets its own agenda (under loose oversight by the Council), estab-lishes its own Working Parties and Expert Groups (who themselves set their own agendas, meeting schedules, and reports). In some respects this decen-tralized and variable architecture could seem like a weakness, and in some respects it is. For example, it poses challenges when the OECD needs to address horizontal policy fields like health or sustainable development. But at another level it gives the organization a certain suppleness. As a network of networks – even internally – it can adapt and morph more flexibly than would other, more tightly coordinated organizations.

The OECD's committee system is widely regarded as its key distinguish-ing feature as an international organization. The MCM is an annual event, and other Ministerials occur from time to time. These meetings are at the highest political level, and are the main agenda-setting events for the dif-ferent components of the OECD. But the day-to-day business of the OECD is conducted by its committees and their subsidiary bodies, and these consist almost exclusively of public servants. Committee meetings consequently are the prime mechanism for building networks – a "fundamental value" of the OECD.[11] One interviewee described a GOV expert group as "part study group, part debating society, part forum for sharing information on what was happening in other countries". It was a "safe space for open dialogue", prin-cipally because only very rarely are non-committee members or formally invited non-state affiliated observers permitted to attend. At the end of the day, members understood that they would have to go home and serve their political masters, but the meetings gave them "a feeling that you were not alone".[12] This was particularly the case in Expert Groups or Working Parties – they consist of specific subject-matter experts, and are less overlaid by diplo-macy and protocol than are committees. But both the PGC and its subsidiary bodies provide a space for those engaged in public sector reform to engage with peers, learn and share experiences. The importance of "not feeling alone" was repeated by several interviewees.[13] Another feature of committees and their subsidiary bodies noted in several interviews was the networking opportunities they create.[14] Two senior government officials who had been engaged with OECD committees and work earlier in their careers noted that it was "hugely valuable" to be able to meet officials from similar political and administrative systems facing similar challenges, and that "there was no remotely similar forum".[15] A comment that was made several times with respect to the PGC and its bodies was that they also provide a platform of support for reformers who seek traction in their home countries – they can air issues at the OECD, and perhaps by getting support, can then use that support with their home government to push a reform agenda.[16] One interviewee recounted an episode where an indicators project had been launched by his home ministry, only to be pilloried by stakeholders. The project was then taken to the relevant OECD committee, which was sufficiently interested in the methodology to launch a Working Group of several countries who were prepared to experiment with the initiative. Within a year or so, the initiating government could point to others who were doing the same thing, making the effort an "international trend", and hence diffusing domestic opposition.[17]

Committee and Council relations are complicated. The Council sets priorities, based on the annual Strategic Overview by the SG, as well as the budget. But each directorate gets its own budget, and committees can set priorities of their own to some extent. The directorate develops a work plan that aligns its activities with Council priorities, which must then get approved. The work of the committees is also vetted by Council – the GOV directorate has to submit major pieces of work (e.g., public governance reviews) to the PGC and eventually to Council. The GOV directorate does not do any work without Council approval – its programme of work must align with the overall OECD strategy, but this is at the broadest level. And the PGC vets and reviews what the GOV directorate does. But since most committees meet only once or twice a year, the actual full committee oversight of the directorates is only periodic, though Chairs and Bureaus maintain regular contact via e-mail. And then there are the subsidiary bodies that also meet and interact with the directorate. This leads to a cascading matrix of agenda-setting processes: from the SG, from Council, from Committees, from Chairs and Bureaus, from subsidiary bodies, and from the Secretariat itself. (And we have not even mentioned the role of councillors from member delegations who keep a watching brief on committee activities and reports, and feed that information not only to the head of delegation but also to "capital delegates" that come as members to attend committee meetings.) There is thus a mix of coordination around key issues, coupled with substantial autonomy for the Secretariat in its day-to-day business.

The membership (as of May 2011) of the three committees associated with GOV is listed in Table 3.1. The committee mandates are listed in Table 3.2.

Table 3.1 GOV Committees Membership (as of May 2011)

Public Governance Committee

Chair: Ms. Katju Holkeri (Finland)
Vice-Chairs:
Ms. Carmel McGregor (Australia)
Mr. Jacques Druart (Belgium)
Mr. Joe Wild (Canada)
Ms. Vassiliki Moustakatou (Greece)
Ms. Ilgin Atalay (Turkey)
Members: Open to all Member countries
Regular Observers (Non-Members):
Brazil
Egypt
Morocco
Ukraine

Territorial Development Policy Committee
Chair:
Mr. John R. Fernandez (United States)
Vice-Chairs:
Mr. Wolf-Dietrich Huber (Austria)
Mr. Paul Leblanc (Canada)
Mr. Eric von Breska (European Commission)
Ms. Odile Bovar (France)
Ms. Maria Kostopoulou (Greece)
Ms. Flavia Terribile (Italy)
Mr. Takeshi Abe (Japan)
Ms. Sara Topelson (Mexico)
Members: Open to all Member countries
Regular Observers (Non-Members):
South Africa
Morocco

Regulatory Policy Committee

Chair: Mr. Jeroen Nijland (Netherlands)
Vice-Chairs:
Mr. Michael Presley (Canada)
Mr. Luigi Carbone (Italy)
Mr. Jang-Ho Park (Korea)
Mr. Carlo Thomsen (Norway)
Mr. Damian Nussbaum (United Kingdom)
Mr. Alexander Hunt (United States)
Members: Open to all Member countries
Observers: None

Source: OECD, On-Line Guide to OECD Intergovernmental Activity. Accessed 16 May 2011 at http://webnet.oecd.org/OECDGROUPS/Bodies/ShowBodyView.aspx?BodyID=863&Body PID=7470&Lang=en&Book=True

Table 3.2 GOV Committee Mandates (2009–2014)

The Public Governance Committee has the following mandate:

I. Objectives

a) The objective of the Public Governance Committee is to assist countries in building and strengthening future capacity for designing, implementing and assessing adaptive, innovative, anticipatory and citizen-focused public policies, institutions and services.

b) The intermediary objectives of the Committee include:

  i.   identifying the current and emerging strategic public governance challenges that governments face, including in a context of global crisis;

  ii. assisting countries in developing and delivering public policies based on a whole-of-government approach and grounded in the core values of the public sector;

  iii. assisting countries in designing and implementing coherent and effective public sector reform policies, including building future capability;

  iv. building and maintaining a body of robust quantitative and qualitative data and indicators on public sector inputs, processes, outputs, outcomes and performance, for carrying out comparative evidence-based analysis;

  v.   assessing the performance of countries' public sectors through peer reviews;

  vi. contributing a public governance and public management perspective on critical public policy issues;

  vii. promoting and providing a forum for policy dialogue, co-operation and exchange of experience among those responsible for the public sector, as well as with other relevant stakeholders, including international organizations and institutions, and the private sector.

Source: Resolution of the Council [C/M(2009)23, item 316, and C(2009)170]. Accessed November 10, 2010 at http://webnet.oecd.org/OECDGROUPS/Bodies/ShowBodyView.aspx?BodyID=863&BodyPID=7470&Lang=en&Book=True

Table 3.2 GOV Committee Mandates (2009–2014) – *continued*

The Territorial Development Committee has the following mandate:

Objectives:

a) The Territorial Development Policy Committee (TDPC) seeks to improve the performance of policies to enhance well-being and living standards in all types of regions by influencing the main factors that: sustain regional competitive advantages; generate stronger, fairer and liveable regional economies; and promote effective and innovative governance.

b) TDPC should serve as a premier international forum for senior-level government policymakers to identify, discuss, and disseminate a vision of development policy that is place-based, multi-level, innovative and geared towards different types of regions. This policy approach focuses on economic growth and competitiveness while integrating environmental and social concerns.

c) The intermediary objectives of the Committee include:

i. Diagnosing policy challenges in different types of regions; comparing cross-territory trends in regional performance, in local finances, and in regional policies; promoting understanding of the linkages between rural and urban areas; and developing and maintaining high-quality and relevant statistical indicators to support policy-making.

ii. Identifying and addressing the current and emerging regional policy challenges that governments face, particularly with the consequences of the global economic crisis and the responses to critical issues, such as climate change, ageing, and migration.

iii. Seizing new regional policy opportunities in key areas such as innovation, green growth, and key national strategies.

iv. Undertaking policy analysis of regional competitiveness strategies, with a view to promoting the best use of under-utilized potential for growth, and better incorporate into regional policy-making the inter-linkage between economic development, social and regional cohesion and environmental and sustainability concerns.

v. Assisting, through the exchange of best practices and peer reviews, members and non-members in designing and implementing coherent regional development policies that are based on a whole of government approach, effective targeting of public investments, and efficient delivery of public services to best support development and other major national objectives.

vi. Examining how the appropriate governance mechanisms can be identified and put in place to improve policy-making.

Source: Resolution of the Council [C(2009)126 and C/M(2009)21, item 242]. Accessed November 10, 2010 at http://webnet.oecd.org/OECDGROUPS/Bodies/ShowBodyView.aspx? BodyID=863&BodyPID=7470&Lang=en&Book=True

90

Table 3.2 GOV Committee Mandates (2009–2014) – *continued*

The Regulatory Policy Committee has the following mandate:

I. Objectives

a) The objective of the Regulatory Policy Committee is to assist members and non-members in building and strengthening capacity for regulatory quality and regulatory reform.

b) The intermediary objectives of the Committee include:

i. promoting an integrated, horizontal and multi-disciplinary approach to work on regulatory quality to increase public policy effectiveness and promote policy coherence;

ii. assessing the potential for regulatory reform to contribute to welfare, sustainable growth, innovation and equity, and developing effective ways to assess and manage risks, collaborating with, or drawing from work of other relevant Directorates in the process;

iii. examining the relationship between regulators and the regulated, and the institutional arrangements for the regulatory process in government to strengthen engagement with public and improve compliance with regulations;

iv. promoting evidence-based decision-making and regulatory transparency to create accessible, predictable and responsive regulations;

v. evaluating and improving regulatory management systems, tools and institutions designed to assure that regulations serve policy objectives efficiently and effectively and improve policy outcomes, including the use of ex-ante impact analysis and ex-post evaluation; and building and maintaining a body of qualitative and quantitative data and indicators;

vi. assessing and providing policy guidance on the components of regulatory quality that affect how regulations are designed, adopted and implemented, and on the functioning of regulatory institutions in Members and non-Members, through peer reviews, comparative studies and evidence of good practices, and promoting the wide diffusion of lessons and examples from them, including in guidelines and principles;

vii. identifying current and emerging regulatory policy challenges and developing strategies to address them by providing a forum for policy dialogue, cooperation and exchange among those responsible for regulatory policy in members and non-members, as well as with other relevant stakeholders including international organizations and institutions, the private sector, and civil society.

Source: Resolution of the Council concerning the Mandate of the Regulatory Policy Committee [C(2009)171]. Accessed November 10, 2010 at http://webnet.oecd.org/OECDGROUPS/Bodies/ShowBodyView.aspx?BodyID=863&BodyPID=7470&Lang=en&Book=True

The committee and sub-group structure for the PGC and TDPC are shown in Figures 3.4 and 3.5. As a relatively new committee, the RPC had no Working Groups or Expert Committees as of December 2010 (though see below).

Figure 3.4   Public Governance Committee

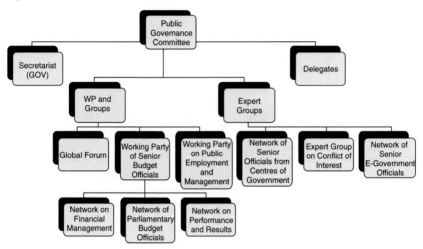

Source: Figure based on OECD, On-Line Guide to OECD Intergovernmental Activity. Accessed 12 November 2010 at http://webnet.oecd.org/OECDGROUPS/Bodies/ListByNameView.aspx?book=true.

Figure 3.5   Territorial Development Policy Committee

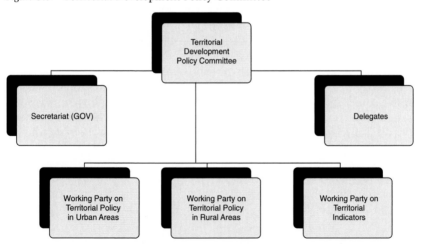

Source: Figure based on OECD, On-Line Guide to OECD Intergovernmental Activity. Accessed 12 November 2010 at http://webnet.oecd.org/OECDGROUPS/Bodies/ListByNameView.aspx?book=true

Under the two major umbrella committees of the GOV directorate (PGC and TDPC) fall a number of working parties and, in the case of the PGC, a number of networks of top officials responsible for the central management systems of government. The PGC embraces the following groups and networks: the Working Party on Regulatory Management and Reform (REG), the Working Party of Senior Budget Officials (SBO), the Network of Senior Officials from Centres of Government (CoG), the Public Employment and Management Working Party (PEMWP), the Expert Group on Conflict of Interest: Ensuring Accountability and Transparency in the Public Service, and the Network of Senior E-Government Officials (EGOV). Under the TDPC fall the Working Parties on Territorial Policy in Urban Areas, on Rural Areas and on Territorial Indicators.

The Working Parties and networks under the PGC have regular observers from the non-member countries of Brazil, Egypt and Ukraine as well as ad hoc observers from time to time. Observers for the FATF,[18] the International Monetary Fund (IMF), and the World Bank (WB) are listed for the Working Party of Senior Budget Officials and the networks on Financial Management and Parliamentary Budget Committee Chairpersons. There are ad hoc observers from the Asian Development Bank (ADB), the Inter-American Development Bank (IDB), the Organization of American States (OAS) and the WB on the Expert Group on Conflict of Interest. Working Parties under the TDPC have regular observers from the non-member countries of South Africa and Morocco, but no ad hoc observers.

As the largest and most important of the three GOV committees, we can look a little more closely at the PGC. As we noted earlier, PGC replaced PUMA in 2004, two years after the new GOV directorate had been created. This was supported by the committee members as a way of strengthening the importance of public management within the OECD (even in 2011, and even with the evident support of the current SG, Angel Gurría, senior committee members still worry a little about the legitimacy and weight of governance within the organization as a whole). There had been some disagreement between PGC and the director of GOV (Odile Sallard) over how to interpret the committee's and the directorate's mandate (e.g., how strong an emphasis on citizen engagement as opposed to the more traditional public management areas that had been characteristic of PUMA).[19] For a time the committee's Bureau (the chair and five vice-chairs) met separately in order to coordinate their agenda in the face of what they considered to be resistance on the directorate's part. Currently, committee members feel that relations with GOV are transparent and cooperative, and once a year (this is in addition to the two full committee meetings per year) there is an "open bureau" meeting of the Bureau itself but also any other members who wish to attend in Paris to coordinate and develop the agenda with GOV.

In 2009 the PGC was reviewed (all committees undergo periodic review) and the resulting "In Depth" report (OECD 2009) (see Chapter 6 for a more extended discussion) concluded that the committee was efficient and effective, but made recommendations on structure, principally the subsidiary bodies.[20] The committee had had a habit of establishing "ad hoc" groups that became permanent, and so one recommendation was to reduce the number of subsidiary bodies. But as we noted above, the relation between these bodies and the main committee is sometimes problematic. In the case of PGC, for example, the networks of CoG and of SBO are virtually independent from the committee, in part due a membership consisting of very senior officials, often more senior than the delegates to the PGC themselves (Matheson 2009). But this is also due to a structural feature of OECD committees – the Working Parties and Expert Groups that they create are not considered "subordinate" but "subsidiary". The PGC is to take a "whole-of-government" perspective, while the subsidiary bodies work in specific areas of expertise. In 2008 the PGC issued a report on improving its committee meetings, and noted there that:

> The Committee decides on the creation and abolition of subsidiary bodies. While these bodies are in principle "answerable directly to the Committee which sets them up and to which they report", they are *subsidiary* to the Committee rather than *subordinate*. Both the subsidiary bodies and the Committee each have their own responsibility. Their relationship is characterized as "mutual dependence": the Committee requires the subsidiary bodies' high-quality substantive work in order to fulfil its responsibilities and tasks. The subsidiary bodies in turn are dependent on the Committee, not only for some of their resources but also for the broader whole-of-government scope and context for their work. ...[The subsidiary bodies] report to the Committee on their collective substantive work rather than providing an account of it. (OECD, Public Governance and Territorial Development Directorate 2008)

Nonetheless, the PGC did adopt several measures to try to improve the links between the committee and the bodies. For example, it decided that each of the members of the Bureau would participate in meetings of Working Parties and other groups, but this has only been partially implemented (for logistical travel and timing reasons). Previously, reports from the bodies were simply oral, and the PGC asked for short written reports. Other improvements had to do with the volume of paper flowing to members and prioritizing the agenda. Up to 2008, PGC members often received as much as 1,500 pages of material just days before a meeting, most of which consequently were not read and so members were often incapable of engaging in discussion, inducing the directorate to stage-manage meetings by "suggesting" questions that members might ask.[21] This has now been improved with the circulation of executive summaries and a tighter focus on key agenda items so that there is more time for discussion as well as informal exchanges. Nonetheless, draft reports from the directorate that come to the PGC for discussion are almost never amended or changed substantially as a result of that discussion.

Committee dynamics can be explored by examining the 42nd session of the PGC in Venice on 16 November 2010, which coincided with a Ministerial meeting on 15 November 2010.[22] This was only the third Ministerial for PUMA/GOV. They have occurred every five years, and set the broad agenda for GOV (directorate and committees). The Ministerial meeting was entitled "Towards Recovery and Partnership with Citizens: The Call for Innovative and Open Government".[23] The one-day meeting was hosted and chaired by the Italian government (the chair was Renato Brunetta, the Minister of Public Administration and Innovation, Italy, and the co-chair was Stockwell Day, President of the Treasury Board of Canada). The global financial crisis and public sector responses to it formed the backdrop to the meeting. The opening plenary addressed the topic of "Governments and Markets: Towards a New Balance". There were three breakout sessions for participants: (1) Delivering Better Public Services under Fiscal Pressures, (2) Towards a More Effective and Performance-Oriented Public Service, and (3) Promoting Open and Transparent Government. The breakout session discussions were supported by the results of a survey conducted in mid-2010 on recent reform initiatives in each of the areas (OECD 2010d). Thirty-two countries (mostly OECD members, but also Brazil, Egypt, and Ukraine) answered the questionnaire. Each of the breakout sessions had a list of questions or themes around public governance:

Better services under fiscal pressures
- How can governments achieve greater productivity at no additional cost in the delivery of public services?
- How to better coordinate with local governments?
- How to build innovative responses for service delivery in partnership with the private sector?
- How can governments deal with ever-increasing public expectations at a time of patchy recovery? How to achieve results and make them known?
- How to reap the dividends of IT? What are the opportunities and challenges of web-based approaches to improve the responsiveness of public services? How to bridge the digital divide?
- What are the options for engaging citizens in the co-production of services? What role can citizens play in driving quality improvement initiatives?
- How to ensure that business supports public sector efficiency? Can we learn from the private sector's experience?

Towards effective and performance-oriented public service
- How can the public sector always be ready for tomorrow? How can Ministers strengthen their strategic capacity?

- How can Ministers foster a performance-oriented public service? Is performance both necessary and sufficient for success?
- What is the role for performance management and evaluation in achieving governments' overall objectives? Do we know how to evaluate performance? What are the appropriate institutional settings?
- How can the public service simplify its processes while spending less? How can government design user-centric services to cut red tape? How can governments exploit the untapped potential of e-government?
- What should be the strategic objectives of public employment policies? How can Ministers foster culture change in the public sector? What is the role of social dialogue?

Promoting open and transparent government
- How can Ministers strengthen citizens' confidence in government, foster greater transparency and openness? What are the key implications for public governance and the public sector?
- What are the challenges of greater citizen empowerment and engagement with civil society?
- How to strengthen and promote integrity in the public/private sector interface? How to reaffirm ethics and core values in the public sector?
- How can governments better address the expectation of an increasingly diverse population? How can the public sector be more inclusive and respond to shifting needs and demands?
- What are the obstacles to maintaining and restoring trust? Is trust a long-term goal or a priority to start with?

The closing plenary session posed questions such as how to strengthen strategic capacity and increase resource flexibility; how to mobilize citizens and the public sector to "build consensus around the reform agenda"; how to work with civil society to "build momentum for change"; and how to share country experiences to promote good practice. Even with only one day, a meeting at this level, with this agenda, and with ministers from governments around the world comparing and discussing experiences (both OECD members and non-members), is a significant networking experience around issues of public governance. Ironically, the themes and questions were hardly new – they echoed, for example, many of the themes in the 2005 review *Modernising Government: The Way Forward* (OECD 2005g): services and fiscal constraint; an effective well-performing public service; transparency. In this respect, some of the issues of modern governance are simply perennials. But looking more closely, we can see some tonal notes that reflect the preoccupations of 2010: coordination with local governments ("local" governments, or cities, are becoming the key nodes of modern economies); citizen "co-production" of services; strategic capacity; ethics and core public sector values; diversity; trust.

The two-page Communiqué from the Ministerial, like most documents of this sort, was both banal and profound. The banality comes from the earnest highlighting of the obvious: the need for leadership, efficiency, effectiveness, integrity, transparency, and preparation. No one could disagree. The more profound and significant elements are embedded less visibly in the text. The Communiqué opens with a reference to the 2005 Ministerial in Rotterdam that was "devoted to strengthening trust in government". With the financial crisis, it was now clear that "improving public sector productivity is crucial to economic recovery". This requires innovation, with a special emphasis on information and communications technology. The first paragraph ended by declaring that "Trust remains an overarching goal, to be built on openness, integrity and transparency". The acknowledgement of key principles is important as well – as we will note in the next chapter, the OECD's leverage is almost exclusively "ideational". As an "ideational artist" it relies heavily on principles, soft standards, and peer comparison. The leadership principle was anchored in partnerships with civil society and business. The efficiency and effectiveness principle was geared towards new technologies, and again the cooperation of the private and not-for-profit sectors. The openness principle underlined the importance of trust for building "support for reform", engagement with social partners, and a reaffirmation of the "core values of the public sector". The preparation principle stated that public sectors "must be forward looking, agile ...". In short, together, these passages and principles reveal a somewhat beleaguered frame of mind due to the financial crisis. At this point, November 2010, there had been successive riots in Greece and France over austerity measures, and Ireland was on the brink of financial collapse. The UK had passed an historic austerity budget in June 2010. These ministers were well aware that at this juncture, public sector "reform" meant draconian cuts, and risked red-hot public outrage. The calls for efficiency and partnerships were not mere formulae, but expressive of a real crisis in the public sectors of the OECD member states.

The second page listed six priorities for the PGC and GOV for the next five years.[24] They were asked to support the Ministers' efforts by:

1. *Providing evidence on government performance.* This was essentially support for Government at a Glance (discussed in the next chapter).
2. *Fostering a more efficient, effective and innovative public sector.* The focus here was on innovation, country experiences that highlighted "agility and performance" such as e-government, human resource management and human capital, budgeting, cutting red tape, partnerships, and evaluation frameworks.
3. *Offering guidance for strengthening trust, openness and integrity.* The point here was to "provide guidance on strengthening integrity, strengthening the public interest, and leveling the playing field for the private sector".

The last sentence called for a strengthening "of instruments for steering relationships with the private sector".

4. *Supporting a whole-of-government perspective through strategic coordination and policy coherence.* This was a call for continued high-level policy dialogue among peers.

5. *The Venice Initiative for Dialogue with Civil Society Organizations.* This Initiative was added to the draft communiqué as a result of dialogue with BIAC, TUAC, Civicus and Transparency International, the four civil society groups that had – for the first time – been invited to attend and participate in the Ministerial. While affirming the importance of continued dialogue among governments, this new directive invited the OECD to "explore the potential for dialogue on best practices of public sector reform with Civil Society Organisations".

6. *Promoting good public governance globally.* This principle asked for a continued emphasis on enhanced engagement, but again had a business twist. "In the interest of broadening the level playing field for business, investment and the mobility of people, the OECD should provide a forum for global policy dialogue with non-member economies, and discuss ways to strengthen and improve public governance".

The Ministerial was held on Monday, 15 November 2010. The PGC meeting (committee members attended the Ministerial as well) was held the following day.[25] The substance of the PGC meeting consisted of a follow-up on the Ministerial, a public governance review of Estonia, a review of Brazil's integrity framework, and a discussion of a new global relations strategy for the PGC that would align more precisely with the OECD's overall enhanced engagement strategy (see Chapter 1). The reviews of Estonia and Brazil followed on the innovation introduced at the 41st session of the PGC in April 2010. This was the first time that the committee had collectively reviewed a country's governance regime – in that case it was Finland[26] – but the committee had decided that these sorts of discussions of different countries' public governance regimes would now become a standard part of its meetings. The Estonia discussion paper, for example, quite forthrightly asked the committee to discuss the challenges of promoting a "whole-of-government" approach in public administration, of building a common societal agenda, and of delivering services effectively.[27]

In GOV parlance, the Estonia peer review was "horizontal", that is, across the entire government and not just sub-sectors. As we will see in the next chapter, these types of reviews are relatively new for GOV – only two (Finland and Ireland) had been conducted previously. The Brazil review on integrity was the first time a country had been reviewed on this subject, so this also was a departure. Sitting at the table were PGC members, observers, and the director of GOV and other directorate officials as required. The meeting opened with remarks by the Italian delegate (since Italy was the host for the meeting), highlighting the importance of the "Venice Dialogue" and redoubled efforts to engage with civil society organizations. Several other countries spoke of the importance of learning from each other. The director-ate, naturally, praised the Ministerial communiqué, and suggested a "reflection group" (all committee members were invited to participate) that would report to the PGC at its April 2011 meeting in Paris.

The morning was devoted to the Estonian review. The discussion had several interesting characteristics that shed light on the dynamics of gover-nance discussions in the OECD. The Estonia delegate spoke to the report, highlighting the challenges that Estonia faced in the financial crisis as a small, open economy. From double-digit growth it had gone to double-digit decline, and had had to introduce major cuts. There were also issues of the competitiveness of the economy and the expectations of citizens. This was the underpinning of Estonia's rationale in requesting a country review of governance by the OECD (such reviews must be requested by the host country). But there was also a "club" aspect to the rationale: Estonia had just joined the OECD and it wanted to engage with the organization. As well, Finland's recent review was a model. This is an important psychological factor in an organization like the OECD – countries compare themselves to the OECD as a whole, but also to subsets of direct comparators to whom they are linked either geographically, economically, or in terms of key characteristics (e.g., size, language, legal tradition).

After a description of the logic of the report by the directorate – a logic that highlighted the specific characteristics of Estonia as a small country, the chair called on two delegates to make formal comments, and then opened the floor to the first of three themes for discussion: the challenges of a whole-of-government approach. The interventions essentially shared country experi-ences on issues like strategic coordination, reform agendas, coordination and corporate leadership among top civil servants, horizontal coordination, bud-geting systems, the balance of centralization and decentralization, and per-formance management systems. The Estonian delegate thanked them all for "sharing their country experiences". The second discussion theme was stra-tegic policy-making and strategic planning. Once again countries intervened to explain their tools and approaches. The final theme was delivering public services effectively. Once again there were lead discussants, and then an open floor for interventions, with often quite detailed examples being provided by different countries about their programmes and experiences.

The afternoon was devoted to the integrity review of Brazil, the first time such a review had been undertaken of any country. Integrity systems concern fighting corruption in government and public administration in everything from hirings to tax administration to bribery (in all its manifestations) to procurement. This discussion had four themes: risk management, increased capability, enhanced efforts to assess the implementation and impact of integrity measures, and increased coordination. Again, though only a small number of delegates actually intervened, the description of their programmes and approaches and lessons was quite detailed. An observer country noted that it had learned a good deal and would be taking this back, and would perhaps seek a similar review by the OECD in the near future.

We can make some general observations of the meeting. As noted, relatively few country delegates actually intervened. The discussion tended to be dominated by about ten countries, which, for their own reasons, place a greater priority in engaging with the PGC. These reasons may be a tradition of solid work in the PGC, a report on a country of interest (e.g., a "comparable" state), or the personal interest and commitment of the delegate. Also, the contributions were almost exclusively about sharing national experiences. There was virtually no detailed commentary on the two reports whatsoever, though written comments were invited by the Chair at the end of each session. In practice, very few written comments are ever received.[28] This would make it appear that the directorate's work does not undergo thorough quality control, at least at the committee level. This is misleading. Directorate staff is highly skilled, and reports are organized and drafted by staff members who have done numerous similar ones in different countries. The country being reviewed also has commented on the reports in detail (the stakes are high since the reports usually end up being public), and sometimes the reports first go to a Working Party or Expert Group for detailed discussion. The reticence on the part of PGC members to engage in critique has to do with the details of the reports – they are quite technical, and not every member of the PGC will have expertise, for example, on integrity frameworks. But, as we noted before, this is a quasi-diplomatic venue, and so delegates have to respect the dignity of other states. There were repeated references and cautions about the uniqueness of each of Estonia and Brazil, and how lessons or experiences were being shared but it would be up to them to decide what to accept and how to implement.

Another interesting feature of the discussion was the general consensus that governance reform was both valuable in itself and necessary in the face of the current financial crisis. The overarching theme of the PGC (both Ministerial and regular) was "innovation and open government" and this theme was couched in terms of the pressures facing public sectors to do more (in the face of citizen demands) with less. It was also clear that "doing more with less" entailed – in the current climate – often major cuts and expenditure reductions for many countries. There was a realistic appreciation that neither reform nor cuts would be politically easy, and so part of the challenge would be to find ways of "making reform happen". There were references, for example, to the serendipity of coming elections, which might provide windows of opportunity to sell a reform agenda. There was also interest in the dynamics of implementation of the reforms, and the two countries were invited back to share their experiences, noting that the OECD was "ready to help".

The final item on the agenda was a discussion and approval of the PGC's strategy for drawing in "enhanced engagement" countries (Brazil, South Africa, India, Indonesia, and China – the EE5) into its work. In Chapter 2 we briefly outlined the OECD's accession and enlargement strategy, and the way in which that was translated into a global strategy for the PGC. The SG had asked all committees to consider ways to enhance participation by the EE5 in their work. The PGC had already taken some actions in this direction, among which were including some of the EE5 in data collection on e-government, integrity, human resources management, and service delivery, and including all EE5 countries in the committee's workplan. Brazil in particular has had a long-standing and deep relationship with PGC. It has undergone a range of reviews (human resources, integrity, regulation and others), and participated in the development of OECD Recommendations on Transparency and Accountability in Lobbying, Integrity in Public Procurement and Managing Conflict of Interest. The other countries are more recent partners in the PGC's work. Committee participation of non-members falls into three categories: full participation (full membership rights and responsibilities), regular observership (attend all meetings of the PGC and subsidiary bodies and make interventions and presentations), and ad hoc observership (attend select meetings by invitation to make a specific presentation). The report recommended that Brazil be offered full participation, that South Africa be offered full observership, and that the other three countries be offered "active ad hoc observership", that is, more regular rather than merely occasional invitations to attend both the PGC and subsidiary bodies. The rationale for this graduated approach was that both Brazil and South Africa were already quite engaged in the OECD as a whole, and so warranted a deeper engagement, while closer relations with the other three countries would help familiarize them with the OECD and the PGC specifically. But the deeper rationale was to strengthen the PGC's capabilities and methods by bringing in more diverse experiences, but also helping ensure "the truly global relevance and impact of the Committee's work".[29]

As mentioned, GOV supports two other committees, the RPC and the TDPC. The RPC was established as a "level 1" committee in 2009, elevating the status of its predecessor, the Working Party on Regulatory Management and Reform.[30] Committee status increased the clout and visibility of the Working Party, and was a reflection of a decision made in 2008 by Council that regulatory issues were of increasing importance.[31] While the work of the committee is clearly related to governance, it has a stronger economic focus due simply to the nature of regulation and its impacts on different economic sectors and economic performance as a whole. Accordingly, the RPC's mandate highlights cooperation not only with the PGC (the two committees as of 2011 have had two joint meetings, the most recent in April 2011 to consider the governance accession report for Russia), but with the Competition Policy, Trade, and Investment committees as well. This kind of cooperation was characteristic of the period when it was a Working Party, and is part of the "DNA" of the RPC. While the RPC has no formal subsidiary bodies, there is a Steering Group on Communication and Perception of Regulation, consisting of a subset of members who are interested in (and willing to pay for) work on the public's perception of the value-for-money of regulation.[32]

The TDPC was created in 1999 from an amalgam of earlier initiatives.[33] In the 1980s and 1990s the OECD had a series of activities dealing with "place-based" policies. There was an Urban Environment activity tied to a Committee on Urban Affairs that was served by the Directorate on the Environment. In another part of the OECD there was a Working Party on Regional Development that was under the Committee on Industry (as it was then). Also there was a group of the Council (these can be created by ambassadors who have an interest in an issue) on Rural Development (which they held was not the same as agriculture). Finally there was a Part 2 budget programme called the Local Initiative on Employment that was connected to the Directorate of Employment and Social Affairs. In 1994 the new director of the Directorate of Employment and Social Affairs, Christopher Brooks, suggested that all these activities be brought together. The proposal was accepted, and the Territorial Development Service was created in 1995 (as a "service" rather than a directorate, it had lower status, but that was because some members of Council had not agreed entirely with the move). Brooks was then asked by the SG to help with his agenda of reform of the OECD, and that was when Odile Sallard was appointed Acting Director and asked to create a new committee for these territorially-based economic activities. The task proved challenging, since all of these different entities had their own constituencies and interests, and were not easy to combine under the umbrella of one committee. The Ministerial that was organized in 2000 in part was designed to provide political legitimacy for this "new logic".[34]

TDPC was established in 1999 to conduct work on regional and place-based policies in an era of globalization when national boundaries were eroding and more competition and trade was taking place among and between subnational regions. The primary task for the TDPC was to provide statistical data on regions, to make them visible to policymakers.[35] But over time it has also become a focal point for thinking about the importance of regional responses to natural disasters like Hurricane Katrina and the Japanese tsunami in 2011. Like the RPC, the TDPC has a more explicitly economic focus than does the PGC. The preamble to its mandate, for example, underscores the importance of "regional policy to promote long-term economic development while addressing major national and global policy challenges, such as fostering innovation and entrepreneurship, confronting climate change, moving towards sustainable development, investing in human capital formation, dealing with demographic issues (such as ageing and migration), and enhancing the effectiveness of public investment and the quality of public services in both urban and rural areas".[36] The TDPC has three subsidiary bodies: a Working Party on Territorial Indicators, a Working Party on Territorial Policy in Rural Areas, and a Working Party on Territorial Policy in Urban Areas.

Global relevance has of course been a key theme in GOV and its committees' work since the earliest days (Chapter 2). This section shows both the advantages and the disadvantages of a highly networked organization. The advantages are that it can couple and connect loosely, at various levels and in various ways, and thus expand the scope of its connections exponentially. The OECD is balancing on several high wires at once – a triad of a Secretariat, a Council, and committees; a substantial autonomy to committees to determine their agendas and plans of work; a host of subsidiary bodies of experts that are only loosely connected and certainly do not "report to" their parent committees; a combination of think-tank and diplomatic international organization. The disadvantages are in corporate coherence. When looked at as a whole, the OECD's agenda is so broad and covers so many fields, it almost defies description (despite the organization's *über*-slogan of "For a stronger, cleaner, fairer world economy"). This is reflected in GOV – it has three committees, each with its own subsidiary bodies, and the relations among those bodies and their committees are often tenuous. The 2010 Ministerial in Venice did establish a five-year agenda for GOV and its committees, but only in the broadest sense. As we argued, there was virtually nothing in that agenda that would have been a surprise five years ago, or even a decade earlier. But, the governance fog nonetheless has some shape, and can be shaped further by the directorate and the committees as they define priorities that are aligned with the broad objectives set in Venice. As well, the strategic importance of a Ministerial – whatever the generalities of the outcomes – should not be dismissed. Initially, there was little interest among member states for a Ministerial, and so they (particularly the United States) had to be convinced. The Ministerial provided a foundation for further elaboration of an agenda, but a foundation with the stamp of approval from the highest authority within the OECD system.[37]

GOV, however, does not encompass all governance-related undertakings in the OECD. As we noted in Chapter 2, the great achievement of the builders of TECO and PUMA was to seize on public management as an area of relevance to economic development. They deliberately had to find a subject matter not being addressed by the rest of the organization, and horizontal management (budgeting, coordination, regulation, citizen engagement, etc.) met the need. But there are other important pockets of governance-related activity in different policy fields that should also be included in the organization's total profile on public sector reform. We turn first to SIGMA, which is in GOV, but separated by a "firewall" for reasons explained in Chapter 2. We then consider several examples of governance-related work outside the GOV umbrella.

SIGMA

Chapter 2 discussed the birth of SIGMA against the backdrop of the collapse of the Soviet Union, the needs of transitional states in central and Eastern Europe, and the evolution of PUMA to that point. In the context of the times, with the Berlin Wall falling in 1989, German reunification a year later, and other Soviet satellites declaring independence, the EU launched PHARE in 1989 (Poland and Hungary: Assistance for Restructuring their Economies), with the goal of preparing those two countries for eventual accession. But the EU had little experience in dealing with the accession process for countries that were in such turmoil and so far below even minimal EU standards. The two organizations came together to create SIGMA in 1991.

SIGMA's first countries of focus were Bulgaria, the Czech and Slovak Federal Republic (as it was then), Hungary, Poland, and Romania. In the first volume of *Public Management Forum* (SIGMA's newsletter), there were six areas of activity listed for the programme: reform of public institutions, management of policy-making, expenditure management, management of the public service, administrative oversight, and information services (SIGMA/OECD 1995: 16). As the EU evolved and expanded, so did SIGMA. But its essential inspiration always remained the same, indeed was amplified, with the growing bulk and complexity of the *aquis communautaire* (over 100,000 pages of detailed standards and legislative requirements in order to accede to the EU). The issue is not simply accepting the EU *acquis* but being able to implement it, and this depends on an effective and efficient public service system and government mechanisms. While gaps will always exist, and certainly exist even in EU member states, the question is whether that gap is systemic. A large part of what SIGMA does is provide *diagnostiques*, advice and projects in very specific areas to build the capacity of states that aspire to join the EU.

In 2010 SIGMA's activities were organized under two broad EU instruments. Under the Instrument for Pre-Accession (IPA) Assistance, it works with four EU candidate countries (Croatia, the former Yugoslav Republic of Macedonia, Montenegro, and Turkey), and with the four EU potential candidates (Albania, Bosnia and Herzegovina, Serbia, and Kosovo [under UN Security Council Resolution 1244/99]). Under the European Neighbourhood and Partnership Instrument (ENPI), it works with countries covered by the European Neighbourhood Policy, with the priority for activities in Armenia, Azerbaijan, Egypt, Georgia, Jordan, Moldova, Morocco, Tunisia and Ukraine. Its work falls into four core areas: legal framework, civil service and justice; financial control and external audit; public procurement; and policy-making.

Public management reform is at the heart of what SIGMA does. While situated in GOV, it does it differently because of its institutional configuration. For example, it provides assessment reports to the EU on the progress of candidate and potential candidate countries. Its projects are more specific and concrete than in GOV's case, since their country partners wish to accede to the EU, and so must conform to the *acquis* through specific legislative and institutional changes.

OECD governance initiatives outside of GOV

In this section we consider examples of governance-related initiatives in three departments (ECO, DCD and DAF) and the SG's office. The SG has room to manoeuvre within the organization, both in terms of being its chief executive officer and in terms of chairing the Council and having a modest budget of his own. But, as noted, the nature of the OECD as an organization gives the SG less leverage that he might wish, with directorates "shielded" to some extent by their connection to committees consisting of representatives of member states. The SG of course steers the organization, but cannot, outside of broad limits, tell them what to do. But he can undertake initiatives within his own office. We will look at three of them.

ECO is one of the OECD's directorates, and is typically seen as the most influential within the organization (Woodward 2009). It issues the regular country Economic Surveys that attract substantial national attention in the target country since they offer authoritative reviews of economic performance as well as economic policy. Recently, along with the usual macroeconomic analyses, ECO has included a chapter in each report on a specific policy field. In the September 2010 Economic Survey of Canada, for example, it had a chapter on "Overcoming Challenges in Health-Care Reform", about as hot-button an issue for that country as one could find. DAC manages development cooperation among the key donor countries (all represented in the OECD), and since governance is a key element of real development, has inevitably addressed public management as part of its mandate. DCD focuses on policies that support open markets, particularly with respect to businesses, and so has worked in the areas of anti-corruption and corporate governance.

Economics department (ECO)

ECO, despite its putative weight within the OECD, is a relatively simple directorate. It only has two committees, and two divisions: one division does single country reviews, and the other produces more focused economic analyses of specific policy areas such as pensions or housing. In contrast to other directorates that tend to be organized around projects and so produce an often bewildering array of publications, ECO essentially only produces country reports and policy-focused reports. Country economic reports are the jewel in the crown, providing macroeconomic overviews as well as often quite sharp recommendations on economic, fiscal and monetary policy. Country reviews used to be issued each year on each country, but now typically come out for any given member every 18 months or two years.[38]

ECO's "The Political Economy of Reform" project was actually launched before the SG's "Making Reform Happen" project (see below), but had a similar inspiration in trying to probe for the determinants of "structural reform" using more formal political economy theory (Williamson 1994; Rodrik 1996), coupled with 20 case studies in three broad policy fields: pension reform, product markets, and labour markets. Ten countries participated (Australia, France, Mexico, Poland, Italy, United States, Netherlands, Spain, Germany, Sweden), and for each country two cases were drawn (in most cases from two different policy fields), one that was judged successful, and one that was judged less successful. The resulting report, while shying away from a "toolkit" approach, did claim to find a "number of striking regularities in the way reform processes unfold" (OECD 2009e: 35). The report's conclusions focused on four areas: exogenous factors; issues related to the scope and timing of reform; public consultation and communication; and the way in which reforms deal with actual or potential opponents of reform.

On exogenous factors, elections and having a mandate from them seemed to be the most important, including the point at the electoral cycle when reforms are introduced (earlier is usually better). Other factors included the weakness of the opposition or strength of the government (though the cases were somewhat ambiguous); the capacity for intergovernmental cooperation in instances of federal states seeking to implement reforms; the business cycle (apparently not that important), and international influences (important primarily in the case of product market liberalization). Timing factors addressed questions of haste and speed. The cases seemed to suggest an average of two years for the adoption of successful cases. Other tips were that appropriate sequencing by tackling easier issues first and building momentum and wearing down opposition seemed to be an ingredient of success. The highlights of the communications and consultation category were not surprising – effective communication and consultation pays off. However, one interesting tip was to ensure the clear communication of the costs of "non-reform". Finally, on dealing with opponents, the report was quite frank in discussing the dynamics of "losers" in the reform process:

> Even if there is a clear consensus that a reform will generate net benefits for the economy as a whole, questions concerning the allocation of costs and benefits are often unavoidable, owning to differences in agents' interests and endowments, the presence in many situations of potential "stranded assets", and uncertainty about individual benefits. Often, the costs of reform are not only incurred up-front, they are also concentrated on specific groups, whereas the benefits not only materialize later but are also both more diffuse and less predictably allocated. (OECD 2009e: 54)

Another example of ECO's contribution to governance and public management thinking and advice within the OECD is the latest versions of its country reviews. Obviously, the reviews have a highly charged policy content simply by virtue of the fact that they review macroeconomic, monetary and fiscal policy and performance. When reports are released they attract significant national as well as international media attention. ECO is not shy to give advice (though the target country of course participates in the review and has an opportunity to see the draft and comment, though changes are made only in cases of error of fact). In the Canadian review of 2010, for example, while the news was generally good about the country's management of the financial crisis and the current state of the economy, the report made blunt and detailed recommendations. Some examples: "Renew the current inflation-targeting agreement without change when it expires at the end of 2011"; "Begin fiscal consolidation in 2011 by allowing temporary stimulus measures to expire as planned"; "Quebec: Wind up the Generations Fund and apply the remaining assets to debt reduction" (OECD 2010g). And just to focus attention, the report also included a table listing previous recommendations and whether they had been adopted or not.

But most intriguing from a public management point of view is the new practice of adding a chapter in each economic review that tackles an important area of public policy, important in economic but also in other terms. In the Canadian case, the OECD decided to include a chapter on "Overcoming Challenges in Health-Care Reform". The health care system has an almost sacral character for Canadians, a defining characteristic of what differentiates them from Americans, since the Canadian system is a single-user (government) pay system and the American system, even with President Obama's recent changes, is still largely private. Canadian consumers of most health care services do not pay at the point of service, but through the broader tax system. The system works reasonably well, but is facing (like most other systems in the world) inexorably rising costs. The OECD chapter is barely 50 pages long, but provides a concise analysis of some of the pressures the system faces. Its recommendations on health were framed in terms of its earlier recommendations in the review on fiscal consolidation, and so while it acknowledged that the policy goal should be a balanced combination of promoting access, quality, and cost containment, it argued that priority should be given to measures promoting cost containment. Among those measures, it recommended eliminating zero patient cost sharing for core services and introducing co-payments and deductibles. If necessary, the foundation of the Canadian health care system, the Canada Health Act, should be revised. In a country where health care is the "third rail" of politics, these recommendations were breath-taking.

ECO does economic analysis, and its core business remains country economic reviews and studies of economically important policy areas. But it has moved into the field of governance, broadly defined, and its country reports now include policy advice that deals with legislation and public management practices.

Development Co-operation Directorate (DCD) and the Directorate for Financial and Enterprise Affairs (DAF)

The Development Assistance Committee (DAC) has been part of the OECD from the beginning (in fact, preceded in 1960 by the Development Assistance Group), providing a forum for the leading bilateral and multilateral donors in the world (at the time, the only donors) to coordinate their efforts. In its current incarnation, the DAC is served by the Development Cooperation Directorate (DCD). The DCD has six divisions (policy coordination, poverty reduction and growth, aid effectiveness, review and evaluation, statistics and monitoring, and aid architecture and financing). All but one – the policy coordination division – deal with the modalities of aid itself, statistics, evaluation, assessment and impact. The policy coordination division deals with broader policy issues relevant to aid: governance and anti-corruption, capacity development, and gender equality, among others. The DCD is involved in a host of development related activities, fora and partnerships, as well as efforts within the OECD to link various development initiatives (one of which is the Development Centre, a distinct entity that works more directly with developing countries, development organizations and researchers and citizens to search for solutions and approaches to development problems).

The DAC is the only committee connected to the DCD, but it is a powerful one. It has 24 members who provide a significant amount of development aid and assistance, and has the World Bank, the IMF and the UNDP as observers. The committee has nine subsidiary bodies. Of those bodies, the most relevant for this discussion is the Network on Governance, or GOVNET. Its responsibilities include "human rights, transparency, accountability, participation and equality, anti-corruption and capacity development in support of these elements of democratic governance".[39] Even though it works on governance issues, it always does so from the point of view of aid donors, aid coordination and aid effectiveness. A good example is a 2008 publication entitled *Survey of Donor Approaches to Governance Assessment* (OECD, DAC Network on Governance 2008). It noted that DAC members were all intensively assessing governance over the past decade as a key ingredient in development but also in donor-recipient relationships, but the overall objective of the report was harmonization and alignment of donor assessment techniques and tools. GOVNET also tries to ensure that aid programmes respect and support human rights, and broad accountability within political systems. This involves supporting institutions such as media, parliaments, political parties, civil society and ultimately trying to help foster free and fair elections. It has contributed to the OECD's anti-corruption drive through the 1996 OECD Recommendation on Anti-Corruption Proposals for Aid-Funded Procurement.

DAC and its various networks are clearly contributing to governance and public management reform within the OECD, but with a focus on donor coordination and efforts. The DAC cooperates in these efforts with other components of the OECD, including GOV and PGC, the Committee on Fiscal Affairs, Tax and Development and the OECD Centre for Tax Policy and Administration (the range of various development activities within the OECD would be the subject of another treatise on intra-organizational networking). Despite this, the DAC is perceived as a "world of its own".[40] This is due to it being a club within a club – originally the richest of the rich nations who had the capacity to provide aid to developing countries. That has changed – other non-OECD countries such as Brazil and China offer significant amounts of aid, and the DAC has adapted by engaging with them and other multilateral players. But it still retains a somewhat insular approach and has not cooperated extensively with GOV, for example. But nonetheless, it does have a significant presence on governance and management issues, albeit from the development perspective.

The Directorate for Financial and Enterprise Affairs (DAF) states its purpose as follows: "The Directorate for Financial and Enterprise Affairs helps governments to improve the domestic and global policies that affect business and markets. DAF identifies policies and best practices designed to keep markets open, competitive and sustainable while combating market abuses and economic crime through international co-operation. It works in the fields of anti-corruption, corporate governance, competition law and policy, investment, financial markets, insurance, private pensions, and private sector development".[41] It supports five committees – Investment Committee, Insurance and Private Pensions Committee, Committee on Financial Markets, the Competition Committee, and the Corporate Governance Committee – and including their subsidiary bodies of working groups, networks, task forces, joint committees forums and so on, supports 30 bodies.

This is an exceedingly broad remit, and with groups working on terrorism insurance, competition and regulation, and bribery in international business transactions. In fact, DAF's mandate is not necessarily "logical" and it is sometimes referred to within the organization as the "directorate of bits and pieces".[42] This is in part because of its evolution. The DAF, like DAC, was there from the beginning of the OECD and has always been responsible for the two binding legal instruments that the OECD has championed around trade liberalization: the Code of Liberalization of Capital Movements and the Code of Liberalization of Invisible Operations (dealing with cross-border services). This meant that in its early days, DAF supported the committees dealing with finance and taxation. Taxation as an issue became large and complex enough that it was spun off as a separate directorate, and as other issues dealing with some aspect of corporate activity came to the OECD, DAF was (partly because of its legal expertise) ready to adopt it as part of its mandate. One example is anti-corruption and bribery. This was started with the Lockheed Aircraft bribery scandal that was revealed in the mid-1970s. Congressional investigations showed that the company had paid millions of bribes to European and Asian political leaders and organizations in order to ensure that they purchase Lockheed planes. One aftermath of the affair was the passage of the Foreign

Corrupt Practices Act that made it a crime for American citizens or companies to bribe foreign government officials. At the time, despite the scandal in the United States and the bribe-receiving countries, the bribery of foreign officials was actually widely condoned in some nation's tax codes, which permitted the deductibility of such bribes as a business expense. Since the United States was the only country with corrupt practices legislation of this type, it wanted others to come aboard so as not to lose a competitive advantage. It went first to the United Nations, but there was no interest and so came to the OECD. DAF, because it had a group of lawyers on staff (due to responsibility for the Codes), agreed to take on the file. It began, in good OECD fashion, to do analytical work, but by that built (along with the momentum of other international bribery scandals) eventually to the 1997 OECD Recommendation on Bribery in International Business Transactions and the 1997 Convention on Combating Bribery of Foreign Officials in International Business Transactions (this was joined in 2009 with the Recommendation of Council on Further Combating Bribery of Foreign Public Officials in International Business Transactions – we discuss these instruments in detail in the next chapter).

The Anti-Bribery Convention is a convention about bribing public officials, and so necessarily deals with issues of public administration and public policy, such as administrative ethics codes, compensation systems, and tax regimes. The anti-bribery review process is one of the most rigorous in the OECD,[43] partly because it is very much in the interests of member states to ensure that there is a level playing field, partly because the members of peer reviews typically have a law-enforcement background, and partly because they collectively have a moral fervour about an issue connected to ethics.

Office of the Secretary-General

Centre for Cooperation with Non-Members (CCNM): The CCNM was established in 2007, though some connection with non-members had always been part of OECD activities. As we saw in Chapter 1, since the OECD was in its early days truly the "club of rich countries" it tried to coordinate international aid through DAC. Even the membership of southern European countries like Greece, Portugal, Spain, and Turkey had a measure of outreach to somewhat unsavoury regimes. With the collapse of communism, the OECD turned its attention (in somewhat of a panic) to "economies in transition" and its engagement was first through the Centre for European Economies in Transition (which later became simply Economies in Transition) and then the SIGMA programme. At this stage, in the mid-1990s, the main OECD focus on non-members (with the exception of DAC) was Europe. Chapter 1 pointed out that after the MAI debacle, Donald Johnston decided that the OECD needed broader global engagement, not only with NGOs but non-members as well, in order to buttress its relevance. A Committee on Cooperation with Non-Members (referred to as CCN here to distinguish it from the CCNM above) was created in 1999 to consolidate various outreach activities, but also shift from "outreach" to "engagement". "Outreach" was seen as more like technical assistance, while "engagement" implied more of a two-way dialogue and interaction. The CCN was given a mandate to review the "strategic orientations and overall architecture of the OECD's co-operation programmes with non-Members", and reported to Council in 2005 on a framework for such cooperation (OECD Council 6 December 2005). The report noted (as we pointed out in Chapter 2) that until the mid-1990s most of the work with non-members had focused on central and Eastern Europe, and had had the character of technical assistance or aid programmes. Starting in the late 1990s (i.e., with Donald Johnston as SG) there was a consolidation of various outreach programmes, diminished emphasis on training and assistance, and "increasing emphasis on policy dialogue". It noted that the "OECD's relations based on an 'outreach model' have evolved into a 'global relations model' based on multiple relationships, mutual influence and partnerships". The CCN recommended the development of a flexible strategy that would provide some coherence to the OECD's global relations activities, and rely a great deal on committees themselves to take the work forward and actualize it. This document was followed by an issue paper for the MCM in May 2006 on the impact of emerging countries on the global economy and on OECD members (OECD Council 10 May 2006). It focused on China and India, with some reference to Brazil and Russia. It outlined the increasingly evident contribution of these economies to global economic growth (almost as much as OECD countries) and their impacts on human capital, foreign direct investment, energy and raw materials, foreign exchange reserves and immigration. It suggested that the OECD could help its members by contributing to improved knowledge about these major emerging economies, influencing policy-making in those economies, and increasing their engagement as responsible stakeholders in the global economy. The third of these is a particularly evocative reflection of the point argued in this book about global coordination around standards:

> So far, our partners in these economies have valued OECD's policy advice, but with few exceptions, their engagement in core OECD work is still limited. The most important challenge for the future of our co-operation may indeed be to encourage major emerging economies to become more active in the processes of international economic co-operation promoted by the OECD, and to participate more actively in the work of OECD committees, several of which have already identified these economies as potential observers. This should help them move closer to OECD standards and disciplines. It would also increase our capacity to influence policymaking and further improve mutual knowledge and understanding. (OECD Council 10 May 2006: 4 emphasis added)

The second contribution had a powerful governance focus as well: "Policy dialogue in the multilateral context of OECD provides reformers in these economies with a range of policy options reflecting the experience of OECD countries themselves. It contributes progressively to building like-mindedness, including on the critical need for public (and private) governance reform".

These documents formed the basis for the OECD's Global Relations strategy of enhanced engagement and accession, discussed in Chapters 1 and 2. The CCNM was created in tandem with, and to provide support to, a new standing committee of Council (one of three created in 2006, the other two being the Executive Committee and the Budget Committee) on External Relations. This committee has oversight on global relations with non-member countries and other international organizations. The CCNM is quite small, with only a handful of staff, but that was due to a strategic decision foreshadowed in the 2005 document to push down responsibilities (and budgets) for relations with non-members to committees.[44] Nonetheless, the combination of the CCNM and the External Relations Committee is an important instrument in a wider governance agenda being pursued by the OECD as a whole, and which while it meshes with GOV, is a distinct site of strategic thinking about influencing non-member states along policy lines, but also encouraging governance reform.

International Futures Programme (IFP): The IFP emerged originally from an informal group founded in the SG's office in the 1970s around planning and evaluation, and was intended to do strategic planning for the organization through auditing the relevance of OECD programmes. This proved to be difficult because of the "territorial way in which the OECD operates" – the directorates were able to resist audited reviews of their programming.[45]

In 1975 the group launched a major project entitled Interfutures – it was meant to be a counterpoint to the Club of Rome, which in 1972 had released its first report, *Limits to Growth* (Meadows 1972). That publication became an instant global sensation, arguing that economic growth faced significant environmental constraints. The government of Japan took the initiative to fund the project, and was joined by 18 other OECD members. The objective was to study the "future development of advanced industrial societies in harmony with that of developing countries" (OECD 1979). The OECD report, *Facing the Future: Mastering the Probable and Managing the Unpredictable* was released in 1979. This was the first real attempt at "foresight" analysis within the OECD, and it was hoped would feed into the work of committees.

The IFP was formally established in 1990 and was intended to do horizon scanning (on a 10 to 25 year scale) on technology, the economy, social developments, and important issues that fall between the cracks of the OECD committee system. Because the IFP operates within the Office of the SG, it does not have a committee in the way that directorates do, which gives it a certain intellectual freedom and agility. As we noted earlier, committees operate on consensus, so this can slow down decision-making and agenda-setting considerably. On the other hand, committees can fight for funds within the OECD budget-setting process, and individual committee members can press their governments to support different projects.[46] As a result, the IFP relies heavily on voluntary grants and contributions from government departments, research institutes, and the corporate sector (about 75 per cent) for its funding. It has among the strongest links to the private sector of any OECD unit. Another result of not having a committee is that the IFP relies heavily on its networks of institutes, governments and companies for ideas and validation of research projects – what they do needs to be funded, and to be funded they have to be relevant.

Two examples illustrate the IFP approach. The first is risk management. Starting in the late 1990s, a number of major threat-events began to happen simultaneously or in close sequence – BSE (bovine spongiform encephalopathy or "mad cow disease", which struck the UK in the late 1990s and the US in 2003), foot and mouth disease (striking the UK in 2001), the ice storm in North America (1998), terrorist attacks (9/11) – and the IFP asked itself what was connecting all these events, was there a thread? They concluded that the key common factor was risk to systems. They had a blue sky meeting with corporations, governments, think tanks, and prime ministers' offices, and produced a report in 2003 entitled *Emerging Risk in the 21st Century* (OECD 2003b). The conclusion was that governments are ill-equipped to deal with systemic threats because of the siloed nature of departments and ministries. The report was well-received, and about a year later governments came back and offered funding, and so a longer-term project was set up with the usual OECD peer review process – being asked by countries to come and conduct assessments of the government of systemic risk management systems (e.g., flooding risks for the government of France, the civil protection system for the government of Italy).

The second example is the space economy. The group had been doing work on space in 2002–2006, but from the point of view of how to use satellites to deal with issues like agriculture, climate change, or fisheries management. They discovered that up to about 2003, governments gave money somewhat uncritically to their space industries, but were now beginning to ask questions about the value-added to the overall economy, and demanded that a case be made from a cost-benefit point of view. The IFP group released a report in 2007 entitled *Space Economy at a Glance* – it produced comparative data for the first time, but also shifted the discussion from the "space industry" to the "space economy" (OECD 2007g).

The IFP works from time to time with GOV, but its mandate is distinct in that it looks at the longer term, and at more exotic policy areas linked to technology – space, infrastructure, the "bioeconomy". Nonetheless, a significant amount of its work has a governance or public management dimension. The most vivid example was a conference held in 2000 (as part of EXPO 2000) and its subsequent publication, *Governance in the 21st Century* (OECD 2001b). That report was couched as "future studies" and had a strong emphasis on the impact of technology, but was explicitly about governance (however, no PUMA directorate staff were on the official list of attendees). Its more recent work on risk management is about how governments as a whole deal with systemic risks, and inevitably deals with coordination across ministries, or what GOV would call "coherence".

Making Reform Happen[47]: Angel Gurría was elected SG in 2006, and at his first Council meeting laid out three broad objectives: enlargement, new work on horizontal issues like migration or climate change that cut across directorates and the OECD committee system, and greater practical application of the OECD's work, or the "political economy of reform".[48] Aart de Geus, who was appointed Deputy SG by Gurría, had been Minister of Social Affairs and Employment in the Netherlands from 2002 until 2007, and had led a major reform effort in the Dutch social security system. Based on this experience, he was interested in leading the project. He and Gurría agreed to launch the project out of the SG's office, but there were several problems. There was no budget, but the SG allocated some of his funds to it. Some delegations were lukewarm to it since it seemed to go beyond the OECD's mandate, and moreover was not tethered to any committee within the OECD system. Also, ECO already had a project underway (discussed above) on the political economy of reform. De Geus pitched the idea to a Centres of Government meeting (as Deputy SG, he is responsible for GOV) in October 2008, and there was support for the idea but not for the title, so he arrived at "Making Reform Happen". ECO came on side because its project and De Geus's were mutually reinforcing, and other directorates (GOV being one of the most important) were engaged by being given resources to hire staff to write contributing chapters. The project faced a challenge in late 2008 when Council decided to cut its funding, but at that point the 2008 budget had already been expended on hiring consultants to draft chapters, and some money had been contributed by a South Korean institute, so they forged ahead. By mid-2009, when the full ramifications of the financial crisis became clear, people within the OECD, including Council, realized that major structural reforms were in the offing for member states, and suddenly the "how" of reform became significant, and funding was restored. The report was released in late September 2010, followed by a conference launch in November.

The project actually had two strands – an analytical one that resulted in the report (discussed below) and an "action" strand. The latter was an effort to link the analytical capacity of the OECD in terms of policy advice to the practical question of implementation. In 2006, for example, the newly elected government of Mexico asked the OECD, the World Bank, the Inter-American Development Bank, the United Nations Economic Commission for Latin America, and the United Nations Development Programme to produce recommendations on a number of priority policy issues in Mexico – effectively to help set the government's agenda. The OECD's contribution was a report entitled *Getting It Right* (OECD 2007e) that covered 15 policy areas (e.g., fiscal policy and tax reform, competition policy, corporate governance of state-owned enterprises, education, health, agriculture, innovation) with the usual OECD approach of benchmarking Mexican experience and performance against its then 30 member states. However, the report also included advice on implementation – the "how" in addition to the "what".

> Another way to shed light on the growth challenge is to look at the institutional environment and the implementation capacity for dealing with reforms and policies. Approving structural reforms and maintaining sound macroeconomic policies are necessary but not sufficient to foster development. Past experience shows that well designed policies at times fell short of delivering the expected benefits because of incomplete or faulty implementation. The privatisation process at the beginning of the 90s was intended to introduce efficiency and competition. This was achieved in many sectors, but not in all sectors even when privatisation took place. There are some other reforms that were good on paper, but their actual implementation is not adequate and therefore misses the intended objective. (OECD 2007e: 13)

Another example was the 2008 Attali Commission on Economic Growth, appointed by French President Sarkozy following his election victory in May 2007. The OECD was asked for a submission to the Commission, which it provided in 2008 (OECD 2007f). In this case the report was more traditionally OECD – it did not discuss implementation strategies – but it had a more responsive, practically oriented, advisory stance than the OECD typically takes. The various directorates which had to contribute to this report as well the Mexican one were unhappy with the time pressures involved and possible effect on the quality of analysis, and so there is now consideration of trying to tie these types of "practical advisories" to predictable political cycles, such as elections, and to produce "country notes" outlining the challenges facing any new government. There are also efforts to mainstream the "practicalities of reform" in the OECD's work, so that there is more explicit acknowledgement and advice on the challenges of implementation.

Making Reform Happen (OECD 2010e) is too detailed a document to summarize here, but our interest is more in the overall approach and the governance aspects. For the approach, the tone is set in the very first line of the Foreword by Angel Gurría: "Structural reforms are at the heart of OECD work" and he follows with an evocative indication of what the publication is about:

> We hope that this report can serve as a "palette" for policy makers who face the challenge of crafting and implementing structural reforms – a

collection of "colours", instrumental in realizing reforms, which deal with issues like communication, evidence, institutions, timing, costs and benefits, and engaging stakeholders. Yet we offer it as a "palette" rather than a "toolkit", for we know well that successful reform is more of an art than a science. (OECD 2010e: 3)

The report takes on some of the most challenging areas of structural reform: opening markets to competition, pensions, tax reform, environmental policy, education, health, modernizing government, regulatory reform and fiscal consolidation. The overview chapter highlights the problem faced by all governments of devising "strategies for securing adoption of such reforms that prevent the opponents of change from blocking reform, but that also address their legitimate concerns about its distributional consequences" (OECD 2010e: 13). The chapter draws some general lessons about reform from the various case studies. The first is the "urgent questions" that would-be reformers should ask as an initial checklist:

1. Do the authorities have a clear mandate for change?
2. What more can be done to demonstrate the need for change and/or the desirability of the proposed solutions to the public and key stakeholders?
3. How strong is the evidence and analysis underlying the arguments for reform?
4. Are institutions in place that can manage the reform effectively, from design to implementation, or is there a need to create/strengthen such institutions?
5. Does the reform have clearly identifiable "owners", in terms of both politicians and institutions responsible for taking it forward?
6. What is the expected timeframe for design, adoption and implementation?
7. What is to be the strategy for engaging those threatened by reform? Can they be persuaded to support it? To what extent can/should their objections be overridden? Should they be compensated for their anticipated losses – and if so, how and to what extent? (OECD 2010e: 16)

Some of the general lessons are perhaps pedestrian: elections (having a mandate), effective communication and evidence, leadership and strong institutions, time, engaging opponents and if necessary "compensating" them. But some are more insightful, such as the discussion of the extent and nature of compensation for "reform losers". For example, reforms that target "acquired rights" or what are perceived as entitlements will be more difficult, as will instances where those rights (through subsidies or economic rents) are capitalized into the value of assets (e.g., taxi cab licences). Compensation for losers will also depend on the capacity losers have to mitigate or adjust to their losses: for those who cannot readily or quickly adapt to, say, pension reform, it is better to implement reforms over a longer period. In cases that affect owners of capital, who presumably can adjust their portfolios more quickly, there is less of a case for long phase-ins (OECD 2010e: 19). Another frank assessment is that "crises often act as spurs to reform", though the report is careful to point out that while crisis can induce risk-taking, it can also induce reaction if the reform threatens existing entitle-ments (programme benefits) or endowments (sunk capital). The current financial crisis, from this perspective, is a bundle of strong incentives to reform, but massive resistance in countries like Italy and Greece. In closing, the chapter reflected on the role of the OECD, and remarked on the importance of "sustained incrementalism" in any reform project:

> The OECD can also play a key role in helping countries meet one of the reform challenges implicit in the findings reported earlier: the challenge of sustained incrementalism. One of the striking features of the sectoral analyses prepared under the auspices of MHR [Making Reform Happen] is the extent to which reform success in many domains requires com-mitment to a series of discrete but co-ordinated reforms over periods that are likely to exceed the lifetime of most governments. While "big bangs" may work for trade or competition reforms, they are unlikely to be suitable for most of the reform tasks facing governments in fields like health care, education, environmental protection or public governance. The OECD thus has a role to play in supporting those domestic insti-tutions that exist to sustain coherent policy reform over extended periods. (OECD 2010e: 33–34)

GOV of course contributed the chapter on modernizing government, but the report is a deliberate horizontal effort that engages most of the OECD's directorates in a discussion on public policy reform, and the practicalities of governance or public sector reform projects.

Conclusion

This chapter has explored the place of public governance, public manage-ment, and public sector reform efforts in the modern OECD. We began with GOV, but GOV is embedded in a bigger organization, and in order to see GOV clearly, we need to take the measure of the OECD as an organiza-tion. This chapter, in conjunction with the last, illustrated several unique features of the OECD. A key observation in this chapter is the decentralized nature of the OECD, but a decentralization of a peculiar sort. To capture that peculiarity, we can conduct a thought experiment. Imagine the OECD as a typical think tank. It would have a president (the SG), a board to which the president would report but the members of which she had some role in selecting. There might be vice-presidents and directors of research areas, but there would be a reasonable flow of priorities and agendas from the centre to the rest of the organization. Of course, think tanks, like universities or research parks, put a premium on creativity and innovation, ineffable and mercurial qualities, so they cannot be command-and-control organizations.

Now we will alter the organizational parameters. Add a layer of members who effectively fund the organization. Then replace the board with the OECD Council, consisting of appointments completely at the discretion of members. On top of that (or below it, more precisely), imagine the replication of this council-like structure with committees. Then to each committee, add subsidiary bodies of Working Parties and expert groups, who are not truly accountable to their parent bodies in any realistic sense. And finally, infuse the entire organization with three qualities: professionalism, informality and protocol. The Secretariat is highly professional, as are most members of committees. Because they focus on the quality of the work, they are informal and flexible, combining and re-combining in teams as necessary, taking on new tasks as needed, and often working long hours to get the job done. But there are spiky points in the organization and the rhythms of activities, points that come from the fact that this business is all about states. The process of the Venice PGC meeting reflected all three of these characteristics.

GOV reflects and refracts these larger organizational characteristics. We described the loose connections among the committees and their subsidiary bodies. The agenda-setting process is what we called a "cascading matrix", combining structure with fluidity. There is an organizational chart and certain protocols about how decisions are to be made, and this provides the scaffolding, but the reality is considerably more indeterminate. Council influence over the GOV committees is relatively light, with the exception of high priority areas like accession. The PGC chair and the Bureau work throughout the year with the GOV directorate on a rolling agenda of items, but because the committees only meet once or twice a year, their members cannot exercise any realistic, detailed control over what the directorate does on a day-to-day basis. In a sense this does not really matter. The director of GOV (in 2011, Rolf Alter) is a conduit for the OECD's larger agenda to the directorate and to the committees, and at the same time a large part of the work (e.g., peer reviews) is fairly routine, though demanding. When new issues come up – how to engage the EE5 in PGC work, accession reviews, Ministerials – there are certain parameters set by the wider organization, and that is complemented by the professionalism of the staff.

The content of GOV's work is both ambitious and amorphous. The ambition echoes that of almost every OECD directorate and is partly self-advertising. If the OECD as a whole is dedicated to creating a "Stronger, cleaner, fairer world economy", how could GOV fail to match that ambition? So, as we saw, GOV was in part designed to move beyond a narrow, internally focused public management agenda to something that embraced "governance", which presumably could include the parliamentary process, rule of law and the judicial system, and civil society. With the exception of better engagement with civil society, it has fudged the first two by continuing to refer to "government" and "governance" when in fact it means mostly horizontal public management systems. Its 2000–2004 mandate, as we saw, was to address "strategic governance challenges", "performance", "elements of good governance". The enlargement process encouraged GOV to be more specific about its version of an *acquis* in developing its "building blocks": budget practices and procedures; human resource management; integrity in the public sector; internal and external reporting; e-government readiness; centre of government; management of regulatory quality; multi-level governance.

The amorphousness comes from ritualistic incantation of the same concepts of governance until they seem almost to lose meaning: consensus, leadership, integrity, change, reform, strengthening trust, productivity, innovation, transparency, efficiency, effectiveness, partnerships, strategy, dialogue, and – the holy grail – whole-of-government. Ritual should not be dismissed. Committee meetings, in part because of the diplomatic nature of the organization, are as much theatre as they are substance. These words, as incantations, serve to remind participants repeatedly about the markers of good governance, in the way that runway lights guide pilots on stormy nights. The lights, and the words, need not have intrinsic meaning, they only need to delineate a space for maneuver.

Two other conclusions may be drawn from the analysis in this chapter. First, the networked nature of the OECD and of GOV is clear. The very decentralization mentioned earlier within the OECD is evidence of a networked organization – as we noted, this provides for both strengths and weaknesses, but it is a key organizational feature. We can see from the way in which GOV and its committees operate that they are quintessential networks as well. The committees and their subsidiary bodies are simply nodes for connections among their participants and for complex interactions with a galaxy of observers and partners and participants. Airline magazines usually have a world map at the back, showing connections that the airline has from its hubs to its destinations. For larger airlines these look like spider webs with strong spines for certain key routes. GOV can be imagined the same way – its hub is Paris, and its networked connections along which information, reports, communication, agreements, and debates flow back and forth radiate out across the world: dense lines to the last accession countries, equally dense ones to Russia; member states; regional groupings; other international organizations located in Washington, Brussels, Geneva, Manila; NGOs and civil society organizations in most of the major capitals of the world.

Second, there is more to governance and public management and public sector reform in the OECD than GOV. The closing sections of this chapter showed a robust agenda in other directorates and in the SG's office itself to make the OECD more relevant, more practical, and more implementation-focused than has been its practice. The advice on making reform happen, while not supported by all member states (since in their minds it steps over the line from advice to deliberately trying to shape agendas) is distinctive in that it goes beyond content to process. The OECD wants to become a partner in the implementation of reform, not simply an "ideational artist" that creates sterile masterpieces.

The references to ritual and to incantation, to the wider scope of governance-related activities within the OECD, may seem to diminish or even belittle the work of policy transfer that GOV does. In fact, what we have reviewed in this chapter is the high altar of GOV's work. The real labour takes place in the daily work that the directorate does with countries and the specific techniques it uses to carry out this work. That is the subject of the next chapter.

4
Networked Tools: How Does the OECD Do Its Governance Work?

In 2010 the OECD published *Brazil 2010: Federal Government*, one in a series of reviews of human resource management in government. The 300-page document is a typical research product of the OECD – rather dry, well-researched, bursting with comparative insights from OECD members and how they manage their public sector human resources. But it is a result of a much more complicated and dynamic set of processes and interactions, of basic tools that the OECD uses to do its work. Brazil is not a member of the OECD, and so there were the initial negotiations over the parameters of the project and the eventual invitation by Brazil for the review. A decision was made to conduct the review in cooperation with the World Bank. Consultants were hired, and internal resources within GOV were mobilized – experts on pensions, job categorization, training and learning, reform implementation strategies, performance management, quantitative and qualitative data generation and analysis. There were study trips by OECD staff to build the initial data scan through meetings with relevant ministries and stakeholders – these included the Executive Secretariat in the Ministry of Planning; Secretariats of Human Resources, of Public Management, of International Relations; offices within at least three other ministries; the Ombudsman Office; the National School of Public Administration; public service unions; the Municipality of Rio de Janeiro; two institutes, and the University of São Paulo. And then in July 2009 came the signature instrument in the OECD toolkit – once the basic data had been assembled by OECD staff, five "high-level officials" (peers) from OECD member countries jetted in from Tokyo, Washington, Paris, Madrid and Ottawa to hear from stakeholders, ask questions, and provide subsequent guidance for the final drafting of the report. There was further drafting and discussion with Brazilian officials, and finally a submission to the PGC, where once again discussion ensued among members, speaking as representatives of member states. As we will see below, these types of reports and research comprise the ultimate "visible" product of the OECD's work, but they are built on a foundation of networked interactions that – if we take the entire OECD and all its directorates and projects as a whole – take place daily in capital cities and ministries across the planet.

As we noted in previous chapters, one of the prime characteristics of the OECD that has attracted analytical attention over the years is the way in which it works. It is an "ideational artist", though as we saw at the close of the last chapter, initiatives such as *Making Reform Happen*, expansion, accession, and global engagement suggest that in recent years the OECD wants to be a more active and direct player on the world stage. But nonetheless, it has no coercive power (indeed, its own rules and culture on consensus make it virtually impossible to impose anything on its members, let alone non-members). It can convene, it can invite exchange, it can review and assess, and it can conduct research. In terms of the causal mechanisms of transfer highlighted by Simmons et al (2008b) that we described in Chapter 1, this means that the OECD cannot rely on coercion or conditionalities in the way that the World Bank or the IMF can. Instead it relies more on mechanisms of policy learning or emulation, or on what Dolowitz calls the "voluntary" end of the spectrum of policy transfer (Dolowitz 2009) that often involves "soft learning" (policy styles and ideas rather than the transfer of hard law or standards), and even "herding" effects, where policies or ideas, once they become popular, attract actors simply because of a subjective sense that these are "leading" or "important" and constitute a "lesson" (Unalan 2009).

This feature of the way that the OECD works has been widely noted (Marcussen 2004; Hansen et al 2002; Ougaard 2004: 86). Aubrey, in one of the first detailed analyses of the OECD, remarked that while these myriad voluntary interactions among peers was an "impalpable process," it nevertheless had the effect of "osmosis" leading to "a diffusion of ideas, a better understanding of one country's policies by responsible officials in other countries, and the anticipation of more sympathetic response by others to these policies (and vice versa). This calls for the periodic personal contacts that also engender mutual appreciation and trust. Participants in OECD meetings agree that this intangible element has given them much better insight and influenced their thinking materially" (Aubrey 1967: 144). Part of some of the scepticism about the actual impact of the OECD (Armingeon & Beyeler 2004; Schäfer 2006) is due to the scepticism of the policy impact of "soft law". We take this up in Chapter 6 on the influence of the OECD on governance and global public management reform, but it should be noted that those organizations with coercive power and the leverage of conditionalites are not necessarily more successful (Woods 2006; Ranis et al 2006; Easterly 2006).

This chapter shifts from the organizational analysis of Chapter 3 to closely examining the tools and processes the OECD relies upon to conduct its work and which form the foundation for its "soft law". These tools will show the primacy of norms rather than rules, of nodal interactions within the broad OECD network, the emphasis on search and information exchange, and flat decision processes and a premium on adaptation. The chapter looks specifically at five tools used by GOV in pursuing global public management reform.

The first is the process of peer review, widely considered to be the hallmark of the OECD and reflective of an emerging reliance on "multilateral surveillance" techniques such as the EU's "open method of coordination". The second is the content of the OECD's governance *acquis*. This is an example of somewhat sharper standards and "more than soft law". The third tool is the recent development of more quantitative measures of governance through a new publication entitled *Government at a Glance*. The fourth is the use of regional cooperation mechanisms with non-members. As we noted in earlier chapters, the OECD has tried to adapt to a different global context by enhancing engagement and broadening its interactions with non-members in different regions of the world. This section will examine the Middle East North Africa (MENA) initiative. Finally, we look at the accession process and the way reviews are conducted on governance issues. Accession is not "normal" business for the OECD, but the process nonetheless casts an interesting light on how the organization sees the application of its own standards, and the measurement and assessment of norms as they apply to accession states.

Peer review

There is a specific logic to peer review that distinguishes it from other types of assessments, judgements, or evaluations. This logic is not unique to "multilateral surveillance" (Schäfer 2006) at the international level, but applies as well to other types of systems, for example, the accreditation of academic programmes. While each element is variable to some degree, in combination they define what a peer review process is. First, there must be a <u>community of peers</u> or members that are willing to comply with certain norms or standards that define membership in that community. Moreover, they have a stated objective of both maintaining existing standards and, over time, improving on them and even developing new ones. Importantly, these norms or standards usually fall short of "hard law", or legally enforceable rules. If they were legally enforceable, then compliance would be achieved through judicial proceedings, not peer review. Second, the members of the community are peers in the sense that they have <u>status equality</u>. This means that despite differences in other characteristics (size, wealth, reputation, etc.), each member is considered intrinsically equal (the word peer has its roots in the Latin *par*, meaning equality of rank or status (Conzelmann 2010: 3, note 1)). Third, the peers that conduct the reviews are presumed to have direct experience of the subject matter of the review, which is the basis of their <u>credibility</u>. For multilateral organizations like the OECD, this means that a governance review on human resources management, for example, will be conducted by representatives of member nations (peers), who will themselves be experts in that particular field. Fourth, there must be an accepted and reasonably <u>objective process</u> of review. This applies both to analysis by the peers, and the fact base on which they make their assessment. This contributes to the fifth element, which is trust. This element is to some degree a resultant of the others – if members are peers and considered equal, if they agree on norms and accept an obligation to comply with them, and if they accept the process, this implies a foundation of trust. Sixth, peer review implies comparison to the other members of the community. This is because the norms or benchmarks of a review are "soft" – they are usually not codified in a way that would permit reference to a clear and explicit standard. Because norms are variable in their application, the process of peer review naturally makes reference to both the norms themselves, but more importantly to the best and worst implementation of those norms. Seventh, because the norms are soft and variable, peer review normally can only make recommendations, and cannot apply sanctions if those recommendations are either ignored or only partly met. Because of this, an eighth element of peer review is discussion and pressure from peers within the community. A ninth element is the opportunity for the target of a review to respond and even sometimes amend (on good grounds) the findings of the review (this would never happen in a court case, for example, without a formal appeal). Finally, a peer review should have some measure of transparency, otherwise it would be impossible for other peers to apply pressure.

At the international level, a number of organizations use peer review in some measure for the enforcement of norms. The World Trade Organization uses it under its Trade Policy Review Mechanism, as do several specialized UN agencies, the IMF, and the European Union (Schäfer 2006; Conzelmann 2010). It also became a key tool in the New Partnership for Africa's Development (NEPAD) through the African Peer Review Mechanism (Nyamugasira & Utoyuru 2008). After the Asian financial crisis, peer review was adopted in 1998 in the form of the ASEAN Surveillance Process (OECD 2008c: chaps. 2, 9) Since 1996, the OECD has worked to create a multilateral framework to deal with tax havens and tax evasion in the form of the Global Forum on Transparency and Exchange of Information for Tax Purposes. The first efforts were around the development of a model agreement on tax information exchange in 2002, followed in 2005 by the issuance of international accounting standards. The G20 meeting in Pittsburgh in September 2009 called for greater tax transparency, and the Global Forum launched the first series of 18 country peer reviews to monitor compliance with the standards.

Forms of peer review, at least in the sense of "governance by disclosure" are also increasingly being used by non-state actors, for example in environmental certification schemes, audits, and benchmarking (Cashore et al 2004; Auld & Gulbrandsen 2010; Auld 2010; Overdevest 2010). However, there "is no other international organization in which the practice of peer review has been so extensively developed as the OECD, where it has been facilitated by the homogeneous membership and the high degree of trust shared among the member countries. The OECD has used this method since its creation and peer review has, over the years, characterised the work of the Organisation in most of its policy areas" (Pagani 2002: 7).

Pagani points out that there is no standardized peer review mechanism within the OECD, though there are some basics that are respected in every version: an agreed set of principles or standards against which the country is to be judged, designated actors to carry out the review, and a set of procedures leading to the final result. Reviews may proceed in terms of decisions taken by subsidiary bodies (committees or Working Groups) within the OECD (though reviews have to be voluntarily accepted by members), Council or Ministerial Council decisions to conduct far-reaching review programmes, or international norms such as provisions in treaties or other legally binding instruments. Performance of a reviewed state can be assessed against policy recommendations and guidelines, specific indicators or benchmarks, or legally binding principles (Pagani 2002: 7–9). Despite the variety in styles of peer reviews across different subsidiary bodies, there are four basic phases: (1) a preparatory phase, which can consist of a self-study, the submission of documents, and responses to questionnaires designed by the Secretariat, (2) a consultation phase by the Secretariat and the peer examiners and the reviewed state, which usually involves site visits, interviews with responsible authorities and stakeholders both within and outside government, (3) a drafting phase, where the Secretariat produces a report based on the data and consultations and advice by the peers, including observations and recommendations (the report is usually shared in draft form with the reviewed country for comment on factual issues), and (4) an assessment and review phase, where the report is discussed in plenary by the subsidiary body and the reviewed state, and usually released publicly.

The different approaches to peer review within the OECD can be illustrated by comparing Economic Surveys with the Development Assistance Committee (DAC) peer review process. The OECD's Economic Surveys are probably its most visible and prominent publications, reviewing each member state's economic performance and policies about every 18 months. The process starts with a questionnaire about recent economic developments, policy frameworks and forecasts (Schäfer 2006: 73–74). This is usually followed by two country visits by secretariat staff responsible for the review. The first is a "structural mission" that can last about a week and is basically fact-finding meetings with officials as well as experts. The staff returns and then drafts a report, which is then taken to the country again in a "policy mission". This second visit is at a higher level, and the OECD staff meets with senior officials to explain core findings or questions. The draft report is then submitted to the Economic Development and Review Committee (EDRC). Two members are designated as reviewers, and lead the discussion with a delegation from the reviewed state. This can lead to some redrafting, but only with respect to factual errors. Finally, sometimes there will be a "release mission" if a country wants it – providing publicity and media attention.[1]

The DAC is the committee of bilateral donors (discussed in the previous chapter), and conducts peer reviews of each of its members every three or four years (OECD 2010e). Two members are designated as "examiners" for each review, who may be members or may be secretariat staff. Designated countries are then requested to submit relevant documentation to the directorate, as well as answer a detailed questionnaire. Since DAC reviews are trying to assess the effectiveness of the member's aid programmes, field visits are then conducted to a country receiving aid by the reviewed member (which selects the country and funds the visits, of which there are usually two). After the field missions, the review team visits the capital of the country under review. Preliminary findings are shared with the reviewed country, followed by a peer review meeting in Paris. Like the EDRC meetings, a delegation from the reviewed country attends and answers questions posed by the review team and other DAC members. This is then followed by an "editorial session" to incorporate the results of the peer review meeting, but the DAC and the OECD make it clear that the scope for revisions is small: "The editorial session is not an opportunity to negotiate the text with the Secretariat and the Examiners. Changes in any of the documents should be kept to factual issues. Any other suggested changes will be considered but not necessarily adopted. For purposes of transparency, any change in language or disagreement with conclusions or recommendations suggested by the Examiners should be raised in the Peer Review meeting itself in order to ensure that only issues that seem legitimate to other Members will be considered".

GOV, as a directorate in the OECD, conducts regular peer reviews as well, and more or less follows the template described above, though with a recent innovation we discuss below. To illustrate a GOV review process, we can describe an actual one that took place recently (the identity of the country is withheld in this example to respect confidentiality).[2]

Country reviews of single sectors (e.g., human resource management, integrity, regulation) usually start at the Working Group level. The directorate provides regular briefings to the Working Groups on their relevant subject matters, and in this case a country delegate approached the directorate after such a briefing and asked for a review in the designated sector. A discussion was then held between GOV staff and country representatives on the scope of the review, setting out the parameters of the project and the agenda. Once that was agreed, the directorate began a literature review and desk studies, but also drew on OECD databanks for comparative information. A questionnaire was then designed, but based to some extent on existing surveys and templates. In this field, GOV does a survey of members every five years, with about 100 questions. The survey was then sent to relevant state authorities in the reviewed country. At about that time, a review team was assembled. Sometimes teams consist only of directorate staff, and peers act primarily as commentators. In this case, the reviewed country wanted (and was prepared to pay for) the peers to make a country visit. As well, the reviewed country designates which member states it wants the peers to come from, and four were selected. However, other member states can also designate a peer if they are interested and prepared to pay for that person, and the directorate cannot say no, highlighting the point made in Chapter 2 about the nature of the OECD as a member organization consisting of states. But it also highlights the point made at the head of this section about the "status equality" of peers. In this instance, one other member state asked to appoint a peer reviewer. Once the countries were selected, the directorate went to delegates from those countries on the Working Group and asked them, as practitioners in the field under review, if they wished to be peer reviewers, or have someone else from their home government appointed. An important point is that all peer reviewers must be formally appointed by their governments, who have complete discretion over those appointments.

The directorate then wrote to the reviewed government authorities with a list of organizations it wanted to interview during the first mission, in some cases actually specifying individuals. The aim was to meet with a mix of high-level officials as well as technical experts. It is the responsibility of the reviewed government to arrange the meetings and deal with logistics. The group of peers and GOV staff arrived and spent a week in the capital. Each day began and ended with a review team plenary, with members dispersed to different meetings with different organizations and experts throughout the day. It was during the evening de-briefings that the team began to see themes and "a narrative emerging". After this first mission, the directorate returned and began drafting the report, which it sent to the peers for comment. They also had a video conference with the reviewed state authorities to hash out questions and issues from the mission. Once the entire review team agreed on the draft report, it was sent to the reviewed country – minus recommendations – for fact-checking. Once it was cleared by the reviewed country, the full report went to the Working Group where it was discussed, and the reviewed state's delegation responded to questions. The report then underwent final editing.

This stage is a complicated and sensitive step in the peer review process. That process rests on trust, and the willingness of recipients of the review to undergo examination and critique. As we noted, the logic of peer review requires transparency, and the OECD's approach is usually to make its full report public. This runs the risk of "naming and shaming" and so a careful balance has to be struck. On the one hand, the OECD has to protect its legitimacy through protecting the quality and integrity of its work. If member states and reviewed states were able to revise and edit at will, the reports would be worthless. On the other hand, the reviewed state pays for the review, and as sovereign states, have a prerogative within an international organization like the OECD to protect their dignity. Drafting becomes a complex process of institutional calibration (Dostal 2004; Gayon 2009). This particular report had to have a careful tone, since the reviewed country "did not want to be lectured to". The report also "had to be diplomatic" – for example, GOV staff saw little evidence of interest in the issue by the current head of state, but much more by the previous one, and so, in the draft introduction, spent some two pages referring to the previous leader, but only one paragraph on the current one. The reviewed country was displeased, and strongly requested that it be more "balanced". The report also had to be careful "not to hurt people's feelings" and so needed to incorporate both critique as well as positive observations about progress.

Once the report was finalized, it was presented to the reviewed country authorities. GOV does not do follow-ups on its peer reviews, unless specifically asked by the reviewed country. However, in the presentation of the report, the directorate stated that it was ready "to accompany you in your journey, and help". This actually yielded a request from the reviewed country for additional support on a specific aspect of the issue under review. But if there is no formal follow-up, what effect does a report like this have? This is where peer review is complemented by peer pressure. The first instance of peer pressure, of course, is the reporting process and the drafting of the final document. The second phase is more subtle but on-going. Each year the Working Group has a *tour de table* where members report on policy developments over the previous year. The reviewed country cannot avoid saying something – obviously broadly positive – about progress on the peer review. This may be simple theatrics, but year-by-year may yield real change, especially if the peer review was instigated by internal reformers in the country in order to get an OECD "stamp of approval" for a pre-existing agenda. And that is what happened – the Minister responsible for the area under review, once he read the report, insisted that all employees in the ministry read it as well.

The preceding was an example of a typical GOV review – it looked at one area of public administration. In a recent innovation, GOV has started to do horizontal country reviews – called "Public Governance Reviews" – that look at the entire system of government.[3] To date they have published three – Ireland (2008), Finland (2010), and Estonia (2011). These reports go to the PGC directly, not to Working Groups, since they cover the whole-of-government. Part of the stimulus to go in this direction was growing dissatisfaction with the traditional "siloed" approach of GOV peer reviews. GOV staff had found themselves doing the same types of reviews year-after-year, but in order to do that, they had to get to know their constituencies reasonably well (e.g., if it was a review of e-government, then the ministries and departments responsible for that sector). But that often led to a sense of capture – review targets would often simply argue that any shortcomings were due to lack of resources, and the OECD staff would not have a sense of the larger governance picture in the country. As Director, Odile Sallard strongly supported the idea of horizontal reviews, having spent a good deal of her OECD career in the Economics Department with its standard economic reviews of countries' entire economic systems.[4] The idea was eventually brought to the PGC in 2007. Conventional peer reviews typically examined one of the eight GOV "building blocks": budget practices and procedures, human resource management, integrity and corruption resistance, open government, e-government readiness, centres of government, regulatory quality, and multi-level governance. The aim behind Public Governance Reviews was to be more comprehensive (reviewing public management reforms across governance sectors), coherent (look at support for whole-of-government objectives), and comparable (using benchmarks that discuss entire governance systems). Each review:

(1) Identifies specific economic, social and political challenges for the country as a whole; articulates the country's policy objectives and priorities as identified in national strategies and policy commitments; and analyses the public sector contribution towards meeting these challenges and objectives.
(2) Makes concrete recommendations for improving the responsiveness and delivery of public policy, including service delivery, at all levels of government, taking into account a whole-of-government perspective and the broader governance context.
(3) Serves to increase dialogue within a country (within government and the public administration, and with parliament, civil society, citizens and businesses), as well as in international fora such as the PGC, about the challenges, successes and future directions for government, both for the country under review, and for PGC members as a whole. (OECD 2010e: 1)

The framework for a typical Public Governance Review touches on the following themes: (1) the case for reform, describing the economic, social and political context of the country, the public service, overview of public management reform efforts, challenges; (2) promoting citizen- and business-centricity, examining the degree of openness in government, social accountability, stakeholder engagement, and improvements in service delivery; (3) ensuring capacity for strategic planning, with a look at agenda-setting and prioritization mechanisms, the degree of evidence-based policy-making, and the stewardship role of central agencies in identifying priorities and communicating them to partners; (4) aligning governance structures and actors, with a review of actors both inside and outside government (including agencies, levels of government, parliament, judiciary, civil society, and the business sector), and how relationships among them might be improved to enhance information flows, coordination and co-delivery of services; (5) incentives and tools for performance, with a regard to how resources can be mobilized to improve responsiveness and building better performance incentives; (6) achieving and sustaining a responsive public service; and (7) one or two sector case studies to illustrate governance issues for the public sector as a whole, and to demonstrate real world issues in terms of obstacles as well as successes (OECD 2010e: 3–7). In practice, the reviews conducted to date have only partially reflected this framework, given that each review has to be negotiated with the country under review.

The philosophy behind Public Governance Reviews as an instrument in the GOV toolkit has at least three distinctive features, apart from the obvious one that they look at entire systems. First, the reports have a more narrative structure than conventional sectoral reviews. This is partly because of the sheer scope of a full governance review – in theory it covers everything, both government and non-governmental structures and actors, and without an overriding theme, risks being unfocused. Second, a new terminology grew from this style of review that emphasized coherence (since these are whole-of-government reviews, the most obvious criterion of assessment is how well the government operates as a whole, or how coherent it is) and "strategic agility". The agility concept was adopted on advice given to GOV staff during the public governance review of Finland, and draws on the 2008 book *Fast Strategy* (Doz & Kosonen 2008). Strategic agility is defined in the Finland review as a "government and public administration's ability to anticipate and flexibly respond to increasingly complex policy challenges, and to determine at what level action is needed (i.e., the whole-of-government level, or a devolved local or sector level). In the public sector context, strategic agility involves the capacity for – and commitment to – strategic insight, collective engagement and resource fluidity. These three elements are inter-related and work together to ensure that the public administration is responsive to the government of the day, with the flexibility and capacity to respond to complex policy environments by anticipating public sector challenges and possible responses. This includes actively consulting and engaging citizens, using evidence-based decision-making, ensuring vertical and horizontal policy coherence, and aligning resources and incentives with outcome priorities" (OECD 2010h).

> **Strategic insight** is the ability to understand and balance government values, societal preferences, current and future costs and benefits, and expert knowledge and analysis, and to use this understanding coherently for planning, objective setting, decision making, and prioritisation.
> **Collective commitment** is adherence and commitment to a common vision and set of overall objectives, and their use to guide public actors' individual work, as well as co-ordination and collaboration with other actors (both inside and outside of government and across levels of government) as needed to achieve goals collectively.
> **Resource flexibility** is the ability to move resources (personnel and financial) to changing priorities if and as needed; to identify and promote innovative ways to maximise the results of resources used; and to increase efficiencies and productivity for both fiscal consolidation and re-investment in more effective public policies and services. (OECD 2010h: 77)

A final distinguishing feature of public governance reviews is the intention to engage a broader governance dialogue, both in the country under review but among other OECD members as well. This reflects the more pro-active posture of the OECD that we discussed in the last chapter in the context of *Making Reform Happen*. Of course, dialogue, discussion and sharing have always been essential parts of the OECD peer review process, but there is a sharper focus in public governance reviews. The framework document for these reviews, for example, states that:

> The purpose of the peer review discussion is to help the country being reviewed to see its system in the light of other countries' experiences and policy choices. At the same time, however, the reviews also have the objective of providing learning opportunities for all involved, as countries share how they have addressed shared challenges and objectives. The resulting discussion, at its best, should challenge pre-conceived notions, and structure the systematic exchange of information, attitudes and views, based on the data and analysis of the Public Governance Review, and the shared values of the PGC. (OECD 2010b: 8)

Governance reviews are also different from an operational point of view. Whereas conventional peer reviews deal with sectors and hence a limited number of agencies and departments, public governance reviews need to engage with key central agencies which have convening power across all of government. This normally means the Prime Minister's office or the Ministry of Finance, or both. These agencies have to have a vision of what they want, and a commitment to the process. In the Irish case, GOV sent a survey to key ministries, and set up a three-level committee system: (1) a high level steering group consisting of very senior officials that only met three or four times a year; (2) a "liaison group" of somewhat lower ranked officials that was more hands-on and operational; and (3) a consultation group made up of business, unions, and some regional and local government representatives. In general terms, once the country requests the review, GOV works out a methodology of areas to explore, and shares that and asks the country if they want anything else. They also have a discussion of the case studies. The country studies done to date each had several cases to make the review more concrete – in Finland there were cases on basic services (primary and vocational education, primary health care); in Ireland the case studies consisted of hospitals, a review of agencies, local waste management, and school planning, and in Estonia, there was a case study on education and one on social services for the elderly.

It is somewhat ironic, given the grave economic and political crisis faced by Ireland in 2010–2011, that only two years earlier the public governance review could state that the country's "economic success story is one that many OECD countries would like to emulate" (OECD 2008a: 11). The overall theme for the Irish report – its narrative – was about the Irish public service and its modernization, particularly around service delivery. The key recommendations of the report were to have better links between central agencies and the broader public service, better integration (interestingly, through more "networked" structures), more serious attention to performance, more focus on on-line services and e-government, better and more flexible mobility for government workers, fresh recruitment into the senior ranks or the public service, and stronger and sustained leadership from the centre of government (the office of the Taoiseach) in order to maintain momentum. By contrast, the Finnish review, as noted above, was organized around the concept of strategic agility, though it too focused on the public service, relationships to citizens and businesses, service delivery and e-government. The government specifically wanted the OECD to examine the Finnish public sector's capacity to respond to horizontal challenges at the state level and across levels of government, in part because – unlike the Irish review – this one took place within the visible context of the global financial crisis. A key question was how well the Finnish "Nordic model" would hold up under pressure. Recommendations were organized around the three dimensions of strategic agility: (1) strategic insight required better efforts at forecasting policy challenges and marshalling stakeholder input and evidence; (2) collective commitment could be improved with better addressing of incentives and values within the public service; (3) resource flexibility demanded more flexibility within the Finnish public service to "move" personnel and financial resources in response to new policy priorities.

The Estonia review was released in July 2011 (OECD Public Governance Reviews 2011), and as the most recent at the time of writing, deserves some more detailed analysis. Again, because of a different governmental context (Estonia was at a different stage of development from Finland or Ireland), a different set of needs as defined by the Estonian government, and the learning process that was going on among GOV staff through each of the reviews, this review differed in important ways from the other two.[5] The GOV team initially wanted to take a similar approach in Estonia as they had in Finland, but soon realized that this was not going to work in the Estonian context. It was only after the first of three study visits that the idea of a "whole-of-government" approach and of "building a common agenda" emerged, in part because of observations about the style of administrative practice in Estonia. A second key influence was also serendipitous – in preparation for interviews, the team asked for background materials and among them was an article by Külli Sarapuu on state administrations in small states (Sarapuu 2010) that ultimately helped frame the overall analysis – Estonia is the OECD's second smallest economy and its sixth most open. Another difference was in the character of the report – the Estonians wanted numerous examples and a very practical tool for use in guiding future reforms, so the report for the smallest country ended up being the longest of the three (over 400 pages – not something likely to be repeated), and the list of recommendations was extremely detailed in comparison, for example, to the Finnish review.

The focus of the Estonian report was on "whole of government" (the title *Towards a Single Government Approach* says it all), with a key observation and question: "... due to its small size, Estonia cannot afford to be fragmented. How can its government act as a single government to efficiently provide seamless and high-quality services to its citizens and businesses?" (OECD Public Governance Reviews 2011: 18). Noting that Estonia had demonstrated "strategic agility" in its response to the financial crisis, the report nonetheless drew on the Sarapuu article to highlight five features of public administration in small states: limited scope of goals and activities; multi-functionalism of civil servants and organizations; informality of structures and procedures; constraints on steering and control; and "personalism" of roles and functions. The result was a "fragmented and decentralized public administration". The report systematically reviewed different aspects of this fragmentation suggesting a variety of ways of overcoming them in the pursuit of more coherence: the creation of more formal or institutionalized coordination networks (citing the New Zealand model); changed organizational culture; the introduction of more robust performance measurement systems to enhance accountability; more mobility within the public service; more stream-lined prioritization in building towards a common agenda (Estonia had over 200 policy strategies at play in its administration); better coordination of service delivery. This analysis yield eight major categories of recommendations under the three broad headings of (1) promoting a "whole of government" approach in public administration, (2) building a common agenda, and (3) delivering public services effectively. In total, the report contained 50 very specific recommendations (e.g., "Amend the Government of the Republic Act to enable machinery of government changes to be made via administrative orders set by the government at the start of, or during, a parliamentary term to best deliver on government priorities and to meet citizen needs"). Contrast the Finland report, with 30 quiet general recommendations (e.g., "Rebuild legislative drafting and analytical capacity in ministries").

Public governance reviews indicate an important evolution in the governance peer review processes within the OECD. They have not replaced the sectoral reviews, but now exist beside them, and have taken GOV into a new direction, while still relying on information exchange and peer participation. That direction is evolving however, as the contrast among the reports discussed above shows. At time of writing, as many as six other countries had expressed interest in Public Governance Reviews, but at the same time there seemed to be less appetite for complete public disclosure of entire systems of governments, warts and all. It might be argued that Ireland and Finland were willing to experiment with the format since they had little to lose as "stars" of the OECD. In Estonia's case, it might have been a combination of wanting to show commitment to the OECD as a newly joined member, and to take advantage of a thorough *diagnostique* as only the OECD is able to provide.

One question about peer review is whether it works, and if so, why it works given that there is little in the way of enforcement mechanisms. While it is not possible to trace exact outcomes, interviews conducted for this book consistently underscored the centrality of peer exchange, discussion, and interaction as a key benefit of the OECD. Peer reviews and peer exchange – given the diplomatic context of the OECD and the delicacy of making recommendations – is unlikely to yield change in the short term. Over time, however, it may have a sensitizing effect as well as an emulation effect. On the question of why countries undergo this type of review, it is likely that the very lack of enforcement mechanisms makes it attractive. Countries have the benefit of an external review, but without the threat of losing sovereignty or being forced to comply with any firm recommendations (Schäfer 2006). Ironically, the willingness to participate candidly in a peer review process in the context of the OECD – as opposed, for example, to the EU – may be a function in part of the low stakes. Reviews are voluntary, and in the OECD context, cannot lead to the authoritative imposition of sanctions or requirements for legislative change. On the other hand, irrespective of enforcement capacities, domestic reformers may see an OECD review process as legitimation for their own agendas.[6]

The OECD governance *acquis*

The conventional references to the OECD as an ideational artist or a practitioner of soft power and multilateral surveillance miss the important point that it is not without some relatively robust quasi-legal instruments. These instruments fall short, of course, of truly legally binding legislation or treaties (though the OECD itself refers to its instruments as "The Acts"), but they are more than mere injunctions, guidelines or pleadings. The response might be that since even these more robust instruments apply only to the OECD membership, their effect is only on a tiny, if well-heeled, club. But firm agreements among this club of leading nations have three characteristics that give them wider scope than just the OECD itself: (1) they are visible "deals" among "leading" nations, and hence have a "brand" attraction (more on this in Chapter 6); (2) many of the stronger agreements are consciously designed to serve as standards or benchmarks, often in the absence of pre-existing ones, and so often tend to "fill the void" and become the only regulatory game in town; and (3) the OECD, as a networked institution, connects with organizations like the UN and the G20, organizations that recognize the usefulness of OECD's capacity to both develop persuasive norms and then police them through the relatively benign mechanism of peer review.

The OECD is a fertile producer of norms, standards, guidelines, best practices, checklists, benchmarks, toolkits, reports, reviews, "glances" (see the next section), and a welter of other publications. The spectrum of its standard-setting capacity runs from the relatively firm (quasi-legal) to the relatively soft (indicators). At the firm end of the spectrum the OECD has several instruments at its disposal.[7] <u>Decisions</u> are legally binding on all OECD members who did not abstain at the time they are adopted. While not international treaties, they entail the same obligations. Recommendations are not legally binding but have "great moral force" for those countries which have not abstained during the vote, with the expectation that they will do all they can to implement its provisions. Declarations are "solemn texts" that lay out policy commitments, and while not legally binding, are monitored by the responsible OECD body for their implementation. Finally there are arrangements and understandings which are negotiated and adopted within the framework of the OECD by a subset of members, and international agreements which are concluded within the framework of the organization and are binding on those who concluded the agreement, but not the OECD members as a whole. At the time of writing the OECD's "Acts" consisted of 28 decisions, 171 recommendations, one agreement, three arrangements/understandings, seven conventions, two DAC recommendations, 25 declarations, and two guidelines.[8]

As we showed in Chapter 2, the strategy of enhanced engagement but particularly enlargement required a clearer sense within the OECD as to what candidate countries were actually acceding to, and what the OECD standards and norms were within each broad policy area. We noted how GOV and the PGC had developed and then elaborated a "building blocks" document that outlined key areas of governance and the existing *acquis*, or body of standards that applied in each area (OECD 2007a). The categories for the building blocks was adopted from the *Government at a Glance* project (see below), and so actually overlooked some important OECD governance instruments. The thematic building blocks and relevant standards as they stood in 2007 were:

> Budget practices and procedures
>> Existing OECD Instrument:
>>> 2001 OECD Best Practices for Budget Transparency
>> Existing PGC Guidance: none
> Human Resource Management (HRM)
>> Existing OECD Instruments: none
>> Existing PGC Guidance:
>>> OECD Country Peer Reviews of Human Resource Management, GOV/PGC/PEM(2006)7
> Integrity and Corruption Resistance
>> Existing OECD Instruments:
>>> 1998 Recommendation on Improving Ethical Conduct in the Public Service
>>> 2003 Recommendation on Guidelines for Managing Conflict of Interest in the Public Service
>> Existing (or forthcoming) PGC Guidance:
>>> Public procurement – a forthcoming publication maps out good practices for integrity in public procurement from both member and non-member countries.

Post-public employment – a good practice handbook is under preparation.

Lobbying – draft principles for enhancing transparency and accountability in lobbying will be reviewed in June.

Ethics Infrastructure and Assessment Framework

Internal and external reporting: Open Government

Existing OECD Instruments: none

Existing PGC Guidance:

Citizens as Partners: Information, Consultation and Public Participation in Policy-Making

Ten guiding principles for successful on-line consultation

Checklist for evaluating public participation

Guiding principles for successful information, consultation and active participation of citizens in policy-making.

E-government readiness

Existing OECD Instruments: none

Existing PGC Guidance:

Analytical framework and methodology to conduct E-government Reviews of OECD countries

Checklist for E-Government Leaders (2003)

Checklist to Evaluate the Economic Case of E-Government

Centres of government

Existing OECD Instruments: none

Existing PGC Guidance: none

Management of regulatory quality

Existing OECD Instruments:

1995 OECD Reference Checklist for Regulatory Decision-Making

2005 OECD Guiding Principles for Regulatory Quality and Performance

Existing PGC and GRP Guidance:

APEC-OECD Integrated Checklist on Regulatory

Multi-level Governance

Existing OECD Instruments: none

Existing TDPC Guidance:

Innovation and Effectiveness in Territorial Development Policy (2003)

From this 2007 list, we can see that the OECD as a body had five instruments on governance, though it should be noted that any decisions or recommendations made by the Council of the OECD come to it from committees and directorates, so these instruments would have originated in GOV and its committees. One OECD instrument was a guide (on budgeting), two were recommendations (on ethics and conflict of interest), and two were principles (a checklist on regulatory decision-making and principles for regulatory quality and performance). The PGC itself of course cannot have any legal instruments, and relies entirely on guides, checklists and principles.

By 2010 this arsenal of instruments had been buttressed by additional ones on public procurement and lobbying, rounding out GOV's "integrity" portfolio. In addition, some areas that are clearly within the "governance" field, such as bribery of public officials, are connected with other committees (e.g., Committee on Fiscal Affairs and the Investment Committee). Two governance areas that have attracted strong OECD instruments are regulation and government integrity, or anti-corruption. We will examine each in turn.

The work on regulation extends back to 1995, when the Council issued its Recommendation on Improving the Quality of Government Regulation (OECD 1995c). The recommendation itself was quite brief, and was a ratification of a proposal from PUMA: it urged member countries to "ensure the quality and transparency of government regulations" by referring to an attached checklist, and invited the Public Management Committee to monitor the application of the checklist and report within three years. So, the heart of the Recommendation was actually the checklist, which consisted of ten questions which were claimed to reflect "principles of good decision-making that are used in OECD countries to improve the effectiveness and efficiency of government regulation by upgrading the legal and factual basis for regulations, clarifying options, assisting officials in reaching better decisions, establishing more orderly and predictable decision processes, identifying existing regulations that are outdated or unnecessary, and making government actions more transparent". The questions concerned: the correct definition of the problem, the justification for government action, whether regulation was advisable at all, its legal basis, the appropriate level of government, costs and benefits, the transparency of effects, clarity and consistency of the regulations, participation of all interested parties, and assurance of compliance. This became the basis for a 1997 report to ministers and subsequently for the 2005 OECD Guiding Principles for Regulatory Quality and Performance (OECD 2005e). It reaffirmed seven principles (which had been proposed in the 1997 report) in typical OECD fashion: prescriptions for market liberalization and deregulation were carefully balanced against public interest considerations, as in principle 5: "Design economic regulations in all sectors to stimulate competition and efficiency, and eliminate them except where clear evidence demonstrates that they are the best way to serve broad public interests". But the Guiding Principles document also illustrates how the norm-setting process takes place. By 2005 Russia had undergone a regulatory review, and Brazil and Chile had been observers in the Special Group on Regulatory Policy. There had been regulatory policy conferences in China in 2003 and 2004, and regulatory reform was part of the Programme on Good Governance for Development in Arab Countries, supported by the OECD and the UNDP. It also was the basis for the 2005 APEC-OECD Integrated Checklist on Regulatory Reform (OECD 2005a). The process to develop this document began in 2000, and of course there is an overlap in membership (seven members of APEC at the time were members of the OECD), but nonetheless, the resulting checklist of self-assessment questions show the migration of OECD norms and standards to other regions in the world.

The foundation for the OECD's integrity agenda is an international legal instrument, the 1997 OECD Convention on Combating Bribery of Foreign Public Officials in International Business Transactions (OECD 1997a). It is the only international instrument that focuses on the "supply side" of bribery transactions, and at the time of writing had been signed by all 34 OECD members as well as four non-members (Argentina, Brazil, Bulgaria and South Africa). It uses peer review as its enforcement mechanism, and is oversee by the OECD Working Group on Bribery in International Business Transactions. The convention provides a definition of the offence of bribing public officials, and has provisions for sanctions, mutual legal assistance, enforcement, and extradition, among other things. The convention is a good example of the OECD approach, not only because of enforcement through peer review, but because it strikes a balance between national sovereignty and international treaty obligations. It seeks (as the commentary on the convention notes): "to assure a functional equivalence among the measures taken by the Parties to sanction bribery of foreign public officials, without requiring uniformity or changes in fundamental principles of a Party's legal system". For example, Article 1 on the definition of bribery states: "Each Party shall take such measures as may be necessary to establish that it is a criminal offence under its law for any person intentionally to offer, promise or give any undue pecuniary or other advantage, whether directly or through intermediaries, to a foreign public official, for that official or for a third party, in order that the official act or refrain from acting in relation to the performance of official duties, in order to obtain or retain business or other improper advantage in the conduct of international business". It therefore provides a definition, but leaves it up to Parties to take their own measures. Article 3 on sanctions refers only to "effective, proportionate and dissuasive criminal penalties" that are comparable to those the Party would apply in the case of attempts to bribe its own public officials. The commentaries that accompany the convention and that are part of it provide more detail, but it is clear that the approach is a flexible one that sets standards, but allows Parties to implement them in accordance with their own legal traditions.

To celebrate the Convention's first decade, the OECD launched discussions on strengthening it in 2007, which resulted in the Recommendation of the Council for Further Combating Bribery of Foreign Public Officials in International Business Transactions (OECD 1997a). This extended (though without legal force as a treaty) the Convention in several ways: awareness-raising initiatives in the public and private sectors; review of tax legislation and regulations that might indirectly support bribery; examination of laws and regulations on banks and other financial institutions to ensure adequate records. It also urged non-members who are major exporters and foreign investors to adhere to the Convention, and instructed the Working Group to provide a forum for countries that have not yet adhered. It also invited the Working Group to "consult and co-operate with the international organisations and international financial institutions active in the fight against bribery of foreign public officials in international business transactions, and consult regularly with the non-governmental organisations and representatives of the business community active in this field". Finally, it included a detailed guide on good practice in implementing the specific articles of the Convention.

There are four key additional OECD instruments dealing with integrity in government, and all four are overseen by GOV: (1) Recommendation of the Council on Improving Ethical Conduct in the Public Service Including Principles for Managing Ethics in the Public Service (1998), (2) Recommendation of the Council on OECD Guidelines for Managing Conflict of Interest in the Public Service (2003), (3) Recommendation of the Council on Enhancing Integrity in Public Procurement (2008), and (4) Recommendation of the Council on Principles for Transparency and Integrity in Lobbying (2010). The "recommendations" of all these documents are at best two or three short paragraphs asking member countries to pay attention to issues of ethical conduct, conflict of interest, integrity in public procurement, and lobbying. These somewhat anemic recommendations are then followed by an annex with guides and principles, again the elements of which are sometimes banal (e.g., provide leadership, enhance transparency, effective implementation). But the banality of the instruments is not the point. Rather it is that these issues are raised at the international level, principles and guidelines are provided, enforcement is then introduced through peer review and follow-up reports, on the basis of which additional guides and toolkits are then developed, circulated, and fed back into an international dialogue. Moreover, these instruments do not stand alone as OECD inventions – as with the Convention on Bribery, they are actively extended into other international organizations such as the World Bank and regional banks, non-member states, and NGOs and the business community.

A close look at the OECD's governance *acquis* shows that it has reasonably clear contours and has characteristics that give it some weight and influence. First, as we could see with the "building blocks", regulatory quality, and integrity fields, there are a substantial number of OECD benchmarks, standards and norms. In the case of the Convention, there is a legally binding treaty. In the other cases, there are recommendations, which, within the OECD system, carry some weight since they emanate as consensual views of the Council. Second, it is important not to see these benchmarks as isolated agreements that exist only on paper. In the OECD system, they serve more as crampons that allow the organization to gain a hold on a slippery policy rock face, and then begin to climb further. This can be through the subsequent publication of additional guides and toolkits that further elaborate the content of the initial recommendations. More importantly, it can be through the elaboration of further recommendations that tackle new but related problems in the same field. This is best illustrated through the "integrity" dossier. It began with the Convention in 1997, the first international agreement dealing with the suppliers of bribes rather than simply the recipients. Once the Convention was signed, it opened a discursive space for international discussion of related themes or variables that affected the broad field of integrity, and so the recommendations on ethics, conflict of interest, procurement, and lobbying quickly followed. But these are also connected to regulatory quality, guidelines on the corporate governance of state-owned enterprises, private sector corporate governance, guidelines for multinational enterprises, and tax law. Taken singly, the OECD's governance instruments may seem anemic, but taken as a collection of instruments that gradually enwrap a field of activity, they become more impressive. Third, the instruments are closely articulated with the rest of the GOV toolkit. Peer reviews, oversight by the Secretariat and PGC, surveys that feed into Governance at a Glance – all combine with the quasi-legal instruments, and indeed are given their legitimacy through them.

Government at a Glance (GaaG)

An interesting development in the past 15 years has been the growth of indicators of public sector performance (Buduru & Pal 2010). It has been driven by a variety of factors. One was the growing realization among international donors like the World Bank and the UNDP that governance, broadly defined, mattered for economic development. In 1996, for example, World Bank President James Wolfensohn reversed the Bank's policy not to address political factors, such as corruption, in development aid (Nanda 2006). The OECD, with its expertise in data collection and analysis, was in the game early as well. A process to develop indicators was proposed by the DAC in 1998 to a joint OECD/UN/World Bank meeting on Agreed Indicators of Development Progress (Knack et al 2003). As Besançon points out: "Measurements matter where clients, foundations, and donor organisations such as USAID, IMF, the Millennium Challenge Account, the World Bank, the UN, or the European Union allocate large sums of money to developing nations and base disbursements on good governance. Such measures show which states have improved and the ones in need of improvement, and show what sectors need more attention" (Besançon 2003: 2). Another driver was the global investment community – it too was putting money into countries, and political risk factors were important ingredients in making investment decisions (Malik

2002). In fact, the business community provided an early market for governance indicators. The Business Environmental Risk Intelligence (BERI) was established in 1966, and the International Country Risk Guide was established in 1980.

In some respects the OECD has a comparative advantage in that it has a long practice of gathering data from members and building indicators of performance across a wide range of policy fields. But this leads as well to a challenge: how to present the mountains of data that it collects coherently and comprehensively. The push by the current SG to make the organization more relevant has led to efforts to not only make the information accessible, but to make it useful as well. One technique that has been used by a variety of directorates has been "... at a Glance" publications that pull together large amounts of data from members in a particular policy field and provide comparative tables and indicators so that readers can easily – and "at a glance" – absorb where their countries line up against other OECD members. These have been enormously popular; for example, there are "at a Glance" publications for society (demographics, unemployment, poverty, social and health expenditures, work and life satisfaction, and in 2009, adult height, risky youth behaviour, and bullying); education (teacher compensation, instruction time, class size, comparison of student performance across different subjects); health (health status, determinants of health, health expenditures, health workforce, access to care). There are also "at a Glance" publications on development aid, the space economy, agricultural policy, national accounts and others.

GOV came somewhat late to the indicators party – the first publication of its "Governance at a Glance" (affectionately known by GOV staff as GaaG) only appeared in 2009, with a second edition in June 2011. The process within GOV to create an "at a Glance" publication actually began in 1999, with an expression of concern about the lack of comparative data by the PUMA Expert Group Meeting on Measuring Productivity (OECD 2005f: 5). The PGC did not formally take the issue up until 2005, when it launched a work programme for GOV to explore, through a series of working papers, the challenges of developing governance indicators, and aiming at a publication in 2009. There was a two-fold interest in launching the project.[9] Members of the PGC wanted a tool that would help them better benchmark and compare performance among countries. They were interested in more than scattered data on different aspects of governance that did not provide a broader and more comprehensive lens. The second driver came from within GOV itself. It too felt that its "products" were scattered and consequently less effective than they might be – certainly in competition with other directorates that had flashier ways of presenting data.

A 2005 discussion paper produced by the directorate for PGC discussion neatly laid out the rationale for the project, but also revealed GOV's broader objectives in positioning itself better to stimulate reform.[10] It started by noting that the "wave of public management reforms" in the last two decades had had "little empirical basis". The project's objectives were a mix of better services to governments and an improvement in GOV's own influence over governance reforms:

17. Improved availability of cross-country data on the dimensions of government will allow a more informed reading of other countries' reforms. Regularly updated data will allow countries to benchmark their own developments – assessing the progress that they have made in their own reform programmes. The data will also enable practitioners to review internal consistency of reforms and the inter-relationships between process reforms and inputs used (is performance-related pay associated with higher wage bills, etc.?).

18. Improving data collection in this area will also have important side benefits. It will open up the field of public administration for broader review – including specialists from other disciplines. It will also encourage the standardisation of terms and definitions, improving the quality of international public management discussions. In the longer term, improved data availability will lay the foundations for a more robust assessment of the impact of different types of public sector reforms.

19. GOV would use the data to leverage greater impact from its own work, by benchmarking developments in public management in its current peer reviews (budget, regulatory, territorial and HRM reviews), facilitating the movement towards an integrated set of public management or governance reviews. (OECD 2005f: 5–6)

The 2005 paper posed some basic questions that were then to be fleshed out in the subsequent working papers. The most important was, what would and could be measured? The overall framework noted that in principle there would be four types of measures: inputs (e.g., wages and salaries in the public sector); processes (e.g., measures which characterize civil service management such as staff mobility); outputs (e.g., number of children in full time education); and outcomes (e.g., perceptions of trust in government, regulatory quality). It acknowledged that of the four, outcomes would be the most difficult. Overall, the project did not envisage the creation of many new datasets, but rather would draw on existing data and surveys within the OECD and GOV in particular, as well as external available datasets (e.g., from the IMF and the ILO). The 2005 discussion paper was followed by phased discussions over the next two years. Three technical papers on the nature of the data to be collected, its sources, and challenges and pitfalls of interpretation and analysis were produced in 2006, which were then combined and published in a 2009 companion volume to GaaG entitled *Measuring Government Activity* (OECD 2009c).

GaaG 2009 had high ambitions of probing the quality of governments among OECD members.[11] It referred to the importance of "good governance" and saw one of its objectives as contributing to a debate about the determinants of "performance". At the same time, the introduction noted the challenges of measuring both outputs and outcomes, and admitted that it was only giving "indications of government activities and performance". GaaG was flagged as a work-in-progress, arguing that over time, as it developed, it could more confidently begin to reflect real measures of quality and of performance. The report consisted of ten chapters: an overview of "future governance challenges", followed by chapters on revenues, expenditures, the "intersection between public and private sectors", public employment, human resource management practices, budget practices, regulatory management, integrity, and open and responsive government. These were deliberately modelled on the "Building Blocks" approach of categorizing GOV activities (discussed in detail in the next chapter). The idea was that GaaG and the Building Blocks would mutually reinforce each other, a scaffolding of governance activities supported by indicators of performance or at least activity.[12]

The "input" chapters (e.g., revenues, expenditures, employment) were fairly standard exercises in gathering existing data, though they were useful in providing common definitions and, on that basis, the opportunity for comparison. The more interesting chapters were the analytical ones. Chapter 1 on future challenges, for example, set its discussion within the context of the global financial crisis and how governments could improve their capacities to deal with its long-term effects. In highlighting the implications of the financial crisis, it noted the importance of evidence-based policy-making (especially around regulatory impact analysis); integrity (the intersection between public and private sectors, conflict-of-interest codes); public procurement; lobbying; better coordination among levels of government; and the important role of robust fiscal projections. The second main section of the chapter asked about the governance challenges for the future, and opened with a direct critique of NPM and three questions that governments were urged to ask themselves in the search for a new governance paradigm. The critique of NPM noted that due "to lack of data and numerous challenges in measuring outputs and outcomes, governments have a difficult time in determining whether the reforms have really resulted in efficiency gains". But it went further:

> New Public Management has exacerbated the traditional separation between politics and administration, between policy decisions and their implementation. Dismantling organisations also sometimes led to a loss of continuity, institutional memory and long-term capacity. The focus on contracting and reporting may have come at the expense of coherence of strategy, continuity of values and connecting public interest to individual motivation. In addition, many governments have not developed sufficient oversight capacity, increasing the threat of provider capture. Often, governments adopted reform instruments or ideas from the private sector or from other governments without regard for the country context and/or

understanding the inherent limitations and weaknesses of these instruments. (OECD 2009b: 33)

In a sober tone reminiscent of *Modernising Government* (see the discussion in Chapter 2), the report asked whether a "new paradigm" was needed: "... OECD member countries may need to reassess what has worked well in past 25 years, what has not and why, what might be discarded from those reforms, what needs to be adjusted, what might be further built upon and what are the conditions for success". The three questions were (1) How can countries achieve a better balance between government, markets and citizens?, (2) What governance capacities or competencies are needed for dealing with global challenges?, and (3) How can a continued focus on efficiency and effectiveness be reconciled with upholding other fundamental public service values? The discussion in connection with the third question was telling. While governments would continue to emphasize performance in terms of efficiency and effectiveness, the concept of performance – in light of the challenges of the financial crisis – would have to be broadened to include a government's ability to uphold "core values such as accountability, transparency and equity".

How well do the more analytical as opposed to descriptive chapters manage to convey quality, performance, and the elements of good governance? Chapter 6 dealt with human resource management practices. The chapter begins by admitting that while "there is evidence that HRM practices can improve performance, there is no agreement or evidence on how specific HRM features do so", and that none of the indexes in the chapter either evaluate the performance of HRM policies or provide information about the quality of work that public servants do. Composite indexes (a single index comprised of several, usually weighted, indicators) were then provided on the extent of delegation of HRM practices to line ministries, recruitment systems (career vs. position based), staff performance management (extend of the use of performance assessment), and the senior civil service (use of separate HRM practices for senior civil servants). All of the data in this chapter were generated through the 2006 Strategic Human Resource Management in Government Survey of OECD members. Chapter 7 on budget practices and procedures relied on a straight-forward set of criteria of what constitutes "well-functioning budget institutions": indicators showing "the extent to which: countries have adopted practices to encourage fiscal sustainability; the public is informed so that fiscal policies and spending priorities can be understood, monitored and evaluated; budgets incorporate a medium-term perspective to ensure that multi-year consequences of spending measures are considered; performance information is used in budget formulation; and the executive can make changes to the approved budget". While the information provided was useful, it certainly fell short of providing a clear view of actual performance. Ireland, for example, which by 2010 was wrestling with a national financial and budgetary crisis, actually exceeded or met the OECD average on most of the indicators in 2009. The final chapter, on open and responsive government, provided one table on legislative institutions related to open government (freedom of information, privacy/data protection, administrative procedures to support accountability of public officials, ombudsman, and independent audit institutions).

The 2011 edition (OECD 2011a) differed from the 2009 version in several important ways.[13] First, the mirroring of chapters in 2009 to the Building Blocks had been criticized as being too much of an "internal" review. The structure of the 2011 edition was changed accordingly: while there are equivalent chapters on human resource management, regulatory governance ("regulatory management" in 2009), and public employment, there are no chapters on integrity (instead, a chapter on transparency in government and another on public procurement), on open and responsive government, or on budget practices and procedures (as defined by the Building Blocks procedural standards). A second difference was the addition of a special, separately authored overview essay (by Allen Schick, University of Maryland) to commemorate the coincidence of the OECD's 50th anniversary with the publication of this edition of GaaG in 2011. The chapter focused on the "leveraging" of resources and institutions by government to achieve public ends, a new world "in which governments network and share power and resources in order to govern ..." (OECD 2011a: 21). It provides a review of key building blocks, but in passing notes that the OECD was never captured by NPM, and that moreover its more recent ambition is to adopt a more whole-of-government and performance-oriented perspective, as evidenced by the Public Governance Reviews. This overview chapter was well received by the PGC, and something like it is probably going to be a feature of future GaaGs.

Third, there were entirely new chapters with a heightened performance focus (a weakness of the first GaaG, which hardly addressed results). For the first time, there was a chapter on public sector compensation in selected occupations (teachers; doctors and nurses; senior management, middle management, professionals and secretarial staff in central government). This was a controversial addition for some countries (unions back home could use these compensation data in interesting ways), as evidenced by the low take-up rate of participation for central government occupations: only 19 of 34 member states provided data (along with Brazil). Despite this, the directorate hopes to include more staffing classifications in the next GaaG. There was also a new chapter assessing "strategic foresight and leadership" capacity among governments. This chapter was shaped by the impact of the financial crisis and the importance of strong, strategic responses to it. It was also shaped by the experience GOV had had to that point in Public Governance Reviews, with their emphasis (particularly with the Finland and the Estonia reports) on the importance of "strategic agility". These are difficult metrics in any case, but of course the OECD was going nowhere near attempting to measure the leadership qualities of different member governments. Instead it relied on measure of "gaps" (e.g., the magnitude of spending reduction required to get to a debt/GDP ration of 60 per cent – pre-crisis levels) and composite measures of the application of so-called strategic tools (e.g., in the human resources sector, the use of performance assessments, capacity reviews, accountability frameworks), and indexes of the appointment process for senior government staff (the degree to which it is politically driven) and numbers of ministerial staff. Finally, there was a new chapter on government performance in selected areas (health and education) drawing on other OECD data from other directorates, and touching on issues of equity and access, especially in health care (using the proportion of public versus private coverage and out-of-pocket expenses).

The technical work that went into the project was impressive, and GOV was well aware of the difficulty of measuring outputs, let alone outcomes of government activity and performance. At one level the effort is notable: it combines the standardized presentation of basic data such as expenditures and revenues, with composite indicators of characteristics of government activity in which the OECD has carved out clear expertise, such as strategic foresight, budget processes, and regulatory quality. GaaG also has a distinctive profile in comparison with the growing universe of governance indicators from other bodies. It does not focus as much on rankings and league tables as much as some others do, for example Transparency International. It can draw on unique datasets within and across the OECD, as well as the tailored surveys to senior public officials in member states. This alone distinguishes it from other "subjective" indexes generated by other organizations that rely on expert but nongovernment opinion. However, at the level of providing useful information about whether governments are actually following good budgetary practice, or actually striving for openness or regulatory quality as opposed to its legislative trappings, GaaG provides almost no help at all.[14] Nonetheless, it has been a success within the GOV constituency. PGC members give it high marks – every year, for example, GOV sends out a survey to committee members on country priorities on governance, and GaaG has been at the top of the list.[15] Within GOV, it has served to pull the directorate more closely together, since all elements within it contribute to the publication. As a simple, clearly presented publication, it gets the international attention that other more specialized GOV publications do not (the 2009 edition has been translated – not by the OECD – into Japanese, Italian, German and Spanish). And it has just begun: the SG's preface to the first report said that the ambition was to eventually include more countries beyond the OECD membership (in 2011 it did), thus offering a "true 'glance' at governance issues across the globe".

Regional cooperation: The case MENA

As discussed in Chapters 1 and 2, the OECD underwent a major housecleaning exercise under Donald Johnston as SG from 1996 to 2006. Part of

Johnston's agenda for the organization was wider global engagement beyond the OECD members, and indeed an eventual expansion of the membership. Those ambitions were realized under his successor, Angel Gurría, through the accession process and enhanced engagement. Indeed, both of these initiatives may be seen as elements of a "re-positioning" strategy under which the OECD seeks to be more globally relevant by engaging with a host of countries and regions, but also serving as a bridge between developed economies and developing ones. As early as 2007, only one year into his mandate, Gurría was referring to the "current transformation of the OECD into a more diverse and global organisation" (Gurria 2007), citing accession and enhanced engagement, but also arguing that the "OECD is gradually turning into an engine of convergence between economies at all stages of development". This expansionist ambition means that now the OECD has relations with some 70 other non-member countries, and organizations like APEC, the World Trade Organization, the UN, and the EU. Regionally, it is engaged in Europe, the Caucasus and Central Asia, Latin America, Africa, and the Middle East and North Africa (MENA). This range of engagement is another networking instrument in the OECD toolkit that facilitates the spread of OECD norms and standards, and encourages convergence to those standards. This section will look at MENA as an example of this type of activity. The MENA project's full title is Initiative on Governance and Investment for Development, and has two major components, one on investment (the MENA-OECD Investment Programme) and one on good governance (Good Governance for Development). We will focus on the latter.

MENA was initially driven primarily by a US interest, after the Iraq War, in working constructively in the region.[16] At first there was even some talk of a new "Marshall Plan", which naturally suggested the OECD. The US was prepared to put a substantial amount of money on the OECD table through a voluntary contribution, even though several member states (especially France, given its colonial history in the region) were reluctant. Eventually the Council agreed, and other major donors came on board (e.g., Canada and Japan). GOV was tasked with supporting the good governance component of MENA (DAF is responsible for supporting the investment side). There was some resistance within the directorate for the additional work that this implied, since while there were new resources, they were not going to GOV. Moreover, there was to be no corresponding decrease in the range of activities undertaken by GOV as part of its existing work plan. As we shall see below, another issue was the pursuit of "good governance" in regimes that top the charts in autocracy and suppression of their populations (which contributed to the "Arab Spring" in 2011). The objections were overruled. The UNDP was brought in to partner with GOV since the organizations seemed to complement each other: GOV had the governance and economic systems expertise required for the initiative, while the UNDP, through its Programme on Governance in the Arab Region, knew key people and organizations on the ground.

The programme design had to be carefully thought out. First, donors were well aware that no MENA states were democracies, so issues pertaining to the political system or civil society had to be dealt with gingerly. If there were to be constructive engagement with the MENA countries, it would have to be primarily on technical grounds. Second, the first phase of MENA (it has been renewed three times, most recently in June 2010 for a five year term, 2011–2015) was to focus on network and trust building. The OECD approach – peer review where countries are treated as equals, evidence based analysis, lesson drawing and experience sharing – were comparatively unfamiliar in the MENA world. Third, the programme had to be demand driven, to build trust and to avoid the connotations of the West imposing its standards and norms. This was behind the organization of the initiative, where MENA states chair the Working Groups.

MENA was launched in 2005 at a conference in Jordan with 18 Arab and North African states, the OECD, and the UNDP. At first the programme was supported by the OECD and the UNDP's Programme on Governance in the Arab Region, but is now also supported by voluntary contributions from Canada, Belgium, France, Italy, Japan, Netherlands, South Korea, Spain, Sweden, Turkey, the UK, the US, and of course contributions by Arab countries themselves. Other international bodies that are currently engaged include the European Commission, the IMF, the World Bank, the League of Arab States, and the Arab Administrative Development Organization. The 2005 meeting resulted in the "Dead Sea Declaration" (the launch conference was held at the Dead Sea in the Kingdom of Jordan) that laid out the nature of the initiative and its working methods. The preamble to the declaration bristled with the language of good governance, reform, modernization, participation, investment, development, effective and efficient public institutions, social justice, fairness and equality before the law, and civil society – the word democracy never appeared. Six themes were identified, which were then taken up by Working Groups: civil service and integrity; judiciary, e-government, administrative simplification and regulatory reform; role of civil society and media in reform of the public sector; public finance; public service delivery and private-public partnerships (OECD 2005b). The 2011 MENA membership of Arab and North African states consisted of: Algeria, Bahrain, UAE, Egypt, Iraq, Jordan, Kuwait, Lebanon, Libya, Mauritania, Morocco, Oman, Qatar, Palestinian Authority, Sudan, Syria, Tunisia, and Yemen.

The MENA system is depicted in Figure 4.1. The six working groups are on civil service reform and integrity; e-government and administrative simplification; public finance; public service delivery, public-private partnerships, and regulatory reform; judiciary; and civil society and media. The Steering Group consists of four Arab chairs, eight OECD co-chairs nominated by member states, and the OECD-UNDP Secretariat. There is also participation by collaborating organizations such as the World Bank and the European

Figure 4.1   MENA Organizational Structure

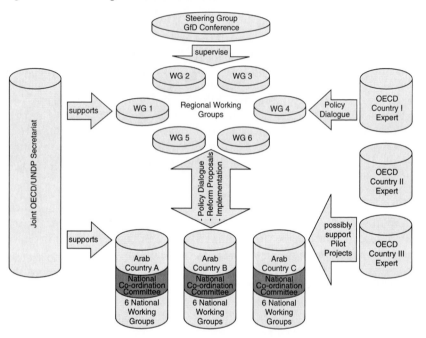

Source: OECD, MENA Key Actors. Accessed 16 May 2011 at http://www.oecd.org/document/6/
0,3746,en_34645207_34645555_34964998_1_1_1_1,00.html

Commission. The Steering Committee meets twice a year, and the regional
working groups meet up to three times a year. In addition, there is an
annual conference for the initiative, and a veritable blizzard of other joint
meetings with the OECD, often in Paris but also in the regions themselves.
On 29 November 2010, for example, there was a MENA conference in Paris
entitled "Towards Gender-Sensitive Regulatory Frameworks: Fighting Legal
Discrimination against Women in MENA Countries". As another example, the
Working Group on Civil Service and Integrity had three meetings in 2010:
national anti-corruption strategies (Cairo), e-procurement and integrity (Rome),
public policy evaluation (Morocco). In 2009 it held conferences on building a
cleaner public sector (Turkey), measuring and planning the workforce (Morocco),
and on integrity (with the OECD, Paris). Each of the working groups also
releases publications and policy briefs. The Working Group on Civil Service
and Integrity has published reports on ways to improve transparency in procurement, and in engaging citizens in policy-making, as well as policy briefs
on conflict of interest and performance pay policies. The Working Group on
E-Government and Administrative Simplification has been equally active,
with six meetings in 2009–2010, and two publications. The Working Group

on Public Service Delivery, Public-Private Partnerships and Regulatory Reform has been the most active of all the groups: 13 meetings in 2009–2010 alone, and it issued a Regional Charter for Regulatory Quality in 2009 (though it was a one-page list of bromides). By contrast, the Working Group on Civil Society and Media has met only once, in 2005, and the Working Group on the Judiciary only twice, in 2005 and 2006. Neither has issued any publications. These two committees have been supported through the UNDP, which is less familiar with OECD practices.[17]

The MENA initiative around "good governance" clearly has a sense of unreality to it, if by "good governance" we mean some measure of actual citizen engagement and open government. The MENA documents pay homage to these principles, as well as other good things such as legal gender equality, but the bald fact is that the MENA member states are among the least free and least transparent on the planet. Table 4.1 provides measures for the 18 MENA members on three standard metrics of governance: Transparency International's corruption index, the World Bank's Worldwide Governance Indicators (voice and transparency), and Freedom House's Map of Freedom of the World. On the Transparency International index, while nearly three-quarters of the 178 countries that are assessed fall below five on a scale of ten, all but three of the MENA countries (Oman, Qatar, and UAE) did. All of the MENA members fell into the bottom 5 per cent of the index. The news was a little better with the World Bank measures on governance, with six countries just above the bottom quintile, with the highest percentile rank going to Lebanon at 35.5, and the lowest to Libya with 2.8. The OECD, by comparison, has an average score of 91.6. The Freedom House survey is equally dismal: of the 18 MENA members, only three were classified as "partly free" (Kuwait, Lebanon, and Morocco), and the rest as "not free". One can quibble with each of these indexes, but the aggregate picture is quite bleak: despite the fine phrases in reports and speeches, the MENA initiative seemed to have engaged with countries at the top of the autocratic food chain. Street revolutions in Tunisia and Egypt in January–February 2011, as well as the protests they sparked in Algeria, Bahrain, Jordan, Libya, Syria and Yemen corroborated these third-party observations (Saunders 2011).

In 2010 the OECD/MENA released a progress report on the initiative (OECD 2010k). Like the Dead Sea Declaration, it flagged the importance of effective governance institutions for increased investment in the region. This was clearly one of the drivers behind the project, besides US patronage – the MENA states themselves understood that investors would hesitate in the face of high and obvious corruption, red tape, inefficiencies, and political instability. The first chapter of the report was crystal clear about the circumstances in the region and the fact that those interviewed for the report (presumably high-level officials) highlighted the fact that MENA countries were falling well behind in the global competitive race with the BRIC's and other developing countries. The report looked at 40 cases of

Table 4.1 MENA Members: Governance Measures

Country	Transparency International (2010: score out of 10 for "highly clean"; rank of 178 countries)	World Bank Governance Indicators: Measure of Voice and Accountability (2010: Percentile Rank [0–100])	Freedom House (2010: Free [F], Partly Free [PF], Not Free [NF])
Algeria	2.9/105	17.5	NF
Bahrain	4.9/48	25.1	NF
Egypt	3.1/98	15.2	NF
Iraq	1.5/175	13.7	NF
Jordan	4.7/50	24.6	NF
Kuwait	4.5/54	31.3	PF
Lebanon	2.5/127	35.5	PF
Libya	2.2/146	2.8	NF
Mauritania	2.3/143	19.9 (2009)	NF
Morocco	3.4/85	26.5	PF
Oman	5.3/41	16.1	NF
Qatar	7.7/19	22.7	NF
Palestinian Authority	N/A	N/A	NF
Sudan	1.6/172	6.2 (2009)	NF
Syria	2.5/127	5.7	NF
Tunisia	4.3/59	11.4	NF
UAE	6.3/28	23.7	NF
Yemen	2.2/146	11.8	NF

Sources: Transparency International 2010; World Bank 2010; Freedom House 2010.

"public sector innovations and reforms". Given the portrait in Table 4.1, there was an almost Orwellian tone to the summary of accomplishments in the past five years:

> MENA countries have achieved impressive results in recent years in reinforcing institutions, modernising legal frameworks and building capacities for improved integrity. The process of dialogue and networking promoted by the MENA-OECD Initiative has actively shared practices and exchanged policy tools. We will continue reinforcing this approach

– we all have much more to gain from fairer and cleaner economies. (OECD 2010k: 5)

The report identified a number of thematic issues: improving the management of human resources (case studies from Bahrain, Egypt, Morocco, and Tunisia); improving the management of public finances (case studies from Egypt, Jordan, Morocco, Tunisia); fostering integrity in the public sector (case studies from Jordan, Morocco, Yemen); ensuring high quality regulation (case studies from Egypt, Jordan, the Palestinian National Authority, Tunisia); administrative simplification (case studies from Bahrain, Lebanon, Tunisia); e-government (Bahrain, Dubai, Jordan, Morocco); public-private partnerships (case studies from Tunisia, Jordan); gender approaches to public management (case studies from Egypt, Morocco, Tunisia); environmental management and the case of water (case studies from Egypt, Morocco, the Palestinian National Authority, Tunisia).

Despite the statements in the Dead Sea Declaration about civil society and engaging citizens, the case studies focused on the sinews of government itself. The report identified four pillars of public governance reform in the MENA and the overall logic of the project:

Public governance in the MENA rests on four interconnected pillars: i) human resources and capacities; ii) public finance; iii) regulatory policies and the rule of law; and iv) policy-making capacity. Reduced to its core, governance reform in the MENA constitutes a broad-based effort to improve government productivity in these areas. The productivity of government resources is widely regarded as being too low in the MENA (or, in other words, the quality of public governance needs major improvements). Thus, the rationale for focusing on these four core resources is clear: improving the productivity of financial and human resources, the rule of law and public policy capacities is fundamental to making progress in virtually every government function. Governments can only improve services and meet public needs if they are soundly managing their public finances, managing and motivating public service employees, and performing both of these functions within a framework of effective rule of law, guided by sound policies. Without these conditions, reform efforts in other areas will be difficult to pursue.

This fundamental logic has driven public governance reform in the MENA over the past decade because the region's governments have recognised the link between better public governance and better economic performance. (OECD 2010k: 35–36)

The MENA initiative is riven with paradox and contradiction – good governance in Yemen, for example, is an oxymoron. The fig leaf of the Dead Sea Declaration covered what emerged as an agenda in effect to improve the efficiency of autocratic regimes. This is indeed "good" governance in a sense – it is good for the autocrats. It smoothes the rough edges of every-day corruption, reduces political risk for investors, improves the investment climate, cuts red tape, and actually can enhance the efficacy of the public administration apparatus. Whether this is "good" governance in the sense that most people would understand, or indeed would be consistent with the corpus of OECD publications on the subject (citizens always come first in these), is another matter. Nonetheless, the OECD has a reasoned response to this critique.[18] First, the OECD has engaged with unsavoury regimes before – in fact, Spain was actually a member under the dictatorship of Franco. Second, the OECD was fully aware that MENA was a technocratic and not a "public governance" initiative, but gambled that small steps forward, for example on integrity and fighting corruption, were better than no steps at all. Third, while the revolutionary winds in countries like Tunisia and Egypt blew away the upper levels of their regimes, the technocratic layers of state administration more or less stayed intact, and it was with these layers that MENA had primarily engaged. Now that these states could truly reform, they had cadres that had been exposed to OECD standards and frameworks, and were open to OECD methods (for example, Tunisian government staff were attending training sessions in Paris as early as March 2011, scarcely two months after the fall of President Ben Ali).

For the purposes of this chapter, however, it is clear that these types of regional projects and alliances extend the OECD network immensely. An organization that started as a Euro-Atlantic alliance around economic development now finds itself engaged on the sands of the Gulf region, dispensing advice distilled from decades of analysis.

The accession process

Accession is not a "normal" tool for the OECD: the last state to accede before 2010 was the Slovak Republic in 2000. Before that there had been a spate of accessions between 1994 and 1996 – Mexico, the Czech Republic, Hungary, Korea, and Poland – with the preceding one, New Zealand, in 1973. The decision to invite Chile, Estonia, Israel, Russia and Slovenia was taken in 2007, and by 2010 all but Russia had become members (it had been reviewed, however, and the governance report was discussed by PGC and RPC in April 2011). We provided some of the background on the accession process in Chapter 2, and how it required GOV to reflect on its "building blocks" for the acceptance of candidate members. The process was governed by a general "roadmap" (OECD 2007d) which laid out basic procedures and results, that was then supplemented by negotiated roadmaps for each of the candidate countries, laying out areas for review and responsible committees. In fact, the so-called tailor-made accession roadmaps were virtually identical, involving reviews by some 17 or more OECD committees and working groups. Candidate countries had to meet the full OECD *acquis*, across all its policy fields and in all its organizational requirements, of which governance was just one standard. In essence, there were really two types of reviews, reflected in the list of committees in the roadmaps.[19] One type was instrument based (e.g., dealing with bribery or investment), and these reviews were often quite minute, even to the extent of examining financial resources and implementation issues. The second type was based on general standards and policies and looked for "alignment" – GOV reviews fell into this category because of the paucity of hard instruments. These reviews did not look for an exact match, but more in the way of commonalities, and they accepted that levels of development differ, and so standards needed to be flexible as well. Both types of reviews involved on-going negotiations with the candidate country over gaps with respect to OECD standards and norms. Chile, for example, had no ministry of the environment and so had to establish one before accession.

What is of interest here is not the unusual nature of the accession process itself, but the fact that it provides another lens on how the OECD does its work, makes its judgements, and spreads its norms and standards. Candidate countries have to submit a request to join after having been issued an invitation, and the process essentially involves gauging the degree to which the country meets OECD standards. This poses an interesting challenge, since as we noted earlier in our discussion of the *acquis* on governance, OECD standards can be quiet vague and elastic. If we take the Convention on Bribery, for example, it was explicitly designed to provide broad principles and definitions, as well as guidelines, but signatories were given the flexibility to reach objectives in terms of their own legal traditions and practices. And this is a Convention – in the cases of recommendations, there are at best vaguely worded injunctions, accompanied by guidelines or checklists. Each of the specific roadmaps contained the same language on the nature of committee/ working group reviews: there would be one group of bodies that could assess the candidate against explicit OECD instruments, and another (including the PGC) which would examine policies in a number of key areas "in which there are few or no OECD legal instruments". The PGC had the following identical mandate in all five roadmaps:

> The Public Governance Committee will review quality of the candidate countries' policies and institutions for public governance as these are necessary for ensuring policy effectiveness, economic development and efficiency and sound fiscal balances, and for maximising the quality of government expenditure. In this regard, the Public Governance Committee has developed a set of Building Blocks and Guiding Elements for Public Governance which will be used as a framework and benchmark tool for policy dialogue on public management issues in accession countries. The Committee will therefore examine:
> a) budget practices and procedures;
> b) human resource management;

c) integrity in the public sector, transparency and accountability, e-government readiness;

d) structure of government, management of regulatory quality and administrative simplification, multilevel governance relations.

As we noted above, despite the lack of explicit reference to the OECD Recommendations over which PGC has responsibility, this list was not devoid of content. But it still left major areas open to judgement: not only are the benchmarks themselves unclear (e.g., what precisely does transparency and accountability mean?), but there is wide variation even among OECD member states, which putatively meet those standards. So in examining the way in which the GOV secretariat applied these standards in the accession process, we get a glimpse into one of the most central parts of the GOV mandate: the assessment of governance sub-systems, the application of standards, and the judgement of whether those standards are met or not.

We can examine the governance accession report on Estonia, Israel, and Slovenia (OECD, Public Governance and Territorial Development Directorate, Public Governance Committee 2009c; OECD, Public Governance and Territorial Development Directorate, Public Governance Committee 2009b; OECD, Public Governance and Territorial Development Directorate, Public Governance Committee 2009a) to get a good sense of the challenges.[20] Every accession report for GOV had the same basic chapters (following the building blocks): structure of government, budget practices and procedures, human resource management, integrity, transparency and accountability, e-government, management of regulatory quality and administrative simplification, and multi-level governance. There were several important general features of the reports. First, since each chapter was drafted by a subject-matter expert (most from within GOV, but some by outside contracted consultants), the chapters are quite variable in tone, structure and approach. Some used models, others referred simply (where possible) to OECD instruments, standards, norms or trends. Second, consistent with the roadmap, the PGC was to provide Council with a "formal opinion on the degree of 'coherence' between the policies of candidate countries and those of OECD member countries" (the formula was the same in the prefaces to all three reports). The approach to determining coherence was couched modestly:

The assessment of "coherence" in this report is intended to provide an indication of how aligned the candidate country's governance policies, institutions, programmes, etc. are with those of OECD member countries. Differences are expected as even OECD countries do not constitute a homogenous group with identical policy practices. The aim is to determine if [Estonia/Israel/Slovenia]'s approach to public governance is consistent with the spectrum of experiences and good practices in OECD member countries. It is not the purpose of this report to provide policy options or recommendations regarding the public governance system in [Estonia/Israel/Slovenia], but rather to identify common trends, reform efforts and challenges experienced by [Estonia/Israel/Slovenia] and OECD countries.[21]

However, there was no detailed definition of what "coherence" with OECD practices and standards might mean. Indeed, the entire accession process for all five countries left this important question both unposed and unanswered, beyond vague references to adherence to market principles and democracy, as well as formal provisions of the OECD *acquis*, which, as we have seen, is quite general in most instances. As we will see in a moment, that led to interesting mental gymnastics in each chapter to arrive at euphemisms to capture what coherence or consistency might entail.

Third, and perhaps most strikingly, none of the chapters made the distinction between formal and informal practices. A country might have the ideal integrity regime on paper (and many do), but its practice might be far from perfect. To be fair, the authors were bound in two senses. While outside sources of information were occasionally tapped, the vast bulk of the evidentiary basis for the report was OECD research, and that research is marked by a heavy reliance on self-reporting (surveys and questionnaires, even in the context of peer reviews) and a focus on formal legal mechanisms. This is linked to the diplomatic tango that is part of even the accession process for non-members: these are states, and states are defined by their legal regimes. To ask and probe about informal realities is tantamount to impugning the testimony of public officials, and hence of the integrity of the state itself. This second point should not be taken too far – committee members did often ask difficult questions, and require concessions. This dynamic was especially evident in the review of Russia, where both the report itself and a number of committee members raised reservations about aspects of governance in the Russian Federation.[22]

The essential question behind accession is whether a country meets OECD standards in order to be eligible for membership. The operative words here are "meets" and "standards". What does it mean to "meet a standard"? Assume for a moment that the standard is crystal clear – as a fanciful example, that the state must have a president. A state either has a president or it does not, and so that would be an easy and unambiguous standard to apply and to "meet". But we saw above that the both the building blocks and the actual governance *acquis* instruments are very much open to interpretation. They consist almost entirely of guidelines that member states must interpret and apply. The OECD is less about the application of mathematical standards, black or white, than it is about engaging in long-term dialogue about those standards and gradually nudging members towards some measure of convergence. But that does not obviate the fact that at any given point, if one has to make reference to the standards themselves, outside of legal instruments they are loose. Adding to the difficulty is the fact that OECD members themselves show considerable variation in reflecting those standards. So, one has ambiguous standards, and a membership that itself is variable in achieving or reflecting them. How to judge, then? There are at least four conceptually rigorous ways in which one could arrive at a conclusion. The first would be to posit an "ideal" OECD state in terms of its fidelity to the OECD *acquis*, and try to measure how close or distant a candidate might be. Some might nominate Finland, since it seems to be at the top of the OECD league tables on most measures. However, since all OECD members have "equal status", and since a degree of variation is to be expected, that is a non-starter. A second might be the "bright line" approach, suggesting that if countries are below a sharp standard, they fail, and if above, even if only marginally, they succeed. The problem is that virtually no OECD governance standards are "bright lines". A third approach might be to try to discern different models or regimes in selected governance areas that characterize different groups of OECD members – all the models would be consistent with the *acquis*, but vary in significant ways without straying beyond the boundaries of membership requirements. A fourth might be to posit an eight-dimensional space structured by GOV's eight building blocks, and plot OECD member positions within that space. If a candidate country fell short on one or more dimensions, it still might remain in the space due to meeting or surpassing some others. This approach is theoretically attractive, but obviously impractical.

Instead, the reports opted for the term "coherence". This is weaker than "consistent", but does imply some logical connection. However, even the idea of "coherence" was rhetorically softened in at least five ways:

1. Softening the meaning of coherence: The only definition in the document of "coherence" was that it actually meant "aligned". But since OECD countries are not uniform, then coherence means consistent with the "spectrum of experiences and good practices in OECD member countries". (Emphasis added)
2. Euphemisms to project coherence tempered by variation: "on par with", "similar to", "akin to", "aligned", "quite similar to", "resembles practices", "not atypical", "in line with".
3. Unspecified references to practices (and hence implied standards) among OECD countries: "spectrum of experiences", "like many OECD countries", "most OECD countries", "commonly used by OECD countries", "common trends", "in many other", "quite similar to those in many OECD", "such as practiced by certain OECD countries", "the trend", "largely in accordance with".
4. Assertions that coherence meant common challenges and aspirations, rather than consistency with practice per se: "experiencing the same problems", "commitment", "a shared interest in a goal".

5. Tolerate inconsistency: For example, (1) despite the evidence in the chapter on multi-level governance that OECD members were clearly going in a different direction than Slovenia, this nonetheless did not render Slovenia "an outlier", (2) the lack of central oversight in Israel over freedom of information implementation.

We are not suggesting that these strategies were deliberately adopted to make a bad case look good. Rather, they arise organically in the very nature of assessing very complex systems and sub-systems of governance, especially against norms or principles as opposed to instruments. Also, in most respects, these three acceded states were "easy" in the sense that even casual intuition would suggest that they meet most standards of what would be defined as a liberal-democratic, free-market society (though Israel's problems with its neighbours made accession more challenging).

Nor are we suggesting that these rhetorical strategies meant empty assessment. In part the very complexity of the exercise – assessing an entire human resource management system in the first place, as against practices in a variety of 30 other countries in the second – means an inevitable degree of aggregation in comments and assessments. But, despite the claim that the exercise would not involve recommendations, in fact all three of the countries had some shortcomings or "misalignment" pointed out in the reports (often in support of changes already underway in the countries). We can draw two examples from each case:

Estonia
- Structure and Coordination of Government:
  o Strategic planning capacity could be improved (para. 32)
  o Improved coordination of sectoral and long-term budget plans (para. 32)
- Human Resource Management:
  o Revising the civil service act (para. 125)

Israel
- Human Resource Management:
  o Strategic workforce planning, delegation of HRM authorities, performance management strategy, etc. (para. 121)
- Integrity in the Public Sector:
  o "Strengthening co-ordination between integrity actors; ensuring continued awareness by public servants of expected behaviour; managing conflict of interests as they arise in unforeseen circumstances; balancing ministries discretion in public procurement with effective controls; initiating partnership with business and non-profit sectors to strengthen integrity; and active monitoring of 'at risk' areas for potential conflict of interests/corruption". (para. 157)

Slovenia

- Human Resource Management:
  - o "There are, however, some elements that represent windows of opportunity to improve the Slovenian HRM practices such as: the complexity of the civil service structure and the salary structure; and the weak link between performance and salary. In addition, clearer recruitment and promotion mechanisms for all civil servants; clearer criteria for assessment; and a comprehensive impact assessment of the reforms may help to increase coherence with OECD countries. Strengthening strategic workforce planning to position the civil service in the future and by ascertaining the skills and competencies necessaries to meet long-term goals; and a change management programme to keep the momentum for reform with a closer dialogue with public employees remain as the pending tasks for Slovenian authorities". (para. 134)
- E-Government:
  - o "Slovenia faces the challenge of identifying a right combination of financial and non financial incentive mechanisms to enhance e-government development in ministries and agencies. The current incentive system in the MPA [Ministry of Public Administration] allows for the possibility to provide financial rewards based on performance as well as on individual participation in e-government collaboration projects. While this can be considered to be a strong tool to enhance a culture of collaboration in the administration, the concrete application and impact will need to be further assessed in light of the government's broader HR strategy". (para. 231)

Conclusion

Ougaard has argued that the OECD is "is an important institutional network – or rather a series of networks – that is part of the evolving global political superstructure" (Ougaard 2010: 45). We made the network argument at the outset of this book, and have tried to show five distinctive networked tools or instruments that the OECD – GOV in particular – uses to achieve its objectives of generating ideas, providing strategic direction, and encouraging convergence around basic norms and principles. It is clear from the discussion in this chapter that these are indeed networked tools, and the OECD is indeed a preeminent networked organization. To revisit the ten characteristics of networks we listed in Chapter 1:

1. *Networks are non-hierarchal, so that "orders" and "commands" are not their basic vocabulary.* We saw that the *acquis* has a few hard spikes that demand compliance (if countries accede to the instrument) but most of it consists of norms, principles, guidelines and such. These are applied (as with the accession reports) in a manner that shies away from "recommendations".

2. *Networks consist of interconnected nodes.* Every one of the tools discussed in this chapter is "nodal". Peer review relies on contributions of experts from member states. The *acquis* is a dense tapestry of agreements or announcements embedded in relations of states and projected outwards both to members and to non-members.
3. *Network nodes need not all be equal, despite the flatness and lack of hierarchy.* The OECD interacts with member states, large and small, with non-members across the globe, with other international organizations of some size and stature, like the IMF and the World Bank and the European Commission.
4. *Network links and connections consist of exchanges.* If one could imagine each communication, report, publication, conference or meeting that the OECD engages in as photons, it would be a blinding blizzard of constantly moving and morphing points of light.
5. *Networks in which the primary exchanges are information (as opposed to money or goods or services) have specific characteristics in themselves: they are open, focus on quality, and are engaged in constant search as old information gets stale.* The GaaG exercise is a good illustration of this characteristic. It took almost five years of cautious technical studies to produce the first GaaG report, which had to be of the highest quality to reinforce and reflect OECD technical credibility. The second edition reached higher. The entire exercise is geared to the production and release of open information that will then influence states.
6. *Networks are typically voluntary. Rules tend to be quite loose, since part of the value of the network to its members comes from a diversity of participants.* The *acquis* and the plasticity of its norms and implementation mechanisms are perfect illustrations.
7. *Networks prefer norms to rules, though they can occasionally arrive at rules that apply to most if not all members.* The *acquis* and the MENA initiative reflect this characteristic.
8. *Networks have no single, final arbiters. To the extent that networks render "decisions" they do so through complex interactions through interconnections and exchanges. Rather than arbiters, networks tend to rely on brokers. Brokers rely on trust.* Perhaps the best illustration of this characteristic is the peer review process. We saw in detail how a balance is struck between trust (peers, an objective process, rigorous data collection that is nonetheless vetted by the reviewed country) and objectivity (the limits to the editing process).
9. *Networks are flexible, often in a condition of flux, change, decline and growth. They can have some institutional boundaries and inner architecture, but in comparison to more hierarchical organizations, they are closer to clouds or schools of fish – they have discernable shape, but are always in motion.* The accession and enhanced engagement processes illustrate this well, as does the regional initiative in MENA. The current OECD leadership

understands quite well that the OECD is an organizational shark: it must keep moving constantly forward or die.

10. *Networks are embedded in environments, and those environments can influence network growth and development, as networks – either unconsciously (e.g., a school of fish reconfiguring itself in the face of a predator) or deliberately – adapt and develop.* Both the accession process and the efforts to engage regionally, both in MENA, but for example also in Southeast Asia, illustrate the logic of adaptation and extension.

In reviewing the instruments that the OECD and GOV in particular have at their disposal, it is striking how "soft" they are in two key senses. First, members and non-members must voluntarily agree to engage in those instruments and processes in the first place. Of course, there may be external pressures, such as the MENA states' realization that they are competing for investment, and that investors assess political risk as well as the complexity of doing business. Nonetheless, peer reviews must both be initiated by the reviewed country and accepted by it. The *acquis* is a patchwork of a few legally binding agreements and a host of pronouncements and encouragements, again, which have to be voluntarily accepted. GaaG relies largely on the voluntary submission of data from member states, and is nothing more than a presentation of comparative statistics whereby governments may – if they wish – benchmark their own performance. MENA is driven by the agreement's Arab and North African states. The accession process hinges on invitations and positive responses to those invitations, though there is a slightly harder edge in that accession does require actually meeting some firm standards (not least, the OECD Convention itself) as well as more nebulous ones (as in the GOV portion of the *acquis*).

Second, there is wide accommodation to national legal traditions and practices, and of course to any eventual implementation of OECD recommendations. As we noted, there are ways to buttress this – for example, in peer reviews, the peer pressure that comes in *tour d' table* committee meetings. But ultimately, the OECD has no enforcement capacity beyond moral suasion and the power of data, and it is well aware that it is tip-toeing through minefields of state protocol and the diplomatic niceties of respecting the sovereign dignity of the states with which it interacts. After all, the OECD could scold more than it does, it could wag fingers, wrap knuckles, or even glare purposively – but it cannot, because it is a state organization dealing with other states, all of which have equal status and dignity. Kept in decent check, this dynamic is not harmful and actually helps the OECD achieve its objectives. But it can become a liability. The insidious absurdity of MENA – promoting "good governance" in places like Libya and Yemen – is coupled with the contortions in the accession reports to somehow mesh quite divergent governance practices with some putative "OECD norm".

This chapter might have given the impression that there is almost no content to OECD norms and principles, just an every-shimmering dance of Northern Lights that gives the impression of substance, but is ephemeral. The hard question is – beyond the conventions and recommendations and decisions – whether the OECD and GOV have, in the more fundamental philosophical sense – a view on governance. In Chapter 1 we cited opinion that the OECD was a key purveyor of NPM in the 1990s, a stalking horse for neo-liberal governance and economic prescriptions, such as structural adjustment (Sullivan 1997: 41). The next chapter will explore this question through a content analysis of key GOV documents and reports. GOV does indeed have a view, but a view that is less one of content than of strategy. Less of a Bible, and more of a playbook.

5
Modernizing Governance: Is There an OECD View?

Its 50th anniversary in 2011 was both a celebration and a time of reflection for the OECD: what, exactly, is the organization about? In the early morning after the high-level delegates had left for their capitals, one could stroll down the quiet rue de Franqueville, and see large posters along the iron fence that guards the main building – like standards raised in medieval times on castle walls, declaring their colours to the world, defining themselves and defying others.[1]

One read:

> Our Mission: Better policies for better lives
> Our Vision: For a stronger, cleaner, fairer world
> Our Values: Ethical, objective, pioneering, bold, open
> Our Means: The OECD measures, analyses, and compares to stimulate better policies for better lives.

On its web page,[2] the OECD describes its core values:

> Objective: Our analyses and recommendations are independent and evidence-based.
> Open: We encourage debate and a shared understanding of critical global issues.
> Bold: We dare to challenge conventional wisdom starting with our own.
> Pioneering: We identify and address emerging and long-term challenges.
> Ethical: Our credibility is built on trust, integrity and transparency.

These are lofty aspirations, easy to dismiss as self-promotion, delusion or fabrication. But the words hang silently in their colours on the gates of the OECD and within its walls, where thousands of staff and visitors pass them each day. Do they amount to a distinctive view of the world – in contrast, for example, to the World Bank or the IMF? Do they seep into the way that the OECD and GOV see governance?

As previous chapters noted, the OECD has the reputation for being the standard-bearer of NPM, particularly in the 1990s (Premfors 1998; Larmour 2005). On the other hand, our own analysis of GOV in previous chapters paints a more ambiguous picture – standards are not that clear, even with "building blocks" and accession reviews. We saw that two key overview and summary reports – *Governance in Transition* (1995) and *Modernising Government* (2005) – had different orientations, and in fact the 2005 version was somewhat critical of the previous one. Moreover, the governance challenges chapter in GaaG 2009 (discussed in Chapter 4) explicitly criticized NPM. Other observers agree with this more nuanced view. Looking at the organization as a whole, they have noted that its siloed nature allows considerable variation in the tone and philosophical foundation of reports and research – for example between the economics side of the OECD and those directorates dealing with social issues (Deacon & Hulse 1997; Mahon 2008).

There are also some other problems in trying to pin down an "OECD" view on governance. First, it is a moving target. We saw that the history of the governance and public management directorate, at least to the mid-1980s, was very much a work-in-progress, with more groping for principles and organizational practices than a firm philosophical view of the world. Second, the directorate is fairly small as a whole, and even smaller in terms of permanent staff. That means that reports and reviews are written in large part by project-based staff brought in for a particular project. The range of publications is enormous – country reviews, reports, guidelines, briefs, occasional papers, decisions and other *acquis* instruments. A decision has to be made as to which set of documents will really express the OECD view. And, as we discussed in Chapter 3, there is actually a variety of sites within the OECD but outside of GOV, that pronounce on governance issues. Finally, the strictures of being a membership-based organization means, as we discussed earlier, that the OECD view is an amalgam of work done within the Secretariat (GOV) and contributions by members on committees and working groups and networks.

However, despite these difficulties, the OECD and GOV continuously use the language of comparison and transfer in terms of standards of at least "good", if not "best", practices. The OECD position on governance cannot be devoid of content – it may draw lines in a wavy and fuzzy fashion, but it draws lines nonetheless. As well, the founding OECD convention referred to "the preservation of individual liberty", and while it has consorted with colonels in the past and sheiks in the present, it is widely agreed both inside and outside the OECD that the organization stands for market-based liberal democracy. The trick is understanding how that content and that commitment is posed specifically as a mode of OECD discourse. We will not pretend that upon a thorough reading of GOV documentation that one will arrive at a clear checklist of hard standards whereby one could easily and unambiguously measure, say, Germany against Chile. As we shall see, however, there is enough content to allow measures between a Germany and Chile, and an Afghanistan or Libya. But checklists and guides – despite GOV's constant production of them – are only part of the real content. Rather, the OECD's view on governance is a composite of rhetorical strategies that posit common threats and challenges to member states – one of which is constantly changing and challenging world – and which creates ideational markers in a dialogical space, as well as inducing constant efforts at reform.

This chapter proceeds by focusing on key documents published by GOV since 2000. In the first part, we discuss a key framework paper published in 2000 that set the agenda for PUMA and GOV as well as the OECD as whole. The second part revisits the *acquis* and provides a more detailed and nuanced discussion of what the different components contain. The third part of the chapter conducts a discourse analysis – setting aside governance principles and standards as such, and focusing more on tone and frames of argument within which those principles and standards are located.

Governance Outreach Initiative (2000)

OECD documents are sometimes like a dance of the veils. They shimmer with seductive platitudes, obscuring any hard spines of content and meaning. The Council's 2000 document *Governance Outreach Initiative* (for this section referred to as *Outreach*) is an excellent example (OECD 2000). Here is the first paragraph of the SG's introduction: "Democratic governance ... that ideal which strives to balance the interests of all individuals in society regardless of colour, creed, wealth or political persuasion; a balance founded on the rule of law which places no one beyond it and applies equally to all in a just and equitable way; which fosters a belief in and support of democratic institutions and enables individuals, families and communities to attain the objectives which they set for themselves while respecting the rights of others to do like-wise". It would be difficult to conceive of, let alone draft, a denser homage to all that is good: balance, non-discrimination, rule of law, equality, equity, families, rights. But SG introductions tend to be florid as a matter of course.

As discussed in Chapter 4, Donald Johnston as SG launched the outreach initiative for the OECD, which SG Gurría then adopted with zeal and extended considerably through enlargement and enhanced engagement. This 2000 document was the first positioning of governance as a key (one of eight) priority for the OECD, and laid out a strategy for outreach to non-members and other organizations on the governance file. It demonstrated a stronger emphasis on networking and engaging the OECD more broadly around the world and more intensively with other actors. Included, for example, were high-level seminars and a Special Dialogue between OECD Ministers and Ministers from non-OECD countries, held before the 1999 OECD Ministerial Council Meeting. *Outreach* included a Statement of

Governance Priorities for the 21st Century – something intended to be a "living document" that would link "good governance" to social and economic development. The cross-directorate initiatives that headlined the document (initiatives from across the OECD and not just PUMA) were:

- Improving the market economy: working with APEC on regulatory reform; undertaking an extensive outreach effort to strengthen competition policy and enforcement in Asia, Eastern Europe and other regions
- Corporate governance: with the World Bank to organize "regional round-tables" to promote the implementation of the OECD Principles of Corporate Governance in non-member countries; roundtables in Russia, Asia and Latin America
- Bribery and corruption: the South Eastern Europe Stability Pact Anti-Corruption Initiative, the Anti-Corruption Network for Transition Economies and the ADB-OECD Regional Forum on Combating corruption in the Asia-Pacific Region; a conference with USAID, PriceWaterhouseCoopers and the US Center for International Private Enterprise on the role of the private sector in fighting corruption
- Public sector reform: PUMA helped organize the Second Annual Global Forum on Reinventing Government in Brasilia; work closely with the Italian government on the Third Global Forum
- Increasing public service capacity (primarily tax policy): with Russia, China, 13 Central and Eastern European countries; Asia Development Bank
- Establishing governance in areas of conflict: regional consultations with the United Nations Economic Commission for Africa (UNECA) and the Organization for African Unity

The bulk of the document consisted of an Annex I that contained a "Draft Statement of Governance Priorities for the 21st Century", and an Annex 2 on the OECD's current governance work, an Attachment A that provided a list (similar to the 2007 "Building Blocks") of documents and links that supported "OECD Governance Best Practices and Policy Lessons", and an Attachment B that outlined key elements of the OECD's work on governance. Together, they provide a rich field of indicators as to what the OECD considered both important in governance (despite its ritualistic incantation that "one size does not fit all") and how it framed best practices. We may see them as successive layers on a watercolour, each one relatively thin itself, but together providing some contours and concentrations of pigment.

The Annex 1 Priorities document began with an emphasis on building capacity in the public sector, the corporate sector, and civil society, and in each case there was emphasis on accountability relations and balance among the three sectors. In discussing the increasing pressures on governments coming from globalization, once again the document highlighted the importance of "promoting openness and accountability". It then moved to common principles of good governance ("successful governance systems tend to display common attributes, upon which can be built clear principles of governance"): legitimacy; rule of law; transparency, accountability, and integrity; efficiency; coherence; adaptability; and participation and consultation.

The Annex 2 Overview of Governance Work and the Key Elements of the OECD's Work on Governance Issues highlighted seven areas of effort across the OECD:

1. Establishing effective institutional and policy frameworks for markets. The goal is market efficiency through corporate governance regimes (reinforcing accountability to shareholders and transparency of financial information), competition policy systems that do not restrict competition in markets (it called for competition agencies to interfere as little as possible with competition but also to fight monopolization and abuses of dominant position), and regulatory reform aimed at balancing market efficiency and the public good (through, for example, government-wide regulatory reform policy, improvement of regulatory practices within the line ministries).

   Under this heading, there was an explicit definition of the elements of effective governance:
   - an institutional and legal framework which supports the emergence of an enterprise-based economy;
   - the development of a competitive environment which enhances the efficient functioning of markets, including effective regulatory policies and strong competition laws and enforcement;
   - a good corporate governance framework providing for transparency of corporate structures and operations and the accountability of management;
   - a performance-oriented and efficient public sector;
   - vigorous action to fight corruption and organized crime;
   - sound national policies and institutional frameworks for environmental management;
   - government investment in people through sound education and training policies, and strengthening social safeguards; and
   - fair, equitable and efficient taxation policies.
2. Managing across different levels of government: Decentralization was leading to problems of policy coordination, accountability, and coherence: "the distinction between who finances, delivers, and administers is increasingly unclear in many programmes". Administrative devolution demanded a "focus on agreed results-oriented performance in order to assure accountability".
3. Managing cross-cutting issues to build policy coherence. The document stated that "Tackling cross-cutting issues and building policy coherence is at the heart of the OECD's mission", though it also noted that exces-

sive coherence could create centralization and rigidity – there had to be a balance.

4. Fostering public sector capacities. The emphasis here was on "strategic capacity". A number of areas where member countries were moving were highlighted, as was work that was consequently done by PUMA to expose best practices and lessons. Regarding <u>user fees</u>, the best practices ranged from "establishing clear legal authority through user charging" through to "developing an effective and efficient collection system" and "improving the delivery of services" to "recognizing equity considerations and concerns in user charging". <u>Evaluation</u> practices included, among others, "defining clear objectives for the evaluation process", "linking the evaluation to the budget process", "involving stakeholders in the evaluation process", and "monitoring the follow-up to the evaluation", On <u>contracting out</u> government services, the document stressed, e.g., "addressing the concerns of personnel who may be affected by contracting out", "monitoring contractor performance", and "developing and maintaining the in-house skill-set" necessary for such monitoring. On <u>budgeting and financial management</u>, the report noted trends toward multi-year budgeting, more efforts to get legislative buy-in, greater prudence in forecasting, greater results and performance focus, and the introduction of accrual accounting systems. On <u>performance management</u>: "devolution of decision-making, accountability for performance, measurement and benchmarking of performance, responsiveness to citizens through service quality initiatives, review of performance through programme evaluation and performance auditing". On <u>human resource management</u>, the report only pointed to the need for a high quality workforce and the OECD's role in disseminating comparative statistics and the provision of comparative analysis.

5. Fostering integrity and fighting corruption. This was the one area (see Chapter 4 and below) where there were concrete instruments such as: (a) the 1997 Convention on Combating Bribery of Foreign Public Officials in International Business Transactions; (b) the 1996 Recommendation which committed all OECD Member countries to put an end to the practice of according tax deductibility for bribes made to foreign officials; (c) the 1997 Recommendation which invited OECD countries to adopt appropriate accounting and auditing requirements, and to deny bribing companies access to public procurement procedures; and (d) the 1996 Recommendation concerning Anti-Corruption Proposals for Bilateral Aid Procurement.

6. Relationships between government, business and civil society: The document identified trust as the basic issue, and argued that trust depends on the protection of public interests such as safety and equity, but citizens' trust in turn would speed up market reforms. It highlighted corporate responsibility such as corporate codes of conduct and the OECD's own

Guidelines for Multilateral Enterprises, which are "recommendations by governments to multinational firms, and aim to ensure that activities of multinational firms are in harmony with government policies and strengthen mutual confidence between enterprises and the societies in which they operate" providing "a reference point for firms developing their own codes of conduct".

7. Governance and economic development. The essence of the initiatives by the DAC was partnerships and local ownership of development efforts around economic well-being, social development, environmental sustainability. The main elements of the partnership component were: "to support institutions and mechanisms which facilitate the empowerment of all people, including low-income populations and women, to enable them to become agents of their own development and contribute to the emergence of strong civil societies; provide support for decentralisation programmes, and enhance people participation at local levels, through the support of grass-roots organisations and groups; to sensitise recipient decision makers and aid agency staff to facilitate the adoption of participatory approaches and responsive government".

Outreach demonstrates an "OECD view" circa 2000, built on two decades of thinking and work on public management in TECO and PUMA and the rest of the organization. Before exploring what the view is, we should address the charge of whether PUMA was merely a mouthpiece for NPM (we addressed this earlier in a more historical context in Chapter 2). The strongest NPM flavour from *Outreach* comes in the section on fostering public sector capacities and the references to fostering free markets (e.g., trusting citizens will make market reforms more feasible). At one level there were visible traces of NPM, but at a more fundamental level the story was more complicated. The first level is that PUMA, while it had a responsibility to lead, also had the general responsibility of the OECD to serve members. Many members at the time (primarily but not exclusively in the Anglo-Saxon world) had been experimenting with a variety of NPM instruments and tools (or ones that could be characterized as market friendly and aiming for a small, down-sized state), from privatization to user fees. PUMA had the obligation to keep its finger on its members' collective pulse, provide data and support, and comparative information about best practices, largely whether it believed these policy initiatives to be the best way forward or not. For example, during the 1990s PUMA published a series of Occasional Papers in public management,[3] and to pick one randomly – on "Co-operative Approaches to Regulation" (OECD 1997b), we can clearly see this logic in how the research is framed. The Foreword to the paper notes how "regulatory reform has become a core element of modern, effective government" and how "almost all OECD countries have regulatory reform programmes". It goes on to say that PUMA's work "attempts to respond to the specific needs of the new reform initiatives.

The purpose is to provide better information – drawn from practical experience, comparisons, and international exchanges – on the benefits, costs, and risks of reform in the policies, management, processes and institutions of regulation". In this sense, PUMA may have appeared to be pushing NPM subjects and techniques, but in fact it was simply reflecting the actions and practices of its members. The same is true with the section on fostering public sector capacity in *Outreach*. PUMA was not recommending user fees, it was simply noting that members were increasingly relying on them, and so provided some advice on best practice.

At a second, deeper level, however, consistent with our earlier analysis in this book, the OECD view was considerably more complex in this period that a simple distillation of NPM. If we look closely at *Outreach* and its various components, we can see three broad categories of concepts and benchmarks that made up the OECD view at that time. The first category was ethical. We see throughout the document an emphasis on accountability – accountability of governments to citizens, of corporations to shareholders, and public servants to the government. This is coupled with openness and transparency – it is hard to see how entities can be accountable if they are not transparent in the sense of providing accurate, regular flows of information.

Also contained in this category is the integrity framework. As we noted in Chapter 4, this has evolved into a robust collection of instruments, but was impressive even in 2000. This was not ethics for its own sake, of course, since corruption redistributes wealth in unproductive ways and hobbles market economies, but the framework nonetheless tried to contain bad behaviour, at this stage principally bribes to public officials. Finally, there were injunctions to support citizen participation and trust-building through initiatives to develop better accountability and reduce corruption. Again, this might be dismissed as pre-emptive strikes on public discontent, but if taken seriously would open up the policy-making process considerably.

The second category is what we might term "frameworks". The OECD is part political and part intellectual. On the intellectual side, irrespective of the policy field – whether it be environment or education or governance – it has a strong bias towards integration and completeness. The intellectual habit of comprehensiveness was noted as long ago as 1959 in Lindblom's seminal article on incrementalism (Lindblom 1959; Pal 2011a). There is nothing that a tidy mind fears more than the ad hoc, the incomplete, and the uncoordinated. This is true in the governance field particularly, where government is often consciously or unconsciously thought of as a "machine".[4] Machines should be well-oiled and their various parts working seamlessly with each other to accomplish their ends. Unsurprisingly, therefore, *Outreach* has a strong emphasis on "coherence". It urges coherence between the market and government, and in economic policies, frameworks that integrate corporate governance, competition policy, and regulatory policy. It worries about the impact of decentralization on the coherence of different levels of government, and at the same time the absence of coherence in dealing with cross-cutting policy issues such as ageing. The references to benchmarking and measurement stem from the same impulse – setting standards and then measuring progress towards them is a mechanism of self-awareness that reduces drift and incoherent behaviour.

The final category was management processes. These have no ethical content, though do reflect a "framework" approach. But they are different since they focus more on the effective management of processes. The emphasis on performance and results is one expression of this – one cannot achieve performance and improve results without relatively sophisticated management mechanisms in place. Where this comes out most clearly is in the section dealing with fostering public sector capacity. Each of the items mentioned (user fees, evaluation practices, contracting out, financial management, performance management, human resource management) is connected to a set of management practices suited to the item that encourage reflective management, control of outcomes, self-correction, and performance.

In combination, these categories and their content form a consistent OECD view on the nature of good governance. If combined well in a system, they would create a "governance sweet spot" of ethical principles and practices; overarching, coherent and coordinated policy frameworks; and solid management of key processes. Figure 5.1 gives a sense of how this might be conceptualized. Even so, there is a certain necessary vagueness in what these might entail in reality. Countries like Finland and Canada probably come close to occupying the governance "sweet spot", but that is not to say that the way

Figure 5.1   The "Governance Sweet Spot"

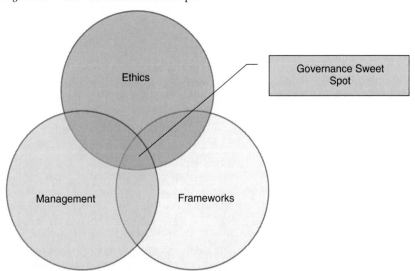

that they arrange their performance management systems, for example, is the only best way. Even countries that might be some distance from the "sweet spot" might have sub-elements of their governance systems that are different yet equivalent in effect.

This was the OECD view in 2000. What was it seven years later as GOV assembled its building blocks?

The Building Blocks (2007)

As previous chapters (see Chapter 2 for a detailed list of the elements) have discussed, the "Thematic Building Blocks for Guiding Elements on Public Governance and Management in Global Relations" (OECD 2007a) was developed as part of an exercise to prepare for enhanced engagement and accession. There were eight blocks in total: budget practices and procedures, human resource management, integrity and corruption resistance, open government, e-government readiness, centres of government, management of regulatory quality, and multi-level governance. We can immediately see an overlap of some categories with the *Outreach* document: multi-level government; integrity and fighting corruption (by 2007 "fighting" had been changed to "resisting"); human resource management; budgeting. Openness was there in *Outreach* as a theme, but not an explicit item. It is not surprising that there is not more overlap, since *Outreach* was an OECD-wide statement of governance work, while Building Blocks was GOV-specific.

We shall proceed by examining each of the building blocks and the instruments that are their foundation. A feature of the approach was that each building block was divided into technical goals of public management reform (three to six), with corresponding institutional arrangements. The emphasis on "reform" is something that we will pick up again in the next section of the chapter.

Block 1: Budgeting

The four technical goals of reform are: (1) aggregate fiscal discipline, (2) effective allocation and reallocation of resources, (3) promotion of efficient delivery of services, (4) budget transparency and accountability. Together, these strive to create systems that permit the government to control expenditures, establish priorities and shift resources as necessary, reduce costs, and subject all aspects of the budgeting and public expenditure system to outside scrutiny. The existing OECD (there was no GOV guidance) instrument was the OECD Best Practices for Budget Transparency (OECD 2002). The first part of that document specified the types of continuous reports that should be issued by governments long with the budget itself – with advice that these contain financial data, but also economic assumptions and information on performance. The document's second part dealt with specific disclosures that these should additionally feature, parti-cularly recommending a clear accounting of tax expenditures. The third part listed practices that would ensure the quality and integrity of the reports, such as internal/external audits, plus public and parliamentary scrutiny.

The GOV building block draws on this document but goes well beyond it. For example, the instrument says nothing about public-private part-nerships or outsourcing, whereas GOV adds a technical goal of effective allocation and reallocation of resources.

Block 2: Human resource management

The three technical goals are: (1) workforce planning and management, (2) core values, and (3) staff performance and capacity. The institutional arrangements to support these goals boil down to planning and monitoring human resources, encouraging merit and clear accountabilities, and a focus on performance. There were no OECD or GOV instruments listed as supports for this building block, beyond country peer reviews of HRM. Accordingly we have selected a recent HRM review of Brazil (OECD 2010j) as an illustration of how the building block is actualized and the sorts of recommendations the OECD makes, based on its implicit views of what constitutes best practice.

The report was divided into four chapters: workforce planning and man-agement, strengthening government capacity, enhancing performance, and a concluding chapter on strengthening reform. On workforce planning, the report highlighted the challenges of an ageing population and dealing with pension issues in the public sector. It suggested that planning in Brazil was "input focused" and not yet enough based on analysing trade-offs. It baldly stated that "Managers' accountability for workforce planning is very weak. Workforce planning needs to be made part of strategic documents and managers need to focus on plans that take an overall strategic view of their workforce (jobs, competencies, future changes) ..." (OECD 2010j: 117). It also criticized a job classification system that was too rigid and did not allow for strategic decision-making and flexibility. It closed with a suggestion to increase the diversity of the public sector workforce.

The chapter on strengthening government capacity argued that staff capa-city was "undermanaged", with limited management of competencies, nar-rowly defined merit selection systems, and rigid and narrow job categories which prevent the optimal use of human resources and limit opportunities for staff to develop their careers through lateral mobility or vertical progression. "The government needs to take a number of measures to develop its civil ser-vice into a fully modern civil service similar to those of most advanced econ-omies" (OECD 2010j: 183). It highlighted limitations in the definition of merit in the Brazilian public service, and recommended an in-depth restructuring of civil servants' job categories and career opportunities, entailing reductions and changes in job categories, the classification system, and procedures for career mobility. The performance chapter closed with the recommendation that in order to respond to pressures to enhance efficiency, Brazil would have to develop more sophisticated systems of staff performance management, including the management of senior staff. Interestingly, it did not recommend an emphasis on performance pay, but rather opportunities for promotions that would be in part performance-based. The closing chapter emphasized the importance of maintaining core values in the public service, even as new values were being added and layered on. The report's discussion of the role of values is important enough to be quoted at length:

> The values embedded in the public service culture, which guide the behaviour of public servants, are an important part of governance. Public service values such as respect for legality, integrity and political neutrality are among the defining features of a democratic society. As such, they tend to be enshrined in the legislation that applies to the public service or in constitutions, supported by codes of conduct, and protected by administrative procedures and sanctions. Well-defined values that lead to consistent government practices are essential to maintaining trust in government. They reflect what the public service is trying to achieve, help design collective and individual objectives, and maintain the collective public service culture.
>
> In OECD member countries these core values include traditional values such as integrity, impartiality, legality, probity and merit and newer values such as efficiency, transparency, diversity and user orientation. Traditional core values usually revolve around three main principles: ensuring ethics and integrity in the public service; securing the continuity of the public service; and guaranteeing the legality of decisions. It is these values that have justified an employment framework for public servants different from that of employees under general labour laws in most OECD member countries.
>
> Broadening the definition of the public service's core values has become a key strategic objective in many OECD member countries as a way to increase citizens' trust in government. Also, with the introduction of more managerial flexibility in public management and less control on inputs and processes, countries have sought to incorporate these values in management processes. Values-based management is viewed as a more efficient way of maintaining core values in the public service than controls that hinder the move towards more performance-based management. (OECD 2010j: 226)

The main recommendations had to do with the implementation of new values and balancing them against traditional ones. In the service of this reform goal, however, this chapter was typical in the level of detailed recommendations it made on the various components of the reform process. It provided exhaustive detail on the public service values and ethics codes in OECD countries generally (based on OECD surveys and reported in GaaG). In analysing the situation in Brazil, after these OECD benchmarks had been reviewed, the chapter was forthrightly critical about rigidities and lack of transparency, highlighting "weaknesses in processes that maintain and strengthen the collective ethos". It made suggestions on codes of conduct and their integration into HRM management, as well as the appropriate division of responsibilities in HRM bodies, again drawing on OECD best practices (especially the delegation of HRM responsibilities from central agencies to line ministries). It criticized Brazil for lacking long-term vision, trained HRM staff, and flexibility in career paths. Finally, it also provided advice (again, with the usual caveat that there is no single formula, and then going on to refer to OECD member experiences) on the implementation of reforms: careful sequencing and an emphasis on a strategic approach, which the report did not see in the Brazilian case. This chapter alone had detailed "in-set boxes" sometimes running several pages with illustrations of approaches to different issues from France, Finland, Canada, Australia, Chile, UK, US, Norway, Spain, Mexico, Ireland, and Korea.

HRM reviews take place regularly, and will differ in their recommendations depending on the country in question. However, from the preceding we can see a template of assessment, an "OECD view" and approach. The building block technical goals were faithfully reflected in the Brazil review, with the addition of a detailed discussion of reform strategies and implementation. When one steps back from the detail, one sees an emphasis on planning, strategy, flexibility, and capacity (both in organizational terms and human resources). Coupled with that is a strong emphasis on systems thinking harnessed to managerial oversight, but balanced with flexibility within the overall system. Even though the building block mentioned core values as one of three technical goals, it is interesting to see the strong emphasis the review placed on traditional public service values, ethics, and the balance with "new values" such as citizen service.

The report was not a whitewash. The criticisms were voluminous, direct, and detailed. It is a good example of the diagnostic power of peer review, discussed in Chapter 4. Not only are peers brought to bear, but there is an almost microscopic assessment of the Brazilian situation in each of the areas. As well, the full weight of OECD practice through specific references to members' systems is relied upon to set what are in effect standards or benchmarks (despite the ritualistic denial that they are). It is true that the experiences cited for Canada and, say France or Norway, in a particular field differ. But there is also no doubt that certain key practices are considered "modern": for example, delegated authorities for HRM management; clear, performance-related and simple classification systems; a strong ethics framework, and so on.

Block 3: Integrity and corruption resistance

As we noted in Chapter 4, the building block of integrity and corruption resistance is one of the most developed in the GOV toolkit, in the sense that it has the greatest number and strongest types of instruments.[5] Some of these instruments were discussed in Chapter 4, so here we will focus on the common content they share in terms of a "view" on corruption and on integrity, as well as the approach reflected in the guide to assessment. We have already noted one key characteristic, and that is that while these are (by OECD norms) quite strong instruments in terms of setting standards, they allow for a great deal of latitude in institutional design and implementation. However, here we are less interested in the technique behind the instruments, and more on the actual content. The overarching commonality is a strong moral stance against corruption, bribery, and inappropriate influence in the policy process, as well as support for ethics and integrity in the public service. Systemic deficits in integrity cripple economic growth and affect state support for markets and economic development, with wealth siphoned off in unproductive ways. The mere fact that there is such a robust set of instruments underscores the seriousness with which the OECD has taken this issue. We shall examine here four of these instruments – ethical conduct, managing conflict of interest, public procurement, and lobbying.

The four instruments all have the same structure – a brief recommendation which is accompanied by a more detailed list of principles or guidelines. The recommendations on ethical conduct (1998) and on public procurement are slightly more detailed in suggesting that countries develop policy frameworks in each case. The ethical conduct recommendation has 12 principles to guide the management of ethics in the public service. A premium is placed on transparency and guidance to public servants, an integration of ethics with other management policies and HRM policies, and accountability. The conflict of interest (2003) guideline is considerably more detailed. It begins by setting out core principles (serving the public interest, supporting transparency and scrutiny, promoting individual responsibility, and engendering an organizational culture intolerant of conflicts of interest). It then provides recommendations on how to develop a policy framework as well as an implementation framework. In both cases, there is a strong emphasis on clear rules, transparency, and partnerships. The public procurement (2008) recommendation is accompanied by ten principles, the first two of which focus on transparency, and the second two on management systems. The next three address compliance and monitoring, and the last three concern accountability and control, and the need to engage with civil society organizations. The lobbying recommendation (2010) also has ten principles, divided among building a framework (rules and guidelines), enhancing transparency (including engaging civil society), fostering a culture of integrity, and mechanisms for effective implement-ation, compliance and review.

Of the four instruments, three have definitions of the phenomenon they are regulating: lobbying, procurement, and conflict of interest. The ethical conduct recommendation has no definition of ethics, and focuses instead on management frameworks. Lobbying is defined as: "the oral or written communication with a public official to influence legislation, policy or administrative decisions, often focuses on the legislative branch at the national and sub-national levels". The procurement principles take the approach of listing violations to integrity (which is defined as behaviour in line with the public interest) such as bribery, nepotism, and fraud. A conflict of interest is defined as "a conflict between the public duty and private interests of a public official, in which the public official has private-capacity interests which could improperly influence the performance of their official duties and responsibilities".

None of these definitions are distinctive or new – in fact, they are widely understood. They do not reflect an "OECD view" per se, except for the fact that the OECD is flagging these issues as of great importance. The deeper resonances are in the way the principles are cast: (1) they consistently push for policy and management frameworks in each of the fields, encouraging a more holistic view rather than disconnected bits and pieces of legislation and programmes, (2) they suggest the integration of the specific policy in question in horizontal ways with other overarching policy frameworks, and (3) they all emphasize transparency and engagement with civil society and stakeholders.

Block 4: Internal and external reporting: Open government

The open government building block has four technical goals: (1) trans-parency, (2) accessibility, (3) responsiveness, and (4) inclusiveness. Trans-parency is designed to ensure that governments will be "exposed to public scrutiny and challenge" and involves legal instruments such as access to information laws but also the regular publication of performance reports and strategic plans. Accessibility demands that governments have independent institutions to provide oversight on access to information (e.g., ombudsmen), but also instruments such as citizens' charters, one-stop shops, on-line services and multiple channels. Responsiveness and inclusiveness are meant to involve the public as broadly as possible.

There are no OECD instruments to support this building block, but there are some principles and checklists. One is the 2001 OECD publication, *Citizens as Partners: Information, Consultation and Public Participation in Policy-Making* (OECD 2001a), which is described as "a practical guide to informing, consulting and engaging citizens in the development of public policy". Two others were parts of *Promise and Problems of E-Democracy* (OECD 2003d) and

Evaluating Public Participation in Policy-Making (OECD 2005d). The first was a guide for officials to give them practical advice on strengthening the relations between government and citizens. The booklet argued that strengthening these relations would lead to better public policy, greater trust in government, and ultimately stronger democracy. Once again, as we saw in previous pages, the OECD instinct is to "build a framework". This was the first recommended step. "When embarking on strengthening government-citizen relations, building a framework is a prerequisite. A framework provides the setting, in which these relations can evolve and be strengthened. It is about the legal rights of citizens to information, consultation and active participation, about governmental policies and about the institutions charged with the tasks. It also covers the evaluation of activities and general capacities to conduct them" (OECD 2001a: 27). It argued that maintaining the right balance between access and privacy required a legal framework with sound legislation, clear mechanisms, and an independent judiciary. The guidelines on consultations supported the idea of "active participation" where citizens "make an active and original contribution to policy-making", and once again, provided tips on developing a framework around the participation.

The key part of *Promise and Problems of E-Democracy* that supports the open government building block is a set of ten guiding principles for successful on-line consultation. The overarching assumption behind the report and the principles was that "Engaging citizens in policy-making is a sound investment in the design and delivery of better public policies and a core element of good governance". The principles were:

1. Start planning early
2. Demonstrate commitment
3. Guarantee personal data protection
4. Tailor your approach to fit your target group
5. Integrate online consultation with traditional methods
6. Test and adapt your tools
7. Promote on-line consultation
8. Analyze the results
9. Provide feedback
10. Evaluate the consultation process and its impacts (OECD 2003d: 10–11)

In contrast, the only component of *Evaluating Public Participation* was a two-page checklist, but oddly, not about the substance of open government, but about the considerations that should go into an evaluation.

In comparison with the integrity instruments, this is thin gruel. Apart from a general acknowledgement that citizen participation and consultation is a good thing, these documents lack any substance, relying instead on advice and on techniques – albeit, advice if which followed would lead to greater participation and in principle more open government as well as a challenge function for civil society actors. Again, somewhat curiously, the whole technical goal of "accessibility" with its call for independent institutions, service charters, one-stop shops – all of which are specific and concrete instruments of public management and service delivery – are never mentioned in these guidance documents.

Block 5: E-government readiness

This building block has six technical goals: (1) e-government vision, (2) establishment of framework conditions for e-government, (3) development of e-government leadership, (4) effective and efficient implementation of e-government, (5) setting up of effective e-government collaboration frameworks, and (6) improving service delivery outputs and outcomes. The approach was to stay away from the technical aspects and focus more on the governance dimension: "E-government is more about government than about the 'e'". The six technical goals yielded 16 institutional arrangements, but the emphasis was on strategies to introduce e-government, supportive legislation for areas like e-procurement, e-commerce, liberalization of telecommunications markets, e-signatures, privacy and data protection. There was also the usual OECD urging for evaluations and monitoring of progress, and clear policies about private sector outsourcing and public-private partnerships.

This building block deliberately ignores transparency, accountability, consultation and public participation, which are dealt with in the open government building block. The e-government block was about services, business processes and e-government coordination. In this respect, the building block relies on checklists. One is for e-government leaders (OECD 2003a): here the emphasis was on alignment and integration of e-government policies with broader public management reform processes; on encouraging a customer focus; and on international cooperation. Another was a checklist to evaluate the cost-benefit case for e-government projects (OECD 2005c).

As dry as all this seems, the cumulative impact of these instruments as well as others that have been developed since them has provided as robust a framework for e-government assessment as the integrity framework. Most e-government reviews address planning and leadership, impact on organizational change, common frameworks and collaboration, user-focus, and monitoring and evaluation. Based on experiences with other e-government reviews, the OECD identifies the existence of a national strategy and strong leadership (since e-government by definition is horizontal, it has to be pushed from above) as key ingredients in e-government reforms.

Block 6: Centres of government

The Senior Officials from Centres of Government (CoG) is an unusual "building block" since it is the only one that does not consist of a substantive core of principles but is rather a network that meets annually to informally discuss a key issue facing OECD governments. There is no OECD instrument or PGC guidance on this building block, and only three technical goals: (1) interface between political and administrative levels (providing advice to senior decisionmakers), (2) coordination of decision-making (ensuring a "whole of government" approach), and (3) preparation for future challenges. The annual meeting in 2009 focused on managing the financial crisis and the 2010 on managing fiscal consolidation and investing in future growth. Previous meetings had discussed "making reform happen" and the question of maintaining public trust.

We noted in Chapter 2 that the CoG was one of the first networks established by PUMA in an effort to tap into a constituency for the directorate's work (it was a similar case with the Senior Budget Officials network). It worked particularly well in the beginning because it targeted the most senior administrative officials in governments, those leading cabinet or Prime Minister's offices, or the administrative body that serves the head of government. These officials were and are the "lonely ones" – they have few if any peers in their home governments, and as advisors have a professional relationship with the head of government and ministers. The CoG network was the first of its type that brought this level of officials together informally to compare problems and challenges and learn what other governments were doing at the highest levels.[6] Meetings have continued to be quite informal in order to encourage exchange. The OECD itself summarizes the work of the CoG as follows:

> The CoG has different <u>levels of output</u>: exchange of experience about how common problems are being addressed and innovations in structure and process; a kind of retreat with peers to think about priorities and operating improvements, and new ideas to bring home; consideration of major governance issues feeding into further work by the Secretariat or into short written think pieces. An important output is also the opportunity to meet, get to know each other and develop the scope for informal contact. The CoG is the <u>only Forum</u> available to this grouping. (OECD n.d.: emphasis in original)

Because of the nature of the network as a vehicle for exchange, it is not governed as directly by principles as the other building blocks are. However, some benchmarks may be discerned from the description of the building block itself and the report of the most recent annual meeting in 2010. From the building block description of the technical goals, we see once again the interest that the OECD has in planning, strategy, coordination, and capacity. The building block refers to ensuring "continuity of procedure, policy and implementation", and "policy coherence and quality". The institutional arrangements call for monitoring functions, "coordination

Table 5.1 Meetings of Centres of Government, 1993–2010: Themes and Sub-themes

YEAR	VENUE	THEMES & SUB-THEMES
1993	Lisbon	Coherence in Policy-Making; Organizing for Change
1994	Tokyo	Managing Cross-cutting Policy Issues; Impact of Globalization on National Policy Coherence
1995	Copenhagen	Impact of Globalization on Policy-Making; Maintaining Ethics in the Public Service: The Role of the Centre
1996	Mexico City	Integrating Multiple Interests into Policy; Managing Relations with the Media
1997	Dublin	Improving Policy Capacities for the Long Term; The Role of the Centre in Public Management Reform
1998	Bern	Information Policy and Democratic Quality; Political/Administrative Interface: The Role of the Centre in Governmental Transitions; Decision-Making for "Mega" Policies (exploratory discussion)
1999	Naples	How to Strengthen Government-Citizen Connections; Free discussion session
2000	Budapest	Government Coherence: The Role of the Centre of Government; Relations between the Executive and the Legislature
2001	Reykjavik	Risk Management; The Public/Private Sector Interface
2002	The Hague	The Public/Private Sector Interface Public Sector Modernization
2003	Madrid	Public Sector Modernization: The Role of the Central Agencies; The Use and Impact of Information and Communication Technologies (ICT) for Decision-Making at the Centre of Government

Table 5.1 Meetings of Centres of Government, 1993–2010: Themes and Sub-themes – *continued*

YEAR	VENUE	THEMES & SUB-THEMES
2004	Istanbul	Using New Tools for Decision-making: Impacts on Information, Communication and Organization; Governance in the Knowledge Society: Implications for the Centre of Government
2005	Lisbon	Governance in the Knowledge Society: Implications for the Centre of Government; Identifying, Anticipating and Managing Risks: Challenges for Centres of Government
2006	Vienna	Leadership in Managing Risk; Strengthening Public Trust by Delivering on Promises: What role for the Centre?
2007	Bern	Strengthening Public Trust by Delivering on Promises: What role for the Centre?
2008	Mexico	Political Economy of Reform: Ensuring Stakeholder Support
2009	Paris	Managing the Crisis: From Recovery Policies to Long Term Reforms
2010	Berlin	Ways out of the Crisis: Managing Fiscal Consolidation and Investing in Future Growth

Source: List provided by OECD.

of government-wide communication", and a role for the Centre of Government throughout the entire policy cycle, from agenda-setting to evaluation, as well as a strategic planning unit that "coordinates among strategic bodies through the administration".

The Summary Report of the September 2010 meeting consisted of only three pages (the network avoids detailed agendas, discussion papers, and detailed reports in order to maintain informality) but still provides insight into an element of the OECD view (OECD 2010f). In what might seem like somewhat self-serving observations, the report argued that continuing uncertainty required continued strong leadership from the centres of government, which were facing unprecedented pressures in "managing complex and often conflicting demands from market, social partners, government agencies, citizens and the international community". It also noted that "maintaining momentum for reform across the whole of government is now a key task for Centres of Government". Table 5.1 list themes for CoG meetings from 1993 to 2010.

Block 7: Regulatory quality

We have already briefly discussed the OECD/PGC approach to regulatory quality in Chapter 4 on networked tools, but here we examine them in terms of substance and content. This building block has four technical goals: (1) broad programmes of regulatory reform, (2) capacity to assess and review regulatory impacts, (3) transparent and non-discriminatory regulatory institutions and practices, and (4) linkages with other policy objectives. Once again, the penchant for frameworks is there: under the first technical goal, the more specific objectives are "to establish clear objectives and frameworks for implementation" and to consider key elements of regulatory policy – policies, tools and institutions – as a whole". Under institutional arrangements, there are calls for "an adequate institutional framework" and effective systems management, as well as three separate calls for transparency. This building block is supported by two OECD instruments (the 1995 Reference Checklist for Regulatory Decision-making and the 2005 Guiding Principles for Regulatory Quality and Performance) and one PGC guidance (the APEC-OECD Integrated Checklist on Regulatory Reform).

The 1995 Reference Checklist has ten questions (OECD 1995b). It is a mix of technocratic, procedural and normative considerations. The technocratic considerations have to do with problem definition, the justification for government intervention, the balance of costs and benefits, and achieving instruments for compliance. The procedural considerations touch on the legal basis for the regulation, the appropriate level of government for the action, and consulting with all relevant stakeholders. The normative considerations include the transparency of the distribution of effects across society, and the clarity and consistency of the proposed regulation.

The 2005 Guiding Principles built upon the earlier effort (as well as a consolidation of that effort in 1997), focusing on seven key principles, but also making more explicit connections with other policy fields such as trade and investment (OECD 2005e). As well, this document was framed in terms of on-going efforts at regulatory reform, and countries needed "to consider the cumulative and inter-related impacts of regulatory regimes, to ensure that their regulatory structures and processes are relevant and robust, transparent, accountable and forward-looking. Regulatory reform is not a one-off effort but a dynamic, long-term, multi-disciplinary process". In addition, this document argued that the concept of regulatory reform had changed in the previous decade: whereas in the 1990s the focus was on "steps to reduce the scale of government" the newer emphasis recognized the importance and necessity of regulation in many instances, and the need to approach regulatory quality from a "dynamic, whole-of-government approach to implementation". The seven principles were:

1. Establish clear objectives and frameworks for implementation. This principle was about institutions, whole-of-government approaches, frameworks, and coordination around the reform effort.
2. Establish clear objectives and frameworks for implementation. This principle encouraged reflection on the costs and benefits and impacts of regulation.
3. Ensure that regulatory institutions and processes are transparent and non-discriminatory. This principle encouraged consultation with all interested parties, transparency, and appeal procedures.
4. Review and strengthen where necessary the scope and effectiveness of competition policy, and promote rigorous enforcement where oligopolistic or monopolistic behaviour risk frustrating reform.
5. Design economic regulations in all sectors to stimulate competition and efficiency.
6. Eliminate unnecessary barriers to trade and investment through continued liberalization, again strengthening economic efficiency and competitiveness, work with other countries to strengthen international rules and principles to further liberalize trade and investment.
7. Identify important linkages with other policy objectives and develop policies to achieve those objectives in ways that support reform. The linkages were to be to policy areas such as safety, health, consumer protection, and energy security.

The final guidance is the APEC-OECD Integrated Checklist on regulatory reform (OECD 2005a), discussed briefly in Chapter 4. It is a self-assessment tool on regulation, competition and market openness. The document had four parts: a horizontal questionnaire on regulatory reform, and then three additional questionnaires on individual policy areas (regulatory policies, competition policies, and market openness policies).

Since the questionnaires built on previous OECD efforts around regulatory reform, there are no surprises in the document. Without reviewing each questionnaire in detail, the common elements were:

1. Integrated policy frameworks.
2. Accountability and transparency.
3. Coordination with all other levels of government, including supranational.
4. Strong management and coordination mechanisms.
5. Adequate capacity.
6. Appropriate legal frameworks.
7. Consultation with stakeholders.
8. Encouraging competition and open markets.

Clearly, this building block had a heavy component of economic policy (regulation and competition policy), and there were a mix of principles that had to do with economic efficiency and effectiveness, as well as the overall governance of regulatory activity.

Block 8: Multi-level governance

This last building block is one of the least specific of the suite. It has only two technical goals: (1) multi-level governance frameworks, implementation and capacity, and (2) relations and cooperation between levels of government for key core functions of public management. The focus was on multi-level coordination between the national, regional and municipal levels of government, with clear distribution of functions combined with effective coordination. The building block calls for budgetary and policy authority at lower levels of government in support of their capacity to develop and implement policies distinct from those at the national level, and contribute directly to regional and local development.

The only guidance for this building block was a 2003 document from the Territorial Development Policy Committee on Innovation and Effectiveness in Territorial Development Policy. It was the result of a high-level meeting in Switzerland, but unfortunately the document is considered confidential by OECD rules of disclosure. However, the annotated agenda for the meeting, which is in the public domain, gives a sense of the considerations that underpinned it (OECD Territorial Development Policy Committee 2003). The meeting had two sessions, the first of which focused on enhancing regional competitiveness in the global economy.

> Regional disparities in productivity, income, employment and poverty are significant, and persistent. Countries need to remove structural obstacles to development and address challenges such as concentrated unemployment,

especially long term unemployment, distressed urban areas, the lack of adequate provision of public services and out-migration in rural areas. A different, more pro-active policy approach is needed to unlock unused potential and invest in the specific assets of regions, thereby improving their attractiveness and quality of life. Creating a new development dynamic calls for better integration of sectoral policies and co-ordination and co-operation across administrative boundaries and between regions within countries and across borders.

The second session addressed the issue of strengthening good territorial governance.

Much of the knowledge needed to develop local assets is dispersed among many different actors at the local and regional levels. As a result, in several countries, responsibilities in the fields of infrastructure and education, among others, have been transferred to the regional or local level. But devolution is not enough. These new institutions need to be empowered to contribute to the process of policy-making and equipped with the competencies to take on new responsibilities. Increasing administrative capacity in local and regional authorities implies upgrading human resources as well as reviewing the legal and institutional frameworks that define functions.

While this quote highlights considerations about devolution or policy responsibilities and building capacity and coordination, it does not provide as clear a set of principles as, say, regulatory quality.

This first part of the chapter has discussed the substantive content of the OECD view, and we have shown that there is indeed a view that has remained relatively stable over the last decade. It does provide benchmarks and tools whereby both member and non-member states can be measured and assessed. In Chapter 7 we will mention aspects of governance that are absent from the OECD view, but which might be incorporated in the future.

However, beyond substantive content, there are discursive strategies. The ideas that the OECD produces have to be sold both internally (to its members) and externally to a wider audience of non-member states, other international governmental organizations, the general public and policy observers. In this process of distributing its ideas, the OECD, like any "ideational artist" must frame those ideas in a persuasive context, a context that breaks through the noise and captures attention and persuades. As we noted in earlier chapters, the OECD is playing on a field increasingly crowded by other international governmental organizations, think tanks, foundations, and NGOs. The next part of the chapter looks at these discursive strategies as another component of the OECD view on governance.

Discourse on governance and management[7]

In 2003 GOV published a series of Policy Briefs (PB) "look at the evolving modernization agenda and how governments can best develop their capacity to achieve, and measure, the desired results". In the series, two publications are of direct relevance, and fed into the third. They were *Public Sector Modernization* (OECD 2003c), and *Public Sector Modernisation: The Way Forward* (OECD 2005h). They in turn both fed into the more detailed study, *Modernising Government: The Way Forward* (OECD 2005g). Since they were written only years apart, and since the first two clearly were drawn upon for the longer report, we will treat them as a group.

It is possible to discern six rhetorical or discursive themes that appear repeatedly in the three documents. Each of those themes is presented and discussed below, with representative examples from each of the documents (each document has multiple examples of each theme). However, they do not stand alone or isolated from each other – their organic relationship, and indeed their rhetorical power, comes from being elements of a larger, master narrative. Each of the documents expresses or reflects that narrative slightly differently, like different translations of the Bible. And yet the main lines of the narrative shine through in all three. It is a complex narrative, since it needs to balance opposing ideas and agendas, not least whether there should be convergence towards some single model or a range of different paths up the mountain. This is the master narrative that can be distilled from the texts:

> In the past years, all OECD countries have faced major pressures for reform – technological, demographic, budgetary, and political. All have undertaken reform, though at varying rates and with varying success. Mistakes were made along the way, particularly with a single-minded devotion to efficiency and to instrumental reform. Certainly, there were major surprises as the pioneers of reform forged ahead on the cold, unforgiving plains of their administrative and political systems. We now know some of the mistakes that were made, principally that there was not enough attention to culture and the fragility of institutions, or to the diverse paths towards modernity. But the pressures have not subsided, and reform and modernization will have to continue. All OECD countries face the same pressures, and they share the same basic principles – how they respond to those pressures and implement those principles will always be a matter of context. Reformers will face challenges, since change is never easy. They must renew their efforts, develop better tools and better calibration, and move forward, ever forward.

Theme 1: Reform is driven by pressure[8]

The animating theme of all three documents, and indeed of the narrative, is the notion of "pressures" that have made reform inevitable and unavoidable (the financial crisis and riots and protests in Greece and Ireland in 2011 have reinforced this point). PB2003 mentions the word pressure 11 times in eight pages; PB2005 four times; WG 43 times in 205 pages of text. While there usually is reference to technology, the key pressures that identified in the texts are budgetary and citizenry. The budgetary pressures are privileged as a historical source of public sector reforms, but were not as prominent as they were in the 1990s. Nonetheless, MG (p. 21) does refer to continuing budgetary pressures due to "demands on social transfer systems" exacerbated by the challenge of an ageing population. But clearly the main pressure that is cited in all three documents is a dissatisfied and somewhat truculent citizenry. The dissatisfaction manifests itself in different ways: demands for more services, demands for more efficient services, disgruntlement about high taxation, a vaguely defined set of inflated "expectations". Though the references are brief, the OECD portrays citizens as somewhat petulant *demandeurs*, whom government officials ignore at their peril. This is not to deny the power of public opinion or public outrage and even demonstrations of violence: the point is the rhetoric and the way it sets up the tone of argument. The nature of the pressure, its legitimacy and its implacable strength, makes reform less a choice than a necessity. Not to reform risks "being out of step" or "not adapting" – in other words to rupture the harmony that should exist between public institutions and citizens.

> With these new challenges, public management is becoming a major policy issue. It is receiving an unprecedented level of attention in OECD countries and beyond, and the pressures for change will not ease off in the decades ahead. (PB2003, 2)

> Budget worries triggered reform in many countries, but the underlying pressure for change came from social, economic and technological developments which left governments increasingly out of step with society's expectations. (PB2005, 1)

> The impetus for change came from many different sources – including the social, economic and technological developments in the latter half of the 20th century – which put pressure on all governments to adapt to new problems, new capacities and new relationships between citizens and governments. The public were increasingly concerned about the quality of the services they received and the choices available to them. Citizens were also increasingly resistant to the government's growing share of the national economy. In some countries, an expectation that taxation would decline became generally accepted across the political spectrum. ... More and more, governments became out of step with a changing society and with an educated and empowered citizenry looking to amend their social contract. (MG, 19)

Theme 2: Surprises and unintended consequences

This is a theme that points largely to the past, but resonates with possible follies in the future, and so reinforces a sense of caution about what is possible. It projects the notion of early "pioneers" (PB2003 refers to "first-generation pioneers" and to "pioneer reformers") who were single-minded in their objectives – building sod huts of reform on the unforgiving prairie of management. They accomplished a great deal, but made mistakes – moreover, ones that in retrospect seem surprising. It is upon their shoulders that modern reformers stand. This manouevre accomplishes several things. As mentioned, it exculpates the OECD from its youthful enthusiasm for NPM, but it also builds a platform for departures, and indeed a wider agenda of reform that engages not simply management but governance more widely. The early reformers may have cleared the forest, but neglected the ecology of the landscape. Ecological management is much more complicated and demanding.

> These reforms have indeed had a major impact but they have also given rise to some unexpected problems of their own. Even a seemingly straightforward action such as simplifying a welfare benefit form and cutting the time taken to process it may, for example, encourage more people to apply for the benefit, increasing the workload and making it more difficult to cut waiting time. While more efficient government is certainly desirable, efficiency alone is not a guarantee of better government. (PB2003, 1)

> The first-generation pioneers of public sector reform also faced the challenge of adjusting to a rapidly-changing world economy. But then the rhetoric of the day identified government itself as "the problem". This led to an impression that there was a single generic cause – "bureaucracy" – to be addressed by a generic set of solutions – "reform" – to arrive at the desired result – "efficiency". This approach suggested a single change from an unreformed to a reformed efficient state, a coherent task with a specific purpose that would be completed when this goal was reached. Since the primary goal was economic efficiency, the pioneer reformers went to work on reducing public expenditure, freeing up the public sector labour market and making greater use of market-type mechanisms in government. (PB2003, 2)

> Most public administrations have become more efficient, more transparent and customer-oriented as a result. But perhaps surprisingly, these changes have not reduced governments' influence in society – indeed, government now has a different but larger presence in OECD countries than 20 years ago. (PB2005, 1)

> Despite these changes – and contrary to the expectations of some reformers – in most OECD countries, public expenditure did not shrink greatly. (MG, 20)

Theme 3: Reform involves multiple goals

This theme is closely wedded to the previous one – the mistakes that were made, principally in the single-minded pursuit of efficiency, were in part due to the complexity of the reform process and the fact that it cannot focus on simply one goal. Multiple goals have to be pursued simultaneously, and consequently balanced carefully. A wider agenda of reform demands more sophisticated tools and analytical capacities.

> To complicate matters, governments are now under pressure for more profound changes to meet the requirements of contemporary society. A concern for efficiency is being supplanted by problems of governance, strategy, risk management, ability to adapt to change, collaborative action and the need to understand the impact of policies on society. To respond to this challenge, member countries, and the OECD, need better analytical and empirical tools and more sophisticated strategies for change than they have generally had to date. (PB2003, 1)

> And openness in itself does not necessarily improve governance, nor does it override all other public values. It should be balanced against other values of efficiency, equity, and responsibility. (PB2005, 3)

Theme 4: The importance of culture/values and the organic nature of reform

This theme is actually an amalgam of three related aspects of governance reform: the organic nature of government, the importance of taking account of organizational culture, and the role of values in organizations. This echoes the complexity theme cited earlier, that public sector reform cannot be mechanistic or purely instrumental, that it must take into account a very broad range of potential interaction effects as well as the less obvious dimensions of organizational behaviour.

The documents do not use the term "organic" but prefer the notion of a "whole of government" approach. In PB2005, this is presented as a "lesson" from two decades of reform efforts – that public administration and governance must be seen as part of an "interconnected whole". This suggests a sort of organizational ecology where changes in one part of the system will ripple through and affect others. This also reflects stronger appreciation of the constitutional integrity of the state. Whereas the reforms in the early 1990s tended to think in terms of "machinery of government" – that is, mechanistically, and in terms of a machine with parts that could be oiled, interchanged, altered, or even dispensed with, the new view being proposed by the OECD is that states have a constitutional personality that is in part founded in law, but is also an artifact of the integral operation of key systems or "levers" such as the budget process, the civil service management process, and the accountability process. These form interactive cycles, and so disruptions or changes in one will reverberate in the others.

An appreciation of the organic nature of government is complemented with an appreciation of the importance of culture within organizations.

PB2003 notes, for example, that "it has long been recognized that the core public service is controlled more by culture than by rules, a situation that is likely to continue despite progress in target-setting, performance contracts and measurement". Moreover, these documents express an appreciation for the historical roots of administrative culture in the OECD countries (e.g., the neutrality of the public service) as something that was achieved over decades if not hundreds of years. In an odd way, this is testament both to the fragility and the resilience of public administrative systems. They are resilient in the sense that they can resist mere technical interventions that do not address real cultural change. Indeed, the documents are forthright in acknowledging that a great deal of the public sector reform movement in the last 20 years was superficial – that it served the interest of certain groups to announce reforms, but not to invoke the pain and resistance of actually following through with those changes. By the same token, reforms that focus on behaviours without addressing the norms and cultures that underpin those behaviours will not be successful. But this notion of culture also signals fragility – if these cultural norms are ignored in the enthusiasm of instrumental change, then what is most distinctive and important about the public sector and how it contributes to modern society, may be lost.

Closely related to the idea of culture is the notion of values. The distinction is not clear in the documents, and the terms seem almost interchangeable, but whereas culture seems to be more connected to organizational norms and practices, values seem more closely aligned with specific democratic governance norms, such as a professional civil service, a dedication to the public interest, or leadership practices.

A key consequence of highlighting culture, values and the organic nature of governance is that public management or "modern governance" is not a goal that will be immediately attainable. It requires long-term commitment, thoughtful implementation, and patience. Moreover, if the interaction effects of an ecological view of governance are taken seriously, then it is likely that reform will be a project without end, since reformation of one part of the system will inevitably perturb other parts, which will then in turn have to be adjusted and reformed, which in turn will feed back and affect the others, ad infinitum.

> The second problem was a failure to appreciate that, despite its size and complexity, government remains a single enterprise. Governments operate in a unified constitutional setting and coherent body of administrative law, and their performance is determined by the interaction of a few crucial levers such as the policy process, the budget process, the civil service management process and the accountability process, all within the ambient political/administrative culture. Because of that, a reform of one of these levers inevitably involves the others. (PB2003, 3)
>
> The third problem was a failure to understand that public management arrangements not only deliver public services, but also enshrine deeper

governance values and are therefore, in some respects, inseparable from the constitutional arrangements in which they are imbedded. (PB2003, 3)

We also need to acquire a better understanding of the time required for serious public management interventions: culture change is not achieved overnight, and may take several years. (PB2003, 3)

Systemic reform in the public sector requires clarity about the behaviour, attitudes and beliefs that are to be changed, an appreciation of how formidable the challenge of cultural change really is ... (PB2003, 5)

Traditional thinking on public sector reform has often seen policy, people, money, and organisations as if they were independent components of public management. This study has made it clear that they are closely interlinked. It is important for reform strategies to take account of the interlinked nature of these components of government. (MG, 201)

Theme 5: Context matters/differences among countries

As we noted earlier, the OECD is widely regarded to have been a key international champion of NPM in the late 1990s, more so than the World Bank for example. *Governance in Transition* (discussed in Chapter 2) was a highpoint in that proselytizing. A decade later the OECD was taking a more subtle approach, and indeed highlighting the divergent paths countries might take on the arduous journey of reform, as well as the importance of context for the reform process (something that we noted in the earlier discussion in this chapter on the Building Blocks). Interestingly, the importance of context is only a minor theme in PB2003, but by 2005 is a major theme of both PB2005 and MG. This is listed as the second key lesson of two decades of reform, that modernization efforts must pay attention to the specific characteristics of each country, and be tailored to circumstances. Similar reform efforts in different contexts will yield different results. In the MG report, context becomes the major finding of the document: "The main lesson the emerges from this review is that modernization is context dependent ..." (MG, 201). It is in this vein the that report is surprisingly critical of the "best practice" movement, because it usually involves the transfer of some universal remedy to contexts that may not be suited to them.

Naturally, if this conclusion were taken to its extreme, there would be little point in cross-country comparisons, or indeed, for the GOV directorate in the OECD. The MG report explicitly recognizes this, and suggests several ways around the conundrum. First, reforms that appear useful should be set against similar systems to see how they might be implemented in similar contexts. Borrowing and policy transfer therefore would occur among families of countries rather than as a movement to change them all towards a single standard simultaneously. Second, it should be recognized that convergence will occur at different rhythms among different countries and for different types of reforms. The report notes for example that strong convergence has occurred among the OECD countries in terms of budgeting practices (interestingly, in part because of an international context where governments pay higher borrowing costs if their fiscal position is considered unsound), but not around accountability and control systems. Third, the only way to assess the potential impact of a given reform is to have a clear sense of the governmental and administrative context into which that reform will be introduced – this requires that governments (perhaps with the OECD's help) should conduct further research on their own internal systems, a *diagnostique* that will prevent the introduction of reform antibodies that might be rejected by the body politic. Finally, more research has to be conducted at the global level in order to understand the micro-dynamics of reform, and measures need to be developed in order to grasp the real impacts on governance systems of any given reform initiative (this foreshadowed *Making Reform Happen*).

> Modernisation is context dependent: OECD countries' reform experiences demonstrate that the same reform instruments perform differently and produce very diverse results in different country contexts. This variation in reform experiences reflects the disparate institutional structures and environments that confront the reformers. A strong lesson to emerge from this review is that modernisation is context dependent. Modernisation strategies need to be tailored to an individual country's context, needs and circumstances. (MG, 22)

> The main lesson that emerges from this review is that modernisation is context dependent: the nature of the problem and the solution are strongly influenced by the national country context. The design of reform strategies must be calibrated to the specific risks and dynamics of the national public administration system and take a whole-of-government approach. (MG, 201)

> One of the main lessons from the reform experience is that there is no single generic solution to the problems of public administration. Countries come from different starting points, with different cultures, and face different problems, so the solutions must also be tailor-made to fit their circumstances. (PB2005, 6)

Theme 6: Change is difficult

This theme is less a single element in the reports than a thread that runs through the entire cloth. The themes of complexity and the organic nature of governance signal that public management reform is challenging at best, and verges on dangerous at worst. The repeated references to past mistakes also highlight the risks associated with reform (these comments are usually balanced with acknowledgements that much was nonetheless accomplished, but the message is clear that despite accomplishments, major mistakes were made). Even the strong emphasis in MG on context is a backhanded reference to the need for care and prudence in proposing best practices. As part of a narrative, of course, this goes well beyond the simple acknowledgement that change is difficult. It helps signal several messages.

First, and somewhat paradoxically, the emphasis on danger and challenge reinforces the sense that reform efforts are necessary, like a pep talk to a SWAT team before it launches a mission. Second, it steels the will. The subtext is that resistance to change is understandable, but irrational. Reformers have to be prepared to encounter irrational resistance, and simply ride it through. Third, it subtly delegitimizes resistance to change, precisely by emphasizing it as a universal reaction. Again, considering it a universal reaction makes it a thought-less reflex; it should be dealt with the same way a doctor deals with a patient's flinching before the needle. Finally, if resistance to change is universal, it is unlikely to be easily overcome, and so reform efforts will naturally stretch over time, and perhaps a very long time, before they are successful. Interestingly, the documents make little reference to building constituencies of support or collaboration – though this does not mean that these more cooperative strategies of change are being ruled out.[9] Instead, governance reform seems a lonely vocation, doomed to opposition, fraught with uncertainty, and potentially disastrous if done incorrectly.

> Major change is uncomfortable and anxiety-producing, and because of this there is a natural instinct to resist it. Dedicated managerial attention can change officials' behaviour but it is only at the point where this behaviour has been internalised by individuals and groups – the point of cultural change – that it is likely to continue without such attention. So a reform that does not reach the critical point of internalisation will slip back to the prior state once the dedicated effort for change relaxes. And that is what happens to many attempted reforms. (PB2003, 6)

> Reforms cannot substitute for hard political choices. For OECD coun-tries, improving the cost-effectiveness and performance of their public sectors will help to reduce pressure on spending. As the past decade has shown, however, this in itself is unlikely to stem the continued upward pressure on expenditure generated by social entitlement programmes and social transfers. Public sector reform is not a substitute for the hard and, in many cases, unpopular choices that politicians have to make in some countries if long-term difficulties are to be avoided. (MG, 21)

> Citizens' expectations and demands of governments are growing, not diminishing: they expect openness, higher levels of service quality delivery, solutions to more complex problems, and the maintenance of existing social entitlements. Reforms to the public sector in the past 20 years have significantly improved efficiency, but governments of OECD countries now face a major challenge in finding new efficiency gains that will

enable them to fund these growing demands on 21st century government. For the next 20 years, policy makers face hard political choices.
Since most governments cannot increase their share of the economy, in
some countries this will put pressure on entitlement programmes. These
new demands on builders of public management systems will require leadership from officials with enhanced individual technical, managerial and
political capacities who think and plan collectively and who can work well
with other actors. (MG, 205)

The documents show a GOV that had travelled some distance from the previous decade. There was an explicit repudiation of some elements of NPM,
and new emphasis on values and organizational culture. There was a strong
emphasis on the importance of context and the dangers of simply transferring models from one country to others, or indeed from the OECD itself to
member states. But the overarching themes were the idea of constant and
implacable pressures on all governments, and that those pressures required
an almost constant pace of reform. Indeed, if we take the Building Blocks
instruments and guides and connect them to the three documents just discussed, it is clear that in governance matters the OECD's constant refrain is
that of the importance of reform. This makes sense if one accepts the assumption of constant pressures. If pressures – of whatever type, but all with great
magnitude – are constant, then the environment within which governments
operate is constantly changing and shifting. Governments that fail to reform
and adapt are essentially failing to evolve, and will become members of a
species doomed to extinction. Of course the other element behind this discursive strategy is that the OECD does indeed have certain standards, as we
saw in the previous section, and part of its mandate is to diffuse those standards to all members and increasingly to non-member states, inviting them to
reform across a broad band of policy fields.

These three documents above were published in the mid-2000s. Has anything changed in the OECD's discourse or rhetoric on governance? The
answer is no, and in fact the discourse we identified above may actually have
intensified due to the global financial crisis since 2008. The crisis has generated enormous pressures, leading to the possible fiscal collapse of countries
like Ireland, Greece, and Portugal, stern budgetary policy by countries like the
UK, and sometimes violent reactions by their populations. Two recent publications that we have already touched on in previous chapters give the
flavour and shows how consistent the rhetoric has been since the mid-2000s.
The discussion paper for the Venice Ministerial meeting of the PGC opened
with a synopsis of government reforms (OECD 2011b). The very first line was:
"As countries are still coping with the far reaching consequences of the crisis,
the public sector is facing acute challenges, with increased demands, and the
need to strengthen leadership, while at the same time facing significant fiscal
pressures". The overview chapter on "Current and Future Public Governance

Challenges" in GaaG (2009) opened with lines that could have been lifted directly from *Modernising Government*:

> As part of broad reform and change agendas, many OECD member countries have been developing and revising their governance institutions, frameworks and tools. The current global financial, economic, social and environmental challenges highlight the unique role of government in serving the public interest. They also direct renewed attention towards the institutions, policies and tools that help government deliver what citizens and businesses need and expect, highlighting areas where further changes may be needed, or where additional consideration may be required on how best to realise reform efforts. Not only are the regulatory rules, oversight systems and procedures for the financial services sector at the forefront of proposed actions by government, but the fiscal crisis has also put the role of governments, the scope of their activities and their effectiveness in advancing the public good at centre stage. In particular, governments are looking at how they can improve their capacity to anticipate and manage risks, and react quickly to complex problems in changing environments. Due to the global nature of these challenges, it is no longer enough to act at the national level. International co-operation and co-ordination is proving to be a critical element of any credible and effective policy response. (OECD 2009b: 20)

Figures 5.2 and 5.3 present word clouds for the introductory chapter of GaaG. They show a pattern that focuses on fiscal pressures and policy responses, a pattern of rhetoric and discourse that clearly show another dimension to the OECD view on governance.

Figure 5.2   Word Cloud of GaaG Introductory Chapter Using Wordle[10]

Figure 5.3 Word Cloud of GaaG Introductory Chapter Using Tagcrowd[11]

addition better budget capacity central challenges change citizens countries crisis current data economic effectiveness efficiency finance financial fiscal future general glance government increased indicator information integrity level long-term making management member oecd performance policy private process projections provide public reforms report require role sector services states sustainability systems values years

Conclusion

As we have noted in previous chapters, the OECD is a complex organization and so it is challenging to try to distill a "view" that it might have on governance. We used the metaphor of a watercolour earlier, and can return to it as a guide through the various layers that make up the OECD view. The first and most fundamental layer of that view is the OECD convention and its reference to the "preservation of individual liberty and the increase in general well-being". This is basically a commitment to a liberal democratic state and a capitalist market-oriented economic system. Those are wide parameters on their own, admitting of much variation. As well, the OECD has been prepared to interpret these basic principles with some degree of elasticity – in the 1960s it had military dictatorships as member states, and more recently has worked with MENA states that are well-removed both from liberal democracy and free markets. But these are the basic standards, the fine but firm lines that are the first layer of colour. A careful reading of key OECD documents on governance – such as *Outreach* – shows that support for the market economy through effective governance is a key objective of the organization. But that is not enough to dismiss the OECD and GOV as mere ciphers for NPM or a raw capitalism. The paradox of supporting modern capitalist economies is that those economies depend on human capital. Progressive and successful market economies will ultimately require policies that support their human capital, and somehow support a measure of individual liberty as well as public administration efficiency.

A second layer of colour comes from the focus on capacity-building and frameworks and efficient processes. As we noted, the OECD constantly supports the building of capacity in all three sectors – government, corporations, and civil society. "Capacity" means well-trained personnel, transparency and accountability. As we noted with the *Outreach* document, if that is unpacked it implies significant initiatives in corporate governance, public administration, corruption, crime-fighting, taxation and regulation. Capacity is also joined to results, performance, and building strategic capacity.

The third layer is the Building Blocks. We have reviewed them in detail above, but the most important point to draw from them is that they are not uniformly grey NPM. They have a strong ethical dimension in the sense that they call for transparency, accountability, openness, and consultation with the general public. To be sure, they contain several more technical elements – budgeting, evaluation of regulations, human resource management, e-government readiness, coherence and centres of government, but they are impressive for their substantive standards and cross-cutting themes.

In terms of substantive content, there is strong continuity between the *Outreach* document of 2000 and the Building Blocks of 2007, as well as the various instruments and guidelines issued throughout the decade. The key substantive topics that have dominated the governance agenda of the OECD are: regulatory reform; competition policy; taxation; integrity and corruption; multi-level governance; budgeting; and HRM. The *Outreach* document referred frequently to corporate governance, while the Building Blocks did not mention it all, though it comes up in some of the instruments and guidelines. Of these substantive areas of agreement, the most focused seem to be budgeting, HRM, and regulatory reform. In looking at the Building Blocks, it is clear that three of them provide only the most general of guidelines: centres of government; multi-level governance; and open government. We noted how the first two lack any substantive instruments or guidance, and in any case the centres of government is actually more of a network that wishes to remain informal. The most that these two building blocks call for is coordination and coherence.

The open government building block does contain specific technical goals such as oversight institutions, access to information, a series of accessibility instruments (e.g., on-line services), as well as checklists (particularly on e-government initiatives to engage citizens), and so has more concrete benchmarks that the other two, but still, considerably less than that for budgeting and regulatory reform. Interestingly, however, the OECD chose open government as the theme for its 2010 Public Governance Committee Ministerial meeting. The theme of the meeting was: "Towards Recovery and Partnership with Citizens: The Call for Innovative and Open Government" and the discussion paper reviewed initiatives taken by a mix of OECD members and non-members (the meeting is discussed in detail in Chapter 3). The discussion paper consisted of self-reporting by the countries based on a questionnaire sent out in mid-2010 (OECD 2011b). The open government component of the questionnaire and the reports did probe about consultation with citizens and e-government initiatives, but most of the responses focused on innovation in services and performance-related public management practices.

The other building blocks had more content, particularly the integrity and corruption resistance block and the regulatory reform block. Table 5.2 provides a summary of the substantive content of the building blocks as a set of specific benchmarks that the OECD would and could apply in assessing states (as it has with the accession process), even given its openness to different legal formats and implementation practices. We can see from this table that the blocks vary in specificity, with some more robust than others. But we can also see that GOV and the OECD do have a "view" on governance, or a set of standards or benchmarks. A country could fall short of these, for example, if in the HRM field it lacked a code of conduct, or

Table 5.2   GOV Building Blocks: Substantive Content

Budgeting
Regular and comprehensive reporting
Mechanisms for effective allocation

E-Government Readiness
Strategy to introduce e-government
Legislation for e-commerce,
    e-procurement
Policies on outsourcing and
    public-private partnerships
Leadership commitment

HRM
Workforce plan
Flexible job classification system
Broadly defined merit system
Broad job category definitions
Staff performance management systems
Codes of conduct and ethics

Centres of Government
Centre of government that provides
    coherence and quality advice
Centre of government engaged in
    entire policy cycle

Integrity
Policy frameworks on procurement and
    ethical conduct
Integration of ethics with HRM
Lobbying legislation and policy framework
Definitions of lobbying, procurement
    and conflict of interest in line with
    instruments

Regulatory Quality
Policy framework on regulation
Legislative basis for regulation
Regulatory transparency
Measuring costs and benefits
Consultation with stakeholders

Open Government
Oversight institutions (e.g., ombudsman)
Access to information
Citizens' charters
Framework for citizen engagement
Privacy legislation and policy framework
E-consultations

Multi-Level Governance
Budgetary and policy authority at
    lower levels
Distinct jurisdictions, coupled with
    coordination mechanisms

had one that departed significantly from the central tendency of OECD members (this might be more difficult to judge). Or even in the area of multi-level governance, if a state were highly centralized without auto-nomies (including service delivery and revenue generation) at the regional or municipal level. Or yet again, if in the budgeting field it did not issue regular reports with comprehensive financial data and economic assumptions.

In addition to these substantive standards, there are cross-cutting themes or broad categories of concepts that shimmer in the background of the building blocks, and are threads that connect back to the *Outreach* document. We have already identified some of these in our discussion of *Outreach*: an emphasis on accountability of governments to citizens and public servants to government; a constant emphasis on "openness" and transparency; and integrity and ethics. Earlier we called this a category of ethical consider-ations. In the building blocks there is an added emphasis on participation and consultation, through e-government and open government initiatives, for example.

We also see a continued emphasis on "frameworks", or, to put it another way, on coherence. There are constant calls for strategies, legislative frame-works, policy frameworks, coherence, and coordination. At one level this is simply an instinct for rationalistic policy-making: that kind of policy-making in principle is self-reflective and self-aware, it has goals and objec-tives and plans on how to meet them. Obviously, the semantic opposites of all these qualities imply incoherence, confusion and a lack of coordination. But there might be another impulse at play here, though this is purely con-jectural. Frameworks are forms of "self-binding" or discipline (Roberts 2010). Governments that are incoherent and uncoordinated can go off in all direc-tions, grow and bloat since they lack the capacity to make policy choices and set priorities. So, the emphasis on frameworks may be evidence of both ratio-nalism and a vestigial preference for limited or at least disciplined governance. This might be linked to the injunction in most of the building blocks to support market mechanisms to the greatest extent possible through good gov-ernance practices – the mother of all frameworks. The OECD view on gover-nance is not simple-minded – the call for markets is balanced by the call for transparency and citizen engagement, but it is there nonetheless as a frank evocation of the key objective of the OECD: global economic growth and development.

Finally, we see a continued emphasis on effective management processes. This arises in the repeated calls for performance measures and results (as in *Outreach*), but also for evaluation, cost-benefit reviews (particularly in the regulatory field), coordination across the policy cycle by centres of gov-ernment, and building capacity through public service training and strong management. The numerous checklists and guides in most of the fields provide questions that policymakers may ask themselves, but in so doing encourage continuous self-reflection and policy awareness.

A fourth layer of colour is one that we have touched up only slightly in this chapter but more in the previous ones – the values that are brought into the organization by its members. The documents that we have focused on in this chapter are products of the directorate – of GOV. They mislead to some degree since the OECD is a member-based organization. The committees – as we saw in Chapter 4 – consist of governmental experts from member countries. There is always a principal-agent tension between GOV and its committees, with the usual outcome that the agent subtly sets the agenda and the terms of discourse. But that is not to dismiss the committees. They can intervene strategically and powerfully and forcefully. The Russian accession is a case in point.[12] It will be challenging since Russia has several technical hurdles to overcome – WTO accession and the adoption of the anti-bribery convention. The later has several stages however – adopting the convention, then a Phase I review of legislation, and then a Phase II review of actual implementation.

The final layer is the rhetorical one – the addendum of meaning and tone. Without these, the documents would be dead letters, simple and silent signposts. Their rhetoric gives context and meaning. And that rhetoric emphasizes pressures, distrust, embattlement, and possible collapse without reform, reform, and more reform. Various paeans accompany this rhetoric.

- We have "experience" and "lessons", but also "difference" and "context". We are all "vastly different" but in "the same boat".
- We have to deal with diversity, fragmentation, and new technologies.
- We have to reform, and we have to be modern. (Lodge 2005)

We take up the issue of how effective the OECD has been as a "transfer agent" (Stone 2004) in the next chapter. Here we have shown that there is a definite OECD "view" on governance. It is a complex layering of ideas and traditions and legacies and actual work that goes on day-by-day – the OECD ministers and committees and directorate personnel are working each and every day, and the amalgam of their efforts is a shifting mercury of opinions and views, occasionally pinned down – if mercury every can be – in documents and phrases and speeches.

Is anything missing from this view on governance? GOV does not discuss constitutions, the rule of law, or war. These are sinews of governance, and for an international organization with a division dedicated to governance, these are major oversights.[13] TECO and PUMA and then GOV evolved progressively to grapple with larger and larger issues of governance. There is a wider horizon beyond the more narrow focus on public management and administrative mechanisms.

6
The OECD's Influence on Governance Issues

Israel acceded to the OECD on May 10, 2010. The original request to initiate accession proceedings had been made by then Prime Minister Shimon Peres in 1993. On the day of accession, Israeli newspapers carried reports of jubilation among the political class. Prime Minister Binyamin Netanyahu said that the accession was a significant advance in the state's international relations: "I'd like to thank the 31 member states for voting for our joining the organization. Any one of them could have voted 'no' and vetoed our inclusion. They chose not to do so", Netanyahu said, adding that "at a time when we keep hearing lamentations over Israel's international isolation", this was a particularly welcome sign of Israel's solid international standing (Hoffman 2010). Defence Minister Ehud Barak also hailed the achievement: "This will bring Israel billions", he said. "It's an important day for the Israeli economy". Uri Gutman, the Foreign Ministry's director of the OECD accession process, said Israel was now a "member of a prestigious organization, but also an organization that has some credibility and influence on the world economy".

The accession was not without criticism (Hever 2010), most obviously from the Palestinian Authority (Hoffman 2010), but had had its own difficulties (Wrobel 2010). In January 2010 the SG visited Israel to present two OECD reports on Israel's macroeconomy and labour and social standards. But he also presented concerns about Israel's compliance with OECD standards in three areas: anti-corruption policy measures, in particular in the defence industry; intellectual property; and exclusion of statistics relating to the territories. Over the course of the two-day visit, Gurría met with Prime Minister Netanyahu, Foreign Minister Avigdor Lieberman, Finance Minister Yuval Steinitz, Industry, Trade and Labour Minister Binyamin Ben-Eliezer, and Bank of Israel Governor Stanley Fischer, as well as with Manufacturers' Association President Shraga Brosh. "Joining the OECD, which includes the major players in the global economy, will enhance Israel's ability to conduct an ongoing dialogue with representatives of these economies; force an upgrade in Israel's public administration; improve Israel's corporate management;

expand trade opportunities, and improve Israel's credit rating" (Wrobel 2010).

Israel may be a special case – it wanted accession in order to open another front for its international legitimacy – and the accession process itself (as noted earlier) is a more robust instrument for the OECD in that it can apply conditions. States that wish to be members need to meet the *acquis*. But it illustrates several key points. The OECD club is still considered an elite club. Joining that club, either through full accession or through adherence to any of its instruments, is both a serious thing but also an exercise in influence by the organization. The existence of governance instruments and the tools that accompany them (as we discussed in Chapters 4 and 5) – while "soft" – are nonetheless international standards in key areas (e.g., anti-bribery, lobbying). Finally, the OECD seems to be universally regarded – despite its "rich country" members – as both prestigious and legitimate. It has gravitas.

This chapter probes different elements of that gravitas. Trying to gauge the influence of an organization, or any exercise of power outside of raw and bloody coercion, is notoriously difficult. The problem is compounded with the OECD due to its non-coercive character, and the fact that it wields only the stick of ideas and the allure of membership. We showed in Chapter 5 that the OECD has developed a handful of international instruments on governance, but they are only a handful. On the rest of its work, how is one to distinguish between the oceans of governance publications and reports that stream from GOV, and actual influence across dozens of countries (both members and non-members)? This chapter approaches the issue from four angles. First, it reviews the standing judgement about the OECD's influence on public management reform, and then reviews assessments by leading academics on the seminal 2005 report *Modernising Government: The Way Forward*. Second, it explores two case studies to assess how the OECD is perceived within governance circles, in this instance Canadian and Finnish parliamentary debates in the last decade. This gives us an empirical sense of how the OECD is perceived by political actors. Third, it analyses data gathered in a survey of public administration academics and practitioners affiliated with the Network of Institutes and Schools of Public Administration in Central and Eastern Europe. These are experts in the field, in both theory and practice, and were asked to gauge the influence of the OECD in public management reform in their countries and their regions. The results were gathered in May 2011, and consisted of 103 responses to ten questions. Finally, we look at an internal evaluation of the PGC's efficacy that was conducted by the OECD itself.

Judging the influence of the OECD and GOV

We noted at the beginning of this book that while there have been very few analyses of the OECD's influence on public management and policy reform, the few observations that exist uniformly agree that the OECD has had an impact. Richard Rose, in the first extended discussion of policy transfer or "lesson-drawing" noted that in a globalized world, inter-governmental and international organizations like the European Community, the OECD and the IMF "encourage exchange of ideas between countries with similar levels of economic resources" (Rose 1993: 105). The OECD has been said to place a premium on "on controlling the 'chain of expertise' – a discursive hierarchy that starts off with the power to define the nature of policy-making problems and then involves the selection of relevant know-ledge and expertise in order to address the problem at hand" (Dostal 2004: 454). It has been branded as a leading and successful proponent of NPM (Premfors 1998; Common 2001; Peters 1997; Sahlin-Andersson 2000; Pollitt 2001). It has shaped "an international community of discourse about public management reform" (Pollitt & Bouckaert 2004).

A unique window into assessments of the OECD's influence on public management reform occurred in 2006 with a special symposium in the jour-nal *International Review of Administrative Sciences* on the OECD's 2005 pub-lication (already discussed in previous chapters) of *Modernising Government: The Way Forward* (OECD 2005g). The symposium brought together six leading observers of the OECD and of public management reform, and collectively the articles provide a sense of how the OECD is perceived in key, informed academic circles. This is a small sample (though the participants are dis-tinguished in the field), and to some extent their very expertise might be expected to induce a certain cheer-leading mentality. The review of the articles shows, however, some healthy skepticism.

Christopher Pollitt's opening remarks as symposium editor signalled the importance of the OECD report: "When the OECD produces an overview of public management reforms in its member states this should be a matter of importance for practitioners and academics alike. For the past decade and a half the OECD's public management service has been a prime node in the growing global network of public management reformers and com-mentators" (Pollitt 2006). However, he also notes that there was a time when PUMA was a pioneer, but that now the "international marketplace for management reform ideas is crowded" (Pollitt 2006: 308). Donald Kettl opened his comments with the statement that the report "frames the state of play in international public management" (Kettl 2006: 313). Haque called it "timely" and noted that it distinguished itself from other OECD pub-lications with respect to a broader, whole of government approach rather than a sectoral one (Haque 2006). Bouckaert also described it as a "solid and important overview" while noting some of its data limitations and perhaps its overly ambitious agenda of setting out principles and "The Way Forward" (Bouckaert 2006). He also had some doubts about the implicit model of governance (primarily performance oriented) that underlay the report – in contrast to possible trajectories of reform to a more neo-Weberian style

(Olson 2006). Premfors agreed with the assessment of the OECD as influential: "For at least a decade and a half, the OECD has been an ambitious and influential contributor to the international debate on public sector reform" (Premfors 2006). Talbot closed the symposium with the same praise for the effort, but strong critiques of the evidentiary basis for some of the claims about trends of reforms.

What can we draw from this collection of articles? First, and most obviously, there is a consensus on the global influence of the OECD/PUMA over the past decade in influencing public sector reform, though the authors vary in their support for the direction of that reform (at least to the extent that it is claimed that the OECD pushed a neo-liberal, pro-market variant of NPM). Pollitt's point of a more crowded field of public sector reform is a telling one, and is reflected in the other articles (Haque and Bouckaert especially) noting international organizations' contributions to public sector reform, particularly in the context of development.

A second point is the uniform praise for the OECD's efforts to provide comparative analysis of public sector reform efforts. We noted in Chapter 2 that this was the result of deliberate efforts within the OECD to build a governance and public management agenda. The Madrid Conference of 1979 was, as we argued, one of the first international comparative meetings to discuss reforms in different jurisdictions. This was more important than it seemed – for the first time, both academics and practitioners had access to a collection of country experiences as well as a reasonable (if not perfect) methodological basis for analysis. We have discussed the impact of PUMA's efforts and the institutional context of the OECD on practitioners, but the influence on the international academic community is also important. That community is relatively small, though has been growing in the past decade as public sector reform gathered momentum and popularity as a continuous movement of "modernization". A small community typically lacks resources, and so the easiest type of research to conduct is on one's own country or perhaps a region. The capacity of the OECD to provide comparative data on its members (and this has simply continued with the GaaG initiative) was a major contribution to at least trying to understand trends across the industrialized states. More recent efforts to provide similar data about non-members has added more value. The PUMA and GOV publications on sectoral public management issues such as performance pay or integrity were often the only in-depth studies available. Its more synoptic reviews (originally as part of an annual series) and most recently its whole-of-government performance reviews provide unique perspectives almost non-existent in the academic literature. As a result, it is usually the case that any academic publication about almost any aspect of public management will contain at least one citation to OECD research. To the extent that the PUMA and GOV managed to avoid an ideological "tag" and maintain the veneer of objective and high-quality research, it tends to be widely cited for empirical data about governance issues. This is influence, though subtle and more in the vein of "wallpaper" than of direct injection of specific ideas.

This does not mean that academic or practitioner views are uncritical, nor would we expect them to be. The symposium articles highlighted some of the limitations of the OECD report. One that we have already mentioned is methodological. The data sources for the report's judgements were often thin or vague – based on self-reporting surveys (still a key tool in the OECD's data-gathering approach on governance issues), for example, or purporting to pluck "trends" from the relatively thin air of a handful of examples of "leaders". Another critique was the depth of conviction that the report showed for a more nuanced culturally, socially, politically and organizationally based approach to understanding reform. We noted in our discussion of the report that it seemed to reflect a better appreciation than *Governance in Transition* did of different trajectories of reform and the importance of country context to what could be transferred and borrowed. Premfors detected the same tone, but argued that it was ultimately only a muted one.

If these articles are emblematic of the global academic community's measure of the OECD's influence, particularly in this one important report, we can conclude that its influence is taken for granted, at least, as Pollitt says, as a "prime node" in the global network of public management reformers. But how do practitioners view the OECD?

Case study: Canadian and Finnish legislative debates[1]

To some extent, influence is in the eye of the beholder. How do politicians themselves gauge the influence and the character of the work undertaken by the OECD on governance and other issues? We could do this anecdotally (as we did at the outset of the chapter with the example of Israel), but anecdotes are scattered and disconnected. Another way is to try to systematically review political discourse over a sufficiently broad time interval that we can see more fundamental patterns and perceptions. An interesting methodology was pioneered by Alasuutari and Rasimus (Alasuutari & Rasimus 2009) for the case of Finland. They gathered data from government bills, legislative initiatives made by individual members of Parliament, and reports and statements from various parliamentary committees. The data were retrieved electronically from legislative datasets spanning 1991 to 2008. They searched for documents that included the word "OECD" somewhere in the text. This yielded 480 documents, or about 3 per cent of the total number of named parliamentary documents in those years. The approach isolated specific sentences with OECD references, and then expanded to include adjacent sentences or even a full paragraph to make the purpose and function of the OECD reference more comprehensible in rhetorical terms (Perelman 1982). As they pointed out, parliamentary debates are not – at least for a lengthy time span – the expressions of any single person. In the aggregate, they reflect national debates about the policy process and echo a sense of what is legitimate and what is not. This is partly due to their "official" character. For better or worse, legislative debates and documents are the collective discourse of a nation, a "discursive field" (Foucault 1972; Pal 1990) about policy issues. They are rhetorical engagements in which each of the various sides is trying to appeal to an invisible public. Indeed, it is the very "public – ness" of these debates that gives them a particular value in understanding the shape and nature of policy discourse (Pal 1994).

The Alasuutari and Rasimus study yielded four categories of references, though they caution that this categorization is not the only one possible. As they point out: "What is essential is the underlying assumption that referring to the OECD is an appropriate device for advancing or justifying the reform in question. Thus the objective is to analyze the uses of the OECD ..." (Alasuutari & Rasimus 2009: 95). The four categories were:

1. Comparisons between OECD countries: "By comparison, an author of the document attempts to illustrate an individual country's ranking order on certain measures".
2. The OECD as a body of expertise: The "OECD as an organisation is considered as a neutral body of expertise".
3. OECD models and recommendations: The "OECD is seen as a source of detailed models and public policy recommendations".
4. Adaptation to global developmental trends: "References in which an author delineates a country's need to accommodate itself to unavoidable global developmental trends ..."

The intent of our research was to replicate the method in the Finnish study to Canada, but that posed some challenges. The Canadian parliamentary website[2] has an advanced search mode that allows specification by the two chambers (House of Commons or Senate), by debates, journals, order papers and notices, by committees, by bills, and by parliaments going back to 1997. Entering the global search term of OECD, for both chambers (House of Commons and Senate) both official languages (French and English), for all committees, bills, and other reports and debates resulted in 20,244 "hits" (on March 14, 2010). To narrow the database, we searched only English references to the OECD in House of Commons debates. This yielded 484 references between October 2, 1997 and July 10, 2009 (the Canadian legislative database does not go back beyond 1997).

This means that there are some important differences between the Finnish and Canadian datasets. The Finnish data only include reports, bills, and statements in committee. The Canadian data excludes those, and focuses exclusively on parliamentary debates (in the House of Commons, the chief law-making body). An interesting question, which cannot be pursued here, is why the Canadian search yielded so many more references to the OECD than the Finnish one did. Nonetheless we believe that the datasets are comparable in that they are windows into national legislative debates that reflect on international standards. To our knowledge, this sort of comparison has rarely been done (Kirejczyk 1999; Sivenkova 2008), but if so then with an exclusive focus on either rhetorical devices as aspects of language (Perelman 1982) and without any reference to the incorporation of international standards and examples. Our approach was to review the Canadian texts and documents, and organize them according to the original Finnish study's four categories. 422 of the 484 references fell comfortably within these categories, though with some nuances that we explore below. As well, however, there were 62 references that did not fit the original four categories, and which reflected distinct aspects of Canadian national discourse. This allows us to explore both the similarities of discursive reference and the divergences that are due to national context.

Comparisons among OECD countries

The Finnish study found that the first and most common type of OECD reference was a direct comparison between OECD member countries. This involved "ranking" of one's own country against OECD members and against international standards or norms, and providing a sense of whether the country was "lagging" or "leading". These notions of the "average", of what constitutes an acceptable standard, of what is "modern" and what is not, are important rhetorical devices in arguments about public policy (Lodge 2005). As noted above, since the OECD is the club of rich and presumably advanced nations, comparing one's own country's performance to the OECD norm becomes an important device in making claims and stating problems. If the OECD can plausibly be portrayed as an international "gold standard" in public policy, measuring oneself against that standard can become a powerful rhetorical advice to either criticize or celebrate government policy.[3] The Finnish data support these observations: statements were made in government documents drawing on the OECD as a measure of either Finland's falling behind or leading. However, aiming at the "average" was not the only use of the OECD as a comparator – it was sometimes argued that it was important to be a leader, i.e., ahead of the average. "This is particularly the case when it comes to themes associated with modernity which indicate qualities like dynamics, advancement and so on" (Alasuutari & Rasimus 2009: 96). More profoundly, the underlying rhetorical logic is that "social change in all advanced market societies proceeds through similar trajectories", thus implying that all advanced countries are more or less amendable to the same reform strategies. This itself becomes a powerful device to encourage universal (i.e., globally similar) strategies, at least for members of the OECD if not for others.

The Canadian data generated 236 references in this rhetorical category, or almost half of the total. As a "club" that constantly issues reports and rankings, it is natural that the OECD will be taken up as a benchmark. So, the language of leaders and laggards that was noticed in the Finnish case is certainly evident in Canadian debates. However, there are some interesting nuances. First, to the extent that the OECD represents rich and developed countries, it is in contrast to poor and developing countries. To somehow fall short of OECD standards therefore is more than just being low on the rankings, it actually carries the danger of pigeonholing the country as in the company of "undesirables" (developing, as opposed to developed, countries).

> The OECD says that we will spend 10 per cent less next year on R and D over this year and the president of Memorial University says that we are acting like a third world country when it comes to R and D. (ref. #6, December 3, 1997)

> In fact the University of Victoria recently did a study that said Canada had one of the worst records in the industrial world and that on 25 environmental indicators we now rank 28 out of 29 countries in the OECD. (ref. #78, May 17, 2001)

Of course, as a member of the OECD and a developed country, this type of rhetorical device can only be used sparely. A more reliable technique is ranking – situating Canada "near the bottom", on whatever scale, is a clear way of attacking government policy. Comparators (those at the top of the list) are routinely credited with greater insight, commitment, determination, vision, and responsiveness to public needs. A variant of this strategy is to put the country in the company of a small subset of other countries that are lagging or not meeting commitments. While being lowest or last, or highest or best, is obviously useful as a discrete ranking device, there is an advantage in being put into the company of others. For critics (e.g., on the environment), this puts Canada in the company of outlaws, for defenders of policy it puts the country in the company of the virtuous. "Keeping company" is a way of establishing more than singularity – it establishes behaviour as part of a pattern, something systemic. It also is advantageous when the country in question is not the worst or the best: if it is in the company of the "worst/best five" then it can be praised or damned by the company it keeps, and not its absolute ranking.

> Canada is one of only two OECD countries that do not have a national grant system. We need to ensure federal funding is provided in cooperation with provincial governments to establish a national system of grants. (ref. #14, May 13, 1998)

The bill would fail to provide any stimulation for the economy at a time of job loss, increasing unemployment, and economic decline in the midst of recession. It would fail to offer any reduction in the national debt at a time when Canada continues to have the third largest debt to GDP ratio in the OECD among the major developed countries. (ref. #89, February 22, 2002)

We are one of the richest countries in the world. We have the OECD's best performing economy, with projections from the OECD that Canada will stay in first place for years to come. (ref. #101, November 8, 2002)

OECD as an expert body

In this set of references, the OECD is relied upon as an organization which is a "neutral body of expertise" – a source of research and statistics which provides raw material to be used by policymakers as they see fit. As Alasuutari and Rasimus point out, there are no overt references to the OECD's authority (i.e., no defences or justifications), but the routine mentions of the OECD's data are themselves indications of the respect that the organization enjoys and its putative neutrality and the quality of its data. This is what we referred to in Chapter 4 as the OECD "brand".

Many of the citations above and in the previous section also reflect this rhetorical trope. Ranking, locating one's country on a scale, and with the company of like countries requires some sort of metric. It is notable that in both the Canadian and Finnish debates the OECD and its data are rarely challenged (more on this below), again an indication of its reputation. At best, opponents will pull out different OECD data on different aspects of a problem in order to debate. For example, the Canadian government routinely cited favourable OECD data or research on its overall economic performance (e.g., low unemployment rates, GDP growth, low levels of debt), while the opposition would seize on OECD studies of taxation that showed that Canada had relatively high levels compared with other OECD members. For the Canadian data at least, the presumption is that the OECD's studies are largely beyond reproach, even if they point to somewhat contradictory performance indicators.

The Canadian data generated 107 citations in parliamentary debates in this category. These types of citations have specific qualities that distinguish them from the first category. For example, they allude to the "reality" or ontological veracity of OECD numbers – since the data come from the OECD, which is a neutral and highly professional research organization, they must be true by definition. Verbal cues in these quotes use devices such as "according to", "predicts" (itself an interesting allusion to the oracular capacity of the OECD), "confirms", "standards", "warnings", "acknowledges" and "condemns" (again, the oracular function). Another interesting device is the "Even the OECD warns ..." The use of "even the" in rhetorical terms is essentially a double maneuver. It suggests, first, that the offence is outrageous (e.g., taxes that are well outside the norm), and that "even" an organization as neutral and dispassionate as the OECD can no longer contain itself and has to make a direct comment. We have underscored the relevant turns of phrase in the following quotes:

> Over the course of the last four years we have put in place the basis for a very solid economic recovery. This is why unemployment has fallen from over 11 per cent to under 9 per cent. This is also why <u>the OECD predicts</u> that Canada will have the highest economic growth rate and the highest growth rate in jobs this year. (ref. #241, February 20, 1998)

> In the recent budget the Liberals should have addressed bracket creep but they did not. This insidious tax constantly pushes taxpayers into higher tax brackets even though their income remains unchanged. <u>Even the OECD</u> called on the government to eliminate this sneaky tax. (ref. #243, March 31, 1998)

> The parliamentary secretary also said that we must have a global approach, because electronic commerce knows no boundaries. <u>This is true</u>. Two or three weeks ago, I had the opportunity, as a member of the Standing Committee on Industry, to attend an OECD meeting, here in Ottawa, on electronic commerce. I was not able to attend all the sessions, but I discussed the issue with the hon. member for Mercier, who did attend.
>
> There were many external factors which those of us on the finance committee felt. Obviously there was the change in terms of the <u>OECD warning</u> us about debt reduction, as well as its admonition with respect to the necessary tax cuts. (ref. #249, February 2, 1999)

> What is the federal government doing? It is keeping this $1 billion in its pockets rather than giving it back to the province that is being used as a model throughout the world. <u>The OECD recently recognized</u> it as such, which is why the federal government decided to implement its national child care program. (ref. #296, November 17, 2004)

OECD models and recommendations

We also found ample evidence of the use of OECD models and recommendations as a rhetorical device in Canadian policy debates. Alasuutari and Rasimus found repeated references in Finnish debates to OECD models as examples of "best practice" for implementation in nation-states, ultimately leading to a desired convergence toward universal standards. As they point out, these models are often based on the experience of individual member states. This is partly an artifact of how the OECD operates – its members constitute the Council as well as Committees and Working Groups, and set the research agenda over a given year. The peer review process is also steered by members (who constitute the majority of review panels). Country studies also consist of experts from member states, and the country under review has an opportunity to comment on the reviews and shape the final report. Thus, the OECD should not be seen as some disembodied entity in Paris, but rather a Petri dish of interacting states and their experts, having an extended global conversation about standards and models. "It is true that OECD-based models and recommendations often originate in the views and definitions of ruling elites in member countries. ... This means that most of the models and recommendations are particularly well-suited to those countries. Nevertheless, in the references in this category the OECD appears as a convenient reference group especially to small or marginal countries, for which it is important to follow the lead of major market economies" (Alasuutari & Rasimus 2009: 98). In this respect, we could anticipate a difference in the tone of the references, since Finland has a special history in the Cold War, and is "smaller" than Canada (one-sixth the population). Canadian political discourse resists the idea of the country as "small" (possibly due to its geographical size, its historical role in the World Wars, its association with the Commonwealth and of course the United States) (Dewitt & Kirton 1983; Welsh 2004).

There were 31 references in the Canadian dataset that fit this category. This is possibly due to the higher technical content of these types of references. They refer not simply to league tables and rankings, which can be easily gleaned from OECD reports, but to more technical standards around specific models and legislative templates. As with the Finnish case, there are references to "model conventions" or legislation, to "standards", "codes of conduct", "rules" and "tools", "norms", "patterns", and "guidelines". A particularly interesting use of this rhetorical device is to couch legislative initiatives as merely routine and unremarkable, since they reflect existing international standards as expressed in OECD models.

> In this exercise we have followed the general outlines set out in the OECD model convention for the avoidance of double taxation. (ref. #345, October 20, 1997)

> We need only think of the bill to implement the land mines convention, which banned land mines and provided for their destruction, the bill to implement the comprehensive nuclear test ban treaty, which I will deal with later, or the Corruption of Foreign Public Officials Act that gives effect to the OECD convention on combating bribery of foreign public officials in international business transactions. (ref. #351, December 1, 1999)

> Even in assessing political risks, the EDC does not take the human rights situation into account, which leads us to say that, before providing its support to a company, the EDC should, as a bare minimum, ensure that the company in question subscribes to the OECD code of conduct relating to human rights. (ref. #352, February 14, 2000)

The member keeps coming back to the Canada account which represents less than 2 per cent and is there to help Canadian exporters on distorted markets. It respects every OECD rule and every OECD country has similar tools. (ref. #355, March 22, 2000)

Bill S-31 is not something radical. It is not rocket science. It is standard, routine legislation to increase our stable of countries with which we have tax treaties and to improve the tax treaties from some of the existing cases. In general, these tax treaties are modelled on a standard OECD model. (ref. #360, November 9, 2001)

Indeed, these treaties, similar to the ones that Canada has with other countries, are patterned on the OECD model tax convention which is utilized by all member countries. Moreover, the provisions in the treaties contained in Bill S-17 comply fully with the international standards that apply to such treaties. (ref. #367, March 11, 2005)

Adaptation to global developmental trends

The fourth category of statements from the Finnish study included references "in which an author delineates a country's need to accommodate itself to unavoidable global developmental trends" (Alasuutari & Rasimus 2009: 98). The logic here is that there are implacable and impersonal trends in public policy and public management/governance at the global level that single countries are unable to control or resist, and so they have to adapt. The adaptation, according to the Finnish data, tends to be couched in terms of harmonization of national legislation and practices, but also in terms of adjusting to the current policy *zeitgeist*, at the time focused on general patterns of deregulation and marketization.

The Canadian data yielded 35 references that fell into this category. In contrast to the first category of references, which seeks to distinguish the country in terms of rankings or the company that it keeps, this set of references was often designed to minimize uniqueness. Again, this makes sense in terms of the logic of the rhetoric – if the global forces being identified are implacable and overwhelming, and if the logic of response is adaptation, then the speaker needs to highlight how there are no other choices. A good way to do this is to say that the country is no different from any others that have had to succumb. At other times it emphasized uniqueness – the country was an outlier and should adapt and follow its OECD partners.

Let me point out that the problems we are facing with our pension system are not unique to Canada. Many OECD countries are also making changes so that their pension systems are more sustainable. Some international organizations have recommended moving toward the increased funding of public plans and that is exactly what we are doing. (ref. #378, October 6, 1997)

While the rest of the countries in the OECD are taking massive steps in terms of tax reduction, the Government of Canada, the Liberal Party of Canada, is taking baby steps. The result is that Canada is falling farther behind and losing its place as a competitive nation. (ref. #391, February 26, 2001)

The government is very much aware of the problems of the international steel market caused by overcapacity and cheap imports. The overcapacity is a global problem that we are attacking on several fronts, particularly in the context of discussions and negotiations with the OECD. (ref. #402, October 3, 2003)

We would not be the first country to bring in measures to ensure that our businesses are not forced to compete with countries or importers that use unfair and unlawful means. The United States, 25 countries in Europe and all the members of the OECD have adopted such measures, all except two countries—and guess which? Australia and Canada. (ref. #415, December 6, 2007)

New potential reference types

Of the total references generated by the Canadian database search, 62 did not fall clearly into the four categories developed in the original Finnish research. Forty of these miscellaneous references did however break out into two reasonably clear categories. The first consisted of references to the OECD as a platform for Canadian global influence. The second was a more critical category of the OECD as a "secret club". Both of these may reflect distinctive aspects of Canadian political discourse and imagination. The search for global influence – Canada's role in the world – is unusual for a relatively small country, but it has bedeviled Canadian debates over foreign policy at least since the late 1960s (Cooper 1997; Nossal 1997). The second category has 15 references, the majority of which are to financial or trade agreements, where the OECD can be portrayed as a club of rich nations forcing the pace of financial globalization to the detriment of developing countries.

OECD as platform for Canadian global influence

All but two of the references in this category were made by government ministers. While in theory it would be just as easy for opposition parties to argue that Canada is not using the potential of the OECD to demonstrate global leadership, that was hardly ever done. Arguing that the OECD is a platform for leadership automatically highlights both the OECD's role, and the specific role of the Canadian government in capitalizing on that resource. It also highlights a key characteristic of traditional Canadian foreign policy, multilateralism. As a relatively small country on the international stage, Canada has always benefitted from stable global rule regimes, and has worked hard (in virtually every international forum – for historical as well as geographical reasons, Canada is an inveterate "joiner") to build those regimes. Despite its lack of coercive power, the OECD is the source of many conventions, agreements, and standards governing specific issues such as subsidies for industries or electronic commerce.

Many of the references cited Canada simply as a participant in a group of like-minded countries who together were dealing with pressing global problems.

> Since 1995, OECD member countries, including Canada, have been negotiating a multilateral agreement on investment, aimed at clarifying the rules governing foreign investments. (ref. #425, November 3, 1997)

> The Canadian government is participating in the OECD and WTO negotiations to eliminate subsidies and remove the barriers that impede the ability of our shipbuilding companies to compete internationally ... We are continuing to meet with industry representatives to fine tune the programs now in place and ensure that the industry takes advantage of them. (ref. #432, May 3, 1999)

> Canada is an active participant in many international fora which are currently studying both the effects and solutions to the issues raised by cyber-crime. These include among others the G-8, the Council of Europe, the United Nations, the Commonwealth Secretariat, OECD and the Organization of American States. (ref. #439, April 6, 2001)

In other instances, Canada was cited not merely as a participant, but as a leader or convenor, and in some cases as a "world leader". The quotes also have the advantage of portraying the government as an actor on the international stage, not simply a recipient of international models and solutions.

> The finance minister and the federal government have been on the leading edge of an OECD initiative that is trying to eliminate harmful tax competition. We also introduced some of the toughest money laundering legislation in parliament last year. (ref. #437, April 4, 2001)

OECD as a secret club

These 15 references break from the others in this survey – while the other four core categories derived in the Finnish research, as well as the fifth possible new one encountered in the Canadian data, more or less laud the OECD or portray it as an example and an international platform for solving global problems, this stream of references takes an overtly critical stance towards the OECD as either a "secret club" or – in what is much the same thing – a "club of rich nations" bent on serving their own interests at the expense of the developing world or the poor. It should be noted however, that 11 of these 15 references were to the Multilateral Agreement on Investment (MAI), and all of these references came from opposition parties (especially the social democratic opposition party, the New Democratic Party (NDP)). The MAI had been launched by the OECD and negotiated over three years from 1995 to 1998. It was to be an agreement among OECD states, but open to accession by others. Critics around the world saw it as conceding too much to multinational corporations, and in this instance the OECD's membership of rich states made it appear to be open to undue influence from corporate interests. The fact that the agreement was supposed to start with the OECD and then spread to poorer nations, simply as a result of those countries depending on investment from OECD members, made the agreement also seem like an attempt to force concessions from the developing world. France eventually decided to withdraw from the draft agreement, effectively killing it (Clarke & Barlow 1997; Henderson 1999).

The "secret club" rhetoric had several key themes. First, there is the idea that the OECD lacks transparency, and that agreements will be made behind closed doors, without democratic participation or, indeed, approval by the legislature (in Canada, international treaties or agreements do not have to be ratified by the House of Commons (Hogg 2006)). Second, some references underscored the "binding" aspect of any agreements through the OECD. Of course, any international treaty is by definition "binding", but this critique took on more force when combined with the first point about the lack of transparency. Third, the MAI was painted as an agreement that benefitted investors (i.e., the rich).

A distillation of these themes, and an astute invocation of emerging global governance regimes that hinge on international governmental organizations like the OECD, was the following statement, again in the heat of the MAI debate (the intervention was from an NDP member):

> Financial globalization has created its own government. A supranational government with its own machinery, influence networks and means of action. I am talking of the International Monetary Fund (IMF), the World Bank, the Organization for Economic Co-operation and Development (OECD) and the World Trade Organization (WTO). These four institutions speak with one voice – echoed by almost all of the major media – in exalting "market virtues". This world government is a power without a society, that role belonging to the financial markets and giant corporations it represents. The effect of this is that real societies have no power. The situation continues to worsen. As the successor to the GATT, since 1995, the WTO has acquired supranational powers and is out of reach of the controls of parliamentary democracy. (ref. #450, December 2, 1997)

These more critical comments on the OECD are outliers – the vast majority fell into the first four categories and reflect a strong sense that the OECD is a global standard-setting organization. The first two categories indicate that the OECD is a reference point for quality in terms of comparative data on what member and even some non-member states are doing, and is judged to be an objective reference point, even among political opponents. We saw in earlier chapters, especially Chapter 4 on the tools that the OECD uses, that its practice and discourse work strenuously to support and reinforce this niche. The second two categories are also complementary – they highlight the point that the OECD is a producer of global standards and norms of best practice and moreover is a window into global, and largely implacable development trends. This is a version of "TINA" – "there is no alternative". Most the references cited above are to models around taxation, education, trade, health rather than governance or public management per se, a point that we take up in the conclusion to this chapter. But the general discourse is still one of global striving for models and regimes in different policy areas that will maximize efficient and beneficial trade and economic development. Sometimes these regimes are given – as in OECD standards on taxation – but in other cases are models that are in the process of being built, and so there is an element of choice and deliberation, but the references in both countries assume that nascent OECD models are worth building and supporting, not just for members but for non-members as well. This is because of forces discussed in earlier chapters, principally that global trade has expanded to such a degree that OECD members see an interest in the spread of the organization's norms to non-members, and non-members see an advantage in adopting those norms and consequently expanding trade.

Canada and Finland are OECD members, and so will be expected to support OECD norms. However, with the exception of the MAI in Canada, even opposition members adopted a similar rhetoric. The consistency of references over a period of more than a decade also suggests an important mental "niche" that the OECD has been able to build over its existence. How does this translate into influence? From a policy transfer perspective (Dolowitz & Marsh 2000; Evans 2009a; Dolowitz 2009), it creates a ready ground for the reception of ideas being generated by the organization. If to some extent the transfer of policy ideas is a matter of "fashion" (Kantola & Seeck 2011) then the OECD has achieved the status of a "fashion setter". We can see the dynamics of adopting what is "fashionable" in at least two of the categories of discourse discussed above: comparison among states (leaders and laggards) and the weight of OECD models and recommendations. Another important factor that touches less on fashion than on the emergent importance of standards in a globalized world (Brunsson & Jacobsson 2000) is the spread of norms of policy practice. Norms have to come from somewhere, and "norm generation" has its own specific dynamic in policy transfer. The "generator" has to have credibility (as long as we are not talking about coercive transfer), and again the discourse that we observed in these two legislatures suggest a strong credibility for the OECD. Both fashions and norms have to be translated and "domesticated" (Massey 2009; Alasuutari

2010), but it helps tremendously if the generator has a credible base from which to start.

A survey of academics and practitioners

Another stratagem to gauge the OECD's visibility and prominence on governance issues is to conduct a survey of knowledgeable academics and practitioners. For logistical reasons, we decided to approach the Network of Institutes and Schools of Public Administration in Central and Eastern Europe (NISPAcee). NISPAcee was established in 1995 to be a network of academic institutions and government departments and agencies. Its original focus was in central and Eastern Europe, but more recently has expanded its membership into central Asia. It has a membership base of over 1,600 individuals. The organization was chosen for several reasons. It has a large membership base of both academics and practitioners who reside in a region still struggling with "transition" and which accordingly should be attuned to governance and public administration in the developed world. As well, SIGMA (discussed in Chapter 3) has been active in the region since 1992, and so there should be a reasonable familiarity with

Figure 6.1 Good Governance Pillars Discussed in Your Country

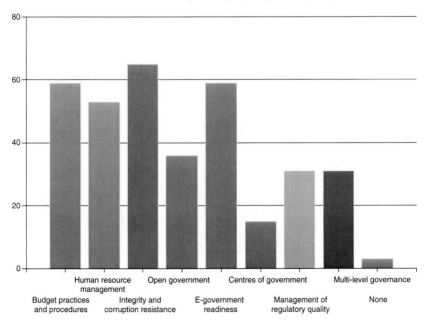

The OECD has eight pillars that it considers important in good governance. Which of these has been studied or debated or discussed in your country? (You may enter multiple responses.)

SIGMA itself as well as the OECD and possibly even GOV (of which SIGMA is a part). The survey was conducted in May–June 2011. There were 103 responses – 73.7 per cent from academics and 24.2 per cent from government, with rest from non-governmental organizations, media, and international agencies. Nine of the ten questions were about the respondent's familiarity with the OECD and its governance work.

Respondents were broadly familiar with the OECD – 83.5 per cent said they were either very familiar or somewhat familiar with the OECD's work on governance and public management. Of those who said that the OECD's work had been referred to by public officials and/or media in their country, 65.6 per cent said that the references were "favourable" – to the OECD as a "neutral and expert" authority. But this was coupled with a question that asked about the OECD's influence on global public management reform: almost half (47.5 per cent) rated it as "medium" whereas almost a third (29.7 per cent) rated it as "small" or low. Two other questions asked about GOV's building blocks and whether these issues are discussed in their respective countries. This is not necessarily a measure of the OECD's/GOV's

Figure 6.2   Leading International Organizations Doing Work on Governance

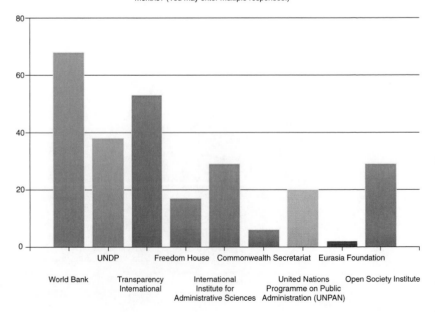

There are several leading international organizations doing work on public management and governance. Which of the following organizations' publications or research have you read or referred to in the last three months? (You may enter multiple responses.)

influence, since it asks about the issues rather than whether it is OECD work itself that is attracting the attention. Nonetheless, it is an indicator of whether these issues resonate with publics in different countries.

We noted in earlier chapters that the governance field is becoming crowded at the international level – at one time the OECD and PUMA were almost alone. Respondents were asked if they consulted the research of other international organizations, with an illustrative list (see Figure 6.2). Heading that list is the World Bank, at 72.3 per cent who consulted its publications in the last three months.

A final question asked about familiarity with the two flagship PUMA/GOV publications that we have discussed elsewhere: *Governance in Transition* and *Modernising Government*. Almost half (43 per cent) of respondents indicated that they had read neither. This is understandable for the earlier document, now over 15 years old, but somewhat surprising for the 2005 version, only six years old at the time of the survey. As we noted above, this group of respondents could be expected to be familiar with the publications, certainly the later one, since they bear directly on governance and public administration issues of relevance in the region. The combination of findings from the survey suggest that the OECD's work on governance, public administration, and policy are well-respected (the "brand") but not necessarily consulted regularly or even drawn upon as a source of inspiration for thinking or writing about governance issues. This makes the issue of "influence" more complicated. If we took the first part of this chapter – the commentaries on *Modernising Government* as the standard for influence and visibility, then there would be no question that the OECD has weight. That was reinforced in the second part in looking at Canadian and Finnish parliamentary debates – the OECD "brand" of high-quality, neutral, and objective data and analysis is rock-solid. Our third section raises some doubts, or at least questions about how the influence of an organization like the OECD is to be weighed.

Evaluation of the PGC

As SG, Donald Johnston's mandate was to reform the OECD in the face of financial pressures and decreasing relevance. One of the changes that was introduced was a regular cycle of evaluations of all OECD committees.[4] An earlier attempt at more regular evaluations had been launched in 1999, with groups of ambassadors conducting the reviews, but it was felt that more professionally based evaluations were required so this system was scrapped and replaced with "In-Depth" evaluations conducted by an evaluation unit located in the SG's office. The "first cycle" of evaluations was started in 2005 and completed in 2011. The "second cycle" will begin all over again, but with a focus on mandate, serving members, and effect and impact. The evaluation of the PGC was completed in 2009, with a formal response by the committee in March 2010.

The following three criteria guided the evaluation: (1) relevance to members' needs in the field of governance, (2) efficiency, and (3) effectiveness. The last criterion explicitly addressed the question of the impact of the committee's work. Over 70 direct interviews were conducted with delegates to the PGC and its working groups and networks as well as OECD officials, supplemented by a survey of different policy communities connected to the committee. Another metric used by the evaluation team was the proportion of "capital-based delegates" serving on the PGC and its subsidiary bodies. The logic here is that countries exhibit a revealed priority for the committee's work by sending delegates from capitals (with all the time and expense associated with that, and usually involving a senior official) rather than appointing delegates from their permanent delegations in Paris. The indicator was the appointment of at least one capital-based delegate to a member's delegation.

The evaluation had mixed results. Overall, the PGC itself was judged to have high relevance in terms of serving members needs and medium to high relevance in terms of impact. On the indicator of capital-based delegates, both the committee and a number of its subsidiary bodies did not fare as well, particularly the Centres of Government network, which had seen a noticeable decline in both the proportion and seniority of capital-based delegates. There was also criticism of the connection between the PGC and some of its subsidiary bodies – as we noted in Chapter 3, the networks of Centres of Government and Senior Budget Officials consist of delegates typically more senior than those on the PGC, and they often have little interest in the committee's work.

Of greatest interest to us here is the assessment of the PGC's effectiveness or impact. The evaluation concluded that the influence of the committee over members' governance and administrative practices was medium to high. This finding was based on the surveys, and asked specifically about areas and "products" where the PGC and its subsidiary bodies had had long-term impact. Among leading areas were conflict of interest guidelines, regulatory reform, and performance measurement. However, while there did seem to be reasonable impact, this was in the absence of concerted communications and follow-up strategies that could enhance impact even further. One of the recommendations from the evaluation accordingly was that the committee develop a communications strategy to fully exploit the potential impact of its work. However, at the same time, the report noted that there had been an increase in recent visits to the public governance and management website at the OECD, suggesting rising public interest in the area.

The report also provided reflections on the longer-term impact of the committee on policy development, as well as specific members' examples from the period 2002–2005 (based on the survey). The summary of longer-term policy effects stated:

186. Comments made by Members replying to the survey indicate, amongst other things, that the Committee's work has the capacity to give

incentives for change and innovation as well as making a systemic overall contribution to the reform agenda and exerting a positive long-term influence by contributing to sustaining the political momentum for public administration reforms. More specifically, in the area of budgeting, the work was cited as shaping policy decisions and serve as a guide to the design of reforms, for example through the introduction of programme budgeting in one Member country and a new structure for performance indicators at ministry level in another.

187. With respect to work on regulatory reform, numerous examples of long-term changes were provided by Members, including reshaping of regulatory frameworks, aligning practices with OECD recommendations, introducing new regulatory policies and tools, initiating policy dialogue on regulatory quality, and pushing forward the agenda concerning better regulation and the reduction of administrative burdens. (OECD 2009: 54 (emphasis in original))

This statement is very much in accord with our previous discussions on the tools and content of OECD products on governance and public management. The most notable aspect is the emphasis on providing incentives for change and innovation, systematic overall contribution, and providing support to sustain the political momentum behind public administration reforms. There are several important dimensions to this. The first, as we noted in our discussion of the rhetoric of OECD analyses, is the emphasis on both the continued necessity of reform and its political risks and challenges. Reform is a necessity in part because the policy context is never stable, it is always shifting, and so governments have to adapt through reform. Financial crises, oil and resource shocks, climate change, ageing of the population, declining public trust, soaring deficits – the list of pressures is endless. Another part of the reform agenda comes from the imperative of improvement and performance in the public sector. The role of the state changed a half-century ago from a night watchman to a primary tool of economic and social progress through effective and efficient public policies. While the health and educational status of a population, or the functioning of its economy, is always affected by exogenous forces, they are strongly affected by the quality of public policy and the quality of state management. Reform becomes an imperative in trying to build and grow societies and economies.

A second dimension is that despite its necessity, reform is always difficult because it is likely to affect stakeholders – both within and outside the state – who have an investment in the *status quo*. Disruptions, even minor ones, can generate resistance. As noted in our discussion of *Making Reform Happen*, the OECD has recognized this in a more overt fashion by not only guiding governments on the content of their reform policies, but on the process of implementing those reforms as well. The OECD's "brand" helps reformers in government point to an external source of legitimacy and inspiration, as well as benchmarks and rankings of the world's most advanced economies and societies. This dovetails with a third dimension that we have discussed in several places – the appetite to be "in fashion" or "modern". This does not afflict all states, but seems to be a factor for many of them. While the OECD and the PGC in particular have recently eschewed the terminology of "best practice" in favour of "good practice"[5] and are more sensitive to different paths to reform, there is still the language of "trends" and central tendencies among members (clear in the accession process).

Some specific examples of PGC/GOV impact on members is provided in Table 6.1. They show that that impact is often less of a "macro-reform" than it is of micro-changes in ministries that quite possibly are under the public's radar. They also show that the influence of the OECD's "products" is often less of a template than an inspiration or broad guideline that serves to inform policymakers in different ministries. This fits with our discussion above and in other parts of this book that policy transfer or diffusion is a more subtle process than simple adoption. While the OECD's work will often be welcomed by domestic reformers, it usually cannot simply be accepted as a whole, but needs to be translated and modified to suit local circumstances (Sahlin-Andersson 1996; Huerta Melchor 2006). And in fact, that translation or editing process takes place at multiple levels and different sites, both within the OECD and outside it among its "targets".

Figure 6.3 provides a schematic model that tries to capture pathways of the OECD's influence. The examples are explicitly from the governance and public management realm, but could just as easily apply to other committees and directorates within the OECD. The schema refers to the types of tools and instruments that constitute the bulk of what GOV and its committees and subsidiary bodies are able to wield – voluntary instruments or guidelines and frameworks rather than the small handful of legal instruments at its disposal (see Chapter 4). The legal instruments have more force, and countries must "sign-on" to detailed provisions, such as in the Anti-Bribery Convention or the accession process. Even so, legal instruments also go through a process of translation within the OECD, among its members, and ultimately provide some scope for adaptation to national conditions by signatories. Despite this, the pathways of influence are relatively clear. They get murkier once we consider other types of "outputs".

In considering Figure 6.3, we can start at the top left with the OECD itself. At the centre of governance and public management activity is the GOV directorate and its associated committees and subsidiary bodies. In the GOV/PGC case, as we saw above from the evaluation report, the committee is somewhat weak in that it has high turn-over of its own Members and loose coordination with its subsidiary bodies (working groups and networks). But as we saw in Chapter 4, almost all publications from this sector involve the committees (one of the three taking a lead depending on the subject matter) and various divisions within GOV. This involves sustained

Table 6.1 Examples of PGC/GOV Impacts on Members (2002–2004)

	Country Examples of Use and Impacts on Policy Development
Austria	• OECD publications on integrity and conflict of interest used in designing a value-based code of conduct for civil servants.
Belgium	• OECD work on administrative simplification had impact through a measurement office created in the Prime Minister's Office.
Canada	• OECD work on administrative simplification shaped approach in designing the Paperwork Burden Reduction Initiative.
Czech Republic	• Used in the design of regulatory impact assessment.
Denmark	• Introduction of accrual accounting. • Inspiration for part of government's work on e-democracy. • OECD publications on human resource management served as benchmarks for reform.
European Commission	• Review of regulatory impact analysis practices helped shape the European Commission's impact assessment tool.
Finland	• Considers the OECD's publications in the area of e-government "the most reliable in the field."
Germany	• OECD publications on human resource management translated and distributed. • OECD products on integrity and anti-corruption distributed to all persons concerned with that field in the federal government.
Hungary	• Adoption of fiscal responsibility law including enhance regulation on transparency and accountability. • OECD studies of e-government in Finland and Norway were "invaluable" in providing materials for the preparation of their own study.
Italy	• Adoption of triennial budget. • Guidelines for promoting e-democracy approved. • OECD work on regulatory governance in a multilevel framework inspired an agreement between the State and municipalities. • Used OECD's regulatory quality indicators. • The e-government strategy drew directly on OECD guidelines in the field.

Table 6.1 Examples of PGC/GOV Impacts on Members (2002–2004) – *continued*

Country	Examples of Use and Impacts on Policy Development
Japan	• Introduction of accrual accounting. • OECD 2004 publication on performance pay translated and published and used as guide.
Mexico	• Adopting whole-of-government approach. • Inspiration for the first government-wide Professional Service Law. • Technical unit in centre of government created to oversee regulatory reform. • Helped government evaluate alternatives to traditional regulation. • OECD products on e-government were used to develop national e-government strategy.
Netherlands	• Principles for citizen consultation adopted.
Norway	• OECD peer review of regulatory quality led to reforms.
Portugal	• Centre of Government concept adopted. • New system introduced linking employment, careers and remuneration. • OECD work on regulatory governance in a multi-level framework inspired a regulatory simplification programme.
Switzerland	• Peer review had "substantial" impact on development of Swiss economic policy.
Turkey	• Introduced regulatory impact assessment as result of OECD review.

Source: (OECD 2009: Table 12). Note that non-response rates to the survey were between 40 per cent and 70 per cent. Respondents were asked to rate specific publications ("outputs") as medium to high.

Figure 6.3 Pathways of Influence and "Translation"

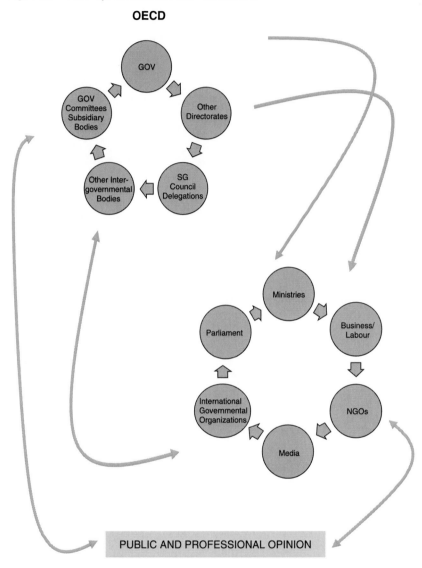

and repeated negotiations over the parameters of work and various drafts of reports as they move from initial to final stages. And of course the various organizations are not static. Delegates to committees and subsidiary bodies change regularly, bringing new people and new ideas and new negotiations and compromises to the table. The directorate is constantly shifting as well, depending on projects.

The directorate and its committees also interact with other directorates in their work, and as we noted earlier, some directorates (e.g., DAF, DAC, and ECO) have important responsibilities in areas of public management not within the GOV/PGC domain. Again, this can involve negotiations over text and interpretation, often balanced by the usual organizational imperatives to maintain some degree of autonomy and independence. All directorates are responsible to the SG and the Council, and this adds another layer of actors in the priority-setting process. We also saw that the SG's office has initiatives of its own in the governance and public management field: *Making Reform Happen* is a good example where the lead was taken by the SG's office in cooperation with directorates, committees, and delegations. The result of the process – even to the level of the final title of the document – reflected negotiations among all these actors. Finally, there are representatives of other international governmental organizations such as the IMF and the World Bank that sit on a variety of committees as observers, but also have both their own input into the process and their own mechanisms of conveying proceedings and developments to their parent organizations. If we put all these players together, it is clear that any single product from the OECD is in fact a complex amalgam of commentaries, discussions, reviews, and cascading matrixes of networked communications. There are, in short, internal influences and counter-influences behind any given document, report, assessment or review.

The figure has arrows on the top right that move down and impact another group of networked players at the national as well as international level, and at the lower left has another arrow that suggests interaction from these players and the various bodies in the OECD. We can begin with the ministries as the main interlocutors with the OECD. The flow of influence here is of course both ways, since ministries/governments appoint delegates both to the Council and committees, as well as the specialized bodies, and OECD products are usually targeted (in the governance area) at ministries. The subtlety here with the governance area is that GOV/PGC have a mandate to maintain a "whole-of-government" approach in their analysis. This had historical roots, as we saw in Chapter 2, in the creation of a constituency for TECO's and later PUMA's work: centres of government, budgeting, human resource management, regulation and so on. So, whereas other directorates tend to have a direct relationship with either one or a limited number of substantive ministries of government (e.g., education, environment), GOV/PGC's ministries are horizontal: prime minister's offices, ministries of finance, human resource agencies, offices responsible for regulatory affairs and e-government. However, as a caveat to this, we should note that one of GOV/PGC's building blocks is multi-level governance, which has brought the committee and the directorate into contact with subnational as well as municipal governments.

The ministries (and other government organizations) are perhaps the most direct pathway of influence for the OECD, but as we noted above, this is a pathway with various filters and transmission mechanisms that compromise the "influence" of any given OECD product. We have noted before that among reformers in any particular government, there will be an openness and even an enthusiasm to engage the OECD as legitimation for changes that will have to be defended and fought for locally. But there is also a logic of sovereignty and "equal status" that makes simple transfer and simple acceptance of OECD recommendations, standards and norms problematic. Even given the reality that international recommendations (as long as they are not legal instruments) will have to be translated for local circumstances, the process of acceptance should show some element of adaptation to avoid the appearance of "being lectured to" by the OECD.

Other local pathways are the media, NGOs, business and labour. Governance and public management rarely make it to the front pages of the media (though accession does attract attention), but work on human resources management, e-government, budgeting, and the work of DAF and ECO do attract the attention of business and labour groups. The OECD as a whole has been working harder to engage with civil society organizations, and we noted in Chapter 4 that at the Venice Ministerial the communiqué explicitly called for a strategy to bring civil society groups more closely into the GOV/PGC process. Legislatures also become a refracting mirror to the release of OECD work and its mention in the media – as we saw in the comparison of the Canadian and Finnish legislative debates. Parliamentarians and political parties parse OECD work in their own ways, which then gets fed back through the media as another layer of interpretation about what an OECD report actually "means".

Then there are the pathways that lead through other international organizations, as well as the governments who are members of those organizations. Many of these same governments and organizations already interact with the OECD as observers on various committees, and so provide a double conduit of influence – they listen and participate in the OECD, and the OECD listens and participates with them. For instance, in Chapter 3 we pointed out that the SBO network has observers from the IMF and World Bank, and also from the Financial Action Task Force (FATF), which itself has 34 states as observers who may themselves act as observers at the OECD (which has observer status at the FATF). The FATF's core members are: African Development Bank, Asian Development Bank, Commonwealth Secretariat, Egmont Group of Financial Intelligence Units European Bank for Reconstruction and Development, European Central Bank, Europol, Inter-American Development Bank, the Organization of American States, the International Association of Insurance Supervisors, the IMF, the International Organization of Securities Commissions, Interpol, the Offshore Group of Banking Supervisors, the United Nations, the World Bank and World Customs Organization (WCO). The Expert Group on Conflict of Interest has ad hoc observers from Asian Development

Bank, the Inter-American Development Bank, the Organization of American States and the World Bank. "Observership" of course does not mean that OECD standards and norms on governance are somehow automatically transferred to these other organizations, but it does illustrate an important network dynamic of constant circulation of information among all the members of the network. It is close to inconceivable that, at some level or in some relevant division of any of these organizations, that they would be unaware of activities, strategies or projects of the others. This is not influence in the conventional sense, but acts as a sort of conceptual wallpaper that surrounds all the players and sets reference points.

A good example of the above is the OECD's Anti-Corruption Network (ACN) for Eastern Europe and Central Asia. It is an outreach programme of the Working Group on Bribery in International Business Transactions, which is a subsidiary body to the Investment Committee (one of six discussed briefly in Chapter 3) of the DAF. Its website states:

> The Anti-Corruption Network was established in 1998. The main objective of the ACN is to support its member countries in their fight against corruption by providing a regional forum for the promotion of anti-corruption activities, exchange of information, elaboration of best practices and donor coordination. The ACN operates through general meetings and conferences, sub-regional initiatives and thematic projects.
>
> The ACN is open to all countries in Eastern Europe and Central Asia. The OECD member states also take part in ACN activities. The main counterparts of the ACN are the national governments and anti-corruption authorities of the participating countries. Civil society, the business sector, international organisations and international financial institutions also take an active part in the ACN.[6]

Target countries for the initiative are: Albania, Armenia, Azerbaijan, Belarus, Bosnia and Herzegovina, Croatia, Georgia, Kazakhstan, Kyrgyz Republic,Latvia, Lithuania, the Former Yugoslav Republic of Macedonia, Moldova, Montenegro, Romania, the Russian Federation, Serbia, Tajikistan, Ukraine and Uzbekistan. The website also notes that: "In addition to national governments, the ACN involves civil society, business, international organisations: the World Bank, the European Bank for Reconstruction and Development (EBRD), Transparency International (TI), Open Society Institute (OSI), United Nations Office on Drugs and Crime (UNODC), United Nations Development Programme (UNDP), Council of Europe (CoE), Group of States Against Corruption (GRECO), the Organisation for Security and Cooperation in Europe (OSCE), International Chamber of Commerce (ICC), Business and Industry Advisory Committee to the OECD (BIAC), American Bar Association (ABA) and others".

Countries submit reports that are then discussed by the ACN, which issues recommendations.[7] Countries respond to those recommendations (and are directly involved in shaping them), and then are expected to implement them. Monitoring reports are periodically issued, indicating the progress of implementation. Gradually, global standards on corruption and bribery leech out from the OECD member states and begin to morph into the legal systems of target states. This yields a loosely coupled or coordinated system of equivalent standards, that then becomes a regulatory regime dealing with such things as money laundering, government procurement rules, commissions to combat corruption, the training of judges and police officers, and so on.

Another example of influence exercised through other international organizations is in the budgetary field. In 2001 the OECD released its *Best Practices for Budget Transparency* (discussed in Chapter 4), which was then incorporated by the IMF in its *Manual on Fiscal Transparency* (2001).[8] Together with the UN's statistical benchmarks in COFOG (Classifications of the Functions of Government) these have become standards of compliance in governmental fiscal reports to the Fund. The standards in turn inform the reporting requirements of donor agencies around the world, as well as private lenders to governments. In a nominal sense these are still "soft" law and voluntary standards, since no government can be compelled to use them. But to the extent the governments seek donor funds, or accession to the EU, for example, they will have to comply with this set of OECD standards, and the larger family of standards of which they are a part.

This is a complicated *tableau* of interactions, to be sure, but it captures the non-linear, networked capacities and activities of the OECD and its member states and partner governments and international agencies. The OECD, specifically in the person of the current SG, Angel Gurría, is well aware that the organization's relevance depends on its service to its members, to the wider international community, and to key global governance institutions. In discussing the OECD's response to the 2008 financial crisis, Gurría said: "Because we responded, that allowed us to connect with, for example, the G20. So now we're a member of the G20, and we're a member ... because we were working on the substantive issues of the G20, not because we asked to join. I mean, we asked to join like crazy, but eventually we were invited because they thought that we were [relevant], that we had merit on the substance".[9] This has been formalized into a strategy of combining efforts with key international institutions to promote "policy coherence":

> We proposed the creation of a network for co-operation on policy coherence, bringing together the international organisations involved in the G20 (IMF, World Bank, FSB, ILO, WTO and OECD). The objective would be to improve co-ordination and exchange of information among international organisations. If we can foster a real cross-fertilisation of ideas, it will help us to stay at the frontier of new thinking and ensure we provide relevant and pragmatic advice to governments in their efforts to

design and implement better policies for better lives. We also need to continue to produce norms and standards which by their quality and credibility can be embraced by the international community. (OECD 2011d: 26)

The SG has made a special point of enumerating his speeches and contacts around the world with other governments and international organizations: his 2011 report listed his visits abroad (50), number of speeches (149), and mentions in media (1,200).

None of this would matter if it did not filter into public perceptions and attitudes. It would all be a game within a game, played by elites. To some extent it is that – *Making Reform Happen* is well aware that stakeholders and vested interests will resist reform. Perhaps this is why the OECD has placed such emphasis on the importance of public trust – it knows that reform is a violation and a turbulence. Certainly, the emphasis on almost constant reform means a result that is almost constant turbulence. Our discussion of the rhetoric of OECD studies on governance shows that the organization is well aware that the reform project is a permanent revolution. Acquiring and retaining public support and public trust is a key ingredient in that project. On one measure – its image of neutrality and objectivity – the OECD has been successful in conveying its message to the public. As we saw in the Finnish and the Canadian parliamentary debates, both government and opposition refer to the OECD as an impartial source of reputable data. To this extent, we can be reasonably sure that that image is conveyed to and accepted by the public. However, any direct sense of how the public perceives the OECD is almost impossible to gauge, particularly, as we have shown above, since the flows of information come from so many different sources and not simply the OECD itself.

Rautalin and Alasuutari (2007) came at this problem through an examination of the interpretation of the results of the OECD's Programme for International Student Assessment (PISA) in Finland. PISA is administered every three years (there have been four assessments, in 2000, 2003, 2006, and 2009). In 2003 there were 43 participating countries, and in 2009 the number had climbed to 65. In each country, between 4,500 and 10,000 15-year olds are examined in mathematical literacy, problem solving, reading literacy and scientific literacy. In 2000 and 2003 Finland was ranked at the top, for example, in the uniformity of achievement among different regions in the country, the equivalence of performance between boys and girls, and the minimal impact of socioeconomic status on educational outcomes. As Rautalin and Alasuutari point out, the PISA studies do not provide any analysis of the factors that contribute to these results, leaving this to national-level institutions. The Finnish Ministry of Education produces more detailed, interpretive studies of the PISA results that links them to teaching materials and methods. The teaching profession also provides its own interpretations.

The study examined the discussion of the PISA results in editorials in the official organ of the Finnish teacher's union, *Opettaja-lehti*. The editorials were generally positive, of course, given that the OECD's results could be presented as a reflection of the excellence of the Finnish teaching profession in the face of only "average" resources, again in comparison to other OECD countries. They argued that "competent and selected Finnish teachers are behind the good results – not the successful planning of education, supportive families or even ambitious students" (Rautalin & Alasuutari 2007: 353). The few weaknesses identified by the OECD were ascribed to lower average unit costs in education in Finland as compared to other participating countries, and so the "good news" of Finnish educational achievement was interpreted as "bad news" about Finland "lagging behind" other countries in their investments in education. While Rautalin and Alasuutari could not come to a clear conclusion of the direct impact of the PISA studies on Finnish education, they do think that the nature of the national debate about education was changed: "the PISA study has caused much discussion about Finnish comprehensive education – not only about its strengths, but also about its present problems – in various forums. ... On the whole, the PISA study has certainly given the teachers and other actors in the field of Finnish education a boost of confidence and the conviction that they are doing at least something right. It has also probably increased Finnish people's respect for the teaching profession" (Rautalin & Alasuutari 2007: 359).

The approach that Rautalin and Alasuutari take is to try to gauge the impact of the OECD on public opinion through its impact on professions in particular policy fields. That approach is replicated by a number of other studies, most of which conclude similarly that the OECD exercises influence through altering policy debate among professional communities, including government – and this is why Figure 6.1 combines "public opinion" with "professional opinion". And most of these studies point out that the OECD is entangled (as the complicated Figure 6.1 suggests) with other international organizations and forces that drive public and professional opinion. Some samples (from not necessarily OECD-friendly analysts):

> The OECD is only one agent among a host of international institutions that, in a complementary manner, have participated in the promotion of a neoliberal world order; nevertheless, it has played a key role. ... The DAC forms part of a complex web of international organizations that have been essential to the globalization of economic and social relations and whose prescriptions have been tremendously influential, particularly in financially dependent developing countries. It has contributed to the formation of a transnational order despite the absence of coercive mechanisms that would enable the DAC to impose its policies and enforce agreed-upon rules. (Ruckert 2008: 110, 111–112)

Since 1961, the OECD has tried to construct an investment regime characterized by progressive liberalization. The efforts are remarkable for their consistency, despite ever-changing personnel and the reluctance of member states to bind themselves to liberalization commitments. Indeed, much of the OECD's work on investment calls into question its basic status as a member-driven international organization. Member governments often have not shared the OECD's end goals on liberalization. ... Yet, the organization is right to suggest that it has achieved a great deal. Members' exchange controls have been completely abandoned (Greece and Ireland were the last to do so in 1994), and there has been a substantial reduction in restrictions to FDI [foreign direct investment]. ... if the OECD has achieved nothing else, it has helped domestic proponents of liberalization pursue their goals. (Williams 2008: 131, 132)

One of the most notable things about the last fourteen years of OECD work on labour market policy is that the record of "policy learning" and transfer has been poor. While some member states, those ideologically predisposed to the Jobs Strategy, adopted OECD recommendations, many did not. Despite OECD efforts, existing domestic institutional arrangements, domestic policy networks, and ideological differences made much of the initial OECD program politically unthinkable throughout Europe, no matter how much credibility the OECD lent its reading of "best practices". (McBride et al 2008: 163–164)

... although OECD ideas made their way into [Danish] domestic debates, they did not play a large role when it came time for serious negotiations inside the Zeuthen Commission. One major exception to this was the concept of structural unemployment, which can be credited in part with helping to pave the way for reform by providing a common problem conceptualization and a focus on a particular (though varied) set of labour market reforms as possible solutions. ... we may not understand the complexities of the OECD's influence if we limit out analysis to a comparison of OECD recommendations and domestic policy. Instead, we need to trace the flow of ideas through the processes of idea transfer, idea acceptance, and idea impact. Such an approach can reveal how ideas are translated in the domestic context. (Grinvalds 2008: 200, 201)

The success of the OECD Guidelines [for the Licensing of Genetic Inventions] lies primarily in defining the policy problem and the most feasible location of policy change. ... this case provides some supporting evidence of the benefits of engaging a broad group of stakeholders in order to generate fulsome policy debate. The recognition of common concerns related to gene patenting raised by these diverse interests intensified the interest and commitment in generating some form of policy solution to the problems identified by health and industry departments in member states. ... the use of the OECD as a forum that created a dialogue between health and industry policy was an important factor in moving towards a workable response. (Drouillard & Gold 2008: 222, 224, 225)

These studies point to influence, but a diffuse and complicated influence. We have cited them at length to both support the threads in Figure 6.1 and to challenge the conclusions of a collected study by Armingeon and Beyeler (2004) that the influence of the OECD on national social policies was minimal. As Rautalin and Alasuutari (2007: 360) point out: "Although the contributors to the study found remarkable concordance between OECD recommendations and national policies, they reject the hypothesis of a strong and direct impact. This is because the concordance can be due to the influence of other international organisations; the national reforms can be caused by domestic challenges; the policy changes can result from new constellations of domestic political power; and, finally, there may have been changes in economic paradigms, not only at the level of the OECD but also at the national level".

Conclusions

Assessing the direct impact of an international organization that does not have any other tools at its disposal except research and reports is difficult. This chapter came at the problem through four lenses. The lens of leading academics was more or less unequivocal: the OECD is a key international node of information and research on public management and governance issues. Its influence in part is a result of its unique ability to provide comparative data from its members and non-members alike. Though the field has become more crowded in the last decade, the OECD still stands out as an important source of research and data about governments and the details of public management. Add to that its research across all its other fields – from the environment to education – and it is virtually unrivalled.

The lens of our case studies of Canada and Finland reinforced this conclusion. The OECD is treated with respect by all sides in government debates – it has the "gold standard" reputation of neutrality, objectivity, and quality. We saw only rare references (mostly tied to the MAI) to the OECD as a secret club of rich nations bent on neo-liberalization of the global economy. The academic sources we cited at the close of the chapter sometimes took this view (primarily on economic issues like taxation or trade), but they all agreed that the OECD has had influence in a variety of policy fields. The NISPAcee survey results cast some doubt on the OECD's influence, and even the OECD's own evaluation of the PGC rated its efficacy as in the "high-medium" range, though as Table 6.1 demonstrates, we can clearly map some direct influences from OECD work to member states. Our final section on pathways tried to trace some of the complexities of the means by which an international organization might impact on domestic policy. That exercise revealed the complexities of those pathways – they are not direct or linear. We need a different language to capture these dynamics.

In a Newtonian world, things have effect and impact because of how they directly collide with other things. We would expect, in this kind of world, to be able to trace some output from the OECD to some result or change in a given government and its policies. Sometimes we do see this – the impact of a convention or a legal instrument, the muscle that the OECD can flex on accession. But these are the exceptions, not the rule. We need another, post-Newtonian way of seeing the OECD and its effects. That perspective has come up in a variety of instances, most directly in a key theme of this book on the nature of the OECD as a network. But we have seen it as well in terms such as "fashion", "brand", and "wallpaper". All of these terms evoke processes in which norms filter or mist their way through complex social mechanisms to have an ultimate effect or impact.

In this respect, the OECD's impact on global public management reform is an effect of ideas, and supports a shift in international relations thinking now about a decade old that emphasizes the impact of norms and normative concerns on public policy-making, norms that have the quality of "oughtness" which involve "standards of 'appropriate' or 'proper' behavior…" (Finnemore & Sikkink 1998: 891). The discovery and persuasive articulation of these norms is undertaken by "norm entrepreneurs", and the OECD is a good example of that type of entrepreneurship: "One prominent feature of modern organizations and an important source of influence for international organizations in particular is their use of expertise and information to change the behavior of other actors" (Finnemore & Sikkink 1998: 899). As we showed in our pathways discussion, these norms are themselves constructed in complicated ways, and move in both directions, from the international to the domestic, and the domestic to the international.

Then, there is an equally complicated process of "translation", transformation or domestication of those norms into local arenas. Alasuutari makes the case that this is more than mere translation, but a "field battle" of various groups and organizations.

> It would be problematic, however, to define domestication in such a way that only processes that make a visible and measurable change to existing practices in accordance with the exogenous model qualify. Instead, in this article we used domestication to depict any process through which a transnational model is turned into practices. From that perspective, it is quite possible that as a consequence of the domestic field battle, the same transnational model may give rise to quite distinct prac-

tices in different regional states, or it may also be that a model's actual effects on the domestic practices are minimal. It makes sense to talk about domestication also in cases in which changes take place at a discursive, not at a practical level. It means that the points and perspectives imported from a transnational context are integrated with the existing framework within which the issue is discussed. On the other hand, as a consequence of local field battles, formal administrative practices may sometimes be changed, but the reform has hardly any effect on the informal rules and rationales applied, so that it does not have any impact on people's lives. In the long run, though, such partial changes probably still spread their influence to other aspects of social reality. (Alasuutari 2011: 14)

Field battles, arrows, mists and ripples. Hardly any sense of impact or influence, of any kind of effect. But let's go micro for a moment. Do any of us have any strong impact or effect on the others around us, except through norms, values, practices and the accommodations of a thousand small acts in specific circumstances? The OECD is no different. Internally it seethes with ambition and horizons of possibility and challenge, balanced by the calm of careful professionals doing their measured work.

Its effect is through the network within which it is embedded. There is a global conversation among elites about governance, and in these days of financial crisis and enormous changes in the public sector, that conversation is more intense and focused. We have not been able to "prove" a specific impact of the OECD on these conversations, but it is hard to imagine a world of governance and public management reform without the OECD as a key player. Perhaps as wallpaper, as a background, as a network – but neither dismissed nor ignored.

We take up network effects and dynamics in the concluding chapter.

7
Conclusion

This book has examined one part of the work that OECD does – governance and public management. The OECD conducts research on many other topics, from the space economy to education, and these areas often gain much more public attention that its research on public management – the PISA results routinely make headlines among both participating and non-participating countries (Ripley 2011). While governance and public management may not generate headlines, we have tried to show that they are nonetheless important for all states and for the OECD itself, despite its historical emphasis on economic development. Even the best economic policies will not achieve their objectives if state administrations are corrupt or inept. One of the contributions of the OECD – not headline grabbing, but a contribution nonetheless – is to reflect on "good governance" practices and circulate research on those practices to governments themselves and to other networks of institutions that focus on governance issues.

Key themes

As we tried to show in the opening chapters, the particular way in which governance issues are discussed globally today had to emerge, and the OECD was part of that emergence and a contributor to it. In 1961 it was far from obvious what good governance and "modern" public management might mean. Single states of course had always engaged in reform activities in the governance and management field, but they did so on their own and with the belief that governance inevitably would reflect local circumstances, and specific national experiences, histories, and institutions. As we showed in Chapter 1, one crucial locus of discussion on what today we would describe as "state capacity" was in the development community and among donors. We showed how the World Bank and other donor organizations began to link economic development to administrative capacity in the mid-1980s, and how there were scattered international meetings (Caiden 1991) on the topic hosted by academic associations (e.g., the American Society for Public Administration). The OECD's signal contribution came with the Madrid conference in 1979, which was crucial in establishing a public management focus within the organization that would be different from the aid and development approach that had characterized TECO to that point. Chapter 2 showed how a public management "policy area" was constructed in the 1980s, culminating in the creation of PUMA and later GOV. This period also happened to be the high-water mark for new public management (NPM), and the OECD contributed to those debates through its leading edge research through the 1990s. It continues to make important contributions to discussions about governance and public management in the eight "building block" areas for GOV and in the other sections of the OECD we discussed in Chapter 3 (though see below for what might be missing from the GOV/PGC agenda).

We also argued that the OECD's ability to influence governments and the international conversation about public management is a result of its unique characteristics as an agent of policy transfer, being part think tank and part international, diplomatic agency. A key strength for the OECD is its membership base and how that membership articulates with the research and other "products" that come from it. Its 34 members are among the richest economies in the world, and together with Russia as a potential accession member and the five countries targeted for enhanced engagement (Brazil, China, India, Indonesia and South Africa) collectively account for 80 per cent of world trade and investment. Members provide funding to keep the organization afloat and increasingly to support specific projects of interest to them. As we pointed out, the OECD's committee system, with its working parties, groups and networks of experts, is seen as a key strength and a distinguishing mark of the OECD in comparison to other international governmental organizations. These committees and groups are populated with practitioner-experts from member states, and so can bring special and applied expertise to bear on public policy discussions. The intermingling of these practitioners, as we noted, is routinely cited as the main benefit of the OECD – it is a venue or a site for informed but practically oriented policy research and discussion. That committee system is complemented by a Secretariat made up of some of the world's brightest and most talented researchers. Of course, these strengths can sometimes serve to weaken the OECD as well. Most decisions are made by consensus, and that frequently slows the process. Larger members, in part because of their funding clout, can sometimes (though not inevitably) steer the OECD where they want it to go. And while accession and enhanced engagement are laudable goals, they do pose the risk of diluting the OECD even further from its original roots in 1961 as essentially a small, homogeneous club of cross-Atlantic members. The OECD "can no longer take support from its members for granted" (Trondal et al 2010: 85).

One of the key themes of this book has been to view the OECD and its work on governance and public management as a "networked organization".

We provided clear evidence of this in several chapters, but especially in Chapter 4 in looking at the tools the OECD uses. The key one is peer review, and again this reflects the unusual nature of the OECD as a combination of research-based think tank and member-based international agency. The OECD does not have a big stick, in fact it has virtually no sticks at all outside of a handful of international instruments. It therefore has to depend on the quality of its work and the voluntary acceptance of the conclusions and recommendations of that work by member and non-member states. Peer reviews need the support of the targeted country, and it is up to the targeted country to implement any recommendations from a peer review. Another example is "at a glance" reports, which rely on countries to provide data that can then be used for comparative purposes.

Chapter 4 highlighted ten features of a globally networked organization like the OECD. Here we will only emphasize the importance of flexible and interconnected nodes, and the circulation and exchange of information. It is its nodal quality that makes the OECD such an important player in so many different global policy networks. It has had to struggle to maintain that relevance (through outreach and engagement strategies), but it has succeeded. Chapter 6 provided different lenses on the OECD's influence, but it is clear that no policymaker could have a serious discussion of fields like education, trade, information technology, e-government, regulatory reform or anti-corruption without referring to OECD work in those areas. The influence of GOV on global policy debates around public sector reform may not be as singularly important as the influence of other directorates might be in their respective policy fields, but this book has shown that it is a prime reference point. If we conceive of global policy networks around governance and public management, they will tend to be organized around sub-themes or topics (e.g., the building blocks). The OECD's contribution through GOV and its committees is that it is a connector to all these nodes of other institutions and players – from academic institutions to professional associations to other think tanks and even private firms that have an interest in governance questions (as information technology companies do).

In reflecting on the nature of the OECD as itself a networked organization and a contributor to other networks, we can see more clearly the contribution it makes to global governance. The OECD now participates in the annual G20 summits, which increasingly appear as a central steering mechanism for the global community. However, even the G20 is not a "global government" and so the mechanisms of coordination have to be more subtle. We introduced the term "isomorphic governance" in the Preface to capture this dynamic, and now we can describe it in greater detail. One key ingredient is what we described in several chapters as the emergence of "public management" as a policy field in its own right through the 1980s and 1990s, an emergence that was partly supported and furthered by the OECD itself. Moreover, it is a policy field where different states can learn from each other – "lessons" and "good practices" – even while there are legitimate reasons for them to maintain unique institutions or practices. We saw how in *Governance in Transition* (1995), PUMA was prepared to be more prescriptive, but softened its tone a decade later with *Modernising Government* (2005). It has maintained that balanced tone ever since, but as we saw in the discussion of the governance *acquis* in Chapter 4 and in Chapter 5, it tries to give due weight to national difference while at the same time developing standards, norms, guides and other tools that can gradually introduce similar patterns of governance practices in different states.

The emergence of "public management" as a policy field therefore assumes that countries can borrow from each other. But this has to be complemented by several other ingredients. First, there has to be, to some minimal degree, a common language or conceptual universe within which there can be shared dialogue. We can see the knowledge production that took place in TECO and PUMA and then GOV as key elements in the development of this conceptual universe. The mountain of studies, reports, conferences and meetings over three decades did not amount to consensus, but did create common reference points so that people could tell that they were talking about the same things when they referred to "open government" for example, even if they might disagree about practice. A complementary ingredient is a desire to "learn lessons" – if no one cares or wants to borrow or transfer policy, there will by definition be no learning. We argued that even in the area of "soft law" in which the OECD specializes, there are several drivers that create a momentum for transferring and learning. One is the impulse we described in Chapter 5 to be "modern". Various analysts have pointed to the appetite for being modern as part of the influence of fashion or fads in all policy areas. Another driver is the importance of "policy search". Policymakers in fact are often much more puzzled and befuddled, especially about severely challenging policy problems, than we acknowledge. The impulse to borrow (or at least see what your comparators are doing) is an impulse to find solutions. Another driver can be competition – states increasingly compete against each other for investments, capital and labour, and their competitive capacity increasingly depends on having the best or at least very good policies, and in the governance area, institutions of high quality that can steer economies and maximize production. If we add all of these drivers together, they provide a constant stimulus to governments to at least look at other policy frameworks if not necessarily borrow them completely. And finally, of course, the case of accession, the OECD does have an ability to demand formal compliance with different elements of its *acquis*.

Once all these ingredients are in play, we can see how a loosely coupled system of global governance can emerge even in the absence of "hard law". The two editions of *Government at a Glance* (GaaG) we discussed in Chapter 4 show that by providing comparative statistics, the OECD encourages governments to look at each other and compare. Exactly the same process takes place with peer review, where the experience of other countries is brought to bear through the participation of peers from those countries (in addition to the detailed comparative work the GOV directorate does – see the discussion of the peer review of Brazil human resource management in Chapter 4). The MENA initiative did precisely the same thing, and indeed that was one of its key challenges – to encourage governments to compare, borrow and reform in a region where those practices were largely unknown.

Now, when governments actually do borrow they are not simply engaged in a straight transfer. Policy diffusion, as we discussed, takes place through a process of translation and adaptation. Even in the case of harder instruments such a the 1997 Convention on Combating Bribery of Foreign Public Officials in International Business Transactions (discussed in Chapter 4), we saw how the OECD combined common definitions and principles with sufficient flexibility in application to avoid "uniformity or changes in fundamental principles of a Party's legal system". It said that the goal was "functional equivalence". In the case of the Convention, state parties do have to meet certain legal obligations, meaning that they will impose a policy regime that has basic points in common with anti-bribery regimes in other signatory states. The reliance on peer review also adds another layer of comparison and borrowing.

From a global governance perspective, these "functional equivalencies" yield similar policy regimes across states, but with no central coordination or imposition "from above". It means that businesses, for example, will face similar policy regimes dealing with bribery of public officials in different countries, and so will have to behave in the same way in all those countries. When governments count and classify their expenditures in the same way (using COFOG), and report on them in similar ways (using, for example, the guides in GOV's budgeting building block), they start behaving in similar ways, again without any overt coordination. The spread of common human resource management practices in government (regarding compensation, promotion, movement through the ranks) means that public bureaucracies begin to resemble each other, and most importantly, that the people who work in those bureaucracies will begin to have similar outlooks on what counts as "good" public service practice.

Naturally, we should not exaggerate the degree of isomorphism that takes place, precisely because there is always a translation process, or more precisely, what Campbell calls <u>bricolage</u>: "The key is to recognize that actors often craft new institutional solutions by recombining elements in their repertoire through an innovative process of <u>bricolage</u> whereby new institutions differ from but resemble old ones" (Campbell 2004: 68). We discussed some of the complexities of this process in Chapter 6, and in some respects research on this process of <u>bricolage</u> at the national level in the face of policy diffusion of ideas and institutions is just beginning. But if institutions mean anything, then they have the capacity to affect the perceptions and ideas of people who inhabit them (March & Olsen 1989), and through that process to change behaviour. To the extent to which there is isomorphism, even if the translation or bricolage does not mechanically reproduce a policy regime at the national level, it will insert similarities in definitions and understandings and consequently engender emerging similarities in practices. For its signatories, the Convention means a common set of definitions of bribery and a common set of practices regarding it. While other OECD governance diffusion processes lack the edge of a legal instrument, in principle the mechanisms are identical.

Another important point that is often overlooked in the diffusion literature is the enormous and constant effort it requires, particularly for an organization like the OECD that lacks the power of conditionalities. We have traced that activity on various dimensions – the creation of directorates in the OECD dealing with governance and public management, the conferences, meetings, speeches, reviews and publications and other activities – the process is never-ending because it is a process of setting standards and altering discourse and debates. In order to do that over time, the efforts have to be continuous as well. The SG's worries on the relevance of the organization in a sense reflect this sensibility. The OECD will not be relevant if it loses its well-earned reputation for neutrality, objectivity, and the high quality of its research. The only way to consistently establish and hang on to this "mind share" is to be a visible producer of neutral, objective and high quality research, to be a vibrant and active node in global policy networks. In a sense, as a "transfer agent" with no leverage except its ideas, it has to show a constant production of those ideas, as well as being perceived to be engaged and active. We noted this organizational imperative in several examples throughout this book. The accession process and enhanced engagement were deliberate strategies to bring important new players on the global stage more directly into the OECD, and to bring the OECD to them. The communications strategies around GaaG are another example – to create a "product" that brings GOV into the increasingly important area of governance indicators and measures. The careful counting of SG's speeches, meetings and trips as listed in his annual report to Council is another, more pedestrian, attempt to provide visible evidence of relevance – as was, of course, the strong desire to be included somehow in the G20. And we noted as well in Chapter 4 in our discussion of the Anti-Bribery Convention, this constant production of materials and connections is part of a "longer game" of policy diffusion. This is another aspect of diffusion theory that tends to be overlooked in the literature – that it is not about "single" victories, but more about a constant reform and improvement process over time. The 1997 Convention was an important milestone, but for those who work in the OECD, it and similar initiatives are simply the platforms for either stronger or wider measures in the future, and so the research activity and reports also prepare the ground for more initiatives down the road.

What we are describing also reflects an interesting imperative within the OECD that consists of a mix of pressure, modernization, reform, and relevance. The theme of "pressure" and even of crisis in most OECD publications – not simply on governance issues, but on climate change, migration, employment, health and education – echoes the approach that we discussed in Chapter 5. The idea is that there is constant and unpredictable pressure on governments, either of a physical nature (as in climate change), an economic nature (rising prices, declining resources), or of human nature (ethical behaviour). Governments thus must constantly adapt in turn to deal with these pressures. As Chapter 5 argued, this constant adaptation is not directionless, but should be harnessed in the interests of modernization (more below), or of regular improvements over what came before either in policy or in practice. As an organization in the service of these governments that need to constantly modernize, the OECD as well needs to be constantly analysing those pressures and constantly providing new solutions or reforms that can be adopted by governments. This makes for a good deal of churn (what Woodward calls "perpetual flux", (Woodward 2009: 4)) within the OECD, but is a key to its relevance (again, only successfully achieved if it is active and visible). And it is also a feature of the networked nature of the OECD – to be relevant and to be able to assess pressures (in a more specific and practitioner-oriented way) the OECD needs to be everywhere it can be at once, harvesting and processing information and research.

The OECD's approach to governance issues

Below, we summarize our specific conclusions about the evolution and content of the OECD's approach to governance and public management, closing with some "macro" conclusions. The final section will raise some questions about what might be missing in GOV's current work.

1. Looked at historically, at least before the creation of GOV in 2002, governance in the OECD was somewhat awkwardly placed. TECO had been carried over from the OEEC as a technical assistance programme for poorer countries on the southern rim of Europe. Despite the clear focus of the OECD on a fairly narrow definition of economic development around trade, balance of payments, etc., TECO (and DAC) represented a dimension of the organization that did pay some attention to governance issues. But in 1961 this could barely be articulated in terms of a global project around public sector or public management reform. The

Technical Assistance Program (TAP) which was overseen by TECO had a different character than development aid (hence the change in 1961 from Technical Assistance Committee to Technical Cooperation Committee) because it provided advice and operational support to members. The initial target countries (originally Portugal, Spain, Greece, Turkey, Yugoslavia, southern Italy and Iceland), because of the prevalence of dictatorships, were in some bad odour within the OECD, and so TAP and TECO were considered lower priorities than other activities, and somewhat marginal to the main business of the organization. Reviewed in 1970, both the programme and the committee faced some limited opposition (the US, the UK, and Japan) but were renewed for another five years with higher financial contributions from the beneficiary states. They were to have been terminated by 1975, but as Chapter 2 showed, were saved by world events that suddenly made them seem more relevant.

2. Possibly the best description for TECO's position within the OECD from 1961 to 1975 was "marginalized relevance". Some of its projects were related to administration, but most were operational ones dealing with capacity-building in economic sectors (tourism or agriculture). That changed, almost accidentally, around 1974 when key people in TECO were convinced by the "Secretary-General's Experimental Activity on Innovative Structures and Procedures in Government" that public management should be the key focus. That happened with the recalibration of the programme in 1975 into the Cooperative Action Program. High-level OECD pronouncements from the period averred that public management would be TECO's special mandate. In the late 1970s TECO itself had to develop a strategy to promote public management within the OECD, as well as determine its core constituencies and competencies. These came together in the 1979 Madrid conference that provided a platform for TECO work through the next decade, some of which, like service delivery, were pioneering.

3. In 1990 there was further evolution away from anything that smacked of donors and technical assistance: the TECO service was replaced with the Public Management (PUMA) Service, and the TECO committee was replaced by the Public Management (PUMA) committee. This was impelled by a 1989 internal study, *Serving the Economy Better*, which was released publicly in 1991. That study incorporated some NPM language, but our discussion showed that it was more nuanced than that, showing respect for political accountability as well as core principles of public law. Or perhaps it is better to say that different parts of PUMA and the OECD had somewhat different views, and so different policy documents tended to put the emphasis on different principles. *Governance in Transition* (1995) represented a high point in NPM within PUMA, but it did not reflect a single point of view – the founding rationale of SIGMA showed a broader consideration of public management

and the needs at the time for economies transitioning from the Soviet model.

4. The establishment of GOV in 2002 was driven by a complicated configuration of forces. Intellectually, GOV was to reflect the new emphasis that SG Johnston had placed on enlargement and engagement and capitalizing on the OECD's comparative advantages in knowledge creation, management, dissemination, and horizontal research. PUMA had had to grapple with the aftershocks of the end of the Cold War, but those had dissipated by 2002. GOV was to focus more on strategic governance challenges, performance, and elements of good governance. But these high-minded rationales were supplemented with more mundane internal factors. Chapter 3 explained that GOV was created through an amalgamation of PUMA and the Territorial Development Service, which had been created in 1995 to support "place-based" economic policies and a committee created in 1999, the Territorial Development Policy Committee (TDPC). Some of this was cost-cutting at a particularly difficult time for the OECD, but there was also a hope that a consolidated directorate serving two committees could rationalize public management efforts within the organization. PUMA remained the main committee until 2004, when its name was changed to Public Governance Committee (PGC). The Regulatory Policy Committee (RPC) was created and added in 2009, though there had been substantial work on regulation in previous years in a Working Party.

5. Chapter 3 discussed the organization of the PGC and the other two committees, with a focus on the PGC. The committee system in the OECD is usually highlighted as one of its distinguishing features, but every committee operates differently, depending on history, policy area, personalities, relations with respective directorates and with subsidiary bodies. Interviews and the "In Depth" evaluation report (2009) revealed a generally effective and efficient committee, but facing some challenges. One is the anomaly that at least two of its networks (CoG and SBO) usually consist of delegates more senior in their government hierarchies than delegates on the PGC. That means that those networks operate almost independently from the committee to which they report. The subsidiary bodies consist of subject-matter experts (e.g., conflict of interest or budgets) while the PGC is to take a "whole-of-government" approach, and these two perspectives do not always align, and so the other subsidiary bodies (and in the OECD system these bodies usually have significant latitude to set their agendas) often are quite independent of the committee. The "In Depth" Review pointed to this problem, and the PGC responded by introducing several reforms to better coordinate with those bodies.

6. The focus on GOV and the PGC and related committees makes a good deal of sense in trying to understand how governance issues are addressed

in the OECD, but it does not include the whole picture (SIGMA, of course, is part of GOV). At one level, it could be argued that almost every area of work in the OECD touches on governance issues in the sense of at least looking at how the organization and capacity of the public sector contributes to policy outcomes, whether they be economic or otherwise. Indeed, that was one of the challenges in the early days of TECO and PUMA as they worked to carve out an area of public management (primarily whole-of-government, the civil service, centres of government) that would be distinctive. However, even if we take those parameters as given, we showed that there are other parts of the OECD – that work with GOV in most cases – where there is a clear governance and public management focus. We reviewed three other directorates – ECO, DCD, and DAF. ECO worked on a Political Economy of Reform project that then dovetailed with the SG's *Making Reform Happen* project. It also issues a new kind of country review that includes a policy chapter, looking at it from an economic point of view, but still addressing governance concerns. The DCD supports the DAC, which through GOVNET conducts work on human rights, transparency, accountability, participation, anti-corruption and democracy development, though as we pointed out, from a donors' coordination perspective. It has responsibility for the Convention on Combating Bribery of Foreign Officials in International Business Transactions, and has a strong focus on how governments can protect their public sectors from bribery. Finally, several examples were provided from the SG's office (Centre for Co-operation with non-Members, International Futures Programme, and *Making Reform Happen*) to show the salience of public management issues there as well. We spent some time discussing *Making Reform Happen* because it suggests a stronger interest by the current SG in more practical advice on the reform front, seeking to give advice on how reforms (which the OECD often has a hand in recommending) can actually be implemented. This has seeped into GOV, with the transfer there of responsibility for *Making Reform Happen*.

7. Reinforcing the argument made in the first part of this chapter, we examined the tools that the OECD uses to generate and apply (or encourage the adoption of) norms. Our conclusion was that, given the limits to the OECD's capacity to impose any of its norms, it has to rely on networked techniques to do its work. This conclusion is a fairly conventional one in the literature on the OECD, going back to as early as 1967 with Aubrey's study (Aubrey 1967). Our analysis in Chapter 4, however, explored some less well-known features of these tools. Beginning with peer review, we showed through comparison of ECO and GOV precisely how they rely on network interactions both within the OECD and with the countries being reviewed. We also discussed the innovation of Public Governance Reviews that look at the whole-of-government. The logic of these reviews

necessarily has to be different, since traditionally peer reviews have been conducted of sectors, such as human resource management. The directorate staff work with the cabinet or prime minister's office, since there needs to be an entry point to all other government ministries. The nature and structure of the reports are negotiated with the countries depending on which themes they would like explored (though the review is still independent). These reviews (only three have been conducted at time of writing – Finland, Ireland, and Estonia) seem nonetheless to have settled on some central concepts to guide the report – coherence, strategic agility, engaging in broader dialogue on governance issues within the country.

We then conducted a close analysis of GOV's eight building blocks, with particular attention to its work on quality regulation and integrity. In both of these cases, we can observe typical network approaches: the recommendations or standards are initially either brief or quite forgiving in their application (e.g., the Recommendation on Improving the Quality of Government Regulation simply provided a checklist). This first, rather weak instrument, was followed by a 1997 report to ministers and ultimately by the 2005 Guiding Principles for Regulatory Quality and Performance. That in turn paved the way for regulatory reviews of non-members, conferences, and applications in the MENA countries and in Asia. The same logic occurred with the Anti-Bribery Convention. Adopted in 1997, it was then strengthened with a Recommendation in 2007. The four additional instruments dealing with integrity are not particularly strong in themselves either, but we noted that they become occasions and instruments for global conversations, become connected to peer review processes, and spread out to other international public and private organizations.

The GaaG project is also clearly a network tool – it provides comparative information from which governments may draw conclusions. It is also an evolving instrument – the comparison between the 2009 and 2011 editions shows responses to the GOV constituency, and the inclusion of more challenging measures of performance such as "strategic foresight".

The MENA initiative is an example of an OECD regional initiative (again, every one will be different). We were critical of the project's gloss on the real governance problems in the region, but concluded that it nonetheless is an example of expanded influence of the OECD.

The accession process mirrors this extension and enhanced networked engagement. We said that it is not a "usual" tool in the OECD arsenal, but it is entirely likely that the organization will consider more accession candidates once Russia completes the process.

8. There are three challenges in coming to any conclusions about an "OECD/GOV view on governance". There first is which OECD, at what period? Our historical analysis shows substantial evolution, reversals, accidents

and organizational surprises over time. A second, even for any one period, is the sheer amount of material and publications that flow from the OECD. We explained in Chapter 5 why they could quite reasonably be expected to be variable. A third is the variety of sources within the OECD that can and will take different orientations to governance issues – the difference between DAF and ECO and GOV, for example. The first two have more of an economic orientation, but will be presenting views on important areas of government policy or public management. We came at the problem from several different angles. The *Governance Outreach Initiative* (2000) document included discussion of governance priorities as well as a summary of work within the OECD over the previous 20 years on governance issues. We concluded that there were three broad categories of concepts and benchmarks that made up the OECD view at the time. One was ethical – accountability of governments to citizens, of corporations to shareholders, and public servants to the government; transparency; integrity. The second was an emphasis on "frameworks" the create "coherence" in government policy outputs and functioning. The third was management processes or practices that emphasize performance and results.

A second angle to determine the "OECD view" was to examine the 2007 building blocks, which capture more or less what GOV does today. Because of their disparity, even though they are all under the governance and public management umbrella, it is a little more difficult to find common themes. Nonetheless, the chapter concluded that, just as with the *Outreach* document seven years earlier, there is a strong ethical dimension to them: accountability, openness, consultation. Core areas or substantive topics are budgeting, human resource management, and regulatory reform. Three of the blocks – centres of government, multi-level governance, and open government – have relatively little content at all. The integrity and regulatory blocks have the most detailed content.

Finally, we looked at forms of discourse on governance, a rhetoric we discussed in the first part of this chapter: constant pressures, citizen distrust, the embattlement of reformers, and possible collapse with on-going reform.

9. In gauging the influence of the OECD on governance matters, one key conclusion is that it gains tremendously from its reputation for objectivity and solid research. Chapter 6 got at this in a variety of ways – we looked at leading public administration academic opinion, for example, the special 2006 symposium issue of the *International Review of Administrative Sciences*. There was clear consensus about the OECD/GOV's influence on public sector reform over the previous decade, and special notice of the OECD's unique niche in providing comparative analysis of those reform efforts. A similar assessment of the OECD's reputation more generally was gleaned from the comparative analysis of Canadian and Finnish

parliamentary debates over a decade. Most references fell comfortably into one of four categories: the OECD as providing comparisons or rankings among countries; the OECD as a body of expertise; the reference to OECD models and recommendations; and the OECD as a source of intelligence about unavoidable global trends. The survey of NISPAcee members was somewhat more complicated since it echoed the idea that on governance issues the OECD has a largely favourable reputation, but that it has only exercised "medium" influence on global public management reform.

10. Beyond reputation, we presented some data from the PGC evaluation about its actual impact on members' public management practices, and tried to map out the complex patterns of influence through "translation" or "bricolage" that likely occur in the real world. The essential contribution of this mapping (Figure 6.2) exercise is that it goes well beyond existing presentations of policy transfer or diffusion, which typically emphasize one-dimensional translation from an external body by a domestic one. Our research on the OECD shows that translation takes place in the first instance <u>within</u> the OECD itself. The second instance is between the OECD (or its directorates and committees) and ministries at the national level, and this is a two-way flow, particularly in the OECD's case with its close and intimate connection and reliance on members and the information that they provide. In fact, as we stressed through several anecdotes, the transfer may be the other way around in many instances whereby reformers at the national level use the OECD as legitimacy for programmes that they wish to pursue in their home governments. The third instance is the pathways for OECD influence through business, labour and civil society groups, as well as parliamentarians and the media. The fourth instance is other international organizations, and the fifth is public and professional opinion.

These form the ten substantive conclusions of this study, but also yield some "macro" conclusions that are worth noting. At the level of understanding organizations, this study has underscored the importance of "process tracing" (King et al 1994) or understanding the evolution of decisions points and their complex inter-linkages over a fairly broad space of time. TECO begat PUMA, and PUMA begat GOV, and understanding the evolution of thinking, as well as acting on that thinking within the OECD, would have been impossible without careful reconstruction (partly but crucially, through interviews) of events and connections along the way. There were accidents of circumstance and character that combined at various key "switching" points along the way. By tracing that story we can see that it actually took some 30 years for governance and public management as a distinct field of activity within the OECD to be established and entrenched – and even today, some PGC members are nervous about the position of the committee and of GOV within the arcane politics of the OECD itself.

Another broad conclusion – or reflection – that emerges from the study is the dynamics of an international governmental organization on a very much more complicated global stage. We are firmly in the camp of those international relations scholars who emphasize the importance of norms and norm-setting as key drivers of global politics (Barnett & Finnemore 1999, 2004; Finnemore & Sikkink 1998; Finnemore 1993). For all the reasons discussed in the book, the OECD is a somewhat peculiar international organization that relies almost exclusively on norm-generation through knowledge gathering, research, and knowledge dissemination. But we would argue that the changing context of the global order today, in contrast to what it was even 20 years ago, with more international NGOs and stronger civil society organizations, with instantaneous communication, with more international players of every stripe, and most importantly with a more complex terrain of states, means that many international governmental organizations rely more and more on being knowledge brokers rather than rule-makers and rule-enforcers. And with that comes certain peculiarities that the OECD, as a quintessential norm-generator and knowledge broker, reveals quite well. One is the importance of reputation. We noted repeatedly that without its reputation, the OECD would lack credibility, and without credibility it loses influence. That reputation comes for high-quality research, which depends on high-quality researchers. But managing researchers is a different enterprise than manufacturing widgets. It involves harnessing creativity and commitment so that the skill and originality of the researcher can shine through in the ultimate product. But there are still organizational imperatives that need to be respected, so norm-generating, research-based organizations like the OECD also experience a tension between the imperatives of internal management and the imperatives of stimulating and supporting creative work. Some of the story of GOV and its predecessors, as well as the larger practices around establishing and "marketing" an organization like the OECD that we saw in Chapter 6, reflect this tension.

A theme touched on in various chapters was the pull of "modernity", both among actors external to the OECD and the OECD itself. One aspect of this must be addressed frankly: it is a rhetorical mechanism to encourage convergence, though it has to be couched carefully. Conservative adherents to orthodox religions (e.g., Hasidic Judaism), for example, are impervious to appeals to "modernize" since their beliefs are grounded in the importance of tradition. The person or group to whom the appeal is being made should at least be open to the idea that it is somehow backward and morally and practically inferior not to be modern. International organizations that can exercise conditionalities do not need to rely on this rhetorical trope, but ones like the OECD do. It prepares the ground for spreading norms by pointing to either a desirable current state ("to be more modern") or a preferred future one ("modernizing"). Accordingly, the governance and public management discourse of the OECD continually used "modernization" as a compass point in divining the preferred directions of change. Of course, it can also rely on the standard of the OECD as the group of "advanced" countries, and use more of a "club joining" metaphor. It is also linked (and as other international organizations conduct themselves more as knowledge brokers we can expect similar strategies) to the repeated references to "trends" and to allegedly widely spread practices as evidence of norms that modern states emulate. The OECD's discourse has always been careful, especially in recent years, to keep a balance with the importance of local experience and context, but it is nonetheless a balance with a powerfully attractive discourse that encourages eventual convergence towards key norms and practices.

What's missing?

We close with a reflection of what GOV might be, rather than what it was and is. Several interviewees expressed some misgivings about GOV and its agenda on governance and public management in the OECD. There were concerns that GOV was not innovative enough, and that in the last decade it had almost deliberately resisted innovations that would take it outside of its "building blocks". It was not looking for "the next big thing", and lacked vision. There were other complaints that its agenda differed little today from what TECO had invented 30 years ago. Some lamented the apparent decline of interest among the most senior public officials, as evidenced by either lack of participation in the SBO and CoG networks or the delegation of junior officials. Several thought that the PGC was actually weaker than PUMA, both *vis-à-vis* the OECD as a whole and with respect to its subsidiary bodies.

There is a measure of truth in these observations. Several members of the PGC itself referred to their own worries about the strength of the committee within the OECD system and in comparison to the heavy-hitters in ECO and DAF. The "In Depth" study, while generally positive about the PGC, also pointed out some weaknesses in its structure and its relations with subsidiary bodies, especially SBO and CoG. The Ministerial in Venice in November 2011 was initially resisted by some member states, and in part it was designed by the directorate to secure greater legitimacy for the GOV agenda within the organization. Its innovations in recent years have been relatively modest. GaaG as a project was started in 2005 and has yielded two reports. Since it was a new venture for GOV, it can be seen as an innovation, but also as imitation within the OECD system of what "sells": crisp, comparative, numerate, and digestible "product". The venture into public governance reviews, and the new highlight on "strategic agility" and "strategic foresight" are also innovations, but not groundbreaking ones.

At the same time, we need to be cognizant of the constraints GOV and other directorates face within the organization. One is the scissor effect of stagnant resources and increased pressure to produce more work. The OECD as a whole has not seen any significant increase in its Part 1 funding in almost a decade. We discussed the pressure that this places on directorates to respond to "voluntary contributions", and the result to have more and more of the directorate's agenda driven by member states and not by research imperatives. The SG's ambitions also add to the pressure on relatively small staff complements to work harder and faster. Another constraint is organizational. Despite our arguments about how the OECD is a networked organization both internally and in its external relations, it naturally has to have some structure. The networking within the OECD definitely takes place across and within directorates, but there are still silos that both reflect and affect thinking about agendas. GOV's divisions mirror its building blocks, and while it is true that innovative thinking can take place outside of organizational structures, those structures do exercise some gravitational effect. To this degree, GOV has some trouble "thinking outside the box" because of the way in which the "box" conditions thinking. Finally, the OECD's nature as a member-based organization means that members have a strong influence on agendas and vision. The extent to which GOV can innovate or explore new visions of governance and public management is conditioned by how receptive members on committees and Council are.

Due perhaps to these constraints, the nature of the GOV agenda on governance and public management is flatter and more truncated than it might otherwise be in at least two senses. The first (and perhaps this is a critique that would be typical of an academic) is that its work and its publications lack a theory of the state or of governance. One can imagine how resistant delegates would be to fund research devoted to this end, but it actually is crucial since it provides the groundwork for all the other work that the directorate and the committee do. What is the object of their analyses? What is government for, and what is it about? Of course, some sort of portrait (not a theory in a more robust sense) is there, but it is thin. One part of that portrait is the mantra of pressures, fiscal crisis, and declining trust that has been part of GOV for 20 years, though the nature of the pressures always changes to suit current realities. Another part of that portrait is the way in which the "public domain" was defined, from a national accounts perspective, in 2007 (see discussion and Table 2.2). The public sector consists of central government, state governments, local governments, social security funds, and "other public sector". The private sector is defined as the "private sector in the public domain" and "other private sector". There is no mention of courts, civil society, the media, or indeed any of the larger complex actors that engage in the "public domain".

The second sense in which GOV's agenda is truncated is the degree to which it seems trapped in categories invented 30 years ago by TECO and PUMA. Its building blocks (budget practices and procedures, human resource management, integrity and corruption resistance, open government, e-government readiness, centres of government, regulatory quality, and multi-level governance) have changed hardly at all since TECO days, especially given the emphasis even today, as we pointed out, on budgeting, regulatory quality, and corruption and integrity. This is not simply a matter of antiquarianism. GOV was in part created to have a broader focus than PUMA did, to move beyond "managerialism". It has taken some steps (strategic agility and foresight) but its research and its work does not differ significantly from what was done at least 20 years ago. A good measure of that is the communiqué released at the Venice Ministerial that we discussed in Chapter 3. The six priorities for the PGC and GOV it outlined for the next five years consisted of the following: providing evidence on government performance; fostering a more efficient, effective and innovate public sector; offering guidance for strengthening trust, openness and integrity; supporting a whole-of-government perspective; dialogue with civil society organizations, and promoting good public governance globally. This is an agenda that has barely changed since *Modernising Government* in 2005.

If GOV (and other parts of the OECD that treat governance issues) were invented today, what would it look like? Certainly it would not ignore issues of open government or budgeting or integrity, but what would an agenda sensitive to the big issues in governance and public management in the last ten years take on?[1]

- The implications of the media, particularly digital media, on governance. GOV has done excellent work on the public administration dimension of "e-government" in looking at service deliver and consultations, but there is much more to consider. The Wikileaks release of hundreds of thousands of internal government documents on the internet was a profound event in terms of the balance of power over information between governments and citizens.
- Innovations in service delivery at the local level, often using data "mash-ups". The mySociety initiative in the UK (www.mysociety.org) is an example of a transparency and democracy non-profit group that builds websites to enable local groups or neighbourhoods to deliver information (communicate with MPs, ask for services) to government. One of these is fixmystreet (www.fixmystreet.com), that allows citizens to identify local street problems and send them directly to responsible local authorities. GOV will launch an "Observatory of Innovation in the Public Sector" in October 2011, focusing on citizen-government service initiatives.
- Parliament and legislatures. GOV has contacts with parliamentarians, of course, but has no sustained research programme on the role of legislatures in modern democratic politics. There may be some obvious reasons to stay away from this area and keep to public management, but from a governance perspective, the comparative analysis of legislatures, what they do, the pressures they face, their potential – all involve key issues of how

the public views politics and hence its trust. At time of writing, a "scoping paper" was being produced on executive-legislature relations.

- Rule of law. As we mentioned, GOV has undertaken some work in this area, and there are clear indications from the early days of SIGMA that rule of law and impartial administration were key ingredients in good governance. But there is a vast terrain of inquiry and comparative analysis that could be conducted here, on the quality of judicial systems, law, enforcement and audit agencies, administrative law systems, constitutional codes, and so forth.

- The security state and challenges to public management and democratic government. The world of governance for OECD members and non-members changed dramatically with 9/11, but one would scarcely know it from GOV publications and research. The enormous security apparatuses erected by states (the US Homeland Security being the most vivid example), the expansion of police power and surveillance, the spending on the military and the changed relation between the military, security services and elected governments, is one of the most pressing questions of governance today. The OECD is inaugurating a High Level Risk Forum in December, 2011, and security will be one of the items on the work programme.

- The intersection of religion and governance. This is an almost impossibly complicated and delicate topic. If looked at the 1970s or even the 1980s, it would scarcely have registered as anything important for governments or public administrations. But today, in more turbulent multi-ethnic and multi-religious societies both inside and outside the OECD, managing social diversity and accommodating different minorities within a rule of law has become a major issue for many governments (e.g., France and legislation against religious symbols).

- The governance of financial systems. This goes well beyond SBO and the budget pillar (Germain 2010). How is financial governance organized at the national level, and internationally? This is not an economic question. It is a governance, and institutional question. How do different governments organize and regulate their financial sectors, and what might the best arrangements be for international supervision of financial transactions? GOV has initiated work on "Financing Democracy" which is connected to its lobbying guidelines.

- Real performance measurement. GaaG has done good work, and in the 2011 edition did move closer in some sections to trying to measure outcomes. But overall, it is a compendium of outputs. What are the actual outcomes of different policies?

The OECD and GOV (and predecessors) have a distinguished history in contributing both to our understanding of governance and public management issues, and to our current governance practices. The balance struck between market liberalism and liberal democracy has varied over time, and while the support for efficient markets has always been a priority, the TECO/PUMA/GOV support for tempering institutions and good governance has always been there as well.

The OECD has been a leader and a builder in key global networks dedicated to public management reform, but as its own prescriptions make clear, it cannot stand still. There is a new frontier of governance challenges and pressures. GOV and the OECD are well aware of that frontier, and are working to adapt and contribute. The organization brings a distinct set of tools, perspectives, and discourse to the global governance conversation.

Notes

Preface

1   Australia, Austria, Belgium, Canada, Chile, Czech Republic, Denmark, Estonia, Finland, France, Germany, Greece, Hungary, Iceland, Israel, Ireland, Italy, Japan, Korea, Luxembourg, Mexico, Netherlands, New Zealand, Norway, Poland, Portugal, Slovak Republic, Slovenia, Spain, Sweden, Switzerland, Turkey, the United Kingdom, and the United States.
2   Interview, 3 May 2010. Quoted with permission.

Chapter 1   Frontiers of Governance and the OECD as an International Organization

1   Interview, 3 May 2010, Paris. Quoted with permission.
2   Interview #101810B.
3   Interview #091410B.
4   Interview #091310A.

Chapter 2   Governance and its Emergence in the OECD

1   Interview #120610A.
2   Interview #091610A.
3   The scale of technical assistance over and above TECO in this period was impressive. By one estimate, about 100,000 experts were sent to underdeveloped countries in 1962 by the OECD, the UN and other bodies. About 40,000 of these were teachers. The official flow of technical assistance from OECD countries alone was $550 million. See Maddison (1963).
4   Interview #091710A.
5   OECD, *Avant-projet de rapport: Examen du programme de cooperation technique* (Paris: OECD, 12 August 1969).
6   OECD, *Summary of a Discussion in the Secretary-General's Office* (Paris: OECD, 2 March 1970).
7   See, for example, *OECD, TECO Review – Turkey* (Paris: OECD, February 10, 1970), and *OECD, TECO Review – Greece* (Paris: OECD, 10 February 1970). An important point as well is that there were two other financial aid consortia of OECD donors for Greece and Turkey, and these consortia were quite directive in their aid and imposed conditionalities. TECO did not, and deliberately tried to foster an approach based more on responsiveness and dialogue. Interview #091610A.
8   Memo, Section IV to M. Ustundag, 19 May 1971.
9   Interview #091610A.
10 Spain withdrew from TECO in 1974, further casting doubt on the traditional *raison d'être* of the programme.
11 Letter from Ravil Kapil to Yehezekel Dror, 11 December 1976.
12 OECD Council, Resolution of the Council Concerning the Mandate of the Technical Cooperation Committee. C(74)211(Final), 29 January 1975.

13 The following paragraph is based on interview #091710A.

14 Letter Ravi Kapil to Ilka Heiskanen, 16 November 1977.

15 There had been intimations and considerable turmoil, of course. Mikhail Gorbachev became General Secretary of the Communist Party of the Soviet Union in 1985 and launched reforms such as *glasnost*, but most notably declaring that the Soviet Union would no longer militarily intervene in its satellites. The Berlin Wall fell in November 1989. The Russian Republic declared sovereignty over its territory in 1989 as well. The Soviet Union finally collapsed after the failure of the August 1991 attempted coup.

16 Interview #091710A.

17 Interviews #091610A, #091710A, #091410E.

18 SIGMA remains very active, though its remit has of changed as some CEE countries eventually joined the EU, others became candidates, and the EU launched the European Neighbourhood Policy with broader outreach to countries such as Georgia. As of 2011, SIGMA's countries of focus were: four EU candidates – Croatia, former Yugoslav Republic of Macedonia, Montenegro, and Turkey; potential EU candidates – Albania, Bosnia and Herzegovina, Serbia, and Kosovo under UN Security Council Resolution 1244/99; European Neighbourhood and Partnership Instrument (ENPI) – Armenia, Azerbaijan, Egypt, Georgia, Jordan, Lebanon, Moldova, Morocco, Tunisia, Ukraine. SIGMA will be discussed in greater detail in Chapter 3.

19 Another key document – space does not permit a discussion – was issued a year later to animate a meeting of SIGMA partners in Bratislava. It is more philosophical than the Programme Orientation document, but raised fundamental questions of the nature of the state system that SIGMA was endeavouring to build, the nature of "control systems" to place checks on an executive and administrative apparatus that historically in former communist states had known no bounds, and the importance of the rule of law. See OECD SIGMA (1993).

20 As good indicator of the change in thinking that had occurred is a 1989 article written by Bob Bonwitt, then the Principal Administrator at TECO and who would go on to direct SIGMA. It was highly sceptical of the "modernization movement". See Bonwitt (1989).

21 A similar review of governance trends was published in 2005, entitled *Modernising Government: The Way Forward*. We discuss it in Chapter 5.

22 Interview #091610A.

23 The GOV accession report for Russia was discussed and approved at a joint meeting of the PGC and the Regulatory Policy Committee in April 2011. The accession depends on Russia first joining the World Trade Organization. Interviews #061411A, 061711B.

24 This 2004 version of the *acquis*, included as an appendix to the Strategy report, was expanded upon in 2007, but the basic principles of the content of the OECD *acquis* were not altered. See OECD (2007b).

25 It should be noted that Russia has been engaged as an OECD observer since 1992, and has undergone several OECD economic country reports since. Moreover it was interested in acceding to the OECD in 1996, according to Donald Johnston. Interview, 9 November 2010, cited with permission.

Chapter 3   Public Management and Governance in the OECD

1 Interview with Donald Johnston, 9 November 2010. Cited with permission.

2 Interview #091010A.

3 "Challenges and Changes: Past, Present and Future: Interview with Secretary-General Donald Johnston", *OECD @mosphere* (sic), 17 July 2005, 3.

4 The following paragraphs are based on Ying (2005) and interviews #091710A, #091610A, #091510B, #091410E, #061511A.

5 Interviews #112310A and #111710A.

6 OECD, C(99)175/Final Resolution of the Council Concerning the Mandate of the Public Management Committee (Adopted by the Council at its 964th session on 9 December 1999 [C/M(99)25]). Cited in Ying (2005: 29).

7 Interview #061411C. It is even difficult now to estimate "permanent" or Part 1 staff, since the new OECD human resource management policy does away with that category. The interviewee estimated that in GOV, roughly 60 per cent of staff were attached to projects.

8 OECD, *Rules of Procedure* (2008), 24. Retrieved on 29 November 2010 from www.oecd.org/dataoecd/19/34/41455263.pdf.

9 OECD, *Rules of Procedure* (2008), rule 15. Retrieved on 29 November 2010 from www.oecd.org/dataoecd/19/34/41455263.pdf.

10 Interview #100810A.

11 Interview #101510B.

12 Interview #100810A.

13 Interviews #091410A, #101510A.

14 Interviews #101510B, #102610A, #040510B.

15 Interviews #081110A, #102610A.

16 Interviews #100810A, #091410A.

17 Interview #110206.

18 The Financial Action Task Force (FATF) was created by the G7 in 1989 to combat concerns about money laundering. In 2010 it had 34 member states and a number of observers. FATF observers may act as observers at the OECD (and the OECD has observer status with FATF): African Development Bank, Asian Development Bank, Commonwealth Secretariat, Egmont Group of Financial Intelligence Units, European Bank for Reconstruction and Development (EBRD), European Central Bank (ECB), Europol, Inter-American Development Bank (IDB), International Association of Insurance Supervisors (IAIS), International Monetary Fund (IMF), International Organization of Securities Commissions (IOSCO), Interpol, Organization of American States (OAS), Offshore Group of Banking Supervisors (OGBS), United Nations (UN), World Bank and World Customs Organization (WCO).

19 Interviews #112310A, #111710A.

20 Interviews #112310A, #111710A.

21 Interviews #111710A, #091410E.

22 The author was permitted to attend and observe the one-day PGC meeting, though not the Ministerial.

23 OECD, *Provisional Agenda, Ministerial Meeting of the OECD Public Governance Committee*. Retrieved on 29 November 2010 from www.oecd.org/document/11/0,3343,en_21571361_45400858_45426123_1_1_1_1,00.html

24 OECD, *Towards Recovery and Partnership with Citizens: The Call for Innovative and Open Government: Communiqué, Ministerial Meeting of the OECD Public Governance Committee*. Retrieved on 29 November 2010 from: http://www.oecd.org/dataoecd/49/52/46340507.pdf.

25 The author was permitted to attend the meeting under condition of confidentiality. The description that follows honours that condition by referring only to the spirit, and not the detail, of interventions.

26 OECD, Compte Rendu Succinct de la 41e Session du Comité de la Gouvernance Publique. GOV/PGC/M (2010l).
27 OECD, OECD Public Governance Review of Estonia: Toward a Single Government Approach, Questions for Discussion. 42nd PGC – Room Document. Paris: November 2010.
28 Interview #111710A.
29 Interview #091410E.
30 Level 1 committees can report directly to Council, whereas lower-level bodies must report through a level 1 committee.
31 Interviews #101510A, #160511.
32 Interview #160511.
33 Interviews #061511A, #061411A.
34 Interview #290611A.
35 Interview #060211.
36 OECD, *On-Line Guide to OECD Intergovernmental Activity*, Resolution of the Council [C(2009)126 and C/M(2009)21, item 242]. Accessed on 5 June 2011 at http://webnet.oecd.org/OECDGROUPS/Bodies/ShowBodyView.aspx?BodyID=863&BodyPID=7470&Lang=en&Book=True.
37 Interviews #120610B, #120610C.
38 Interview #091410B.
39 OECD, *On-Line Guide to OECD Intergovernmental Activity*. Accessed 26 June 2011 at http://webnet.oecd.org/oecdgroups/Bodies/ListByNameView.aspx.
40 Interviews #061411A, #310311A, #061511A.
41 OECD, Directorate for Financial and Enterprise Affairs, http://www.oecd.org/department/0,3355,en_2649_33725_1_1_1_1_1,00.html. Accessed 26 June 2011.
42 Interview #061511D.
43 Interviews #061511D, #061511E.
44 Interview #091410A.
45 Interview #091510A.
46 Interview #091510A.
47 After *Making Reform Happen* was released at a conference in November 2011, further responsibility for it was transferred to GOV.
48 The following narrative is based on interviews #091610B, #120610B.

Chapter 4   Networked Tools: How Does the OECD Do Its Governance Work?

1 Interview #091410B.
2 The following is based on interviews #091710B, #040510A, and #120610D.
3 The following is based on interviews #091510B and #091410E.
4 Interview #290611A.
5 Interview #160611D.
6 Interviews #040111B, #110206.
7 See OECD Legal Instruments www.oecd.org/document/46/0,3746,en_21571361_38481278_40899182_1_1_1_1,00.html. Accessed 12 February 2011.
8 The full list of OECD instruments may be found at http://webnet.oecd.org/oecdacts/Instruments/ListByTypeView.aspx. Accessed 12 February 2011.
9 Interview #091410C.
10 The following discussion draws on (OECD 2005f).
11 The following based on (OECD 2009b).

12 Interview #290611A.
13 Interviews #061411B, #290611B.
14 There are also significant methodological problems with the data that we cannot discuss here, though they are addressed in some measure in the two publications. To name only three: (1) most of the data come from surveys of governments, and there is no real vetting of how these surveys are completed or who completes them, (2) there is reliance on composite indexes, and it is not clear why and how certain indicators are combined into the composites, and (3) in many cases there are no common definitions of key terms (e.g., civil service) among member and partner states. The report did not ignore these issues – see for example the discussion in Annex E of the 2011 GaaG of how it dealt with problems in composite indicators.
15 Interview #091410C.
16 Some parts of this discussion of MENA are drawn from interviews #032611A and #091710B.
17 Interview #032611A.
18 Interview #032611A.
19 Interview #040111A.
20 The accession reviews conducted by different OECD bodies and submitted to Council are confidential, and declassification requires the agreement of both the country in question as well as the OECD. The author requested declassification of the reports for Estonia, Israel and Slovenia. The Chilean government wishes to keep its report confidential, and at time of writing the accession process for the Russian Federation was still underway. This section relies on the reports as well on interviews #091410D, #120610D, #040510A, #091410C, #091410E.
21 This was identical (paragraph 4) in each of the three reports, with only the country name differing.
22 Interviews #040111A, #120610A, #110206.

Chapter 5   Modernizing Governance: Is There an OECD View?

1 The posters were viewed on 17 June 2011. The lists of terms were in French, and their order differs slightly from web-based publications by the OECD.
2 OECD Core Values, http://www.oecd.org/pages/0,3417,en_36734052_36734103_ 1_1_1_1,00.html. Accessed 1 July 2011.
3 The PUMA Occasional Papers series started in 1994, superseding a similar series that had been launched in 1990. The PUMA series produced 22 papers between 1994 and 1998.
4 The government of Canada has a division in its Cabinet Office (the Privy Council) called "Machinery of Government".
5 They comprise: *OECD Convention on Combating Bribery of Foreign Public Officials in International Business Transactions* (1997) (OECD 1997a); *OECD Recommendation on Improving Ethical Conduct in the Public Service including Principles for Managing Ethics in the Public Service* (1998) (OECD 1998); *OECD Recommendation on Guidelines for Managing Conflict of Interest in the Public Service* (2003) (OECD 2003e); *OECD Recommendation on Enhancing Integrity in Public Procurement* (2008) (OECD 2008b); *OECD Recommendation for Further Combating Bribery of Foreign Public Officials in International Business Transactions* (2009) (OECD 2009d); *OECD Recommendation on Principles for Transparency and Integrity in Lobbying* (2010) (OECD 2010i). These were supplemented by a guide for assessment entitled *Public Sector Integrity: A Framework for Assessment* (OECD 2005i).

6   Interviews #102610A, #310311A.
7   Parts of the following discussion were previously published in Pal (2008). Reproduced with permission.
8   The documents will be referred to in this section as PB2003, PB2005, and MG.
9   As we saw in Chapter 3, both GOV and the OECD have taken stakeholders and their support for reform more seriously in recent years, as in *Making Reform Happen*. Engaging stakeholders and other institutions to support the reform process was a key theme in the Centres of Government meeting in September 2008, for example. See (OECD 2010f).
10 Wordle: www.wordle.net/.
11 Tagcrowd: http://tagcrowd.com/.
12 Interviews #040111A, #061411D, #160511. The PGC and RPC had a joint meeting in May 2011 to discuss the Russian governance accession report.
13 At time of writing, GOV was engaging in work on the rule of law.

Chapter 6   The OECD's Influence on Governance Issues

1   This section draws on research for an unpublished paper coauthored by Pertti Alasuutari and Leslie A. Pal.
2   Canada, Parliament of Canada, http://www2.parl.gc.ca/search/refine/Advanced. aspx?Language=e.
3   A perfect example from Canada comes in recent references to how well the country – comparatively – fared under the financial crisis of 2008. References were constantly made to IMF and OECD reports and comparators. See Pal (2011b).
4   The following discussion is based on interviews #160611B, #111710A, #091710A, #290611B.
5   Interview #040510A.
6   OECD, *Anti-Corruption Network for Eastern Europe and Central Asia*, www.oecd. org/document/14/0,2340,en_36595778_36595872_36959886_1_1_1_1,00.html. Accessed on 8 July 2011. The author was engaged by the ACN in 2004 in a country review of Ukraine.
7   The Working Group on Bribery has is a decision rule of "consensus minus one". This means that the country that is being assessed cannot block the decision of the rest of the group. It is a unique decision rule within the OECD structure. Interview #061511E.
8   International Monetary Fund, *Manual on Fiscal Transparency*, available at www.imf. org/external/np/fad/trans/manual/index.htm. Accessed on 7 July 2011.
9   Interview with Angel Gurría, 3 May 2010. Cited with permission. The OECD is not actually a member of the G20, but rather a supporting organization, like the World Bank and the IMF.

Chapter 7   Conclusion

1   We are not implying that there has been no thinking on these issues within the directorate, and will give some examples in the next sections of impending work that should be visible in 2012. Moreover, we realize that, given the constraints we described above, these suggestions may be completely unrealistic. But that might be why they could be useful.

Bibliography

Àgh, A. 2003, "Public Administration in Central and Eastern Europe" in *Handbook of Public Administration*, eds. J. Pierre & B.G. Peters, Sage, California: 536–548.

Alasuutari, P. & Rasimus, A. 2009, "Use of the OECD in Justifying Policy Reforms: The Case of Finland", *Journal of Power*, vol. 2, no. 1: 89.

Alasuutari, P. 2011, "Social Change as Domestication of Global Trends". Unpublished ms.

Alasuutari, P. 2010, "The Domestication of Transnational Models". Unpublished ms.

Armingeon, K. & Beyeler, M. (eds) 2004, *The OECD and European Welfare States*, Edward Elgar, Cheltenham, UK.

Atkinson, M.M. & Coleman, W.D. 1992, "Policy Networks, Policy Communities and the Problems of Governance", *Governance*, vol. 5, no. April: 154–180.

Aubrey, H.G. 1967, *Atlantic Economic Cooperation: The Case of the OECD*, Published for the Council on Foreign Relations [by] Praeger, New York.

Aucoin, P. 1995, *The New Public Management: Canada in Comparative Perspective*, Institute for Research on Public Policy, Montreal.

Auld, G. 2010, "Assessing Certification as Governance: Effects and Broader Consequences for Coffee", *The Journal of Environment and Development*, vol. 19, no. 2: 215–241.

Auld, G. & Gulbrandsen, L.H. 2010, "Transparency in Nonstate Certification: Consequences for Accountability and Legitimacy", *Global Environmental Politics*, vol. 10, no. 3: 97–119.

Barbezat, D. 1997, "The Marshall Plan and the Origin of the OEEC" in *Explorations in OEEC History*, ed. R.T. Griffiths, OECD, Paris: 33–48.

Barnett, M.N. & Finnemore, M. 2004, *Rules for the World: International Organizations in Global Politics*, Cornell University Press, Ithaca, N.Y.

Barnett, M.N. & Finnemore, M. 1999, "The Politics, Power, and Pathologies of International Organizations", *International Organization*, vol. 53, no. 4: 699–732.

Batliwala, S. 2002, "Grassroots Movements as Transnational Actors: Implications for Global Civil Society", *Voluntas: International Journal of Voluntary and Nonprofit Organizations*, vol. 13, no. December: 393–408.

Bennett, C.J. 1997, "Understanding Ripple Effects: The Cross-National Adoption of Policy Instruments for Bureaucratic Accountability", *Governance*, vol. 10: 213–233.

Bennett, C.J. 1992, *Regulating Privacy*, Cornell University Press, Ithaca, New York.

Bennett, C.J. 1991, "What is Policy Convergence and What Causes It?", *British Journal of Political Science*, vol. 21: 215–233.

Besançon, M. 2003, *Good Governance Rankings: The Art of Measurement*, World Peace Foundation, Cambridge, MA.

Bonwitt, B. 1989, "Reform of Public Administration: From Tasks to Goals", *International Review of Administrative Sciences*, vol. 55: 211–228.

Börzel, T.A. 1998, "Organizing Babylon – on the Different Conceptions of Policy Networks", *Public Administration*, vol. 76, no. 2: 253–273.

Boston, J. 1996, *Public Management: The New Zealand Model*, Oxford University Press, Auckland.

Bouckaert, G. 2006, "Modernising Government: The Way Forward – A Comment", *International Review of Administrative Sciences*, vol. 72, no. 3: 327–332.

Brunsson, N. & Jacobsson, B. (eds) 2000, *A World of Standards*, Oxford University Press, Oxford.

Buduru, B. & Pal, L.A. 2010, "The Globalized State: Measuring and Monitoring Governance", *European Journal of Cultural Studies*, vol. 13, no. 4: 511–530.

Caiden, G.E. 1991, *Administrative Reform Comes of Age*, W. de Gruyter, Berlin.

Campbell, J.L. 2004, *Institutional Change and Globalization*, Princeton University Press, Princeton.

Cashore, B.W., Auld, A.G. & Newsom, D. 2004, *Governing through Markets: Forest Certification and the Emergence of Non-state Authority*, Yale University Press, New Haven, Conn.

Cerny, P.G. 1997, "Paradoxes of the Competition State: The Dynamics of International Globalisation", *Government and Opposition*, vol. 32: 251–274.

Christensen, T. & Laegreid, P. 2008, "NPM and Beyond: Structure, Culture and Demography", *International Review of Administrative Sciences*, vol. 74, no. 1: 7–23.

Christensen, T. & Laegreid, P. (eds) 2002, *The New Public Management: The Transformation of Ideas and Practice*, Ashgate, Hampshire.

Cini, M. 2001, "From the Marshall Plan to EEC: Direct and Indirect Influences" in *The Marshall Plan: Fifty Years After*, ed. M. Schain, Palgrave Macmillan, New York: 13–17.

Clarke, T. & Barlow, M. 1997, *MAI: The Multilateral Agreement on Investment and the Threat to Canadian Sovereignty*, Stoddart, Toronto.

Common, R. 2001, *Public Management and Policy Transfer in Southeast Asia*, Ashgate, Aldershot.

Conzelmann, T. 2010, "Beyond the Carrot and the Stick: The Authority of Peer Reviews in the WTO and the OECD", *ECPR Standing Group for International Relations*, 9–11 September 2010: 1.

Cooper, A.F. 1997, *Canadian Foreign Policy: Old Habits and New Directions*, Prentice-Hall, Scarborough, Ont.

Crawford, B. & Lijphart, A. 1997, "Old Legacies, New Institutions: Explaining Political and Economic Trajectories in Post-Communist Regimes: Introduction" in *Liberalization and Leninist Legacies: Comparative Perspectives on Democratic Transitions*, eds. B. Crawford & A. Lijphart, University of California Press, International and Area Studies, Berkeley, Calif.: 1–39.

De Jong, M., Lalenis, K. & Mamadouh, V. (eds) 2002, *The Theory and Practice of Institutional Transplantation: Experience with the Transfer of Policy Institutions*, Kluwer Academic Publishers, Boston.

Deacon, B. & Hulse, M. 1997, "The Making of Postcommunist Social Policy: The Role of International Agencies", *Journal of Social Policy*, vol. 26, no. 1: 43–62.

Denhardt, R.B. & Denhardt, J.V. 2003, *The New Public Service: Serving, Not Steering*, M.E. Sharpe, Armonk, N.Y.

Dewitt, D.B. & Kirton, J.J. 1983, *Canada as a Principal Power: A Study in Foreign Policy and International Relations*, Wiley, Toronto.

Dolowitz, D.P. 2009, "Learning by Observation: Surveying the International Arena", *Policy and Politics*, vol. 37, no. 3: 317–334.

Dolowitz, D.P. & Marsh, D. 2000, "Learning from Abroad: The Role of Policy Transfer in Contemporary Policy-Making", *Governance*, vol. 13, no. 1: 5–25.

Dolowitz, D.P. & Marsh, D. 1996, "Who Learns What from Whom: A Review of the Policy Transfer Literature", *Political Studies*, vol. 44, no. 2: 343–357.

Domergue, M. 1968, *Technical Assistance: Theory, Practice, and Policies*, Praeger, New York.

Dostal, J.M. 2004, "Campaigning on Expertise: How the OECD Framed EU Welfare and Labour Market Policies – and Why Success could Trigger Failure", *Journal of European Public Policy*, vol. 11, no. 3: 440–460.

Dowding, K. 2001, "There Must be an End to the Confusion: Policy Networks, Intellectual Fatigue, and the Need for Political Science Methods Courses in British Universities", *Political Studies*, vol. 49: 89–105.

Dowding, K. 1995, "Model of Metaphor? A Critical Review of the Policy Network Approach", *Political Studies*, vol. 43: 136–158.

Doz, Y. & Kosonen, M. 2008, *Fast Strategy: How Strategic Agility will Help You Stay Ahead of the Game*, Pearson Prentice-Hall, Edinburgh Gate, Harlow.

Drouillard, L. & Gold, E.R. 2008, "The OECD Guidelines for the Licensing of Genetic Inventions: Policy Learning in Response to the Gene Patenting Controversy" in *The OECD and Transnational Governance*, eds. R. Mahon & S. McBride, UBC Press, Vancouver, B.C.: 205–225.

Dunleavy, P. et al 2005, "New Public Management is Dead – Long Live Digital-Era Governance", *Journal of Public Administration Research Theory (Transaction)*, vol. 16, no. 3: 467–494.

Dunlop, C.A. 2009, "Policy Transfer as Learning: Capturing Variation in What Decision-makers Learn from Epistemic Communities", *Policy Studies*, vol. 30, no. 3: 289–311.

Easterly, W. 2006, *The White Man's Burden: Why the West's Efforts to Aid the Rest have Done so Much Ill and So Little Good*, Penguin, New York.

Eisfeld, R. & Pal, L.A. (eds) 2010, *Political Science in Central and Eastern Europe: Diversity and Convergence*, Barbara Budrich, Farmington Hills, MI.

Evans, M. (ed.) 2004, *Policy Transfer in Global Perspective*, Ashgate, Aldershot, England.

Evans, M. 2004, "Understanding Policy Transfer" in *Policy Transfer in Global Perspective*, ed. M. Evans, Ashgate, Aldershot, England: 10–42.

Evans, M. 2009a, "New Directions in the Study of Policy Transfer", *Policy Studies*, vol. 30, no. 3: 237–241.

Evans, M. 2009b, "Parting Shots", *Policy Studies*, vol. 30, no. 3: 397–402.

Evans, M. 2009c, "Policy Transfer in Critical Perspective", *Policy Studies*, vol. 30, no. 3: 243–268.

Farazmand, A. 2004, "Sound Governance in the Age of Globalization" in *Sound Governance: Policy and Administrative Innovations*, ed. A. Farazmand, Praeger, Westport, Conn.: 1–23.

Finnemore, M. 1993, "International Organizations as Teachers of Norms: The United Nations Educational, Scientific, and Cultural Organization and Science Policy", *International Organization*, vol. 47, no. 4: 565–597.

Finnemore, M. & Sikkink, K. 1998, "International Norm Dynamics and Political Change", *International Organization*, vol. 52, no. 4: 887–917.

Foucault, M. 1972, *The Archeology of Knowledge*, Tavistock, London.

Freedom House 2010, *Map of Freedom of the World*. Available: http://www.freedom-house.org/template.cfm?page=363&year=2010&country=7950 [6 February 2011].

Gayon, V. 2009, "Un atelier d'écriture internationale: l'OCDE au travail. Éléments de sociologie de la forme 'rapport'", *Sociologie du Travail*, vol. 51: 324–342.

Germain, R.D. 2010, *Global Politics and Financial Governance*, Palgrave Macmillan, Houndmills, Basingstoke, Hampshire.

Griffiths, R.T. 1997a, *Explorations in OEEC History*, Organisation for Economic Co-operation and Development, Paris.

Griffiths, R.T. 1997b, "'An Act of Creative Leadership': The End of the OEEC and the Birth of the OECD" in *Explorations in OEEC History*, ed. R.T. Griffiths, OECD, Paris: 235–250.

Grinvalds, H. 2008, "Lost in Translation? OECD Ideas and Danish Labour Market Policy" in *The OECD and Transnational Governance*, eds. R. Mahon & S. McBride, UBC Press, Vancouver, B.C.: 188–202.

Gurría, A. 2007, *Making the Most of Globalisation: The OECD and the MENA Countries*. Remarks to the Egyptian Council for Foreign Affairs, Cairo, Egypt, November 27, 2007.

Haas, P.M. 1992, "Introduction: Epistemic Communities and International Policy Coordination", *International Organization*, vol. 46, no. 1, Knowledge, Power, and International Policy Coordination: 1–35.

Halligan, J. 2010, "The Fate of Administrative Tradition in Anglophone Countries during the Reform Era" in *Tradition and Public Administration*, eds. M. Painter & B.G. Peters, Palgrave Macmillan, Basingstoke: 129–142.

Hansen, H.K., Salskov-Iversen, D. & Bislev, S. 2002, "Discursive Globalization: Transnational Discourse Communities and New Public Management" in *Towards a Global Polity*, eds. M. Ougaard & R. Higgott, Routledge, London: 107–124.

Haque, M.S. 2006, "Modernising Government: The Way Forward – An Analysis", *International Review of Administrative Sciences*, vol. 72, no. 3: 319–325.

Heclo, H. 1978, "Issue Networks and the Executive Establishment", in *The New American Political System*, ed. A. King, American Enterprise Institute for Public Policy Research, Washington, D.C.: 87–124.

Heclo, H. & Wildavsky, A. 1978, *The Private Government of Public Money*, Macmillan, London.

Henderson, D. 1999, *The MAI Affair: A Story and its Lessons*, Royal Institute of International Affairs, International Economic Programme, London.

Hever, S. 2010, *The Economy of the Occupation: A Socioeconomic Bulletin: Israel and the OECD*, Alternative Information Centre, Jerusalem.

Hoffman, G. 2010, "PM Celebrates Israel's OECD Accession", *The Jerusalem Post*, 10 May 2010: T19.

Hofstadter, R. 1963, *The Progressive Movement, 1900–1915*, Prentice-Hall, Englewood Cliffs, N.J.

Hogan, M.J. 1987, *The Marshall Plan: America, Britain, and the Reconstruction of Western Europe, 1947–1952*, Cambridge University Press, Cambridge.

Hogg, P.W. 2006, *Constitutional Law of Canada*, Thomson Carswell, Scarborough, Ont.

Hood, C. 1998, *The Art of the State: Culture, Rhetoric, and Public Management*, Clarendon Press, Oxford.

Huerta Melchor, O. 2006, *Understanding International Agents of Policy Transfer: The Case of the OECD and Mexican Administrative Reform*, Ph.D. diss., University of York: Department of Politics.

Jacoby, W. 2001, "Tutors and Pupils: International Organizations, Central European Elites, and Western Models", *Governance*, vol. 14, no. 2: 169–200.

Judt, T. 2001, "Introduction" in *The Marshall Plan: Fifty Years After*, ed. M. Schain, New York, Palgrave Macmillan: 1–9.

Kahler, M. 2009, "Networked Politics: Agency, Power, and Governance" in *Networked Politics: Agency, Power, and Governance*, ed. M. Kahler, Cornell University Press, Ithaca: 1–20.

Kantola, A. & Seeck, H. 2011, "Dissemination of Management into Politics: Michael Porter and the Political Uses of Management Consulting", *Management Learning*, vol. 42, no. 1: 25–47.

Kettl, D.F. 2006, "Modernising Government: The Way Forward – A Comment", *International Review of Administrative Sciences*, vol. 72, no. 3: 313–317.

Kettl, D.F. 2005, *The Global Public Management Revolution*, 2nd edn, Brookings Institution Press, Washington, D.C.

King, G., Keohane, R.O. & Verba, S. 1994, *Designing Social Inquiry: Scientific Inference in Qualitative Research*, Princeton University Press, Princeton, N.J.

Kirejczyk, M. 1999, "Parliamentary Cultures and Human Embryos: The Dutch and British Debates Compared", *Social Studies of Science*, vol. 29, no. 6: 889–912.

Klijn, E. & Skelcher, C. 2007, "Democracy and Governance Networks: Compatible or Not?", *Public Administration*, vol. 85, no. 3: 587–608.

Knack, S., Kugler, M.K. & Manning, N. 2003, "Second-Generation Governance Indicators", *International Review of Administrative Sciences*, vol. 69: 345–364.

Laking, R. & Norman, R. 2007, "Imitation and Inspiration in Public Sector Reform: Lessons from Commonwealth Experiences", *International Review of Administrative Sciences*, vol. 73, no. 4: 517–530.

Lane, J. 2000, *New Public Management*, Routledge, London.

Larmour, P. 2005, *Foreign Flowers: Institutional Transfer and Good Governance in the Pacific Islands*, University of Hawai'i Press, Honolulu.

Lee, C.K. & Strang, D. 2008, "The International Diffusion of Public Sector Downsizing: Network Emulation and Theory Driven Learning" in *The Global Diffusion of Markets and Democracy*, eds. B.A. Simmons, F. Dobbin & G. Garrett, Cambridge University Press, Cambridge: 141–172.

Lindblom, C.E. 1959, "The Science of 'Muddling Through'", *Public Administration Review*, vol. 19, no. 2: 79–88.

Lodge, M. 2005, "The Importance of Being Modern: International Benchmarking and National Regulatory Innovation", *Journal of European Public Policy*, vol. 12, no. 4: 649–667.

Lynn Jr., L.E. 2001, "Globalization and Administrative Reform: – What is Happening in Theory?", *Public Management Review*, vol. 3, no. 2: 191–208.

Maddison, A. 1963, "The Role of Technical Assistance in Economic Development", *OECD Observer*, no. 7: 2–8.

Mahon, R. 2008, "Babies and Bosses: Gendering the OECD's Social Policy Discourse" in *The OECD and Transnational Governance*, eds. R. Mahon & S. McBride, UBC Press, Vancouver, B.C.: 260–275.

Malik, A. 2002, *State of the Art in Governance Indicators*, UNDP, Geneva.

March, J.G. & Olsen, J.P. 1989, *Rediscovering Institutions: The Organizational Basis of Politics*, The Free Press, New York.

Marcussen, M. 2004, "Multilateral Surveillance and the OECD: Playing the Idea Game" in *The OECD and European Welfare States*, eds. K. Armingeon & M. Beyler, Edward Elgar, Cheltenham, UK: 13–31.

Marin, B. & Mayntz, R. 1991, "Introduction: Studying Policy Networks" in *Policy Networks: Empirical Evidence and Theoretical Considerations*, eds. B. Marin & R. Mayntz, Westview Press, Boulder, CO: 11–23.

Marsh, D. & Smith, M. 2001, "There is More than One Way to do Political Science: On Different Ways to Study Policy Networks", *Political Studies*, vol. 49: 528–541.

Massey, A. 2009, "Policy Mimesis in the Context of Global Governance", *Policy Studies*, vol. 30, no. 3: 383–395.

Matheson, A. 2009, "Networking of Senior Budget Officials" in *Networks of Influence?: Developing Countries in a Networked Global Order*, eds. L. Martinez-Diaz & N. Woods, Oxford University Press, Oxford: 197–220.

McBride, S., McNutt, K. & Williams, R.A. 2008, "Policy Learning? The OECD and its Jobs Strategy" in *The OECD and Transnational Governance*, eds. R. Mahon & S. McBride, UBC Press, Vancouver, B.C.: 152–169.

Meadows, D.H. 1972, *The Limits to Growth: A Report for the Club of Rome's Project on the Predicament of Mankind*, Universe Books, New York.

Murray, D.J. 1983, "The World Bank's Perspective on How to Improve Administration", *Public Administration & Development*, vol. 3, no. 4: 291–297.

Nanda, V.D. 2006, "The 'Good Governance' Concept Revisited", *The Annals of the American Academy*, vol. 603, no. January: 269–280.

Nello, S.S. 2001, "The Impact of External Economic Factors: The Role of the IMF", in *Democratic Consolidation in Eastern Europe, Vol. 2: International and Transnational Factors*, eds. J. Zielonka & A. Pravda, Oxford University Press, Oxford: 76–111.

Nossal, K.R. 1997, *The Politics of Canadian Foreign Policy*, 3rd ed., Prentice Hall Canada, Scarborough, Ont.

Nunberg, B. 1999, *The State After Communism: Administrative Transitions in Central and Eastern Europe*, World Bank, Washington, D.C.

Nyamugasira, W. & Utoyuru, S.A. 2008, "Leveraging the Peer Review Process for Greater Ownership of Reforms to Promote Investment for Development: The Case of Uganda", *OECD Global Forum on International Investment VII*, OECD, March 27–28, 2008: 1.

OECD n.d., *Network of Senior Officials from Centres of Government (CoG)*, OECD, Paris.

OECD August 12, 1969, *Avant-projet de rapport: Examen du programme de cooperation technique*, OECD, Paris.

OECD 2011a, *Government at a Glance 2011*, OECD, Paris.

OECD 2011b, *Innovative and Open Government: An Overview of Recent Initiatives*, OECD, Paris.

OECD 2011c, May 2011 – last update, *OECD 50th Anniversary Vision Statement C/MIN(2011)6*. Available: http://www.oecd.org/ dataoecd/36/44/48064973.pdf [4 June 2011].

OECD 2011d, *Secretary General's Report to Ministers 2011*, OECD, Paris.

OECD 2010a, December 16, 2010 – last update, *DAC Information Note on the Peer Review Process for Peer Review Participants*. Available: http://www.oecd.org/document/60/0,3343,en_21571361_37949547_37976444_1_1_1_1,00.html [19 January 2011].

OECD 2010b, *Framework for Public Governance Reviews: Draft Framework for Policy Dialogue (41st Session of the Public Governance Committee)*, OECD, Paris.

OECD 2010c, *Global Relations Strategy for the Public Governance Committee, 2010–2014*, OECD, Paris.

OECD 2010d, *Innovation and Open Government: An Overview of Recent Initiatives: Ministerial Meeting of the OECD Public Governance Committee*, OECD, Paris.

OECD 2010e, *Making Reform Happen: Lessons from OECD Countries*, OECD, Paris.

OECD 2010f, *Meeting of Senior Officials from Centres of Government: Ways Out of the Crisis: Managing Fiscal Consolidation and Investing in Future Growth. Summary Report.*

OECD 2010g, *OECD Economic Surveys: Canada*, OECD, Paris.

OECD 2010h, *OECD Public Governance Reviews: Finland: Working Together to Sustain Success*, OECD, Paris.

OECD 2010i, *OECD Recommendation on Principles for Transparency and Integrity in Lobbying*. Available: http://www.oecd.org/document/48/0,3746,en_2649_34135_44644592_1_1_1_1,00.html [30 March 2011].

OECD 2010j, *OECD Reviews of Human Resource Management in Government: Brazil 2010, Federal Government*, OECD, Paris.

OECD 2010k, *Progress in Public Management in the Middle East and North Africa: Case Studies on Policy Reform*, OECD, Paris.

OECD 2010l, *Compte Succinct de la 41e Session du Comité de la Gouvernance Publique.*

OECD 2009, *In Depth Evaluation of the Public Governance Committee. C(2009)35*, OECD, Paris.

OECD 2009a, *Annual Report 2009*, OECD, Paris.

OECD 2009b, *Government at a Glance 2009*, OECD, Paris.

OECD 2009c, *Measuring Government Activity*, OECD, Paris.

OECD 2009d, *OECD Recommendation for Further Combating Bribery of Foreign Public Officials in International Business Transactions*. Available: http://www.oecd.org/document/13/0,3746,en_2649_37447_39884109_1_1_1_37447,00.html [30 March 2011].

OECD 2009e, *The Political Economy of Reform: Lessons from Pensions, Product Markets and Labour Markets in Ten OECD Countries*, OECD, Paris.

OECD 2008a, *OECD Public Management Reviews: Ireland: Towards an Integrated Public Service*, OECD, Paris.

OECD 2008b, *OECD Recommendation on Enhancing Integrity in Public Procurement*. Available: http://www.oecd.org/document/32/0,3746,en_2649_34135_41556768_1_1_1_1,00.html [30 March 2011].

OECD 2008c, *Shaping Policy Reform and Peer Review in Southeast Asia: Integrating Economics Amid Diversity*, OECD, Paris.

OECD 2007a, *Building Blocks and Guiding Elements for Public Governance and Management in Global Relations*, OECD, Paris.

OECD 2007b, *The Concept of the OECD "Acquis"*, OECD, Paris.

OECD 2007c, *A General Procedure for Future Accessions*, OECD, Paris.

OECD 2007d, *A General Procedure for Future Accessions C(2007)31/FINAL*. Available: http://www.oecd.org/officialdocuments/displaydocumentpdf? cote=C(2007)31/Final& doclanguage=en [13 February 2011].

OECD 2007e, *Getting It Right: OECD Perspectives on Policy Challenges in Mexico*, OECD, Paris.

OECD 2007f, *Le pari de la croissance: Contribution du Secrétarie Général de l'OCDE aux travaux de la commission Attali*, OECD, Paris.

OECD 2007g, *The Space Economy at a Glance*, OECD, Paris.

OECD 2005a, *APEC-OECD Integrated Checklist on Regulatory Reform*. Available: http://www.oecd.org/dataoecd/41/9/34989455.pdf [12 February 2011].

OECD 2005b, February 6–7, 2005-last update, *Declaration of the Good Governance for Development in Arab Countries Initiative "Dead Sea Declaration"*. Available: http://www.oecd.org/dataoecd/36/36/34945817.pdf [14 February 2011].

OECD 2005c, *E-Government for Better Government*, OECD, Paris.

OECD 2005d, *Evaluating Public Participation in Policy-Making*, OECD, Paris.

OECD 2005e, *Guiding Principles for Regulatory Quality and Performance*. Available: http://www.oecd.org/dataoecd/24/6/34976533.pdf [12 February 2011].

OECD 2005f, *Management in Government: Feasibility Report on the Development of Comparative Data*, OECD, Paris.

OECD 2005g, *Modernising Government: The Way Forward*, OECD, Paris.

OECD 2005h, "Policy Brief: Public Sector Modernisation: The Way Forward", *OECD Observer*, vol. November: 1–8.

OECD 2005i, *Public Sector Integrity: A Framework for Assessment*, OECD, Paris.

OECD 2004, *A Strategy for Enlargement and Outreach*, OECD, Paris.

OECD 2003a, *Checklist for E-Government Leaders: Policy Brief*. Available: http://www.oecd.org/dataoecd/62/58/11923037.pdf [30 March 2011].

OECD 2003b, *Emerging Risks in the 21st Century: An Agenda for Action*, OECD, Paris.

OECD 2003c, "Policy Brief: Public Sector Modernisation", *OECD Observer*, vol. October: 1–8.

OECD 2003d, *Promise and Problems of E-Democracy: Challenges of On-Line Citizen Engagement*, OECD, Paris.

OECD 2003e, *Recommendation of the Council on OECD Guidelines for Managing Conflict of Interest in the Public Service*. Available: http://acts.oecd.org/Instruments/Show

InstrumentView.aspx?InstrumentID=130&InstrumentPID=126&Lang=en&Book=False [30 March 2011].

OECD 2002, *OECD Best Practices for Budget Transparency*, OECD, Paris.

OECD 2001a, *Citizens as Partners: Information, Consultation and Public Participation in Policy-Making*, OECD, Paris.

OECD 2001b, *Governance in the 21st Century*, OECD, Paris.

OECD 2000, *Governance Outreach Initiative: Progress Report and Next Steps*, OECD, Paris.

OECD 1998, *Recommendation of the Council on Improving Ethical Conduct in the Public Service Including Principles for Managing Ethics in the Public Service*. Available: http://acts.oecd.org/Instruments/ShowInstrumentView.aspx?InstrumentID=129&InstrumentPID=125&Lang=en&Book=False [30 March 2011].

OECD 1997a, *Convention on Combating Bribery of Foreign Public Officials in International Business Transactions*. Available: http://www.oecd.org/ dataoecd/4/18/38028044.pdf [12 February 2011].

OECD 1997b, *Co-operative Approaches to Regulation. Public Management Occasional Papers, No. 18*, OECD, Paris.

OECD 1995a, *Governance in Transition: Public Management Reforms in OECD Countries*, OECD, Paris.

OECD 1995b, *The OECD Reference Checklist for Regulatory Decision-Making*, OECD, Paris.

OECD 1995c, *Recommendation of the Council on Improving the Quality of Government Regulation, C(95)21/FINAL*. Available: http://acts.oecd.org.proxy.library.carleton.ca/ Instruments/ShowInstrumentView.aspx?InstrumentID=128&InstrumentPID=124& Lang=en&Book=False [12 February 2011].

OECD 1992, *SIGMA: Support for Improvement in Governance and Management in Central and Eastern European Countries (Programme Orientation)*, OECD, Paris.

OECD 1991, *Serving the Economy Better*, OECD, Paris.

OECD 1987, *Administration as Service: The Public as Client*, OECD, Paris.

OECD 1980a, *Activities of OECD in 1979*, OECD, Paris.

OECD 1980b, *Strategies for Change and Reform in Public Management: Proceedings of the Symposium "Managing Change in Public Administration", Madrid, 1979*, OECD, Paris.

OECD 1979, *Interfutures: Facing the Future: Mastering the Probable and Managing the Unpredictable*, OECD, Paris.

OECD 1977, "The Technical Co-operation Service", *OECD Information*, no. 40: 1–7.

OECD 1963, *The Organisation for Economic Co-operation and Development*, OECD, Paris.

OECD, *Convention on the Organisation for Economic Co-operation and Development*. Available: www.oecd.org/document/7/0,3343,en_2649_201185_1915847_1_1_1_1,00 &&en-USS_01DBC.html [2 July 2011].

OECD Territorial Development Policy Committee, 2003, *High-Level Meeting – Annotated Agenda: Innovation and Effectiveness in Territorial Development Policy (Martigny, Switzerland)*, OECD, Paris.

OECD Council 6 December 2005, *A Framework for OECD Relations with Non-Members. C(2005)158/Final*, OECD, Paris.

OECD Council 10 May 2006, *Impact of Some Major Emerging Economies on the Global Economy and on OECD Countries. C/MIN(2006)4*, OECD, Paris.

OECD Public Governance Reviews 2011, *Estonia: Towards a Single Government Approach*, OECD, Paris.

OECD Public Management Service and Public Management Committee 1999, *Governance and Public Management: Background Paper, 19th Session of the Committee*, OECD, Paris.

OECD SIGMA 1993, *Ensuring the Regularity of Administrative Acts: Issues Paper, Bratislava May 10-11-12 1993*, OECD, Paris.

OECD, DAC Network on Governance 2008, *Survey of Donor Approaches to Governance Assessment*, OECD, Paris.

OECD, Public Governance and Territorial Development Directorate 2008, *Public Governance Committee, Improving Committee Meetings: Note to the Bureau of the Public Governance Committee. GOV/PGC(2008)4*, OECD, Paris.

OECD, Public Governance and Territorial Development Directorate, Public Governance Committee 2009a, *Accession Assessment Report: Estonia*, OECD, Paris.

OECD, Public Governance and Territorial Development Directorate, Public Governance Committee 2009b, *Accession Assessment Report: Israel*, OECD, Paris.

OECD, Public Governance and Territorial Development Directorate, Public Governance Committee 2009c, *Accession Assessment Report: Slovenia*, OECD, Paris.

Olson, J. 2006, "Maybe it is Time to Rediscover Bureaucracy", *Journal of Public Administration Research and Theory*, vol. 16, no. 1: 1–24.

Ougaard, M. 2010, "The OECD's Global Role: Agenda-setting and Policy Diffusion" in *Mechanisms of OECD Governance: International Incentives for National Policy-Making?*, eds. K. Martens & A.P. Jakobi, Oxford University Press, Oxford: 26–49.

Ougaard, M. 2004, *Political Globalization: State, Power and Social Forces*, Palgrave Macmillan, New York.

Overdevest, C. 2010, "Comparing Forest Certification Schemes: The Case of Ratcheting Standards in the Forest Sector", *Socio-Economic Review*, vol. 8, no. 1: 47–76.

Pagani, F. 2002, *Peer Review: A Tool for Co-operation and Change*, OECD, Paris.

Pal, L.A. 2011a, "Assessing Incrementalism: Formative Assumptions, Contemporary Realities", *Policy and Society*, vol. 30, no. 1: 29–39.

Pal, L.A. 2011b, "Into the Wild: The Politics of Economic Stimulus" in *How Ottawa Spends, 2011–2012: Life Under the Knife (Again!)*, eds. C. Stoney & G.B. Doern, McGill-Queen's University Press, Montreal and Kingston: 39–59.

Pal, L.A. 2008, "Inversions Without End: The OECD and Global Public Management Reform" in *The OECD and Transnational Governance*, eds. R. Mahon & S. McBride, UBC Press, Vancouver: 60–76.

Pal, L.A. 1994, "Advocacy Organizations and Legislative Politics: The Effect of the Charter on Interest Group Lobbying over Federal Legislation, 1989–91" in *Equity and Community: The Charter, Interest Advocacy and Representation*, ed. F.L. Seidle, Institute for Research on Public Policy, Montreal: 119–157.

Pal, L.A. 1990, "Knowledge, Power and Policy: Reflections on Foucault" in *Social Scientists and the State*, eds. A. Gagnon & S. Brooks, Praeger, New York: 139–158.

Pal, L.A. & Ireland, D. 2009, "The Public Sector Reform Movement: Mapping the Global Policy Network", *International Journal of Public Administration*, vol. 32: 621–657.

Perelman, C. 1982, *The Realm of Rhetoric*, University of Notre Dame Press, Notre Dame: IN.

Peters, B.G. 1997, "Policy Transfers between Governments: The Case of Administrative Reforms", *West European Politics*, vol. 20, no. 4: 71–81.

Peters, B.G. & Pierre, J. 2001, *Politicians, Bureaucrats and Administrative Reform*, Routledge, London.

Pickel, A. 1997, "Official Ideology? The Role of Neoliberal Reform Doctrines in Post-communist Transformation" in *The Grand Experiment: Debating Shock Therapy, Transition Theory, and the East German Experience*, eds. A. Pickel & H. Wiesenthal, Westview Press, Boulder, CO.: 212–228.

Pierre, J. 2010, "Administrative Reform in Sweden: The Resilience of Administrative Tradition?" in *Tradition and Public Administration*, eds. M. Painter & B.G. Peters, Palgrave Macmillan, Basingstoke: 191–202.

Pollitt, C. 2001, "Clarifying Convergence: Striking Similarities and Durable Differences in Public Management Reform", *Public Management Review*, vol. 3, no. 4: 471–492.

Pollitt, C. 2006, "Modernising Government: A Symposium: Editor's Introduction", *International Review of Administrative Sciences*, vol. 72, no. 3: 307–308.

Pollitt, C. & Bouckaert, G. 2004, *Public Management Reform: A Comparative Analysis*, 2nd edn, Oxford University Press, Oxford.

Pollitt, C., Thiel, S.v. & Homburg, V. 2007, *New Public Management in Europe: Adaptation and Alternatives*, Palgrave Macmillan, New York.

Porter, T. & Webb, M. 2008, "Role of the OECD in the Orchestration of Global Knowledge Networks" in *The OECD and Transnational Governance*, eds. R. Mahon & S. McBride, UBC Press, Vancouver: 43–59.

Premfors, R. 2006, "Modernising Government: The Way Forward – A Comment", *International Review of Administrative Sciences*, vol. 72, no. 3: 333–335.

Premfors, R. 1998, "Reshaping the Democratic State: Swedish Experiences in a Comparative Perspective", *Public Administration*, vol. 76, no. 1: 141–159.

Radin, B. 2006, *Challenging the Performance Movement: Accountability, Complexity, and Democratic Values*, Georgetown University Press, Washington, D.C.

Ranis, G., Vreeland, J.R. & Kosack, S. (eds) 2006, *Globalization and the Nation State: The Impact of the IMF and the World Bank*, Routledge, London.

Rautalin, M. & Alasuutari, P. 2007, "The Curse of Success: The Impact of the OECD's Programme for International Student Assessment on the Discourses of the Teaching Profession in Finland", *European Educational Research Journal*, vol. 6, no. 4: 348–363.

Reichlin, L. 1995, "The Marshall Plan Reconsidered" in *Europe's Post-War Recovery*, ed. B. Eichengreen, Cambridge University Press, Cambridge: 39–67.

Rhodes, R.A.W. 2007, "Understanding Governance: Ten Years On", *Organization Studies*, vol. 28, no. 8: 1243–1264.

Ripley, A. 2011, "The World's Schoolmaster", *The Atlantic*, no. July/August: 109–110.

Risse-Kappen, T. 1994, "Ideas do not Float Freely: Transnational Coalitions, Domestic Structures, and the End of the Cold War", *International Organization*, vol. 48, no. 2: 185–214.

Risse-Kappen, T. 1995, *Bringing Transnational Relations Back In: Non-state Actors, Domestic Structures, and International Institutions*, Cambridge University Press, Cambridge.

Roberts, A. 2010, *The Logic of Discipline: Global Capitalism and the Architecture of Government*, Oxford University Press, New York.

Roberts, A.S. 1996, *So-called Experts: How American Consultants Remade the Canadian Civil Service, 1918–21*, Institute of Public Administration of Canada, Toronto.

Rodrik, D. 2006, "Goodbye Washington Consensus, Hello Washington Confusion? A Review of the World Bank's Economic Growth in the 1990s: Learning from a Decade of Reform", *Journal of Economic Literature*, vol. 44, no. 4: 973–987.

Rodrik, D. 1996, "Understanding Economic Policy Reform", *Journal of Economic Literature*, vol. 34, no. 1: 9–41.

Rose, R. 1993, *Lesson-Drawing in Public Policy: A Guide to Learning across Time and Space*, Chatham House Publishers, Chatham, N.J.

Ruckert, A. 2008, "Making Neo-Gramscian Sense of the Development Assistance Committee: Towards an Inclusive Neoliberal World Develop Order" in *The OECD and Transnational Governance*, eds. R. Mahon & S. McBride, UBC Press, Vancouver, B.C.: 96–113.

Sahlin-Andersson, K. 2000, "Arenas as Standardizers" in *A World of Standards*, eds. N. Brunsson & B. Jacobsson, Oxford University Press, Oxford: 100–113.

Sahlin-Andersson, K. 1996, "Imitating by Editing Success: The Construction of Organizational Fields" in *Translating Organizational Change*, eds. B. Cznarniawska & G. Sevon, Walter de Gruyter, Berlin: 69–92.

Sarapuu, K. 2010, "Comparative Analysis of State Administrations: The Size of State as an Independent Variable", *Halduskultuur – Administrative Culture*, vol. 11, no. 1: 30–43.

Saunders, D. 2011, "'Day of Rage' tests Libya's Gadhafi", *Globe and Mail*, 16 February 2011, Toronto: A16.

Savoie, D.J. 1994, *Thatcher, Reagan, Mulroney: In Search of a New Bureaucracy*, University of Toronto Press, Toronto.

Schäfer, A. 2006, "A New Form of Governance? Comparing the Open Method of Co-ordination to Multilateral Surveillance by the IMF and the OECD", *Journal of European Public Policy*, vol. 13, no. 1: 70–88.

Schimmelfennig, F. 2002, "Introduction: The Impact of International Organizations on the Central and Eastern European States – Conceptual and Theoretical Issues" in *Norms and Nannies: The Impact of International Organizations on the Central and East European States*, ed. R. Linden, Rowman & Littlefield Publishers, Boulder, CO: 1–29.

Schmitter, P.C. 1996, "The Influence of the International Context upon the Choice of National Institutions and Policies in Neo-Democracies" in *The International Dimension of Democratization*, ed. L. Whitehead, Oxford University Press, Oxford: 26–54.

SIGMA/OECD 1995, "SIGMA", *Public Management Forum*, vol. 1, no. 2: 1–16.

Simmons, B.A., Dobbin, F. & Garrett, G. 2008a, "Conclusion" in *The Global Diffusion of Markets and Democracy*, eds. B.A. Simmons, F. Dobbin & G. Garrett, Cambridge University Press, Cambridge: 344–360.

Simmons, B.A., Dobbin, F. & Garrett, G. (eds) 2008b, *The Global Diffusion of Markets and Democracy*, Cambridge University Press, Cambridge.

Simmons, B.A., Dobbin, F. & Garrett, G. 2008c, "Introduction: The Diffusion of Liberalization" in *The Global Diffusion of Markets and Democracy*, eds. B.A. Simmons, F. Dobbin & G. Garrett, Cambridge University Press, Cambridge: 1–63.

Sivenkova, M. 2008, "Expressing Commitment when Asking Multiple Questions in Parliamentary Debates: English-Russian Parallels", *Journal of Language and Social Psychology*, vol. 27, no. 4: 359–371.

Smith, R.E. 1962, "Harvard Hears of the Marshall Plan", *The Harvard Crimson*, no. May 4: 1–6.

Smith, K.E. 2001, "Western Actors and the Promotion of Democracy" in *Democratic Consolidation in Eastern Europe, Vol. 2: International and Transnational Factors*, eds. J. Zielonka & A. Pravda, Oxford University Press, Oxford: 31–57.

Stone, D. 2008, "Global Public Policy, Transnational Policy Communities, and Their Networks", *Policy Studies Journal*, vol. 36, no. 1: 19–38.

Stone, D. 2004, "Transfer agents and Global Networks in the 'Transnationalization' of Policy", *Journal of European Public Policy*, vol. 11, no. 3: 545–566.

Stone, D. 2003, "The 'Knowledge Bank' and the Global Development Network", *Global Governance*, vol. 9: 43–61.

Stone, D. 2002, "Knowledge Networks and Policy Expertise in the Global Polity" in *Towards a Global Polity*, eds. M. Ougaard & R. Higgott, Routledge, London: 125–144.

Stone, D. 2000, *Banking on Knowledge: The Genesis of the Global Development Network*, Routledge, New York.

Stone, D. & Wright, C. (eds) 2007, *The World Bank and Governance: A Decade of Reform and Reaction*, Routledge, London.

Sullivan, S. 1997, *From War to Wealth: Fifty Years of Innovation*, OECD, Paris.

Thatcher, M. 1998, "The Development of Policy Network Analyses: From Modest Origins to Overarching Frameworks", *Journal of Theoretical Politics*, vol. 10, no. October: 389–416.

Transparency International 2010, *Corruption Perceptions Index 2010 Results*. Available: http://www.transparency.org/policy_research/surveys_indices/cpi/2010/results [6 February 2011].

Trondal, J., Marcussen, M., Larsson, T. & Veggeland, F. 2010, *Unpacking International Organizations: The Dynamics of Compound Bureaucracies*, Manchester University Press, Manchester.

Turner, M.M. & Hulme, D. 1997, *Governance, Administration, and Development: Making the State Work*, Kumarian Press, West Hartford, Conn., USA.

Unalan, D. 2009, "An Analytical Framework for Policy Transfer in the EU Context", *Policy and Politics*, vol. 37, no. 3: 439–452.

Vreeland, J.R. 2007, *The International Monetary Fund: Politics of Conditional Lending*, Routledge, London.

Watts, D. 2003, *Six Degrees: The Science of a New Age*, W.W. Norton, New York.

Watts, D. 1999, *Small Worlds: The Dynamics of Networks between Order and Randomness*, Princeton University Press, Princeton, N.J.

Weaver, C. & Leiteritz, R.J. 2005, "'Our Poverty Is a World Full of Dreams:' Reforming the World Bank", *Global Governance*, vol. 11, no. 3: 369–388.

Wedel, J.R. 1998, *Collision and Collusion: The Strange Case of Western Aid to Eastern Europe, 1989–1998*, St. Martin's Press, New York, N.Y.

Welsh, J. 2004, *At Home in the World: Canada's Global Vision for the 21st Century*, HarperCollins Publishers, Toronto.

Westney, D.E. 1987, *Imitation and Innovation: The Transfer of Western Organizational Patterns to Meiji Japan*, Harvard University Press, Cambridge, MA.

Williams, R.A. 2008, "The OECD and Foreign Investment Rules: The Global Promotion of Liberalization" in *The OECD and Transnational Governance*, eds. R. Mahon & S. McBride, UBC Press, Vancouver, B.C.: 117–133.

Williamson, J. 1994, "In Search for a Manual for Technopols" in *The Political Economy of Policy Reform*, ed. J. Williamson, Institute for International Economics, Washington, D.C.: 11–28.

Williamson, J. 1993, "Democracy and the 'Washington Consensus'", *World Development*, vol. 21, no. 8: 1329–1337.

Wolfe, R. 2008, "From Restructuring Europe to Constructing Globalization: The OECD in Historical Perspective" in *The OECD and Transnational Governance*, eds. R. Mahon & S. McBride, University of British Columbia Press, Vancouver, B.C.: 25–42.

Woods, N. 2006, *The Globalizers: The IMF, the World Bank, and Their Borrowers*, Cornell University Press, Ithaca, N.Y.

Woodward, R. 2009, *The Organisation for Economic Co-operation and Development (OECD)*, Routledge, London.

Woodward, R. 2004, "The Organisation for Economic Cooperation and Development", *New Political Economy*, vol. 9, no. 1: 113–127.

World Bank 2010, *World Wide Governance Indicators*. Available: http://info.worldbank.org/governance/wgi/sc_country.asp [16 February 2011].

World Bank 1997, *World Development Report 1997: The State in a Changing World*, World Bank, Washington, D.C.

World Bank 1983, *World Development Report*, World Bank and Oxford University Press, New York.

Wrobel, S. 2010, "OECD 'a Platform for Our Other Face'", *Jerusalem Post Online*, 19 January 2010: T18.

Ying, C. 2005, *How and Why did the Influence of the OECD on International Public Management Vary Over Time? Research on the PUMA/GOV from an Internal Perspective Over the Last Fifteen Year*s, MA thesis, Erasmus University Rotterdam, Rotterdam.

Index